Wednesday, May 17

Dear Jerry,

That last letter must have made me sound like a very grim and weary person so I want, first of all, to amend that picture, not only because a depression is so boring but also because I am really quite cheerful; it is the people around me who seem miserable—spiritless, at least...why are they always sleeping? When I am unhappy, then, it is only because I am so rarely find people to be happy with. Happy? Well, not quite—joyful. (I bet that sounds like one of those awful posters they tack up on the walls of church youth group coffee houses, but I mean it really.) It is the dilemma of my life that friends matter terrifically to me, that I like to like people, but find so many so unlikeable. I was not raised by my parents so much as I was sharpened, schooled and burdened with a critical sense I can never turn off. I wear it like a pair of X-ray glasses or—do you know Andersen's Snow Queen fairy tale?—that snow-child with the chip of glass in his heart, who saw the ugliness in everything. What all this comes down to is that landscape—no, yes, I know the word well, the people who it revers to very little—well, landscape are, to me, a rare and valuable group of just a few. Finding one—a kindred spirit, perhaps; I don't use the phrase lightly—makes me happier than I can say.

   Do you know, this letter comes harder than it should. I feel the burden of maintaining your faith in my writing; competition, almost, because your own letters are so fine and here is mine, with a dash in every sentence. I've used my quota already: no more.

James Barringer

JOYCE MAYNARD has been a reporter for *The New York Times,* a magazine journalist, NPR commentator, and syndicated columnist. She is the author of seven novels, including *To Die For, Labor Day,* and, most recent, *After Her,* as well as four books of nonfiction. Maynard's bestselling novel *Labor Day* has been adapted for film by Academy Award–nominated director Jason Reitman and stars Kate Winslet and Josh Brolin. *At Home in the World* has been translated into ten languages. The mother of three grown children, Maynard makes her home in Northern California.

Also by Joyce Maynard

After Her

The Good Daughters

Labor Day

Internal Combustion

The Cloud Chamber

The Usual Rules

Where Love Goes

To Die For

Domestic Affairs

Baby Love

Looking Back

"When Picador announced last year that they were publishing *At Home in the World*, Jonathan Yardley of *The Washington Post* condemned her as 'reckless' and *The New York Times* questioned whether anyone should write about 'America's most private citizen.' The subtext behind these articles was 'Keep quiet, little girl; you're not the big important writer he is.' Fortunately Maynard ignored them. Her confusion, suffering, and the lasting impact of her brush with a powerful older man show us the dark side of the Pygmalion myth."
—Cynthia Kling, *Harper's Bazaar*

"Maynard has written, in a completely unpretentious manner, a poignant, deep memoir in which a very bright woman looks back at her life and reveals truths that most of us would rather never have to face. . . . I thought the book was wonderful, compelling, honest, and right on target."
—Jeffrey M. Masson, author of *Dogs Never Lie About Love* and *When Elephants Weep*

"*At Home in the World* reads like a companion piece to Mary Pipher's penetrating *Reviving Ophelia*, a study of the painful and crosswired contradictions that still plague ambitious girls."
—Chris Kraus, *The Nation*

"*At Home in the World* is not a sleazy tell-all memoir about the author's affair with a famous (and famously reclusive) man. It's actually an earnest . . . autobiography that, in the course of tracing the author's coming of age, delineates her first serious love affair, one that happened to be with the author of *The Catcher in the Rye*. . . ."
—Michiko Kakutani, *The New York Times*

"Many, mostly male literary critics abhor her egocentric material and call her self-absorbed and silly. I see her as one of America's literary pioneers."
—Barbara Raskin, *The Washington Post Book World*

"[Maynard] has an interesting and disturbing story to tell, and she tells it simply but vividly. . . . She also captures the innocent strivings of a precocious young girl remarkably well."
—Marion Winik, *Newsday*

"In her very shamelessness; in the unrelenting thoroughness of her self-exposure; in her determination not only to tell the truth but to tear it open and eviscerate it and squeeze it until it is bled dry—Maynard is surprisingly powerful."
—Larissa MacFarquhar, *The New York Times Magazine*

"*At Home in the World* is a memoir that demands reading for the outstanding pleasure to be found in a writer who has the courage to show herself inside out."
—Julius Siegel, *The San Francisco Chronicle*

At Home
in the World

a memoir

Joyce Maynard

PICADOR
—
NEW YORK

www.picadorusa.com
www.twitter.com/picadorusa • www.facebook.com/picadorusa
picadorbookroom.tumblr.com

Picador® is a U.S. registered trademark and is used by St. Martin's Press
under license from Pan Books Limited.

For book club information, please visit www.facebook.com/picadorbookclub
or e-mail marketing@picadorusa.com.

Endpaper photographs are from the personal collection of the author.

Frontispiece: Cover of the April 23, 1972, issue of *The New York Times Magazine*.
Copyright © 1972 by The New York Times Co. Reprinted by permission. *The New York
Times Magazine* cover photograph of Joyce Maynard © Ted Croner. Used by permission.

"An 18-Year-Old Looks Back on Life," printed in the April 23, 1972,
issue of *The New York Times Magazine*. Copyright © Joyce Maynard.
Reprinted by permission.

Designed by Gretchen Achilles

The Library of Congress has cataloged the first Picador edition as follows:

Maynard, Joyce, 1953–
    At home in the world : a memoir / Joyce Maynard.
        p. cm.
    ISBN 978-0-312-20229-3
    1. Maynard, Joyce, 1953– 2. Women authors, America—20th century—
Biography. 3. Salinger, J. D. (Jerome David), 1919– —Relationships with
women. I. Title.
PS3563.A9638Z47 1998
813'.54—dc21   98-28066
                                                                                        CIP

Picador ISBN 978-1-250-04644-4

Picador books may be purchased for educational, business, or promotional use.
For information on bulk purchases, please contact Macmillan Corporate and
Premium Sales Department at 1-800-221-7945, extension 5442,
or write specialmarkets@macmillan.com.

First published in the United States by Picador

First Picador Paperback Edition: October 1999
Second Picador Paperback Edition: September 2013

D 16 15 14 13 12 11 10

To my sister, Rona, with admiration and love.

And to Audrey, my firstborn child and only daughter,
who may think that her father and I brought her into the world.
But truly, she is the one who brought me here.

Preface to the 2013 Edition

I WAS GETTING off a plane when I learned the news: J. D. Salinger was dead.

I was fifty-six years old, and with the exception of one brief meeting on his doorstep, thirteen years before—an encounter that lasted no more than five minutes, in which I found myself the object of a greater wrath than any I'd ever known—nearly four decades had passed since the last time I had spoken with the man.

But I had loved him once, and more even than loved, had worshipped him. I had grafted his view of how a person should be so utterly onto my sense of who I was in the world that there existed a time when I no longer knew who I was, separate from Jerry. Everything I believed came from him.

He told me what movies to watch, what music to listen to, what food to eat. Jerry told me what to think, and write, and not write, what was real and what was false. He told me who to be, and, because I adored him, I wanted to be that person.

The relationship lasted just eleven months, and ended forty years ago, when I was nineteen years old. But absent as Salinger has been all my adult life, he has remained an almost daily presence in it. This is not a fact of my choosing.

At first (when I was nineteen, then twenty, then twenty-one) Salinger haunted me because I longed so desperately to earn back his good opinion of me. I kept his voice in my head: offering up opinions of everything he loved, and everything he condemned, and for a long time his views were simply mine. This was true even though on his list of the condemned was my own self.

To the girl I was then, Jerry Salinger remained the wisest and best person I'd ever known, or ever would—the purest, the most enlightened, the funniest. He had written once, early in our correspondence, that I was a wonderful writer, and the most lovable girl. When he told me, a year after, that I was a shallow, worthless person, I believed that too.

I got over this. But even after I moved on to build another kind of life, I continued, as many people did and many do still, to adhere to the code he'd laid down long before, that to speak of him constituted an unforgivable crime, and proof of one's own reprobate soul. To a stunning degree, for a period of nearly five decades, Salinger managed to convince not only those around him but the rest of the world as well that his words and actions should be exempt from scrutiny. He might write someone a letter. But she must never say she received it. He might break her heart—or wound it badly, or even derail her. But she must never mention it happened.

For twenty-five years I did not speak of him, or what his presence in my young life had cost me. Then I did speak of it, and that cost me dearly too.

I did not seek out J. D. Salinger. He wrote me a letter. I was eighteen years old. He was fifty-three.

Eight weeks after receiving that first letter, I walked out of the world of my own making and into a world that was his. When he was finished with the chapter that had me in it, I no longer knew where I belonged—if such a place even existed. The fact that, at the age of nineteen, I believed I might never know love again, is a part of my story. But far more significant is the fact that my life did not end at age nineteen. Neither does the story that unfolds in these pages—a story I felt moved to write when my only daughter reached the age of eighteen.

Salinger was the first man with whom I shared a sexual relationship, and his assessment of me as a girl (never a woman) shaped my view of my own sexuality for a long time. Here my story is far from unique: it belongs to so many young girls who give themselves over, young, to a man of vastly greater age and power and, in the course of doing that, abandon themselves. And then believe it is their obligation to remain silent.

Twenty-five years later, I gave myself permission to tell my story.

"Oh, you're the one who wrote that book about Salinger," people have said to me over the years since.

"I wrote a book about me," I tell them. "Salinger chose to make himself a part of my story."

My story. Not his.

I have not spent the last four decades consumed with J. D. Salinger, or haunted by the year I spent with him. In certain significant ways, I was shaped by that time, and by Salinger. But more so, by my parents, by my father's love of art and my mother's love of language and my early passion for both. And by my father's drinking and the unhappiness of their marriage.

The failure of my own marriage is a large part of my story, as are the lessons of divorce, and the experience of raising my children and supporting my family, after. My story contains books and music and places I've traveled and the friends I've made there. When I reflect on what it is that made me the woman I am now, those are the things I name first.

Not J. D. Salinger. My experience with Salinger, and the manner in which it ended, left me shattered and lost for time when I was young. But I reclaimed myself. I never saw myself as a ruined person, or a victim. I did not cease to trust, or to be hopeful, or to seek love, and love back. Also, I never stopped being a writer.

Many things have happened between that day Jerry Salinger put those two fifty-dollar bills in my hand and told me to clear my things out of his house, and this one. I have broadcast political commentaries on the radio and worked as a newspaper reporter. I married and gave birth to three children. I made a good home in New Hampshire, then watched our good home fall apart when my husband and I entered into an angry and bitter divorce. I wrote a few books. I fell in love a few times. I traveled to Africa. I sat by the bedside of my dying mother. Buried my father. Fought with my sister. Made peace with her.

In the fifteen years since the publication of this memoir, I've written seven more novels and a few hundred essays. I built a home in a Mayan village in Guatemala, on the edge of a deep lake, looking out to a volcano. I taught a few hundred people (a thousand, probably) how to make a good pie the way my mother taught me. With their father—my former husband—I've watched our three children launch themselves into the world, managing despite all the old battles to take nobody's side and love us both, and to make brave, interesting, and adventuresome lives of their own, and to forgive us both the many ways we fell short. All of this has contributed to the story of my life, far more than J. D. Salinger did.

Like many people my age, I have known a few big successes and an equal measure of large and occasionally brutal failures. One year, when the Department of Energy announced its intention to locate a high-level nuclear waste dump in my beloved state of New Hampshire, I helped to organize the resistance that ultimately defeated that effort. I adopted two older children from Ethiopia, and then learned, painfully, that I was not the parent they needed, and searched for—and found—the couple who could be. If that sentence reads simply enough, the events it describes were not.

Still, the old story dogged me. It didn't matter that I'd turned thirty, and then forty, and then fifty. I would surpass the age Jerry had been when I knew him, and yet I would still be, to many people I encountered, the girl who lived with a famous writer. When a book of mine was published, the reviewer would speak of *The Catcher in the Rye,* and of the ancient history of my connection to its author. And so it came to seem I needed to tell the truth about what happened, so I would never need to tell it again.

There are many things to say about me (good and ill) besides the fact that for a brief time in my late teens I was the follower (a more apt word than "lover") of a famous man. But to excise the story of Salinger from the rest, out of a sense of obligation to protect the great man's secrets, would have made it impossible to know myself, or to be known, or to pursue what every human being deserves— the simple right to tell her story.

I was forty-four years old when I wrote *At Home in the World,* having at that point maintained my career as a writer for twenty-five years. For seven years I'd published a weekly newspaper column about my experiences, never mentioning Salinger. A novel of mine—*To Die For*—had recently been adapted into a film. Still, when this memoir was published in 1998, many people expressed the view of me as a "leach" (the word selected by Maureen Dowd in *The New York Times*) who had made her living off the flimsy story of a brief girlhood affair.

"The only good thing about *At Home in the World,*" one critic wrote, "is that now we'll never have to read another book by Joyce Maynard again."

It was the view of many of my critics (and I seemed to have nothing but critics that year) that because my story involved that of a great man who demanded not to be spoken of, I owed him my silence. The attacks, not only on my memoir, but even more so on my character, were brutal, intensely personal, and relentless. *The Washington Post* called *At Home in the World* "the worst book ever published." I was labeled an exploiter, a "predator." I lost count of the times I was described as "shameless."

At a literary gathering the winter after this book's publication (a rare event to which I'd been invited to read, thanks to the insistence of a powerful friend), a stunning thing occurred. As I took the stage to speak, an entire row of highly respected literary types got up from their seats—en masse—and exited the hall. Their message was clear: what I had to say did not deserve to be heard. Their sense of my story, and their outrage that I'd written it, would be preserved.

And in many quarters it still is. Five years ago, when I brought the unsold manuscript of my novel *Labor Day* to the agent who would ultimately decide to represent me, he agreed to try and sell it, but with one proviso.

"I know this will sound harsh," he told me. "But I'd like to submit this piece of work without your name on it. So people will read it free from . . . preconceptions."

Many editors expressed interest in buying that novel. Later, when it was revealed that the book had been written by me, a number withdrew their offers. Or lowered them substantially.

I'm looking now at a photograph well known to me, of the girl I was at eighteen, taken on a sunny day in late March 1972, at the Yale University library, with my messy hair and my red sneakers and my too-big man's watch flopping on my too-thin wrist. At the time this photograph was taken, I remained ignorant of the fact that this was precisely how a character named Esmé wore her watch too, in a short story by a writer whose books I was aware of but had not read.

I was exploding with optimism back in those days—a girl more naïve in some ways, even, than most eighteen-year-olds, though possessed of large ambition and an abiding curiosity—hunger, really—to find my place in the world. In April of 1972, when that photograph of me ran on the cover of *The New York Times Magazine*, with an article by me inside, speaking with a certain affected world-weariness of "growing up old," it caught the attention of the author of that short story.

I was already a girl with troubles in her life: a father I loved deeply who drank too much, a mother I adored who—blocked from achieving a career of her own—had poured her vast energies into seeing that I had one, to the exclusion perhaps of my ability to define for myself what my dreams might have been. Like many young girls inhabiting complicated families, I was eager to please the people I loved. Sometimes at the expense of my own well-being.

Still, I was a hopeful and optimistic person, and a trusting one. The afternoon I opened Salinger's first letter to me—inspired by my article and the accompanying photograph, perhaps—I possessed a fundamental belief that the world was a good place, and that a wonderful life lay ahead of me.

You will be exploited, he warned me in that letter. There remained one person and one only—a *landsman*—who understood me. This was him.

By July, I'd moved in with him, and in September I gave up my little off-campus apartment and my scholarship and withdrew from Yale. Like many young girls—even the modern kind, who may (as I did) call themselves feminists—I still believed that the path to happiness was true and undying love.

Thirteen months from that sunny afternoon when the *New York Times* photographer, Ted Croner, took my picture at the Yale Library, I had my picture taken again. The relationship with Salinger was over now. He'd instructed me to depart from his life as suddenly and irrevocably as he had summoned me to enter it.

The photographer focusing his lens on my face in May of 1973 was Richard Avedon—assigned by *Vogue* magazine to create a portrait of Twelve Significant Women of the Year. Flattered that I'd been included (and then guilty for feeling this way, knowing—as I always did—what Jerry would say about this), I made the drive down from New Hampshire into Manhattan to have my photograph taken by another great man. I think I believed he might make me beautiful.

Little resemblance exists between the impishly smiling girl in the red sneakers on the cover of *The New York Times Magazine* the spring of 1972 and the one captured on film by Richard Avedon just a year later—a wary, sad-eyed exile, her face puffy from too much crying and too many containers of boysenberry yogurt—who believed that the one person she'd ever known who understood the truth about life had found her unworthy of spending his with her.

Although I had consented to the Avedon sitting, I did little to promote that first book of mine, *Looking Back*, published in May of 1973. I withdrew from much of the tour that had been planned for me, and retreated to the farmhouse in New Hampshire I'd bought that heartbreaking spring with the proceeds from the book. There, with black flies swarming, I planted a patch of Early Girl and Jet Star tomatoes in the hopes that somehow, if I did a good enough job of replicating the kind of life Jerry valued, he'd value me again.

He never did, of course. All that summer, tending my weedy garden, I imagined a day when he'd drive up the road to my house for lunch, sit on the porch with me, share a meal I'd made, and then—remembering how much he'd loved me once—he'd take me back.

When—after I begged him—he consented to stop by that August on his way to Concord, he brought his twelve-year-old son along.

"We'll have to pass on lunch," he told me, glancing over the plate of my just-harvested tomatoes, arranged in the pattern of a flower. "You've got yourself a great setup here, kiddo."

Five minutes after his BMW had pulled up in front of the house, the two of them were off down the road again, and except for that other brief and scorching visit on my forty-fourth birthday, that was the last time I saw him.

I am sometimes asked about J. D. Salinger's reaction to this book. Not surprisingly, he never made any public statement about it. I could guess at his response, but the larger truth is this: decades have gone by now since I have lived, as I once did, under the long, bone-chilling shadow of his disapproval. It took me some hard years to reach this place, but how J. D. Salinger might have felt about how I live ceased to matter to me.

After he died, a lot of reporters called me up to ask for a comment. I had none to offer. The stab of sorrow I felt, hearing the news, was not for the raging and bitter man who'd shaken his fist at me on his doorstep that day we spoke for the last time, the man whose most withering assessment had been to tell me, "The problem with you, Joyce, is . . . you . . . love . . . the . . . world." I grieved for the person I'd known forty years earlier, the voice that spoke to me from the letters I couldn't rip open fast enough at the Yale post office, I was so eager to hear what he had to say.

It was the voice of Holden Caulfield speaking to me. Embodied—though I could not understand this yet—in the person of a fifty-three-year-old man, sitting at his typewriter at a high desk on top of a hill in Cornish, New Hampshire, with a dachshund at his feet and Glenn Miller playing in the background.

That voice has inspired a few generations now, but its power over readers—young people in particular—endures. When you ask these readers what it is they love best about *The Catcher in the Rye*, what they will likely note is that when they first encountered the book (so often, this will have been in the teenage years) it had seemed to them that Holden Caulfield—and therefore, Salinger—had been the first and perhaps the only person in their life who understood how they felt.

I understand what these passionate, devoted readers mean. I fell in love with the voice of Holden Caulfield too when I was young—though I hadn't read the book at the time. For me, the voice of Holden Caulfield spoke to me through J. D. Salinger himself.

This was a man I loved deeply once, with whom I once supposed—in the boundless innocence of youth—I would live my life forever. Ours was a story of two unlikely teenagers—a young girl trying to be older, a middle-aged man in search of youth—whose paths crossed briefly and, for me, at considerable cost.

His choice to enter my life caused the loss of some things that I never got back (a Yale education was one; youth, another). But he also gave me some extraordinary gifts. Central among those: wise counsel about the importance, for a writer, of being true to herself. The necessity to disregard in equal measure words of harsh criticism and extravagant praise. "One day you'll cease to care anymore whom you please or what anybody has to say about you," he told me. "That's when you'll finally produce the work you're capable of."

It was a grave mistake, giving myself over as I did to J. D. Salinger when I was eighteen, and to mistake what he wrote in those letters as something other than a brilliant fiction writer's construct of who he might like to be, what he might imagine, if we were characters in a story, not human beings living out their lives beyond the page.

But I was not wrong to recognize in his words the dark, brutally honest insight of the man who sent them to me, or the humor. Even now, after all these years, I can still remember the pure joy of seeing my name on the outside of an envelope addressed to me in his hand. I remember the beating of my heart when I made my way to Hanover to meet him for the first time, and I spotted him standing on the porch of the Hanover Inn, waving to me like a shipwrecked sailor catching sight of land. I sat in the front seat of his BMW that day, as he raced along the highway bringing me to his house for the first time, with Mt. Ascutney looming before us, and—it seemed then—no heights beyond our grasp. Neither one of us could stop talking, and I thought we were just at the beginning of the most wonderful lifelong conversation. I fell in love with words on a page, and transferred my affection easily and utterly to the man who wrote them.

If he were alive today, Jerry would be ninety-four years old. In November, I will turn sixty.

A few months before then, just seven weeks from the day I write these words, I will return to New Hampshire again—a different hillside, in a different town—for my wedding to a man I believe to be my true and long-awaited partner. All three of my adult children from my first marriage will be there to celebrate (dancing wildly, no doubt, and very likely performing rap numbers and poems they will make up on the spot, flipping into headstands, performing cannonballs into whatever body of water is closest at hand). Many friends will come to celebrate, some from great distances. There will be pie.

Sometime after this, near the end of this year, I will make my way to a movie theater and slip into a seat to watch a film made from that novel of mine from a few years back, *Labor Day*, whose sale once appeared contingent on concealing the fact that it had been written by the shameless former teenage lover of J. D. Salinger. It's a coming-of-age story of a sort, featuring a couple of characters, no longer young, who've known heartbreak and loss but still believe that love is possible, as well as goodness. They don't live happily ever after, exactly, but there's a hopeful ending to their story.

I believe in those. It was true of the eighteen-year-old girl I once was, and it is true of the woman I became. Difficult though things may get around here, I do still love the world.

May 2013

"Real isn't how you are made," said the Skin Horse. "It's a thing that happens to you. When a child loves you for a long, long time, not just to play with, but REALLY loves you, then you become Real."

"Does it hurt?" asked the Rabbit.

"Sometimes," said the Skin Horse, for he was always truthful. "When you are Real you don't mind being hurt."

"Does it happen all at once, like being wound up," he asked, "or bit by bit?"

"It doesn't happen all at once," said the Skin Horse. "You become. It takes a long time. That's why it doesn't often happen to people who break easily, or have sharp edges, or who have to be carefully kept. Generally, by the time you are Real, most of your hair has been loved off, and your eyes drop out and you get loose in the joints and very shabby. But these things don't matter at all, because once you are Real you can't be ugly, except to people who don't understand."

—*from* THE VELVETEEN RABBIT *by Margery Williams*

At Home
in the World

Introduction

WHEN I WAS eighteen, I wrote a magazine article that changed my life. The piece was called "An Eighteen-Year-Old Looks Back on Life." It was published in *The New York Times Magazine* with a photograph of me on the cover. In it, I described growing up in the sixties, expressing a profound sense of world-weariness and alienation. I spoke of wanting to move to the country and get away from the world. "Retirement sounds tempting," I wrote.

Among the hundreds of letters I received after the article ran was one expressing deep affection for my writing, and concern that I might be exploited in the months and years to come. J. D. Salinger wrote to me from his house, high on a hill in the country, where he had retreated many years before.

I embarked on a correspondence with Salinger that spring. I fell in love with the voice in his letters, and when school got out, I went to visit him. Within a few months I left college to move in with him. For most of that year I lived with him, in extreme isolation, working on a book and believing—despite the thirty-five years separating our ages—that we would be together always.

Shortly before the publication of my book, *Looking Back*, the following spring, J. D. Salinger sent me away. I remained desperately in love with him.

For more than twenty years I revered a man who would have nothing to do with me. J. D. Salinger was for me the closest thing

I ever had to a religion. What happened between us shaped my life in many ways long after he left it. But I put the experience away, just as I'd put away the packet of letters he'd written me.

I endeavored to move on with my life. A month after I left Jerry Salinger's house, with the money I'd earned from the sale of *Looking Back*, I bought a farmhouse on fifty acres at the end of a dead-end road in a little town where I knew nobody. I lived there alone for two and a half years.

I got a job as a newspaper reporter in New York City. I fell in love and married. My husband and I had a child, and then two more. We built a pond on our land where, winters, we would skate together in the moonlight. My husband made paintings, sometimes of me. Then he didn't paint me anymore.

I published magazine articles and books. I worked hard, drove carpools, cooked meals, went to hundreds of soccer and Little League games, read to our children and played with them and sat on the beach with my eyes locked on the tops of their heads in the water. My husband and I fought, and struggled to stay together.

My father died. I wrote a lot of magazine articles and newspaper columns to support my family. I cared for my mother when she was dying, and fought so bitterly with my sister about our mother's care that I could not attend the funeral. That week, my husband and I parted.

I left the house at the end of that dead-end road. My husband and I didn't fight over the house, but we went to war over custody of our children. I fell in love again, and when that love affair ended, I loved other men. Some of them were good choices, at the time. Some terrible.

I made a new home. I made good friends and lost some. I wrote another book. My sons taught me how to throw a baseball. My daughter hung roses over her bed, and taught me by her own example what it is to be a hopeful and optimistic person who greets the world with open arms.

I planted flower gardens. We got a dog. I taught many women, and a few men, how to bake pies the way my mother taught me.

I swam long distances across many New Hampshire lakes and ponds, with the crawl stroke learned from my father.

I turned forty. I sold a book I'd written to the movies, and worried about money a little less for a while. I wrote another book. Now and then I still got so angry about some relatively minor frustration that I would dump a gallon of milk on our kitchen floor. But it didn't happen as much anymore.

My sons grew taller than I was. My daughter knew some things I didn't. I sold the house I'd bought after my marriage ended, and laid most of our possessions in the yard, had a giant tag sale, and then moved with my children to a town in California where we didn't know anybody. We made a new home and new friends there. That was two years ago.

Because I have frequently made myself a character in my work, I wrote about most of these experiences. More and more over the years, I learned to trust my readers with the truth. I published stories and articles about aspects of my experience that some people would have considered shameful or embarrassing. I wanted to tell the story of a real woman with all her flaws. I hoped, by doing that, others might feel less ashamed of their own unmentionable failings and secrets.

Two years ago my daughter Audrey turned eighteen, the age I was when I left home to go to college, and the age I was when I got that first letter from J. D. Salinger.

Audrey was a high school senior. We were still living in New Hampshire. After that year I knew it was unlikely my daughter would live at home ever again.

I had always believed in encouraging my children's independence. But now, out of nowhere, I felt a wave of terrible anxiety for her. All through the years when so many of my friends had fought bitterly with their adolescent daughters, Audrey and I had gotten along. The year she turned eighteen, we didn't.

She was breaking away from me, and I saw myself turning into a hovering and controlling woman. What if I hadn't taught my daughter everything she needed to know as she ventured into the world? I had only a handful of months left. I wasn't ready to let her go.

When I was Audrey's age, I had suffered from eating disorders. It had been a very long time since I had last stuck my finger down my throat or binged on a whole carton of ice cream. Now I found myself looking at my own beautiful daughter and panicking if I saw her turning to food for escape or comfort. "You've eaten half that container of Häagen-Dazs," I'd say, my own stomach tightening, and reach across the counter to put the carton away. One day I started shoveling the ice cream into my own mouth so she wouldn't eat it, all the while believing I was trying to save her.

I stood on the sidelines at her cross-country track meets, waiting for her to cross the finish line, and realized I was breathing with her. I watched the slow ending to what had been an extremely tender and long-lasting relationship with her boyfriend and wept, myself, at their parting. Once when she was at school I entered her bedroom and started to read her journal—the very thing I had vowed, when I was twelve, I'd never do to any child of mine, because my mother did that to me. I stopped myself, but I couldn't control the frantic feeling.

"I just don't want to see you get in situations where you might get hurt," I told her.

"The only situation where I'm getting hurt," she said with unfamiliar sharpness, "is the one you're creating. *What's happening to you?*"

Many things were happening. My firstborn child, my only girl, was nearly as old as I was when everything changed for me.

In my senior year in high school, I left my New Hampshire public school to enroll as a day student in Phillips Exeter Academy, a highly competitive prep school with a hundred-and-ninety-year tradition of educating boys. Unable to face meals in the dining hall, and filled with anxiety about college, about boys, about pleasing my parents, and my teachers, I took to eating little besides peanut butter and chocolate, and gained ten pounds. My mother— a lifelong dieter herself, who had always taken pride in my skinniness—remarked on this. I began to diet and exercise so rigorously that by the spring of my senior year I weighed 88 pounds.

I sent applications to Harvard, Princeton, and Yale. I spent days bent over a legal pad, refining my answers to the essay questions. I never truly asked myself: Did I want to attend these schools? I only knew I wanted to get in.

My daughter is nothing like the driven young woman I was then. A good but relaxed student, a young woman with a healthy body who's smiling in nearly every photograph I have of her, that college-application season she spent her weekends riding her snowboard in the mountains of New Hampshire and Vermont with her many friends. She had no interest in attending Ivy League schools.

She wrote her college essay one afternoon when the snow conditions were lousy, and said maybe she'd polish it up if she had the time. I said her writing needed work. There was nothing I knew better than how to write an essay like this. We'd work on it together, I said, as my parents had done with me.

My daughter kept putting this off. The deadline was approaching, and everything in her applications was complete but the essay question. Not a day went by that I didn't ask her: When are we going to work on it?

The week the applications were due, she was still putting me off. Then it was the final day for getting her applications in the mail. "Come home after your first class," I told her. "I'll be waiting." I was trying to sound more casual than I felt.

Noon came and went. One o'clock, two o'clock. She wasn't home. At two-thirty I turned on my computer and typed her essay myself. At three-thirty, the new version was mostly done. A little before four my daughter walked in the door. She took one look at what I'd done and her face was neither relaxed nor smiling.

"How could you?" she said, looking over my shoulder at the computer screen.

"These aren't my words. I am not you," she said, taking me by the shoulders. "I'm not the Girl Wonder who writes her autobiography when she's eighteen. I don't even want to be."

"I only wanted to help you," I said. "I wanted to spare you

pain. I wanted to keep you safe. I wanted you to go to a college where you can be happy."

My daughter was as angry as I've ever seen her. "You stole my voice," she screamed. "You're trying to take over my life. *Get out. Get out.*"

I knew she wanted to hit me, but she couldn't. When I reached to hug her she pushed me away. We ended up on the floor, wrestling, our legs wrapped around each other. Our arms gripped each other's shoulders. "I don't want to hurt you," she said. "But you have to stop this. I'm stronger than you now."

We were evenly matched. She was younger, and had been running cross-country all that fall. But I had given birth three times, and had a kind of endurance and capacity for pain she couldn't know. We rolled around on the floor for several minutes until we were both dripping with sweat. Then at the same moment, both our bodies went limp, and we lay there in each other's arms, weeping.

That night Audrey completed her essay without assistance from me. She mailed her applications the next morning, one day late.

The blurring of boundaries between my daughter and me is a lifelong problem between us, as it had been for my mother and me. But it wasn't until Audrey turned eighteen that I became so confused trying to keep our two stories straight.

I know what triggered the crisis between my daughter and me. It was observing her extreme trusting nature, her lack of defenses against injury, her seemingly inextinguishable hopefulness. I found myself reliving my own dashed hopes when I was that age. Her face became my mirror. Her body, my body. Her nineteenth year, mine.

We survived it. Audrey took a year off before college to work at a ski resort and go snowboarding. I left the state of New Hampshire where I'd lived all my life and moved, with her younger brothers, to Northern California. But something had changed in me that year. I had caught a glimpse of something in my daughter's face that haunted me.

*　　*　　*

I don't tell them everything, but my children have heard enough to know I lived with enormous worries, growing up. When I was their age, I was already sending my stories to magazines. I spent my Saturday nights, more often than not, in the company of my parents. I never slept late. I knew I had to get up early and start writing.

More than anything, I wanted to raise children who would have a different kind of childhood from mine. Even when I was still a child myself, I reflected on the kind of mother I would be. I wanted my children to have a home that felt like a safe place for their friends to come, with no fear that an alcoholic parent might come careening into the room and deliver a lecture on the hopelessness of the human condition, or that their mother would inquire into the intimate details of their sexual lives, as mine used to, in the guise of interviewing them for some magazine article she was writing.

Maybe it was faith I wanted to give them. Having grown up, myself, with a bone-deep sense of separateness, I wanted my children to feel at home in the world.

The lives of my three children have included their share of sorrow. Still, all three appear to possess the belief that life is more likely to go well than badly. It's something of an amazement to me that I am related, by blood, to three people who see things with a fundamentally optimistic attitude.

"Sometimes it seems to me life is an endless series of good-byes," I said to Audrey a while back.

"That's funny," she said, looking genuinely surprised. "To me it seems more like a series of hellos."

For years I'd made daily deals in my head: *Let my children be safe. I will ask no more.* And still, terror that one day one of them might be hurt clutched at my stomach. Now I imagined what I'd feel if a literary legend thirty-five years her senior asked of Audrey what was asked of me when I was her age. I pictured my daughter living through the kind of devastation I had experienced at nineteen, and the shame that had followed it.

For all those years, I had never looked critically at Jerry Salinger. I had always believed I owed him my never-ending silence, loyalty, and protection. It came to me as a new thought that the girl he had invited into his life with that first letter he wrote deserved certain things, too.

All my life I had been trying to make sense of my experiences without understanding a crucial piece of my history. I couldn't have said, two years ago, what it was in how I had lived before meeting Jerry Salinger that made his power over me so vast and enduring. I couldn't have said how the events of that year I spent with Jerry shaped what I went on to do with my life. Now it was hitting me in the image of my daughter. All these years, I had been holding on to secrets that kept me from understanding or explaining myself. I knew it was time at last to explore my story.

Chapter One

THE HOUSE WHERE I grew up, in Durham, New Hampshire, is the only one on the street with a fence surrounding it. That fit. Our family—my mother, my father, my older sister, Rona, and I—never belonged in that town. Or anywhere else, it seemed to me, but in that house, with one another, like a country unto ourselves, a tiny principality with a population of four. Arguably three, since my sister tried to remove herself as much as possible.

There was a phrase we used in our family: "one of us." We didn't use it often, but what it meant was that we'd encountered a person who might get inside the fence and enter the fortress of our family. No one ever did, fully. The only ones who were truly "one of us" were ourselves.

My father comes into my room just after six every morning and wakes me with the snap of my window blinds. "Time to get up, chum," he says. Four decades since he lived there last, you can still hear England in his voice. Years later, when I'm in my thirties and beyond, and he's long dead, I will sometimes be at a movie and Sir John Gielgud appears on the screen, and, though he looks nothing like my father, the sound of his voice will be enough to make me cry.

There's no unkindness in the way my father wakes me. He simply believes it's an unconscionable waste to stay in bed when the sun is shining. Or even if it's not. My whole life, I have been unable to sleep late.

Every morning, my father brings my mother coffee in bed, then comes back down to make his breakfast. He'll be eating it when I come down the stairs. Porridge, maybe, or an egg. He always reads while he eats breakfast. It might be the letters of Harold Nicolson, or the journals of Simone Weil. Although he knows *Paradise Lost* by heart—eighteenth-century literature is his field of specialty, and he teaches it at the University of New Hampshire—he may still read over a passage from Milton that he'll be lecturing on today. Sometimes my father will read the Bible at breakfast—another book he knows well.

My father's parents were British Fundamentalist missionaries who left the Salvation Army because of its excessively liberal teachings to join a sect known as the Plymouth Brethren. The second to last of their seven children, my father, Max Maynard, was born sometime around the year 1900, in India, where his parents had come to proselytize. Of the many mysteries that surround my father's family, the first concerned the date of his birth. He claimed his parents told him they were so occupied with the Lord they hadn't written it down. I never met my father's parents, or any parents so consumed with God that they'd forget the year of their child's birth. If nothing else, the story told me something about my father's perception of them.

As a small child, my father had loved to act and sing, but his deepest passion was for painting. He had known for a long time that he wanted to make art, but hadn't dared ask his parents for paints. When he was ten, he finally got himself a paintbox, which became his most treasured possession. He painted and read constantly, and with so much reckless abandon that he broke the inviolate rule of his household, to observe the Sabbath with no activity but reading of the scripture. His older brother saw him painting and reported the news to their parents.

His father called him to his study.

"Bring me your paints," he said, and when my father delivered them, his father placed them in his desk drawer and slammed it shut. "For one year, Max, you shall not paint," he said.

My father broke with the church and with most of his family when he was a young man, having emigrated from England by now and settled in British Columbia. While most of his brothers and sisters pursued a life within the church—one, Theodore Maynard, becoming a moderately well-known Catholic theologian—my father took up with a group of early modern artists in Victoria who were regarded as a radical bunch. One, a much older woman painter named Emily Carr, would become the mentor and inspiration of a group of young modern artists in the twenties and thirties. Several among this group would later become celebrated in Canada, part of what was known as the Group of Seven.

From the little I've been able to gather of those early years of his—decades before I came on the scene—my father led a bohemian life: making art, making love, making poetry, and waking up with a terrible hangover the next morning. He was a handsome, dashing man—blue-eyed, blond-haired, compactly but athletically built, with the broad shoulders of a powerful swimmer. He had a cleft chin and a strong jaw, but what probably melted the hearts of women, more than his good looks, was his ability to draw and write for them. He could dash off light verse or a romantic sonnet in flawless iambic pentameter, illustrated with a funny or erotic drawing of a couple in mad embrace, or a caricature of himself, on bent knees, holding out an armload of flowers.

When I was sixteen I learned my father had been married once before his marriage to my mother. Although that news came as a terrible shock, the stories of my father's many flamboyantly romantic escapades in Manitoba and British Columbia were almost a source of pride and legend in our household. I think my mother actually derived some pleasure out of the sense of my father's romantic and rakish past. He used to say she had probably saved his life; it was all so reckless and undisciplined before she "whipped him into shape."

He met her in Winnipeg, where he had fled, on the lam from some romantic disaster. He was hired by the University of Manitoba as a last-minute replacement for another professor—the only reason he could have gotten an academic job with no more in the way of credentials than a bachelor's degree.

His lack of formal training in literature hardly kept him from establishing a reputation as a riveting lecturer. My mother—at nineteen, in her senior year as the English department's top student—was assigned the job of being his assistant, with the task of reading student papers. Partly, it was supposed, she was serious and sensible enough to withstand his attempts at seduction. She had already earned a reputation as a single-mindedly driven young woman, headed for a brilliant academic career.

My mother labored over her first batch of essays with elaborate corrections and comments. After she'd delivered them, he stopped her outside his classroom to compliment her on the job she was doing.

"But you mustn't trouble yourself with tracing plagiarisms as you have," he told her.

"I didn't trace them," she said. "I recognized the sources."

Where my father's story has tended to be murky (relatives we never meet; an ex-wife I learn of only well into my teens; vague talk of a former career as a cowboy, a radio announcer, a diving instructor), my mother's is so well known to me, from her own rich retellings, it has taken on the aura of mythology.

She was born Freidele Bruser, the second daughter and last child of Jewish immigrants who fled the pogroms of Russia for Canada in the early part of the twentieth century. Her father was a shopkeeper and a dreamer—a tender-hearted, not particularly practical man who once opened every box of Cracker Jack in his store to give my mother the particular treat (a tin ring) she longed for. The store—a whole series of them, always named The OK Store—went bankrupt regularly.

My grandmother, a woman of fierce ambition and pride in her children, particularly my mother, launched Freidele in the study of elocution, the oral presentation of poetry, popular in rural areas during the Depression. From the age of four, my mother was hustled to the front of grange halls to recite verses—sometimes comic, sometimes sentimental and tragic—in a voice that was not simply loud but strikingly clear, and capable of bringing the crowd to great laughter or tears.

All through my growing up, my mother recited poetry to me. In the middle of dinner or driving to the store or hearing me describe an incident that happened on the playground at school, she plucked lines from her head—maybe Shakespeare, maybe

Milton—that referred in some way to what was going on in our lives. For as long as she lived, whenever I needed a line of poetry for a paper, or a debate speech, and, one day, for my wedding, I only had to ask my mother.

There was more to my mother's encyclopedic knowledge of literature than the fluke of her photographic memory. She loved poetry, most of all reciting it out loud. Even when she wasn't quoting poetry, its rhythms were present in her speech, as they were in my father's.

For both my parents, I think there was a sensual pleasure in shaping the words of Keats or Donne or Yeats or Dylan Thomas or Wordsworth. Neither one of my parents played a musical instrument. For them, language was music. They loved the sound of the human voice delivering the best the English language had to offer.

They loved rhythm, meter, timbre, inflection. They were performers who knew instinctively when to take the breath, when to lower the voice very slowly, or pause, or linger over a syllable— and they did it so well, even a person who didn't speak a word of English would know, just listening to them, that this had to be poetry, and pay attention.

My mother won the golden Governor General's Award at the age of sixteen for being the top graduating senior in all of Canada in the year 1938. That earned her a full scholarship to college at the University of Manitoba in Winnipeg. She'd lived in small prairie towns all her life.

My mother was eighteen (Fredelle now, not Freidele) when she met my father in Winnipeg. He called her Fredelka and courted her with sonnets he wrote her, sketched beautiful drawings of her, and the most elegantly humorous cartoons of himself on his knees, beseeching her to accept his suit. But she was Jewish; he was not. Her parents had told her she must never marry a Gentile, and she had never disobeyed her parents.

But the same qualities in my father that made him such an unacceptable candidate for a husband in her parents' eyes were, no doubt, part of what drew my mother to him. He was a dark and dangerous character who distrusted conventions of every sort, and the most romantic man she'd ever met. He introduced her to modern art and classical music. All her life, she'd been the good daughter. He was the Bad Son. She fell wildly in love.

My mother was my grandmother's favorite, and as the favorite, she carried the responsibility to heap honor and glory—the Yiddish word is *naches*—at her mother's feet. Because her mother sacrificed everything for her—so she could have her elocution lessons, so she could go, as her older sister did not, to the university—it went without saying that my mother's mother was entitled to complete loyalty and devotion in return. Her life, her accomplishments, her successes, belonged not to her alone, but also to her critical and hugely demanding mother.

Every summer she returned home to the prairies of Saskatchewan to work in her father's store. My father began courting her by mail, but her parents withheld his letters to her. He got himself a radio show in Winnipeg, and read poetry to her over the airwaves, under the pseudonym of John Gregory. But his voice was unmistakable. On Valentine's Day, 1943, he sent her this:

> *Not all the loveliest words will go*
> *In rhyme with "dear Fredelle"*
> *But all the fondest thoughts I know*
> *Are subject to that spell.*
> *Like honey dripping from the comb*
> *In streams of amorous sweet they come.*
> *My lily flower, my luscious peach*
> *My pretty octopus, my leech*
> *My swordfish whose sharp-pointed dart*
> *Runs precious panic through my heart*
> *My biblio-vandal whose least look*
> *Rips all the pages of my book,*
> *My dazzling jewel by whose glare*
> *The very sun is in despair,*
> *My arching sky, my curving earth,*
> *My death, my life, my second birth,*
> *My sun-warmed field, my shady tree,*
> *My time and my eternity,*
> *My cigarette, my nicotine*
> *My coffee, tea, and whole cuisine*

> *My loaf of bread, my jug of wine*
> *All this and more, sweet valentine!*

Knowing she had to find a Jewish husband, she went to graduate school in Toronto to put some distance between herself and my father. A young Jewish man, recently back from a distinguished career in the army, courted her. He was intelligent, kind, deeply in love—a man who had all the signs of becoming an excellent husband and a good father. But there was none of the romantic excitement with Harold Taubman that my mother felt for Max Maynard. Every day came a new letter from him, in his exquisite artist's hand, on nearly transparent onionskin, sometimes decorated with drawings.

Reading these letters now, from a distance of more than fifty years, I am struck by the wit and extravagance of my father's expression to my mother. But I see something else too. These are not so much the letters of a man who burns for a flesh-and-blood connection to a woman as they are the words of a man in love with the idea of such a romance. There's an unreality to his fervor. My father has made himself into a character who might have been created by the romantic poets. He is drawn relentlessly to the impossible, the tragic, the unattainable. The vision of life without Fredelka inspires him with nearly suicidal despair. But never in all the hundreds of pages he writes does he realistically envision a life *with* her.

Hearing of Harold Taubman's proposal of marriage and my mother's anguish over the decision, my father sent her another poem:

> *I simply can't make a decision*
> *On the one hand the talk's circumcision*
> *And all it implies*
> *On the other: revise,*
> *Change outlook, have faith and some vision!*

She held him off for five more years. In 1946, she left Toronto for Ph.D. studies at Radcliffe, where she earned a doctorate, summa cum laude. She wrote her dissertation on the concept of chastity in English literature. She liked to say she was the world's foremost authority on the chastity belt.

My father sought a job as close to Cambridge as he could to be near her. The job he found was at the University of New Hampshire in Durham. Weekends he traveled to Cambridge, begging her to marry him. Seven years after he'd begun courting her, she said yes. Her parents were broken-hearted. It was the first time in my mother's life that she had failed to please her mother.

This is as much of my parents' story as I hear growing up. The next part I learn only later.

Although my parents had written hundreds of pages of letters to each other, they had lived in different cities, separated by hundreds and sometimes thousands of miles for most of that time. They knew each other largely through words on a page.

The day my mother moved into my father's bachelor apartment, she found empty vodka bottles hidden in a third-floor closet—an experience she describes with comparisons to the story of Bluebeard's bride opening the door to the forbidden room and finding her life destroyed forever by the discovery of what lay inside. That very day, she also came upon a letter he'd written his ex-wife—no doubt while drunk. "I've made a terrible mistake," he wrote. "I've married a clever little Jewish girl."

Until she moved in with my father, my mother knew almost nothing about liquor, coming from a family where wine was touched once a year at most. But having flown in the face of her family to marry my father, my mother could not tell her parents the truth— that the marriage was in trouble from the beginning. She kept the fact of my father's drinking hidden not just from her family but from everyone she knew—and, as much as she could, from herself.

By the time my sister was born, in 1949, my mother's once-boundless hopefulness about her own bright future was vastly diminished. By my birth, in 1953, her marriage was in many ways already finished.

"You were conceived the last time we made love," my mother eventually tells me, years later. Her words strike me with something close to physical pain.

I have a photograph of my mother when she must have been

a new bride in Durham. She is sitting on the porch of the little apartment my parents rented. She's not yet thirty. My mother had always said she was simply smart, that her older sister Celia was the beauty. But the young woman in this photograph is, like the older woman she will become, exotically beautiful. She wears a simple cotton dress, pushed down over her shoulders. Her body—which she always worried about, and tried to slim down—is not heavy so much as ripe. (In an era when women were encouraged to bottle-feed their babies with formula, she insisted on breast-feeding.) She has curly black hair and dark eyes of unmistakable intelligence, and her skin is so brown that when she was younger, she was more than once denied entrance someplace when she was thought to be, in the word of the time, *colored.*

It isn't just my mother's romantic hopes that are dashed early. Wife of the fifties, she can't get a job. The University of New Hampshire has a strict policy against hiring faculty wives. When she applies for high school teaching jobs, they tell her she doesn't have the right credentials; she needs education credits. She could go back to school, but she sees no way to study, pay for school, and care for her children.

As a young faculty wife in a small New Hampshire town in the late forties and fifties, my mother doesn't know what to do. Bursting with ambition and energy, the lone Jew in a world of blue-blooded WASPs, far away from her family, inhabiting a lonely and difficult marriage, my mother pours her prodigious energies into the too-narrow space of domestic life: baking, sewing, entertaining, shopping for bargains, growing flowers, canning vegetables, and raising her two daughters to have what she had not: fame, fortune, career success, access to the big and glittering world of the city.

My mother has always been a wonderful writer and story-teller, but these days the only writing she does takes the form of letters home to her parents in Manitoba, and to a couple of old friends from her Radcliffe days, Marion and Phyllis. Recognizing, as she must at this point, that these letters may be her truest forms of expression, she keeps carbons of the hundreds of pages she writes: funny stories about her husband and children and life as a faculty wife in a small New Hampshire town, tirelessly looking for an outlet that might give more direction to her life. A letter she writes to the Sunbeam Appliance Company, in 1959, remains, as they all do, in her correspondence file:

> *Dear Sir:*
>
> *I want to express my total disenchantment with Sunbeam vacuum cleaners and with the kind of repair service provided under your one-year warranty.*
>
> *In May of this year, after carefully studying the analyses in Consumer Reports, I purchased a Sunbeam canister cleaner, Model No. 635, confident that I was acquiring a top-quality machine and a "best buy." From the first, the vacuum seemed long on noise and short on suction, but I tried to persuade myself I must be mistaken. In October, the cleaner developed a roar like that of a jet plane; it smelled and felt hot when operating, had lost suction almost completely. I took the machine to the place of purchase, for repair under the warranty. My vacuum departed and was gone ten weeks—a long time for a housewife to be without a cleaner.*
>
> *Last week my Sunbeam returned, with cord neatly folded and a fresh new bag inside. Happy, I plugged it in. Imagine my surprise. The machine roars like a jet plane, it smells and feels hot when operating, it has no suction at all. Pins and fluff on the carpet before vacuuming are not disturbed by the mighty assaults of the 635.*
>
> *There seems no point in returning this ruin for further "repairs." Evidently—after five months' use—I must purchase another vacuum cleaner. It will not, I think, be a Sunbeam. Since I clean my house once a week, I figure it cost me something over $4.00 for every whirl with my magical Touch 'n' Lock. A more appropriate motto might be Touch At Your Own Risk.*
>
> *Sincerely....*

Money is a theme of my mother's letters. Our family is always coming up short and searching out new avenues for earning it. Even more, my mother keeps looking for ways to make use of her inexhaustible energies.

* * *

"You know I've always said I wouldn't sell if I were starving," she writes to her parents, in the summer of 1954. "But I am now engaged as a salesperson of the *Book of Knowledge* encyclopedia. Who knows, I may discover I have capacities I haven't explored. If nothing else, the whole thing should provide me with invaluable literary material. . . ."

My mother works hard selling the *Book of Knowledge*, and earns a set for our family. But the huge commission checks elude her. In another letter, written a few months later, she mentions to her parents that she's applying for a Guggenheim grant to work in England and Wales on research concerning Dylan Thomas, who has recently died.

"It is unlikely that Guggenheim will greet my application with cries of joy (and large checks)," she writes. "Chief against it is the unlikelihood of any committee viewing seriously a researcher who comes accompanied by two small girls and a diaper pail. . . ."

She doesn't get the grant. In the years that follow, my mother's letters to her parents no longer mention academic and scholarly aspirations. They are breezy, chatty, and lighthearted—reports on my sister's activities and mine, mostly, and English department gossip.

A single letter to an old Radcliffe friend, Phyllis, comes closest to offering a glimpse of the frustrations my mother must have felt during her years as a New Hampshire housewife:

> *You asked if I were happy. Ten years ago I would have had a definite yes or no. Yes, I think I am; but I am a different person, and I no longer think of happiness in terms of either utter serenity or perfect ecstasy. . . . I would say that I understand the Ode to Melancholy and Wordsworth's Intimations much better than I did ten years ago. I think I am in some ways a "better" person, and yet less a person. . . . I am afraid that you will find me not at all the girl you remember. Overweening personal ambition is no virtue; but while I had it, I could have danced on a bed of nails.*

* * *

Though our family's resources are modest, my mother makes it possible for me to have adventures she could only have dreamed of in the tiny prairie towns of Saskatchewan where she grew up. With her loathing of Walt Disney (who, in her view, bastardized so many of her favorite books) she would never have taken us to my dream destination, Disneyland, even if money hadn't been an issue. But she brings my sister and me, by bus, to operas and the ballet in Boston. She enrolls us in dancing classes and French lessons. She seldom takes us to children's movies—I see *Old Yeller* and *Pollyanna* with friends and their families—but she does take us to *Death of a Salesman, Who's Afraid of Virginia Woolf?* and many Bergman films. Afterward, she spends an hour or two critiquing the actors' performances, the direction, the script.

Our family is always short of money, and though my father seems oblivious, my mother worries constantly about bills. She tutors French and Latin for a dollar an hour. She takes substitute teaching jobs and teaches English composition at a nearby air force base, where I am sure she enjoys the attentions of her students, all men. She gets a job teaching high school English.

My mother's a born teacher, also a born performer—funny, confident, genuinely interested in her students, prodigiously energetic. She counsels them on their writing, also their relationships with their boyfriends, their girlfriends, their parents. There must be at least a dozen students who stop by our house on a regular basis. I know all their names and also their stories.

She likes to hold classes in our living room. Wearing one of the full-length silk or wool caftans she has designed and sewn for herself, she serves homemade cookies while students read their writing out loud, and everyone—but especially my mother— offers comments and criticisms.

I never miss the chance to sit in on these sessions. I'm so proud of my glorious, brilliant, funny, outrageous mother. I take in every word she tells her students about writing. In between these classes, I sit beside my mother on our couch when she's marking student papers, and read all her comments in the margins. Her comments are often longer than the student's original paper.

To a student who comes out with an unfortunate cliché, she will be funny but ruthless. "Are you sure, Cynthia, that you want to say your heart soared like a piece of popcorn on the stove? Let's think this through...."

"Linda, Linda, Linda," she begins. "Would you really like me to tell you how many papers I read, every year, that begin with 'Webster's Dictionary defines....' I don't think you would, as a matter of fact."

"No need to go on like this, Rick. You're taking the reader to the bathroom!" she says.

By the time I'm twelve or thirteen, I've heard enough of my mother's comments that when one of her students reads a paper, I know just what she'll say. Everytime I sit down to write, I hear her voice.

As my sister and I grow older, our mother creates an unexpected new career for herself as a writer for women's magazines. She starts out writing articles for *My Baby* magazine and *Baby Talk*—chatty, helpful stories about toilet training and sibling rivalry. She sends *Good Housekeeping* a story called "A Jewish Girl's Christmas," about her experience as the lone Jewish child at a Christmas celebration of Gentiles in her little prairie town, at which she, alone, received no present. A few weeks later comes the letter: The magazine is publishing her story in its Christmas issue. I have seldom seen my mother happier.

With her first magazine check, my mother buys our family a Danish modern teak table. Her choice is telling. Mealtimes in our family are the most important event in our day.

In all the years of my growing up, we never once go to a resturant. At least once a week my mother points out how much better and more cheaply we could eat at home. "I bet this meal would have cost ten dollars if we'd gone out," she says, setting out the brisket. "Eleven, with tip."

She loves the ritual of a family meal, and sees to it that we eat together every night. She's a good cook—a "peasant cook," she calls herself. Everyone who's tasted her pie says it's the best they've ever had. But the real attraction of meals at our house is the conversation. Recounted by my mother, a trip to the grocery store or a conversation with the paper boy becomes a three-act comedy or drama, with my mother in the starring role. If she has less than total reverence for strict veracity, she maintains complete respect for the rules of good storytelling and comic timing. I so love the sound of my mother's voice regaling us with her adventures over dinner, I can hardly imagine taking in food without it.

My mother's next purchase with *Good Housekeeping* money is a Danish modern desk. Up until now, she has worked on our living room couch or spread her papers on the dining room table. Now she sets up an office in her bedroom. She gets an electric typewriter and a file cabinet. In manners similar to the way my father purchases art supplies, my mother stocks up on notebooks and pencil sharpeners and stamp dispensers and brightly colored file folders. She gets stationery printed with her name, FREDELLE BRUSER MAYNARD.

Until now, the only places I've ever been are Manchester, New Hampshire, for our annual back-to-school shopping trip; Ogunquit, Maine, two times a summer, to the ocean; Boston, to the ballet or the opera with my mother; and Winnipeg, Canada, to visit my mother's parents for six weeks every summer—a trip on which my father never accompanies us.

My grandmother's one-bedroom apartment is very hot and stuffy, and my grandmother seems to take all my mother's attention, and not to have much interest in my sister or me. I don't know kids my age in Winnipeg. Every day, we have to take a city bus to the nursing home to visit my grandfather, who doesn't even recognize my mother anymore. My mother's cousin Ernie and his wife, Naomi, always bring my sister and me to the Canadian Exhibition and take us on the rides, which is something we don't do in our family. Otherwise, these trips are spent doing little besides visiting relatives, most of whom are very old. Because of this, for a long time I actually suppose Canada is a Jewish country, like Israel.

In the summer of 1964, my mother announces that she's taking us to New York City for the World's Fair. I'm thrilled and amazed, since we never visit the kinds of places other families do. We'll stay with our old friends, Joe and Joan McElroy, and my mother will visit her editor at *Good Housekeeping*.

I'm craning my neck to catch every sight as our bus pulls into the Port Authority Terminal. It's nighttime when we arrive in New York, and my mother wants my sister and me to go straight to bed when we get to Joe and Joan's, on East Thirtieth Street, but I can't sleep. I love the sound of traffic and the lights blinking out the window.

The next day my mother takes us to Flushing, Queens, for the World's Fair. But it will be Manhattan I love, not the fair. We go to Chinatown and Little Italy and the Museum of Modern Art, so I can tell my father I saw the Picassos. Joan introduces me to two friends of hers, and my mother tells me they're lovers. She has told me about homosexuality before this, but I've never actually met someone who's openly homosexual. What interests me most about Don and Phil is that they don't seem embarrassed. So much embarrasses me. I can't imagine how it could be that they wouldn't feel the need to keep their story secret.

The next day my sister goes to Greenwich Village, and my mother brings me with her to meet Betty Frank, her editor at *Good Housekeeping*. I have only ridden in an elevator a handful of times on our annual Boston trip. My mother is wearing a suit, and I'm wearing my best dress. Betty shows us the test kitchens and a room full of free products that have come in the mail. "Maybe someday you'll come and work here," she says to me.

The world opens again. The summer I'm twelve and my sister sixteen, our mother takes the two of us and my cousin Gail to Mexico—after spending a full year not simply saving the money, but studying Spanish. "Never go anywhere you can't at least make an honest attempt at speaking the language," says my mother.

We don't take a tour. We cross the border in a train known as the Aztec Eagle, and stop in towns where few Americans venture—certainly no women traveling alone with three young girls. We ride Mexican buses and tromp through the dusty streets of villages where we never see another American, in search of some artisan my mother's read about in one of her books on Mexico. As usual, my father is not part of our trip, but my mother has brought along a drawing of his—the doodle of a horse, done in red pen at an English department meeting. In the tiny village of Teotitlán del Valle, she locates a weaver who will take my father's design, made on a three-by-five card, and weave a woolen rug from it. A year later, the rug arrives: a perfectly rendered, three-foot-by-five-foot woven version of my father's design. One day, years from now, it will hang on the church wall at his memorial service.

Good Housekeeping gives my mother her first regular writing job: ghost-writing a monthly advice column by a famous psychologist. My mother has no training in psychology, but the psychologist doesn't seem that knowledgeable herself, from the looks of the background material she sends my mother—clippings from old articles in *Reader's Digest* and *Coronet* magazine, usually.

Around this same time *Good Housekeeping* gives my mother a second job: writing first-person stories for a monthly feature called "My Problem and How I Solved It." One month she adopts the persona of a woman who discovers that her husband is a compulsive gambler, or homosexual, or unfaithful, or impotent. Another month, her son has been discovered to be taking drugs, or her teenage daughter announces she's pregnant, or her mother has cancer, or she does herself.

The one problem my mother never tackles in the pages of *Good Housekeeping* is Alcoholic Husband. She never touches that subject with my sister and me, either. For all the years I live in that household, with two dazzlingly articulate parents who can talk in fully formed paragraphs about any aspect of English literature, religion, art, or politics, my mother never discusses my father's drinking. Never a mention of liquor. Never the word *vodka* spoken. Never *drunk, drinking, hangover.*

Intuitively, I recognize the irony of living in a household in which my mother is dispensing psychological wisdom to families about relationships, marriage, child-raising, even as our own family continues to skirt the terrible, unmentionable issue of my father's drinking. In our family, where so much apparent freedom of expression exists that I knew, at age five, the meaning of words like "sodomy" and "misogynist" and "anti-Semite," I am in my teens before I know what an alcoholic is. The only other person I've ever observed drunk is a character on *The Jackie Gleason Show*, Crazy Googenham. Kids I know at school think he's very funny, and like to imitate his slurring speech and staggering gait. He never makes me laugh.

I know my father's been drinking when I open our front door and hear Mozart horn concertos. The particular recording he favors is an old LP of Dennis Brain on the French horn. The record is very scratchy, probably because my father is so often drunk when he puts it on. More often than not the needle skids over the grooves a couple of times before he gets it right. Then he sits in a Danish modern chair we have, with his back to the hi-fi and his arms raised, conducting an imaginary orchestra in our living room. "Killed in his thirties. Car accident," he tells me of Dennis Brain. "But the music! Jesus Christ, the music he made. What this man accomplished!"

Then he may sigh and stand in front of the painting of his that hangs over our fireplace, *The Woman in the Red Hat.*

"He who hath wife and child have given hostages to fortune," he says. It's a line he quotes to me regularly. Oddly, though I understand the quotation refers to the sacrifice of art for parenthood, I never suppose my father resents or regrets my existence. I know he adores me and delights in everything I do. Now, as he says this, I show him a drawing I've been working on.

"Wait here, Daddy," I say, though I know he's going nowhere. I run and get a couple of my mother's silk scarves and put on my leotard. Then I'm back. In our living room, to the music of those horn concertos, I whirl around the room, dancing for him.

My father wants to spend his days painting and considering the nature of art, the definition of beauty, the existence of God. He spends every Wednesday afternoon in the English department meeting instead, discussing fine points of grading systems, the pros and cons of requesting new chairs for the department office. The doodles he draws on three-by-five note cards during these meetings tell the story: exquisite drawings in red ballpoint pen of mountains, horses, trees, beaches—beautiful, unpopulated landscapes or angry abstract scratchings. One drawing from those department meetings I remember with particular clarity. It's a rooster, head thrown back, eyes burning, with an arrow piercing its breast. My father.

A group of students have circulated a petition demanding that courses like Eighteenth-Century Literature be replaced with others featuring the work of minorities, dissidents, rock poets, and political activists. A member of the English department my father likes and respects has been denied a promotion for failure to publish. (That my father himself does not receive promotions is a fact we all learned long ago.) On days like these, my father goes straight up to his attic studio when he gets home from the university and pours himself a glass of vodka. If we can keep him from having that first drink, the night will go all right. If he has that one, we all know, he will have others.

His temper can be ferocious and his words to others, when drunk, are often brutal. But my father is never anything but tender and melancholy toward me when drinking. When he's drinking he talks about his family, his younger sister Joyce in particular, who died young, of diabetes, and whose many letters, in the years before her death, he had left unanswered. "Joyce, Joyce, Joyce," he sighs. I am never sure, when he does, which one of us he's talking to.

My father would never raise a hand to me, sober or drunk. I cannot remember a time when I was so young I didn't know it was my job to take care of him. I have friends, growing up, but my chief companion is my father.

We pretend nothing's wrong. There are two stories: the way life really is in our family, and the way we make it look to the world. We have a day life and a nighttime life. In our day life there is a father who puts on his oxford shoes and tweed jacket and corduroy pants and fedora hat every morning and mounts his ancient three-speed bicycle to ride to his office at the university, where he has been passed over every year for promotion for lack of an advanced degree. My daytime father is trim, handsome, fastidious, funny, brilliant, and courtly. His clothes are old, even shabby, but there's enormous stylishness and grace about him. This father can hold a room transfixed, and often does, with his withering assessment of Dwight Eisenhower ("a second-rater") or Norman Vincent Peale ("a vulgarian"), his analysis of a poem by Eliot, a drawing by Rembrandt, his thoughts on the Epistles of

Paul, or his unexpected affection for *Gilligan's Island*. My daytime father is formidable to the point of inspiring fear in those who don't meet his standards of excellence. But for one who does— and I fall in that category, and my sister too, though she has little use for it—he is the most thrillingly appreciative audience and supporter.

But there's the other father, Nighttime Daddy, whose behavior, especially in my later years at home, spills out with growing frequency into the daytime hours. This father is unshaven, unkempt, red-eyed, and ranting. My nighttime father sleeps in a separate room from my mother, in a single bed surrounded by clothes in piles on the floor, library books that have been overdue for years, student exams, half-marked, with pages flung in all directions, half-finished letters to old friends in British Columbia he hasn't seen for fifteen years. My nighttime father is rageful and depressed—a man who might become convinced, at ten o'clock one night, that his problems at the university all stem from our not owning a better car, or his not having a particular kind of raincoat (which will result in his riding the bus to Boston the next day to buy it. Though he leaves the coat on the bus. And forever after my mother regales friends with the story).

My nighttime father once thrashes around for hours trying to catch a bat that has gotten into my sister's bedroom, and when he finally gets it, but accidentally kills it in the process, he plunges in such despair he buries his head in his hands. Nighttime Daddy often brings me to the attic past my bedtime to look at half-finished paintings. There are always bits of construction paper taped on these paintings, representing elements of the landscape he's still shifting around. Now, at close to midnight, I stand barefoot and shivering in the attic as he moves the bits of construction paper from one spot in the landscape to another. What do I think about this rock? That branch? That cloud? "It's good there," I say. "Don't you think this might be better, old chum?" he says, moving the rock again. I agree, then go back to bed.

Although we never discuss the specific exploits of Nighttime Daddy, Rona and I are well acquainted with the circumstances most likely to bring on his emergence, and we do what we can to avoid them. We tell friends not to call the house after eight o'clock for fear they'll wake our father, who goes to bed very early, unless he goes to bed very late. When he's awakened by a phone call, he may deliver a terrifying lecture. "Jesus Christ! What in God's name are you doing calling at this hour?" It's eight-thirty.

My own behavior never sets my father off, but certainly my sister's does, if she's ill mannered, or dismissive of his criticisms, or if she ignores him altogether, which is her approach wherever possible. If we play our music loud, or bring home an English paper with a teacher's comments that reveal the mediocrity of the instruction we're receiving at our school, that will be enough to send our father to the vodka. Rona adopts the strategy, early, of staying in her room, away from trouble, as much as possible—reading mostly, and playing her guitar. I do the opposite. If I stay close by, keeping an eye out for danger, maybe things will be all right. I will tell Daddy anything to keep him happy. If I am pleasing and lovable enough and keep my father entertained, as he seems to be in my company—sketching and working on reports and taking walks—he won't need to climb the stairs to the attic.

When I ask Daytime Daddy to help me with a report on dinosaurs, he drives with me to the library to assemble research materials—never simply an entry or two from the encyclopedia either, but stacks of books. Home again, we set to work executing the most magnificent posters and pencil renderings of a triceratops the fourth grade at Oyster River School has ever seen. But if the project extends past the hour of six P.M., and he has his first drink, Nighttime Daddy takes over. Midnight finds me barely able to keep my head up while my father redoes the chart depicting the span of the Mesozoic and Jurassic periods.

"I can't keep up this sort of thing," he says, his head in his hands. "I'll be destroyed in the morning." Suddenly he flings the stack of file cards we've assembled for my oral presentation across the room. "Jesus Christ!" he rails. "We need more time to do this properly! We haven't even got to the pterodactyl."

My sister makes the choice, very young, to disappear into a world of books. Even as a small child, she sits for hours reading and thinking.

I read my Beverly Cleary books and Nancy Drews. But I am never a *reader*. Oddly, for the child of two people whose house is filled with books and who seem to have a substantial portion of English literature committed to memory, I find my solace in television.

From the moment we get our set—in 1960, when I'm not quite seven—the life I observe on the screen becomes a crucial part of every day. Except for times I'm playing with my dolls or drawing, I live in our TV room.

I watch everything: *Romper Room* (though I'm too old) and *Truth or Consequences, Art Linkletter,* and *Bozo.* I will watch *Bowling for Dollars* or *Jack LaLanne,* if I have to. I watch *Death Valley Days* and *Highway Patrol.* But what I really love are the family situation comedies: *Ozzie and Harriet. Pete and Gladys. Make Room for Daddy. Donna Reed. Leave It to Beaver.* Over the years, the list will grow to include *My Three Sons* and *The Dick Van Dyke Show* and my particular favorite, *The Andy Griffith Show.*

I Love Lucy, though I watch it, actually interests me less than the others. Lucy and Desi are, like my parents, an unconventional couple. What I mostly look for from television—situation comedies especially—are the glimpses it gives me of what I imagine to be normal, all-American life.

This is why I love the Anderson family on *Father Knows Best.* The father on that show seems so wonderfully ordinary. I love it when the husbands go off to work in their suits, and come home at dinnertime, give their wife a peck on the cheek, and go in the den to read the paper. I love the mothers in their shirtwaist dresses with aprons on, their tidy kitchens, their preoccupation with their children and the bridge club.

In these families, if anybody's behavior gets out of line, it's the children. Beaver Cleaver gets into scrapes all the time. So does Opie on *Andy Griffith,* and Kitten on *Father Knows Best,* and Rusty on *Make Room for Daddy.* When the kids make mistakes, though, the parents are nearly always wise and sensible—stern, maybe, and even angry. But you always know what to expect from them.

I never get tired of watching these shows. I don't care if I turn one on and it's a rerun. In fact, I like it when the episodes become familiar.

There is a little ritual I perform, watching these programs. I tell nobody this, but I have memorized not just the names of the cast members, but every single name that appears on the credits. I whisper them under my breath as the last bars of the music play, ending with "Glenn Glenn Sound."

The one thing that's guaranteed to get my father drinking is my mother's absence. She doesn't take trips often. But every year, the week between Christmas and New Year's (the week of my father's birthday, though how old he will be no one can say), my mother takes the bus to Princeton, New Jersey, to spend a week in the company of several hundred English teachers from around the country, marking the essay question on the college board exams. My mother experiences her annual trip to Princeton as the one week out of fifty-two when she gets to live anything close to the academic and scholarly life for which she's been trained.

It isn't Florida or Hawaii, but this is also the closest my mother ever comes to taking a holiday, the only time she gets to stay in a hotel, or eat in a restaurant, or function not as a faculty wife but as a teacher. Where in Durham my mother has never had much success making friendships with the stay-at-home faculty wives, in Princeton she is much admired among the other teachers, having earned a reputation for regaling the group with comical readings from her favorite examples of terrible student writing.

My mother loves her college board trips and looks forward to them all year. All year, I dread them. Christmas is a hard time for my father anyway with the memories it evokes of his dead younger sister and his abandonment of the church. He endures my mother's and my sister's and my celebration of December 25, with our Santa decorations and piles of presents and flashing lights, but he is horribly depressed by the spectacle. "I am living with vulgarians," he explodes, having spent the last hour stuck in the traffic caused by crazed holiday shoppers. "Jesus Christ! The world's gone mad!"

From the moment my mother gets on the bus headed for Princeton to the moment she walks in our door again five days later, Daddy will be drinking. All around us, happy-looking families continue to celebrate the holidays. Our house sparkles with lights. But the cheer of the season is out of keeping with what's going on at our house. Christmas carols and a recording of the *Messiah* in which the needle sticks in a certain groove and endlessly repeats the same three measures. Our beautiful tree, tilting loopily, or, as it did one year, crashing down as my father lurched into its branches, leaving him lying in a glittering mess of broken ornaments and strings of blinking lights.

One terrible night, during one of my mother's Princeton trips, two policemen show up to tell my sister and me that our car has been left in the middle of the road with the headlights on and the motor running. By this time our father's in the attic and we know better than to go get him. This is a small town in the sixties. Policemen still look the other way about certain people's tendency to tie one on now and then. They pull our Buick into the driveway for us since neither Rona nor I is old enough to drive. Twenty-five years later, my sister names that night as one of the reasons she didn't get a driver's license until past her fortieth birthday. How could she ever believe the roads could be safe?

The winter I'm sixteen, my parents take a vacation to Mexico—the only vacation I ever remember them taking together. My sister is long gone by now, attending university in Canada. I'm a junior in high school. Still, my mother hires a college student to come and stay with me at our house so I won't be alone. I do not say it to her, but this is what I'm thinking: *It's not being alone here that's scary. It was all those years you left me with Daddy*.

My mother is in no way a religious Jew. Still, she is utterly, culturally Jewish.

Years before the Holocaust, my mother had already absorbed from her mother a view that saw the world divided in two: Gentiles and Jews. All her life my mother still saw the division between *us* and *them* wherever she looked. She was pregnant with me the summer Julius and Ethel Rosenberg were executed—an event that loomed large in her imagination. That same year she was asked to serve with my father as chaperone of a dance held at a fraternity where Jews were not allowed admission.

My mother experiences the world of the fifties—particularly

from her little corner of small-town New Hampshire—as hostile and alien to someone like her. She has come to view her own husband as quietly, reproachfully anti-Semitic, in his uneasiness over her rich, highly spiced cooking, her overly dramatic home-sewn dresses, her dark skin. Never one to celebrate a Sabbath or attend synagogue or mark Passover, she conveys the oddest mix of messages to my sister and me about our split-down-the-middle heritage. She calls herself Jewish, but never speaks of us that way, though neither are we Christian.

My mother celebrates Christmas with more energy than most Christians I've known. But our family Christmases, filled with music and wonderful food and decorations, always leave my father disheartened.

"You've turned the birth of Christ into a pagan ritual, Fredelle," my father says. "A celebration of *mammon*."

It has been almost half a century since my father belonged to the Plymouth Brethren, or any other church. Still, he reads his Bible almost every day. His speech is filled with the rhythms of the Old Testament.

My father loves language, but teaching English literature at UNH is not what my father intended for his life. "Castration!" he calls it, in one of his early letters to my mother, during their courtship—back when he thought he'd be leaving academic life soon.

If he isn't reading his Bible at breakfast, my father studies some art book he's checked out of the library. Taking a spoonful of his porridge, he pores over a reproduction of Cézanne or Raphael or Caravaggio. Years before, when I was very young, he traveled alone to Florence. I know, as he looks at his art books, he's remembering that trip.

More than anything, my father loves art. I can't remember a time when I didn't know, as clearly as my name, the central fact of my father's life: that he wants to paint, and that he can't make a living doing it. At the university, he also teaches a humanities course in which he's known for creating chalk renditions of the Old Masters on the blackboard. El Greco one day. Titian the next.

But apart from what he draws for students and the huge,

mural-size pictures he makes with a stick in the sand on our twice-annual family trip to Maine, the art my father makes is seldom viewed by anybody besides my mother, my sister, and me. Not being a member of the university art department, he is not permitted to show his paintings in the annual show of faculty work in the arts center on campus. He enters his paintings in the town art exhibit instead. His bold, slashing landscapes of dead trees and craggy rock formations on the Canadian coastline and back roads in New Hampshire always look out of place among the still lifes of pussy willows and bowls of fruit. Although they are priced cheaply, nobody ever buys one.

Now and then some visitor to our house will comment on my father's paintings. In our living room is a single haunting portrait in oils he calls *Woman in a Red Hat* that people mistakenly suppose to be my mother (as, years later, when it hangs in my house, they will think it's me). In our front hall are a couple of exquisitely rendered line drawings. One is of my mother in a chair, mending a shirt. This is my favorite drawing. I love to imagine the scene in which my father sketched it.

The other line drawing that hangs in our house must be a self-portrait, because my father calls it *Myself When Young.* But the man in this drawing—though he bears a certain odd resemblance to my father—appears so frightening I don't like to look at it. He is bare chested, and very thin, with the skin stretched over his bones, and his face is skull-like and deeply melancholy. He stands in a landscape that might as well be the surface of the moon—no trees or houses in sight. It is a portrait of desolation.

Nobody has a father like mine. There are times when I wish I didn't have a father like mine either: when he takes me swimming at our town pool, and puts on his bathing cap before entering the water, or when we go for walks and he not only carries a walking stick himself, but instructs me on how to swing my own, smaller stick, in rhythm with his. Times like those, and many other times, I wish for those other, golfing, barbecuing, pipe-smoking fathers who live at my friends' houses, or inside our TV set.

But I'm also protectively proud of my father. Nobody else's father writes funny limericks on the spot the way mine does, or sits on the side of their bed at night, reciting Wordsworth or Yeats, in a voice as good as any actor in the Royal Shakespeare Company. Nobody else's father can deliver, on the spot, his views on the drawings of William Blake or the definition of beauty.

He is not a large or particularly athletic person, like some people's fathers, but his power with language allows him to take possession of a room. Many times, in my later years at school, when I'm writing a debate speech or engaged in some kind of political discussion or preparing a report, I'll ask my father to provide me with the language for my beliefs. Moments like this, he quotes from the Bible, or from literature—as, all my life, I quote him.

And nobody else's father can draw like mine. Any time I need a drawing, whether it's of a girl on a bicycle or the musculature surrounding the heart, all I have to do is ask him and he'll render the image perfectly. Draw me a hand petting a kitten, I say. Draw me a soldier dying on the battlefield at Gettysburg. *Done.*

For him, love of art is inseparable from love of the outdoors— not raw wilderness, but the landscape of a dirt road cutting through a barren landscape, abandoned boats lying on a shore, an orchard or (a theme he returns to several times in his work) a church in the woods. My father possesses a pure love of light, and trees, the curve of a hill, the angle of a barn roof—shadows and colors. Weekends, as early as I can remember—age five or six maybe—we head out to the horticulture farm of the university with our walking sticks. Now and then, my mother and sister come, but often it's just the two of us under the experimental apple trees sketching a field of cows or a stretch of abandoned railroad tracks.

Sometimes, walking along the path on our way, my father stops so suddenly it seems as though he's been jolted by electrical current. He points his walking stick toward the sky.

"Look at that, chum," he says.

"What?"

"See how the light hits that branch?" he says. "Study that cloud formation."

Now and then my father, who doesn't like to drive, rides the Trailways bus to Boston or New York to see a particular show

of paintings—Van Gogh or Picasso, or the Flemish masters—
and comes home so moved he's almost weeping. He teaches my
sister and me to recognize all the painters' names and styles of
painting. Sometimes when he's drunk I'll hear him on the phone
late at night, talking to the one artist friend with whom he
has stayed in contact, Jack Shadbolt, now a celebrated painter in
Canada.

"He who hath wife and child hath given hostages..." I hear
him say, the old refrain.

We have a routine, Saturday mornings. Nearly every week,
with our dog Nicky, who goes with my father everywhere, we go
together to the art supply store, in Dover. My mother complains
that Daddy has plenty of art supplies already, but there's always
something we need: a new box of Cray Pas, a sketching pad.
Charcoal. A tube of the new acrylic paint he loves.

We go to the liquor store next. I stay in the car. Then we stop
at the newsstand on Main Street for a bag of freshly roasted Spanish peanuts.

In the afternoon, we take one of our excursions: sketching or
looking for horseshoe crabs on Great Bay, or cycling along the
paths through the campus at the university, studying the construction of some new building, or stopping at the art gallery to look
at an exhibition there. We often stop by the experimental livestock
barns at the university to visit a bull we particularly like. He's so
large, and so angry-looking in his small pen with its iron bars,
with foam coming out of his nostrils, pawing the dirt with a huge
hoof. We are sad, watching him. One week, when we stop by the
bull's barn, his pen is empty. We ask the man where the bull is.
"He got too big," he says. "We had to put him down." My father
is very quiet the rest of the day.

In summer, he and I cultivate a garden patch over at the
university, where he teaches me how to plant tomatoes (sideways,
so the root system will be well supported), and how to build a
good squash hill, and the secrets for tall corn. *"Nine bean rows
will I have there, and a hive for the honey bee,"* he recites, as
we draw our hoes across the soil. *"And live alone in the bee-loud
glade."*

Every spring, when the brooks melt, we make paper boats and

load them into our bike baskets, and launch them in the little stream out behind the university arts center. We jump back on our bikes and follow the course of the stream as it winds through the campus, watching to see if our boats make it through the underground culverts and cheering when they do. If I have a particular report for school, we stop at the library. Once, when my report is on the eyeball, we stop in at the biology department, where my father has a colleague who gives us a glass jar filled with cow's eyes we bring home and dissect up in my father's studio. To him, the lens seems beautiful and jewel-like. We study the iridescent tissue of the retina for a long time.

My mother possesses more energy than anyone I've ever met. She can whip up two dresses in an evening—one for me; one, matching, for my doll. The next day, she sews a third matching dress, this one in her size. One day I announce that two small stuffed animals of mine—a bear and a rabbit—have married and are now expecting a baby; she sews the rabbit's maternity dress. A few weeks later, when I come home from school, she rushes me upstairs. "Lucy's in labor," she says. The offspring she extracts from under the doll bedcovers, no larger than my thumb, looks like a cross between a rabbit and a bear.

She can make up a poem on the spot, recite Lady Macbeth's blood-on-the-hands speech, or any of a couple dozen others, critique debate arguments, conjugate Latin verbs, grow zinnias, bake miniature doll pies in pop bottle caps. One day I discover, when I get home from fourth grade, that my glasses have fallen out of my bookbag somewhere along the mile-long route between our house and Oyster River Elementary School. My mother sets out immediately to retrace my route, but discovers that, this very day, pavers are laying down sand along our road to make a sidewalk. So my mother gets her rake, and rakes the sand in search of my glasses. Halfway down the street, she finds them.

When I tell my mother I need a sweater for a particular toy bear of mine (the rabbit's husband, three inches tall), she knits one on toothpicks. Having been identified as a picky eater who hates the junior high school cafeteria, I am met by my mother outside the front of the school building every day at noon and whisked home for lunch, where the special kind of soufflé that represents one of the few foods I will eat is currently in the oven, timed to come out at the moment of my arrival home.

My mother greets me at the door, when I get home from school, wearing a full-length gown of her own design with antique jet beads around the collar and cuffs. She has been working on magazine articles, but she sets her work aside when I walk in the door. She wants to hear about my day.

As I get older, this includes wanting to hear everything about whatever sexual things might be going on with me. I tell her nothing. More accurately, since it remains unimaginable not to tell my mother everything, I make sure there's nothing to tell. The only things going on for me, sexually, happen in my head, which is the one place my mother can't get to.

When I'm fourteen, she still comes into the bathroom when I'm in the tub. "Look at those little nips!" she says, laughing. "I think you're finally starting to develop." She doesn't buy me a bra, though. Years after the other girls in my class have theirs, I continue to wear undershirts—the reason I hurry to be first in the locker room for gym class, so I can get one of the two bathroom stalls and change there.

Often, on Sundays, we take a drive to a country store a few miles out of town that sells a particular kind of anadama bread we like for toast. My mother has a standing order for two loaves. But there's another part of our ritual visit to Calef's Country Store. We never leave without spending a few minutes in the section that features a bunch of old-timey books. One that my mother opens regularly (but never buys) is called *Jokes for the John*. On the drive home, or later, at dinner, my mother (the same woman who also quotes Shakespeare and Chaucer) regales us with dirty jokes. My sister says nothing. My father says "Please, Fredelle. Restrain yourself. The *girls*."

Who else has a mother who taught her the meaning of the word *cunnilingus*?

How is it I forgive her? She means no harm.

Every morning, I come into bed with her for what my mother calls "cuddle time." I do this when I am very little. My own children will one day come into bed with their father and me when they're young, too. But for me, the practice of getting into bed with my mother in the mornings continues into junior high. Maybe longer, but my sister left home when I was thirteen, and since she is the one who remembers what happened, I only know for sure that it was still going on then.

Rona felt sufficiently uncomfortable about what went on at cuddle time that she spoke to our mother about it, she tells me later. "I told her I thought it was inappropriate," she says. Another family friend who sometimes came for visits, Ellen, told my mother the same thing. Our mother dismissed their comments, Rona says. "Joycie just can't get enough snuggling," my mother laughed. "Can you imagine what she'll be like with men?"

What I remember: my mother's dark skin and full breasts, showing through the worn, almost transparent nightgowns she sleeps in, the once-luxurious but now faintly shabby hand-me-downs from her sister Celia; the smell of her and her black hair that I like to style because it's so curly, and my own is straight. She kisses me on the lips and I kiss her back. There are names for the kinds of kisses we share. *Suction. Cutie. Movie star.*

She may comment on my body, check to see if I have any pubic hair yet, make a joke about my pink, childish nipples. She calls me "triangulo," because she says that's the shape of my bottom. "Look at your legs," she says. "People will think you've been in a concentration camp."

(Later, though, when I fill out a little, this will also be a subject of discussion. "I'm tipping the scales at 105," I write to her, from camp. "I can't come home, for sheer shame!")

Whenever my grandmother comes to visit, she brings a tin of a strange green ointment called Zambuk, available only in Canada. My mother sees nothing odd or hurtful in applying Zambuk to my vagina, at night, as late as junior high. My guess is that her mother probably had done the same with her, though what the Zambuk was supposed to do is never clear to me.

For my sister, the story is different. What Rona remembers is walking past our mother's bedroom to the bathroom, listening to my mother and me cuddling, but taking part in none of it.

We all knew, in our family, that Rona didn't like to be touched.

One day, when I come home, I see she has left out a copy of our local paper, turned to the sports page, which is rare in our family. She has drawn an arrow, in red magic marker, to a photograph of a high school football player in uniform. With her marker, she has drawn a circle around the boy's crotch, with an exclamation point.

"Can you believe this, in the paper?" she says. I know right away what her problem is, because I know my mother. She doesn't know football players wear athletic cups. She thinks this boy must have a very large penis—thinks he's having an erection, in fact, for all the world of sports fans to see—and she had to point it out.

My mother suffers from other frustrations. Despite her determined optimism and cheerfulness, her dreams, not only for romantic love but also for a career, were crushed a long time ago. She has her magazine career, and her teaching, but her biggest hopes rest with her daughters now, and because I am a more willing and responsive recipient, she places her most ambitious expectations on me.

She is a lifelong dieter, never wholly successful in her battle; I will be slim. I will receive the best education. I will be loved by a wonderful man. I will not have to worry about money as she does. I will see the world beyond New Hampshire.

Though my father was a champion diver as a young man, and he still possesses a surprisingly strong body and a forceful crawl stroke, he is not a follower of organized sports. In our family, we do not own a single ball or piece of sporting equipment besides our croquet set. I am twelve years old when I point out to my parents that I would like to learn to ride a bicycle—an idea that has never occurred to them. This earns me a reputation as the family athlete. My sister never learns to ride a bike.

My mother and father coach my sister and me to write. Before we knew how to form alphabet letters ourselves, we gave dictation. We spoke; our mother wrote down what we said and told us how to make it better. Soon enough, she gives us a typewriter.

Our family sport takes place in the living room. There in a

circle of shabby furniture, surrounded by my father's paintings, my sister and I read our manuscripts aloud for our parents. With file cards and yellow legal pads in hand, they take notes and analyze, one line at a time, every metaphor and choice of adjective. They talk about the rhythm of our sentences, the syntax, the punctuation. My father is a careful and demanding editor, but my mother's criticism is the most exacting. Her instruction is incomparable, but it carries a price. My mother is teaching us not just how to write, but what to say. Back in that living room, I am adopting more than my mother's punctuation and sentence rhythms as mine. On the page, I could not differentiate between my own feelings and my mother's.

My sister, Rona, is regarded as the real writer in our family. I like drawing better, and dancing, and acting in plays and playing the guitar and singing folk songs. But I'm acutely aware of my father's story, too. I know well that the fact that you love to do a particular thing doesn't mean you can earn a living by it, or that anyone will ever acknowledge your talents. Singing and dancing might make me happy, but are less likely to make me successful—something that matters a lot in our family.

Partly in anticipation of its future significance, my mother has typed what we've written, as far back as preschool days, and saved every poem and story in suitcases—one for my sister, one for me.

My childhood suitcase features not just the usual Mother's Day verses and school book reports but a three-act play, written when I was nine, chronicling the life and loves, including the sexual peccadilloes, of Henry VIII. There are hand-drawn fashion magazines in the suitcase, and tragic folk songs, and comedy routines, and the beginnings of several novels. Dozens of poems. Earnest, idealistic reflections on the Goldwater-Johnson election of 1964 (the year I turned eleven) and school busing and the Vietnam war. When I'm seven, my mother gives me a mimeograph machine for my birthday, and I begin producing a newspaper that I sell door-to-door on our street. It would never occur to me that our neighbors wouldn't be interested to read what I write. Or that I shouldn't charge a nickel for it. Later, a dime.

My mother schools me young to view my writing as valuable. She conveys another lesson too: Whatever happens in my life, I can look at it as *material*.

When my sister is thirteen or fourteen, our mother encourages her to enter the *Scholastic Magazine* writing contest. She wins—that year, and again, for years after that, collecting prizes of $25, $50, sometimes even $100.

The *Scholastic* prize money sounds to me like a fortune. As soon as I'm old enough, I also enter the *Scholastic* contest—feeling, now, the pressure to match my sister's early successes or top them. I enter in every division available to me: fiction, essay, poetry, dramatic script. Through most of junior high, and into high school, the month before the *Scholastic* deadline and the week when prizes are announced will be two of the most important times of my year. If I win only one award, I will be disappointed.

When Rona's sixteen, our mother mails a short story of hers called "Paper Flowers" to the *Ladies' Home Journal*. The magazine buys the story for $500. The story will later be named as an honorable mention in the annual volume of *Best American Short Stories* for 1964. At age eleven, I'm proud of my sister, but also consumed with a need to match her achievement, and with an anxiety that I might not be able to.

In the fall of 1965, just before my twelfth birthday, I start keeping a diary. I write in it every night—entries that sometimes go on for five or six pages. In my journal, I talk about all my darkest secrets: My embarrassment that my mother is still giving me baths. The jealousy and competition I feel toward my sister. My impatience with my classmates at school, my longing for a close friend, and my sense of having no one who understands me, except for my mother. I write about my secret and shameful interest in boys, my wish that I could attend dances, and my belief that my mother would never in a million years guess that I could care about such things. I am consumed with a desire to win contests, earn money, earn recognition from the world and, above all, from my parents. I also worry about death, the meaning of life, the universe.

Sometimes, in my diary, I will refer to my father as being "stormy" on a particular night. So stormy, in fact, that one night he takes away my diary entirely, and sends me to bed, until my mother steps in to rescue me. "Stormy" is a code word for the word I don't dare write even in my diary: *drunk.*

SEPT. 5, 1965
...Today I listened to a Judy Collins record. Oh, music excites me so. But listening to the record, and Rona playing the guitar, I feel so hopeless and far behind....I never seem to get anything done or polished enough. My slow typing. My dreadfully inadequate, repetitious choreography. Mummy would say this diary is completely without form or direction. Oh dear.

SEPT. 6
...I think a lot about dying these days, and how I have an image of myself as the center of things, like the universe revolving around the earth! Oh, but I am so inconsequential! I must do something....

SEPT 7
...I have always thought of our family as a kind of divine circle, speculating even on close friends, and their limitations—their not being wholly correct. I realize now that even Mummy has flaws! I guess truly no one can come into the "divine circle" except me. One is always so alone!

SEPT 9
...I desperately need to talk to someone, but everyone I talk to is part of my depression so I can't talk to them, of course. How little I have in common with these people....

SEPT. 27
...I must do something. I must win Scholastic Contest this year!

OCT. 6

How sad for Daddy not to have any family of his own other than us. I often notice Daddy talking about being a bachelor and REALLY PAINTING. What a lot he gave up for Mummy. It must often be sad for him to have given up the full cultivation of his talent. He thinks of art constantly! I don't think that I'll marry a man so much older, if I can help it.

OCT. 7

Reading Maria Trapp's autobiography of the Trapp Family Singers. It has a lot of religious overtones. How simple it would be to be religious. How safe....

OCT. 11

...People are always such a disappointment....

OCT. 14

I feel depressed about a space travel article I read. It talked blithely of underground living and space migration to stop the population explosion. And to think I may well live to see this day, where all purpose goes out of life, and one's goal is merely survival. To misquote Anne Frank, "I still believe all men are good." Are they?

NOV. 17

Daddy just started an awful scene. He took away my diary (it was only 9:15) saying it was too late for me to be up writing. Luckily, Mummy came to the rescue....A father should be a steady person, not necessarily happy and well adjusted, but steady. If he punishes you because he's had a bad day or his shoulder hurts, no reprimand will be meaningful....

NOV. 11

...Today in math the problem of infinity was brought up. Does space go on and on and on?...If not, does it stop all of a sudden, as people once thought the Earth did? And what

would lie beyond? Nothing. What is nothing?...I am so little and inconsequential....I must make my mark!

NOV. 28

I finished Gone with the Wind this morning. How I cried, at Bonnie's death, Melanie's goodness, and alas, Scarlett's alone feeling, with no shoulder to cry on. A ruined life. I was particularly moved because, oddly enough, Rhett reminds me of Daddy, and therefore he seemed closer to my heart. I realize this book is sentimental, with no shape or symbolism or form, but any book that can create such a vivid picture of so sad an event has got to have something. It is the best book I've ever read.

DEC. 1

Daddy is stormy tonight and wants me to go to bed, so I must hurry....

A few nights later I note my father's upsetting behavior again. This time I call it what it really is.

DEC. 8

When I came home last night, Daddy was drunk and moody—you could smell liquor on his breath all down the hall. For some people, life is so easy, so secure. Fathers in crew cuts, nice and dull, who bring home the paycheck. Not so here.

The December 8 entry marks the first time I have used real language to describe my father's drinking. The next night, when I open my diary to write again, there is a letter stuck inside the pages, written on a yellow legal pad. My mother's handwriting:

My Dearest Joyce,

Yes, I did look at your diary this morning....Actually, because we are so close in feeling and temperament, I haven't learned much I didn't already know. I understand very well you longing, in a way, for a steady, crew-cut, run-of-the-crowd father. (Do you think I haven't wondered ruefully, at times, what it would be like to have that kind of husband?) But of course if you had that kind of father, you wouldn't be you. Round and round the circle goes. You really do have an extraordinary (and extraordinarily difficult) father— and in life one pays for everything. Remember the little mermaid, and what it cost her to walk on land with little human feet? Everyone has some problem; this is ours. And it's not, after all, disastrous. When Daddy is drunk he is sad, disgusting, embarrassing, pitiable...all these things. But not mean or cruel or violent. And—this is the important thing— whatever follies he commits at midnight, he gets up in the morning, goes to work and—as you would say—brings home the paycheck—i.e., meets his responsibilities. Read around a bit in the lives of painters and poets and you'll see that this is not a bad score.

After some twenty years, I think I have as good an answer as possible. There is no use indulging in self-pity. ("Why did this happen to me? Other people have it so easy.") And there is certainly no use complaining, attacking, berating—or even speaking about the matter. There is nothing I could say to Daddy that he hasn't said to himself. Try to imagine what it must be like to live with the knowledge of one's own dreadful fallibility. Positively speaking, there are just two things one can do—try to avoid situations which you know will aggravate the nerves; and accept, without struggle, the fact that this is how it is. You'd be surprised at the serenity that comes with acceptance. I used to—at awful moments—cry and accuse and attempt to stop the avalanche. This was painful and utterly futile. Now I just turn out the light and go to sleep, knowing that tomorrow the coffee will be made and the cereal cooked as always.

One final observation. If you work things out mathematically, our lot is not so bad. Twenty-four hours a day, seven days a week—168 hours. Say, on an average, six of those hours are unpleasant—I make it 3.36% of the time.

And all the other times? You have a father who is highly intelligent, gifted, sensitive, witty, gentle and absolutely devoted to you. How many children can say as much?

More than thirty years later, with a daughter of my own, I reread my mother's letter to me, at twelve, with the deepest kind of sorrow. It's misguided enough for a parent to tell her child she cannot speak of her most painful feelings. But my mother goes further than that. She tells me I must not even acknowledge my feelings to myself. She requires me to support her denial. She has even provided mathematical proof: scribbled calculations in the margin, allowing her to arrive at the figure of 3.36% as the portion of my life in which I am actively affected by my father's drunkenness.

The twelve-year-old who reads my mother's letter in her diary that night recognizes none of this. I acknowledge only the brilliance and wisdom of my mother's reasoning. I am so accustomed to my mother's invasions, I don't even recognize the invasion—only her supreme and matchless understanding of me.

DEC. 9, 1965

Dear Diary,

Today I found a note in my diary that Mummy wrote me. She has read it. And, oh, how she understands me! And what use is a secret if it isn't one? She has upheld the tradition—the infallible, the God in my life, knowing all! Right now I'm crying too much to go on writing. Let me go to sleep.

As I enter my teens, my father's "stormy" times will become nightly, not occasional events—the percentage of the drunkenness rising. But after the diary episode, I will not speak of my father's drinking again to my mother or anyone else for many years, or even write about it in the most secret place.

Every now and then, some night when my father's drinking, he will stumble into our kitchen to fix himself "a spot of tea" and leave the kettle on the stove with the burner on. In the morning, we'll come downstairs to find a little silver-colored coin that used to be our teakettle. I have a collection of these. For the purpose of her storytelling, my mother transforms Daddy into someone resembling Mr. Magoo. Only with better eyesight.

I never speak with my mother about the fact that she read my diary or that after the night of December 9, 1965, I never write in it again. From now on I focus my writing energies on the kind of writing that wins prizes and makes money.

When I am eight or nine, I write to the president of CBS, informing him of my availability to replace the child actress Angela Cartwright in her role as the daughter on *The Danny Thomas Show*, if she should ever become unavailable. At fifteen, I write to the Children's Television Workshop, suggesting that they include a teenage character on *Sesame Street* and, if so, that I get to play her. That same year, I write a letter to *Seventeen* magazine, proposing that I write an article for them, and enclose samples of my work. The magazine buys a short essay I write. I receive a check for $100.

After that first sale, I pursue more assignments with *Seventeen*. I send off proposals, as my mother taught me. I begin getting jobs: a roundup of summer camp options for teenagers, a report on wedding fashions. I travel to New York to meet with editors, pitching a long list of possible topics. I still don't plan to become a writer. But I believe that writing may provide me with a ticket to New York City, the place I've wanted to get back to ever since our trip to the World's Fair.

I have friends at my school. I act in plays. But I have never shaken the feeling that I'm an alien in this place. More than anything—fame or success or writing prizes—what I long for is a sense of fitting in somewhere. Maybe it will be New York.

I am also thinking a lot about boys. At dances I stand on the sidelines, wishing someone would ask me. A boy at school says, "Did you get the license plate number of the tractor that ran over your face?" For days after, I study my reflection in the mirror. I know I'm not beautiful, but I had supposed I was cute. I must be wrong. Certainly no boys are calling me.

In my junior year, something happens that seems to me more wonderful and surprising than any debate team trophy or writing prize. A boy asks me on a date, but this one is smart and confident and funny and well liked at our school. I cannot imagine why he would have sought me out.

Jim is seventeen, a year older than I. He's tall and solid as a tree trunk, a boy who commanded the soccer goal at Oyster River High School for four years. This fall, I begin attending those games. Because so many of the players on the team are graduating seniors, there is a deeply significant atmosphere surrounding these games that even a person like me who hadn't been following the team's career would have picked up on. This group of boys is playing their last games together. They have never played better. That October they will win the state championship in their division.

Jim has curly blond hair, glasses, and a sharp wit, but unlike me, no burning ambition. He has no apparent interest in applying his fine intelligence to winning any prizes besides the only one that mattered to him: to successfully defend the space between Oyster River's goal posts. He has lived in this town all his life, and plans to attend the University of New Hampshire next year. He likes to barbecue steaks and play air guitar along with Jimi Hendrix and go out in a little boat he has on the bay.

Shortly after the soccer team returns from the championships with their trophy, and following a week of nonstop celebrations in which even I participate (though unlike nearly everybody else at these gatherings, I don't drink or smoke pot), Jim asks me if I'd like to go for a drive with him one evening. His car is famous at our school: a Model A Ford he and his dad have fixed up.

We drive out to Great Bay, site of so many of my sketching trips with my father. On a back road, with no other cars in sight, he pulls over the Model A. In a clump of bushes he clearly knows well, someone has hidden a six-pack of beer. He opens the back of the car and takes out an old stadium blanket, also a pillow. Taking my hand and carrying the beer and the blanket in his other, he leads me through the woods to a clearing where he lays down the blanket. We lie down. He opens two beers. It's chilly here, but he has wrapped his soccer jacket over my shoulders. He takes off his glasses and kisses me.

All that winter and spring, I am Jim's girlfriend. After school now we head to a diner downtown where Jim and a bunch of friends, mostly soccer teammates and their girlfriends, drink Cokes and fool around. One of the boys in the group has a family-owned cabin in the woods where we go, once the snow comes, to drink rum-laced hot chocolate and ride toboggans. I'm terrified of the steep hill and the speed of the toboggan run, but when Jim sits behind me and wraps his arms around me, I feel safe enough to go down the hill with the others.

He possesses a quality rare among high school boys: an appreciation for irony. He loves a few things: his car, his boat, beer and rum, Jimi Hendrix, his soccer teammates. He does not dream of New York. And he seems to feel, for me, the nicest combination of passion and affection. We neck for hours: on his stadium blanket, in his parents' basement, lying on dunes at Ogunquit beach, in the backseat of his Model A with the tattered old window shade pulled down.

That spring, I learn that Phillips Exeter Academy, the prestigious boys' prep school a couple of towns over, will accept a handful of female students for the first time in its one-hundred-and-ninety-year history. For years I've watched with envy and resignation as so many of the brightest, most ambitious boys in my school headed off to Exeter in ninth or tenth grade. (Not Jim, though he would have been smart enough. "Why would I want to go to prep school?" he laughs. "Do they have a better soccer team?")

A few days after Jim's graduation, he picks me up and we head to the town pool, which is not yet open for the season. Jim's best friend on the soccer team, Greg, is taking off the next morning on a hitchhiking trip across country. A group of friends has decided to celebrate his departure with an illegal swim.

Except for my few sips of beer with Jim, I have never broken the law. Now he lifts me up so I can climb the fence with the others. We strip down to our underwear and jump in the familiar waters I know from a dozen childhood summers when my mother brought me here, or when my father embarked on his ceaseless quest to teach me a proper crawl stroke. The diving board isn't up yet, but Greg is performing cannon balls off the stone wall at the deep end.

The stars are out. The water's very cold. We're all shivering. Jim passes around his flask of rum. Greg asks him one more time to come along on the hitchhiking trip. "Why would I want to go someplace else?" he says. "I like it here."

The knowledge that I'll be attending Exeter has changed things between us. I still feel excitement at the sound of his car horn outside my house on Saturday nights, and we still take the rum or the beer and the blanket out into some field or other. But the relationship feels finite and terminal now. I never say it, but as we head into the summer I am thinking I should begin my life at Exeter unattached and available for what I imagine to be some wonderfully sophisticated, prep school–style affair.

Three weeks after he took off on his hitchhiking trip, Greg returns from California. Once again, a group goes out to celebrate. Just boys this time. For some reason, Jim doesn't join them.

On a stretch of two-lane road I will find myself traveling every day the next fall as I make my way from Durham to Phillips Exeter Academy, the car with Jim's friend Greg and a half dozen other friends, mostly soccer teammates, misses a curve and slams into another carload of teenagers. Everyone in both cars is killed.

I don't learn this news until the next night, when Jim shows up at my door for our usual Saturday night. I had gotten us tickets to see a Shakespeare play, so I'm more dressed up than usual. Getting into the car, I'm telling him what I've heard from my mother about the production. Jim is uncharacteristically silent.

"I don't think I can go to the play," he says, as the Model A heads down my street.

"What's the matter?" I ask him.

We drive to a patch of field out by Great Bay, where we lay down the blanket and put our arms around each other. Although I have seen my father in a state of despair, when drunk, I have never seen a boy or man cry before.

Jim is never quite the same after that. The next couple of

times I see him, he's drinking—straight Scotch this time, not beer. There's a sharp, bitter edge to him. He seems unreachable.

I get a waitressing job at Ogunquit and rent a room a few blocks from the beach. Jim drives up to see me once, then no more.

I show up for my first day of classes at Exeter that fall thinking that maybe I have finally found a community where I belong. Far from feeling the need to keep their talents concealed, as a person was wise to do at my old public school, the Exeter boys flaunt their intellectual and artistic obsessions. For the first time in my life, I don't need to conceal the intensity of my interest in accomplishment or success. The school is filled with young men in suit jackets and ties, every bit as driven as I am. More so.

But though Exeter provides more academic excitement than anything I've ever known at Oyster River High, the social atmosphere at the school, in its first year of coeducation, is tense and strained. There are only ten girls in the senior class, and nobody knows what to do with us. Now and then, in a classroom, a teacher will ask one of us for the female point of view. Most of the boys, intimidated by the scarcity of female students, steer clear of us.

My mother asks me every day now, when I come home, what boys talked to me, whom I like. I am self-conscious, embarrassed, and paralyzed. I think about boys all the time now, but the more I do, the less able I am to behave in anything close to a relaxed and comfortable way. The whole area of sex becomes increasingly scary and unnatural.

There is a small group of rebellious types on campus who have made the choice not to attend college at all next year, but to go off into the country someplace and start a farm. They wear overalls with their ties and jackets, and they play Bob Dylan's "Nashville Skyline" a lot. Listening to them, I feel a wave of longing for the boys on the soccer team. As brilliantly as the Exeter boys hold forth in the snack bar or the couches in the art gallery discussing Nietzsche or Sartre, they seem sheltered and unworldly compared to my old crowd that spent winter afternoons at the cabin, or, most of all, Jim, in the backseat of the Model A.

*　　*　　*

I am too uncomfortable to attend meals in the dining hall. I live on peanut butter sandwiches and candy bars instead and put on weight. "Your face certainly is getting round," my mother says one day. "I guess we don't need to worry anymore about that concentration camp look of yours." Another time she asks me, "Do you know how many calories are in a tablespoon of peanut butter?"

I decide to cut my intake of food down to the barest minimum. From January, when the last of my college applications are mailed—to Harvard, Princeton, and Yale—until graduation in June, I do little at the school but attend my classes, send article proposals to magazines, and rush home in time to go, with my mother, to the Elaine Powers exercise salon. I go to bed with Saran Wrap around my abdomen and see my weight drop thirty pounds within a space of five months. By spring, I have received my acceptances to all the colleges and decided on Yale.

I send a proposal to Doubleday for a how-to book I want to write about making dollhouse furnishings, which I have constructed since childhood. I am given a contract and a check for $1500, and I buy a jigsaw and a bunch of hand tools and balsa wood.

I also buy myself a platinum blond bubble-cut wig. It's part of my plan to transform myself into a completely different person. I love it that I am unrecognizable now, even to myself.

The week after my Exeter graduation, weighing 88 pounds and wearing my blond wig, I hitchhike to Boston, apply for a secretarial position at a mail-order catalogue, and get the job, not mentioning my plan to leave in the fall to begin my studies at Yale. I rent a room on Beacon Hill for the summer. I make myself a schedule that calls for me to get up at six, write for an hour, walk two miles to work, type at the office from nine to five, walk home, exercise till eight, work on my dollhouse book, eat an apple and an ice cream cone, and go to bed by ten-thirty.

The word *anorexia* is not known to me at this point. But the condition is.

Chapter Two

WE LIVE LESS than two hundred miles from New Haven, but I take a Greyhound bus to college. My parents don't drive on highways when they don't have to.

The fact that I enroll myself at Yale—that I take a cab from the bus station and haul my trunks and stereo up three flights of stairs to my dormitory room—will seem stranger to me years later than it does now. In the fall of 1971, I look around with some envy at the many other freshmen who have come accompanied by one parent or another, usually both.

Nineteen seventy-one to seventy-two is the third year of coeducation at Yale. So while the university has yet to graduate its first coeducated class of seniors, I have supposed that the situation here will be a good deal less awkward for girls (few of us call ourselves women yet) than it was at Exeter. But when I arrive, Yale still has the feeling of a basically male school that has *let girls in.* A female student walking across the Old Campus gets noticed, even if she isn't, like me, lugging a large trunk, and dressed as I am in a short, home-sewn A-line shift in a style that would not seem unusual for a girl heading out to a Brownie troop meeting.

There are a thousand students in our freshman class—fewer than two hundred of us female. The day we arrive, we all get a book featuring the photographs of our fellow freshmen and their campus room numbers. In the book, I am listed with my real first name of Daphne, though I never go by this name. When I am greeted as Daphne, as I am with some frequency during my first weeks at Yale, I always know it must be because somebody has been studying the face book. Why am I surprised? I pore over it myself. Still, the idea is unsettling, to think of being judged on the basis of our pictures in the book—mine not particularly good-looking. Of course, it could be worse. One girl I know gets several calls a day for no other reason than because she and her room-mates live in room number 69.

Yale in the fall of 1971 seems to be the scene for some kind of mating ritual whose rules I don't understand, though I long to participate. I know I should be thinking about areas of study as I make my way around the campus, buying notebooks and texts and signing up for classes. But what I am thinking about is the search I have been on for as long as I can remember, to find somebody who will rescue me from my alienation.

This has less to do, for me, with actual physical hunger—what my classmates call, to my great embarrassment, *horniness*—than with emotional longing. My own body is shut down, un-awakened. What I want is an intimate friend.

The male freshmen are scattered among many dorms around the campus, but the girls in our class have all been placed in a guarded dormitory, Vanderbilt Hall. I share a three-room suite—two tiny bedrooms with two bunkbeds in each, and a common room—with three other girls: Shana, Pat, and Susan.

I'm the skinniest I've ever been the day I arrive on campus. I change my outfit three times before going to the dining hall that first day, and when I do, I set nothing but an apple on my tray. When, after circulating the room a few times in search of a safe place to sit, I find none, I put the apple in my bag, abandon my tray, and head back to my room. For much of the year, this will be my pattern: solitary trips to the dining hall, tense search for somebody to sit next to, followed, more often than not, by a retreat to my room for a snack of fruit or granola.

At college, most people sleep late on weekends, but my father's training has made it impossible for me to stay in bed much past sunrise. Early in the morning I climb down the ladder from my top bunk and walk through the campus. Often I write letters to my parents. Because my mother views all my writing as valuable and significant, she saves these letters.

My reports from Yale are transparently envious. My wisecracking barely conceals the longing, loneliness, and isolation. Although I go to movies and the occasional concert with people I call friends, I can't shake the sense that there is no one here to whom I can turn with my truest feelings.

Things are very quiet right now on the fourth floor of Vanderbilt. I'm the only one up now; the girl across the hall has only just gone to bed. I saw her emerge from her bedroom while I was in the bathroom, hand-in-hand with a tousled pursuer. She rushed up to the sink next to mine, once he'd left, to remark on how he had this fantastic chess set and they'd played (I'll bet!) for hours. Time sure flies, etc., and she sure does love chess. So that's what they call it. All this while supposedly washing her hands. They looked clean enough to me.

Now and then, as the months pass, I talk in these letters about classes I'm taking. Mostly to please my father, I discuss Milton and Spenser and medieval art history. But my preoccupation—my obsession, really—is with sex. The offhandedness with which so many of my classmates describe their sex lives, and their apparent sophistication, has left me feeling like a mutant.

With my parents, I adopt our family's tone, which is jocular, prudish, and above-it-all. I write about the habits of my classmates as if I were Margaret Mead, observing the behaviors of some South Sea Island tribe.

Pat—the conservative-looking microbiology major—spent most of yesterday in her room with some Bob fellow, a different Bob from the day before. Occasionally they'd come out to change the records. Then they'd have these oddly stiff little intercourses—the verbal variety—and back to the bunk bed. They can't talk to each other.

I like Shana's style a bit better. She seems to be making

a fantastic number of conquests. Even three flights of stairs
do not discourage her nightly parade of suitors. We don't
bother going to the door now, when it knocks. We just call
out "Shana's not here." She never is.

I tell nobody about my father's drinking. Or about my anxieties
concerning my virginity. My friend Joanie's mother is diagnosed
with lung cancer freshman year—a fact she tells me only twenty-
five years later. Another woman gets an abortion—also unknown
to me at the time. One has some kind of breakdown that renders
her virtually unable to leave her dormitory room, so her roommates bring meals to her bed. We speak of none of this.

Of my casual friends that year, two are men who eventually
come out as homosexual. But though we spend many hours together in our freshman year, talking about drama, and music, and
our courses and papers and friends, neither of these boys ever
raises the issue of his sexual preference with me. Both of them
go through the motions of courting women.

So there is this odd juxtaposition of experiences. I have a
roommate who makes love with her boyfriend in the bottom bunk
while I lie stiffly awake, on the bunk above them, waiting for it
to be over. Boys drift into our bathroom at all hours of the day
and night, only partially clothed.

When her graduate student lover is visiting, Shana sits on his
lap. He puts his hand down her shirt while the rest of us go on
reading our *Oxford Book of English Poetry* on the couch across
from them. But when he's gone—and he hasn't called in five
hours, and none of the rest of us is supposed to make a phone call
for fear of tying up the line—there's nothing free or easy or
relaxed about her. She might as well be a sorority girl from the
fifties, worrying about getting a date for the prom.

By the time I arrive at Yale, I've cut my caloric intake down
to under a thousand calories a day and I'm stepping on and off
the scale after every meal and trip to the bathroom. So are many
girls in Vanderbilt Hall. I live on a campus with one of the great
libraries, and a faculty filled with brilliant scholars, a gym with a
wonderful pool, and movies and plays and lectures and concerts

every night, but the subjects that receive the greatest portion of my attention, besides my lack of a boyfriend, are food and my preoccupation with being thin. Although I give no thought to acquiring physical strength, I start every day with a hundred sit-ups, and I do another hundred before I go to bed.

Nineteen seventy-two is the year the Equal Rights Amendment will be drafted. It's the year *Ms.* magazine is launched. The first women's studies courses are being designed at Yale. But I doubt many of the women in my class truly see ourselves as powerful or independent, or suppose that we have ultimate control over our own lives.

"Our feminist act was getting into Yale," my friend and Yale classmate Jessica says, years later. For me, getting into Yale seemed like my arrival at a destination, when it was actually just the starting-off point for the rest of my life.

"We had no language for what was happening then," Jessica reflects. It wasn't just anorexia that didn't have a name yet, either. "The sexual revolution was happening," Jessica says. "So we knew that now we could say yes. But we didn't really understand we could say no."

It was not regarded as outrageous or particularly unusual on the Yale campus of 1971–72 for a graduate assistant or even a tenured professor to have an affair with a student. "It was just one of the things you'd know about certain teachers," Jessica says to me. "This one smoked a pipe. This one had long hair. This one slept with his students. Nobody talked about sexual exploitation or harassment."

These were times when the idea of an older man pairing up with a younger woman was viewed less as disturbing than romantic. A few years earlier, in his fifties, Frank Sinatra had married Mia Farrow—a particularly innocent-appearing and waiflike twenty-year-old. The year before we entered Yale, the prime minister of Canada, Pierre Trudeau, age fifty-one, had suddenly announced his marriage to a twenty-two-year-old.

Being of comparable age ourselves, my female contemporaries and I were hardly going to take the view that a twenty-year-old, or an eighteen-year-old, was ill-equipped to make sound romantic judgments and life choices. We knew everything we needed to. We were smart enough to get into Yale. We could do anything.

By Thanksgiving of our freshman year, one of my roommates, Shana, has moved out of our quad to live with the graduate student discussion leader for her philosophy class.

I remain a virgin. I think about my virginity all the time. I also believe that the fact of my sexual inexperience and awkwardness is as obvious to everyone around me as if I were sporting a giant letter V on the front of my shirt. I say as much, in fact, in an article I will publish the following summer in *Mademoiselle* magazine on the subject, titled "The Embarrassment of Virginity." I am too embarrassed to speak to a boy I like in the dining hall, or set my tray down beside a stranger. But I can publish an article in which I talk about the fact that I have never had sex. More and more, I live my life on paper.

I had begun sending articles to magazines while I was in high school, but now—in spite of a full course load at Yale—I pursue assignments more doggedly. I'm still working on my book about dollhouses with my friend Joan McElroy. I enter the *Mademoiselle* magazine guest editor contest—the same contest that Sylvia Plath won when she was at Smith College, which inspired her to write *The Bell Jar* about her summer in New York City, her wild ambitions, her eating disorders, and her nervous breakdown. I have also taken on an assignment from *Seventeen* magazine to go to the White House for the purpose of interviewing Julie Nixon Eisenhower—daughter of our current president.

In preparation for my trip to Washington, D.C., I come home for the weekend so my mother can sew me an outfit. We pick out a sailor dress pattern, and buy red, white, and blue fabric—white for the dress itself, a blue panel in the front, with a red bow.

I have grown up in a family that regards Adlai Stevenson as the only truly worthy candidate of the last twenty-five years. To my father, Nixon is a warmonger and a vulgarian. But at the direction of my editor at *Seventeen*, we confine our discussion to safe topics: Julie's favorite recipes, her taste in movies, what it's like living in the White House. I do not mention Vietnam.

We sit on silk-upholstered settees—me, Julie Eisenhower, and the other young girl selected to participate in this interview. We chat with great politeness about almost nothing. Julie Nixon Eisenhower, with the hairdo of my old Midge doll, keeps her ankles crossed. I take careful notes, and afterward, we pose together for a portrait.

I suggest a new topic to my editor at *Seventeen*: a profile of the Miss Teenage America pageant. She says *Seventeen* would only be interested in such a piece if it could be written by an actual participant in the pageant. What my editor has in mind is a first-person account of competing, from the point of view of a contestant.

I know I can never become Miss Teenage New Hampshire. So I conceive of another way to participate. I call the director of Miss Teenage America—a name I get, after placing a number of calls to CBS Television, which carries the pageant. I tell him I'm on assignment from *Seventeen* to cover the pageant, but that the magazine would like me to present the story from an insider's view. Perhaps they could make me some kind of judge? No problem.

I miss the last week of classes before my Thanksgiving break for the purpose of flying to Fort Worth, Texas, where I can enact what must surely rate high among the fantasies of a self-perceived teenage outsider: I get to sit in judgment, literally, of fifty very pretty, popular, and apparently self-confident girls, just a year or two younger than I am.

From Fort Worth I fly on to New York City, where my Yale friend Marguey has been chosen by the Junior League as one of the twelve debutantes to come out that season. To me, having lived all my life in a small New Hampshire town, this is a thrilling event. Marguey, who attended the Lycée Français in New York and lives on Central Park West, has told me how much she hates having to do this, but her grandmother left her money in her will for her introduction to New York society. She has to put up with it.

My mother has made me a gown for the event, using an old taffetta dress of hers from the fifties, completely reconstructed to fit my smaller body. I change into my dress at Marguey's family's penthouse while Marguey's mother finishes hemming her own dress, bought at Bergdorf's that afternoon. The whole family seems to have a kind of casual offhandedness about the evening that I can't imagine possessing.

We ride in a taxi with her brothers and her parents to the Plaza hotel, where several of our group disappear almost immediately into the bathrooms to smoke pot. I long to dance, but I know nobody here besides Marguey's brothers, and, unlike the others here, I have never taken ballroom dancing lessons. I stand on the sidelines talking to Marguey's aunt.

There at the Plaza, with the orchestra playing and the couples swirling around the room so beautifully, I make the wish that I will one day live in New York City myself, and come to the Plaza with a partner of my own, who will sweep me out onto the floor in a beautiful store-bought dress. I do not smoke pot in the ladies' room, though I stand there with the girls who do, and I slip a Plaza hotel ashtray in my evening bag, a souvenir for my mother.

By Christmas, I have applied for permission to be relocated in what's known as a psychological single—a room in a different dormitory, across the campus, with no roommates.

When I come back from Christmas break, I try out for a play. This one is an original musical called *Punks*, written by a pair of students. The story bears a certain similarity to *Bye Bye Birdie*: a rock star returns to his hometown for a weekend, where the townspeople greet him with adulation.

The part of the rock star is played by a graduate student in the art school, an androgynous-looking young man named Buddy who has a reputation on campus as one of the coolest and hippest students. Rumor has it that Buddy is friendly with Tennessee Williams and Andy Warhol. Some people are even saying that Andy Warhol's coming to see *Punks*.

I have been cast in the role of a young girl who idolizes the rock star played by Buddy. I have very few lines in this play. Mostly I am called to writhe around in a state of excitement every time Buddy makes an appearance. In my one big scene, I sit to one side of him while he performs a song, and I gyrate in a chair.

Though I do not understand this at the time, the director's instructions that I rub myself against the back of the chair and look ecstatic have required me to masturbate onstage.

Also in this production is a young man named Steve, an art student a year ahead of me. He's a quiet person; I doubt we exchange more than two sentences throughout the rehearsal period, although he has made a strong impression on me. He is one of the most handsome young men I've ever seen, in an extremely all-American, wholesome way. One night after rehearsal, out of the blue, he suggests that I come with him to a dance. He takes me to a church hall where an old-timey band is playing polka music, and we whirl across the floor. The next time I see him at rehearsal, though, he says nothing.

After twenty-five years, my father is retiring from the University of New Hampshire.

To honor the occasion, my mother has asked the university to give him a show of his artwork in one of the galleries at the arts center he and I used to visit so often on our bikes. The dean of the faculty responds with regret that since my father is an English professor, and unaffiliated with the art department, this cannot be arranged.

So my mother arranges a show of my father's paintings at our house. She has the floors refinished and repaints the downstairs woodwork. My father busies himself with framing and deciding which of his hundreds of unseen paintings and drawings will hang in which locations around our house. He has a lifetime's body of work—most of it seen by almost nobody but my mother, my sister, and me.

I come home from New Haven for the show. My sister, eight months pregnant, flies in from Toronto. Our house looks beautiful. For days, my mother has been preparing appetizers. She has been worried that the excitement of the show would be too much for my father, "set him off" (the code to describe what happens when he hits the vodka). But though he is visibly agitated, my father manages to remain sober, even as I pass around the trays of wine and cocktails.

My mother wears one of her full-length, bead-trimmed gowns

for the event. For the first time, my father looks old to me—shorter than I'd remembered, and faintly sad in the bright plaid shirt my mother has bought for the occasion that she said would look "jaunty." Many of his paintings are marked with price tags of $100. He sells a few and comments, later, on the wonderful stash of cash he's taken in—over $800—but something about the sight of him, counting up the checks, upsets me so much I have to leave the room.

I deliver my article about the Miss Teenage America pageant to *Seventeen*. The magazine buys it, but I'm not happy. The article I've written—filled with a lot of smart, biting language of a sort that seems to me very clever—has been cut from twenty pages down to six or seven, with all the meanest writing eliminated, so that what's left is a bland and not unapproving report of teenage beauty pageants.

I am so upset by this that I send a photocopy of my original story to an editor at *The New York Times*, Lester Markel, whose name I get from the masthead of the newspaper. I enclose a letter in which I introduce myself and make known to Mr. Markel my availability for future assignments from the *Times*. Perhaps, I suggest—particularly in light of the fact that this is an election year, and there is so much talk about the significance of the youth vote—he might like me to write an article about what young people are thinking about on college campuses these days? In which case, I would be uniquely well equipped to tell the readers of the *Times* what that might be.

A week later a letter turns up in my Yale mailbox, not from Lester Markel, but from Harvey Shapiro, an editor at *The New York Times Magazine*, to whom Mr. Markel has evidently turned over my original note.

Dear Miss Maynard,
     Please go ahead with a 3,500-word personal essay about what it is like to be eighteen years old in this country. Are you optimistic, pessimistic, or what? What do you think about the scenes around you and the scenes you have recently been through? How do the various ideological move-

*ments in this country speak to you, if at all; for example, do
you consider yourself a liberated woman or not, and why?*
*The piece should be based on your own observations—
of yourself and of your peers.*
*We will look for it in several weeks, as agreed. If you
want to talk about it as you go along, please don't hesitate
to call me collect.*

All my life I have associated writing with my parents' house.
Every entry I ever produced for the *Scholastic Magazine* contest
was produced in my bedroom. Every time I finished writing something there, I would call to my parents. My father would make
tea and my mother would set homemade cookies on a plate and
wheel a tea cart with the tea and cookies and cups into our living
room. I would read out loud to them while my mother made notes
on a legal pad and my father jotted down his suggestions on file
cards. Then they'd take turns delivering their criticisms, and I
would write down what they said, and go back up to my room
and work some more, implementing their suggestions, until I was
ready to call them and read again from the revised version of my
piece. Finally they both agreed I had done my best, and my
mother would type my work and mail it to the contest.

When I learn that I have an assignment from *The New York
Times*, I know that to be successful, I have to go back home to
write. That Friday afternoon, after my last class, I head out to the
highway—Route 91 North—and stick out my finger. Soon a car
picks me up.

The driver is a very fat man with a familiar smell of alcohol
on his breath. While driving along the highway he says he has a
brand-new gun in the car and tells me to take a look at it. "Big
motherfucker, huh?" he says. I look in the backseat. Sure enough.

Somewhere in Massachusetts, he says he's hungry and we pull
into a truck stop. I drink a glass of water while he has a couple
of hamburgers and a huge pile of fries. After he's done, he says
he's tired from all that food and needs to take a catnap. Just an
hour or so.

For about ten minutes I sit in the car while the man rests,
although I can see he isn't really asleep. At one point, he turns

sideways in the seat in such a way that his leg presses up against mine.

It's nearly dark by now, and I still have at least a hundred miles to cover. I tell him I think I'll try to find another ride, if he doesn't mind, and get out of his car. He doesn't try to stop me as I walk out to the side of the highway again.

The next person to pick me up, a few minutes later, is a trucker. He's going to Portland, Maine, he says, but he doesn't mind taking me right to my doorstep, because a young girl like me really shouldn't be hitchhiking like this. You never know what kind of person you are going to run into. There're a lot of perverts in this world.

"You don't believe me, but you would if you saw some of the movies they're making these days," he tells me. Then he begins to tell me about these movies. There's this one, called *The Nurses*, that has made a particularly big impression on him. He can describe every scene, including what each of these nurses' breasts looked like. His descriptions go on from Springfield, Massachusetts, to Durham, New Hampshire.

Just when he gets to my house, the trucker leans over in his cab and kisses me, sticking his tongue in my mouth. He tells me again that it's not safe to hitchhike. I jump down out of the cab and run up the walk to our house, where my parents are waiting for me.

They know I have hitchhiked home—this is my usual method of transportation, and they have never objected—but I don't tell them about the man with the gun, or the trucker who watched porn movies. My mother has cookies and milk waiting, and my father has a couple of new paintings to show me in the attic. Our dog, Nicky, is very happy to see me. Curled up on the living room couch, I munch slowly on a cookie and listen as my parents reflect on my *Times* assignment. "We've got an interesting topic to work with here," my father says.

The next morning I get up at six, take out my legal pad and start writing. I write all day and into the evening. Sometime Sunday morning, I call to my parents that I'm ready to read them what I've written, and my father puts on the water for tea. My parents offer their critiques. I take notes. My father drives me to the bus in Portsmouth.

A few days later, I finish typing my article and mail it to *The New York Times,* and I get a call from Harvey Shapiro that the paper will be running my story the next month. They need a photograph of me, and are sending a photographer to the Yale campus.

The next week Harvey Shapiro calls again, suggesting that I might like to come into New York to go over the edited version of my story there. I take the train to New York and walk over to the *Times* offices. Harvey Shapiro introduces me to the editor in chief of the magazine, Lewis Bergman. Several other editors come in to say hello and tell me how much they'd liked my piece.

"Oh, by the way," I say, "do you happen to know what you can pay me?"

"Seven hundred fifty dollars."

This is good news.

I remember two other things about my visit that day. One is that my piece has to be cut quite a lot, and, as usual, this upsets me. I am so disappointed about the part that has to go that I ask Lewis Bergman whether there's any chance I could use some of the money from my fee to buy space in the magazine, same as an advertiser might, for the purpose of extending the length of my article. This is not possible, he says.

The other thing I remember: The word "penis" appears in my article—surprising, since I am not even sure I've ever said the word out loud.

The copy editor points out to me, with some amusement, that I have misspelled this word. I have spelled it "penus."

Chapter Three

MY ARTICLE, TITLED "An Eighteen-Year-Old Looks Back on Life," runs in the Sunday *New York Times Magazine*, April 23, 1972. In it, I talk about the various social, cultural, and political experiences that influenced me and my generation, and the ways those experiences contributed to what I present as a premature world-weariness evident in myself and my contemporaries.

Reading this article twenty-five years later makes me uncomfortable. The girl who wrote it possessed a precocious facility with language. But what strikes me now is that there is a nearly insufferable tone of presumptuousness running through the article. The voice I adopt in the opening paragraph, and maintain throughout, speaks not only for myself, but for my generation. *"Mine is the generation of unfulfilled expectations,"* I say. "According to whom?" I would ask now. What gave me permission to speak for all young people?

> We inherited a previous generation's hand-me-downs and took in the seams, turned up the hems, to make our new fashions. We took drugs from the college kids and made them a high-school commonplace. We got the Beatles, but not those lovable look-alikes in matching suits with barber cuts and songs that made you want to cry. They came to us like a bad joke—aged, bearded, discordant. And we inherited the Vietnam War just after the crest of the wave—too late to burn draft cards and too early not to

be drafted. The boys of 1953—my year—will be the last to go.

In the article, I talk about the national events that shaped my generation's world view—the Cuban Missile Crisis, the Kennedy assassination. "Like over-anxious patients in analysis, we treasure the traumas of our childhood," I write. But I never mention the real traumas of my childhood: my father's drinking, my mother's reading my diary, the years of Mummy-baths, and our family's inability to discuss any of it.

The truer and more honest parts of the piece have to do with my feeling about television, my passion for Joan Baez and Jackie Kennedy, my longing for religion. But throughout the article, as I read it now, I can hear my parents' voices—my mother's in particular—shaping not just the rhythm of my sentences but even, far more disturbingly, my ideas. "An Eighteen-Year-Old Looks Back on Life" is the work of a quintessential Good Daughter, the ultimate gesture of a girl desperate to please her parents.

In the section on marijuana, I talk about how I don't smoke pot—reason enough to call my credentials as a youth spokesperson into question. I adopt a prim, puritanical tone where drugs are concerned. About sex, I am even more guarded.

We all received the "Sex at Yale" book, a thick black pamphlet filled with charts and diagrams and a lengthy discussion of contraceptive methods. And at the first women's assembly, the discussion moved quickly from course-signing-up procedures to gynecology, where it stayed for much of the evening. Somebody raised her hand to ask where she could fill her pill prescription, someone else wanted to know about abortions. There was no standing in the middle any-more—you had to either take out a pen and paper and write down the phone numbers they gave out or stare stonily ahead, implying that those were numbers you certainly wouldn't be needing. From then on it seemed the line had been drawn.

But of course the problem is that no lines, no barriers, exist. Where five years ago a girl's decisions were made for her (she had to be in at 12 and, if she was found—in—with her boyfriend . . .), today the decision rests with her alone. She is surrounded by knowledgeable, sexually experienced girls and if she isn't willing to sleep with her boyfriend, somebody else will. It's peer-group pressure, 1972-style—the embarrassment of virginity.

For much of my article, I engage in personal storytelling. When I get to talking about sex I revert to the third person. I cannot bring myself to say that this embarrassment I observe is my own. As for my obsession with dieting and being thin, the other issue that has haunted me for at least a year, probably longer, I cannot bring myself to mention it.

Reading this article twenty-five years later, I realize that the fundamental dishonesty of the voice speaking in this early article of mine is a function of my own deep sense of shame and secrecy. I wanted so much to be, on paper, a person readers could like and identify with and trust. I wanted to be an all-American girl, the Miss Teenage America of print. I never supposed, in 1972, that anybody would have cared to hear the voice of the girl I really was, a girl who did two hundred sit-ups a day, a girl whose first thought every morning, for as long as she can remember, is "What worthwhile project will I create today?"

Maybe it was my years of television watching that contributed to my total lack of faith in a reader's ability to accept a narrator who didn't seem to have emerged from my own naïve idea of the all-American family. So the voice I adopted was not even a truly female voice at all, but the most generalized, nonspecific Voice of American Youth. If I could be that person, on paper at least, I might actually succeed in transforming myself into somebody readers could accept as a normal, happy, well-adjusted, and trust-worthy narrator. More than that, even, if I could sound like such a person on paper, I might actually become her.

I take a bus home from New Haven the weekend my article is published. It's my Sunday morning ritual with my father when I'm home to drive into town with him to pick up the Sunday *New York Times* and our half-pound of freshly roasted Spanish peanuts.

This time we buy three or four extra copies of the paper, then stop at the store, as usual, for milk.

In the passenger seat driving back to Madbury Road I flip through the sections to find the one with my piece in it. I'm on the cover of the magazine section, photographed sitting cross-legged on the floor of the Yale library in my bell-bottomed jeans wearing a ratty gray sweater and red-and-white checked sneakers. I'm wearing an oversized man's watch, which fits so loosely on my wrist that it has slipped in such a way that the face of the watch is visible. Weight conscious as I am, I eye the photograph anxiously for any sign of a double chin, a stomach. But there's none of that—in fact, my face is very thin, and I have starved myself so long I am now nearly flat-chested. Still, I look nothing like the fashion models I envy. My hair is lanky and my bangs are unevenly cut. I'm smiling in the photograph, but there are dark circles under my eyes.

With the publication of this article, I have not simply accomplished something for my own self. I have vindicated the sacrifices and the terrible disappointments my parents have suffered over the years. All morning the telephone rings at our house, with my parents' friends and colleagues congratulating them.

I ride the bus back to New Haven later that day, arriving at my psychological single alone and in the dark. I don't see or talk to anybody that night. The next day, when I walk into the freshman dining hall, I feel the stares of my fellow students as I take my place. *Who do I think I am? What makes me so special?*

There are also students on this campus with sufficient self-confidence and generosity of spirit that they don't spend time resenting or probably even thinking about me. But for others, the publication of my *New York Times* story has established me on campus as an object of resentment and distrust.

If my classmates don't embrace me for my accomplishment, in the world of New York City that I've longed to be part of, many do. Within twenty-four hours of the publication of my piece in the *Times*, I'm getting phone calls from magazine editors inviting me to come into the city to have lunch. It's my mother's dream for me come true.

Under normal circumstances, I would pick up my mail at the

Yale Station post office, where I have a box. But Tuesday morning following that weekend I open the door of my dormitory room to find a couple of mail sacks filled with letters from all over the country. Hundreds.

I dump them on my bed and start reading. Some of the people who have written tell me how much they enjoyed my piece. Many are angry, sour, hurtful letters accusing me of being shallow, glib, presumptuous, sickeningly ambitious.

There are more letters from editors and television producers, congratulating me on my work and expressing an interest in meeting me. *Call my office,* they say. *I'll take you to lunch.* A movie director invites me to the Palm Court at the Plaza hotel. Several editors write to ask if I have a book contract. Senator Hubert Humphrey writes to tell me I'm a credit to my generation.

Most of the letters in the mailbags are from young men around my age who tell me they are my soul mate. They also listen to the same music, felt the same feelings I did growing up, the same alienation in high school, the same isolation, the same longing for love.

"I believe I see in you the farsighted, deep-searching qualities of a person who can both laugh and cry at Garbo, cautiously admire Dr. Hannah Arendt (whose book is reviewed in May 7's *New York Times Book Review*), assess the difference between Jung and Freud, or parry Germaine Greer with a paradox or two," writes one young man. "Enlightenment is as close and as far as the indomitable electron."

"This is the third letter to you I've written," writes another (also male). "The first two didn't get mailed. They sounded too much like love letters. . . . Your article really did something to me, or maybe it was the cover picture of you. You touched some very deep place within me like I've never been touched by words and pictures before."

"Your article gave me the same feeling I got the first time I saw *Hair*. It was as though I was watching the movie of *Woodstock* or walking for hunger or talking about Gene McCarthy again. Come out to California and I'll take you for a ride on the Hollywood Freeway. Well, Jesus, I mean you didn't expect a red-blooded American boy of twenty to write you a whole letter without one come-on did you?"

Then there is another letter. I could easily have missed it. After I read this one none of the others matter.

The envelope is hand-addressed. The paper inside, a single sheet, is the kind used for sending air mail to Europe—thin, almost transparent. I can tell from the typing that this letter wasn't typed by a secretary on an IBM. The spacing's irregular. Some letters drop below the line slightly. Some float. The return address says Cornish, New Hampshire, a small town sixty or seventy miles north of the one where I grew up. The salutation reads "Dear Miss Maynard."

The author of this letter explains that the nature of what he says must be kept totally private. Like me, he says, he is half-Jewish, right-handed, and lives in New Hampshire.

At this point I am only skimming over the words, I have so many letters yet to read. A line in the second paragraph makes me stop. Referring to a photograph that accompanied the *Times* article, featuring me in a Minnie Mouse costume sitting alone as usual at a high school dance, the author of this letter makes a wry, self-deprecating joke. I'm startled. Whoever this person is, he has come out with the kind of remark I'd make myself.

The writer says he figures I'll be getting a lot of intriguing mail in response to my article in the *Times*. He urges me to be careful before signing up for any of the stuff they offer me. Reading his list of the types of people I'm apt to be hearing from, I feel as though this person has been looking over my shoulder just now at the stacks of letters from publishers, magazine editors, news programs, television talk show producers, and Hollywood. He has correctly identified them all.

The writer of this letter tells me he is speaking from an unfortunate wealth of personal experience when he cautions me that the people making me offers to do this or that are not likely to demonstrate even the smallest measure of true concern about me or the gift he tells me I possess. My writing should be allowed to develop quietly and without haste, he says, rather than being plastered over the pages of a bunch of magazines. He suggests that I be highly skeptical about editors and New York types. He says he wants me to know that I could be a real writer, if I would just look out for myself, as no other person is likely to.

I am sitting in my dormitory room as I read these words. There's a Janis Joplin poster on my wall and ivy curling in my window, and a little wooden desk where someone carved his initials years before. I can see my portable typewriter, and my stereo and my stack of Bob Dylan and Joni Mitchell records, and my sagging single bed, and the window looking down on the Yale Old Campus quadrangle, where other girls sit on the grass beside boys with guitars, or playing Frisbee or blowing bubbles. I can hear Paul Simon on somebody's stereo, through an open window, playing the song that never seems to stop that spring, "Me and Julio Down by the Schoolyard." I hear showers running, the sounds of young voices on the stairs. I see boyfriends and girlfriends hand in hand, walking across the quad to classes or to the dining hall, where they will eat meals together, and go to the library together, and to movies, and later, probably, back to somebody's room.

I am struck by two things as I read what the writer has to say to me. One is, simply, that I love the voice that comes through in this letter. The other is that I believe this stranger with the extraordinary voice seems to *know me*. I know as I read his letter that I will never be one of the people down in that quadrangle playing Frisbee, and I probably know I won't ever quite become the successful New York City personality/media star/girl-about-town the writers of so many of these other letters suggest that I become.

The author of the letter concludes with apologies for taking such a dark view of things, but the fact is, he likes my writing quite a bit, and he has experienced the dangers as well as the appeal of youthful success. He signs his letter "Sincerely." The signature reads *J. D. Salinger*.

On the campus where I live—on any campus, anywhere young people can be found, or people who used to be young and remember how it felt—there is probably no writer whose name carries more cultlike significance than J. D. Salinger. My classmates who were envious of my early publication would be even more envious and resentful if they knew he had written to me. I don't tell them.

I am probably one of the very few people on the entire Yale campus—or any campus in 1972, or any year for the nearly two decades before—who has not read *Catcher in the Rye*. Or the *Nine Stories*. In fact, I haven't read any book by Salinger. I have a general sense of his avoidance of publicity, but I know nothing of his legendary solitude. A letter from Bob Dylan or Johnny Carson or Peter Bogdanovich (whose movie *The Last Picture Show* had recently inspired me to write a fan letter myself) would have mattered more to me than a letter from Salinger.

Still, I am impressed with the name. The fact that a famous man has conferred approval on me thrills me. This is less about any ambition to become a writer than it is about my longing to please.

Having won the prize of his approval and admiration, I feel joy, but also anxiety: Now that he has told me what a fine writer I am, I must consider every word I put on paper with a new kind of self-consciousness.

I spend a long time composing my response to J. D. Salinger's letter on my yellow legal pad. When I'm done I type it carefully. Like my mother, I place a piece of carbon paper and a second sheet underneath.

"I will remember your advice every day of my life," I write back. "I read your letter over and over, and carried it in my pocket all day. I no longer need to read it. I know it by heart. Not just the words, but the sentiments expressed. . . ."

I know instinctively that I don't need to appear overly literary in my letter to J. D. Salinger. I sense that part of what attracted him to me was my lack of interest in the literary world. This man has no need for another adoring reader and fan to analyze and discuss his work.

Neither do I need to pretend to be in possession of a New York or even Yale brand of sophistication. I am a New Hampshire girl. I know how to plant a hill of corn; I recognize the call of a flicker. I have more to say about *The Dick Van Dyke Show* than Thomas Pynchon. I have never been to Europe.

I tell J. D. Salinger that I like to ride my bicycle into the countryside outside New Haven. I don't have many friends here, I tell him. I make dollhouse furniture. I listen to a lot of music and I draw. I don't like writing all that much. I love acting in plays, and hope to be an actress someday.

I am also working hard in my letter to maintain J. D. Salinger's original high opinion of me as a writer and observer of the world. So I entertain him with stories of my world—a glimpse of my Yale dormitory, my English class, the dining hall, the play I'm acting in.

I don't fit in very well in this place, I tell him. I do not need to pretend with this man, as I would with boys my age, that I am cool or knowledgeable about things that make me enormously uncomfortable. Where, all year, I have tried to act like other girls, with this person about whom I know virtually nothing I feel I can speak in something approaching my real voice.

His first letter was dated April 25—two days after the publication of my article. I received it on the twenty-seventh or twenty-eighth and mailed my response the next day. His next letter is dated May 2. He writes to me from a plane headed for New York City, rather than waiting till his return to answer my letter to him.

He thanks me for writing and calls my letter nice—twice. He offers a kind of regretful apology about his compulsion for privacy. I would never have thought to compare myself to J. D. Salinger, but he compares himself to me, observing that I seem more levelheaded than he was at my age. Even so, he cautions that a glimpse of fame can distract a writer, so it might be just as well if I like acting best. His guess, though, is that what I will always be is a writer.

He signs off with a weather report and the news that he and his twelve-year-old son Matthew recently attended a baseball game at Dartmouth. Reading this, I get a comforting picture of J. D. Salinger as an all-American dad.

Once again, I write back immediately. I tell him about the letters I continue to get in response to my article. I tell him about a new assignment I have taken on for *The New York Times Magazine*— the story of a junior prom in the upscale suburban town of Cheshire, Connecticut, and about my fears that I will not be able to do as good a job with this story as will be expected of me now.

The "Letters to the Editor" page in the *Times Magazine* has come out with a number of highly critical responses to my original article there. I am wounded by these, and shaken, I say. I never expected that anybody reading what I wrote would take such a dislike to me.

Again, J. D. Salinger writes back at once. I'm flattered that he, too, has studied the letters to the editor, and hates the ones critical of my piece. It never ceases to amaze him how vicious and envious people can be. I can feel his indignation as I read this, and I thrill to his protectiveness of me, and his praise. He has never been more sure of anything, he tells me, than that I am a natural writer. I should write what I want, and what I have to write, and let nobody tell me what that is or plant doubts in my head. Nobody's opinion of what I do should matter to me but my own. I am a girl with a beautiful life ahead of her, he tells me.

He signs off with the suggestion that I can call him Mr. Salinger if I like, but most people call him Jerry.

The letters keep coming and keep speaking to my needs. He knows the terrible effect of unsolicited letters to a writer; probably no writer alive has received more letters than he has.

I understand already what he means when he tells me that a stranger's words in the mail are a powerful thing in the way they come to occupy your mind. Although I have had only the smallest taste of criticism, I have already been wounded by the words of complete strangers coming through the mail.

It's not just the critical letters that are a problem either, Jerry points out. The letters of praise can be dangerous too. Watch out, he tells me, for those readers who tell you everything they love about your work, because the minute they say this they're influencing you (whether you want to be influenced or not) to offer up more of the same, when what a writer needs to do is remain true to his own heart.

I had written to Jerry about the brush-off I'm receiving in the Yale dining hall. He is practically spitting as he responds. Once again, he has accurately gauged what I've been experiencing—the backbiting of certain classmates, the sudden friendship of others who never paid any attention to me before, and now want to know the name of my agent. He knows the whole thing is sickeningly unamusing. A cruel invasion. Death to a writer's work.

J. D. Salinger tells me he grew to detest his relatives when he became successful. Not that he held any affection for them before. He could bend my ear with stories of relatives suddenly turning up on the scene during the period (no doubt after the publication of *Catcher in the Rye*) when he first became anointed as a celebrity. It makes me feel worldly and sophisticated when he tells me we'd have to be drinking Scotch together before he could stomach that tale. I have never sat over drinks with anyone at this point, unless I count my father.

In his letters, he appears to be talking about me. Reading what he has to say now, I see something else. His letters are about himself: His early success. The pain he endured. The invasion of his privacy, and the attempts of others to appropriate his life. His comments about readers' responses to a writer's work and the world of publishing—the world, period—crackle with contempt.

Standing in the sunlight outside the Yale post office, ripping open my latest letter from Cornish, I take in everything he tells me as the purest kind of truth. I certainly do not observe—and won't, for a couple of decades—that the letters Jerry Salinger now sends me constitute precisely the kind of danger he has warned me about: unsolicited praise to a writer, from a reader, telling me everything he loves about my work, everything he wants to see more of. In nearly every letter, he assures me he's no sage. Then he gives me more advice. Even as he tells me I must never think of pleasing people, there is one person I want to please, more than any other. Him.

I continue to attend my classes that spring. I write papers and study for exams. But I am not engaged in any of it anymore. I act in another play—a jazzed-up production of *Measure for Measure*. I ride the train to New York City more than once on the invitation of the various magazine and book editors who have called, suggesting that we meet at some expensive restaurant and discuss some project that would have thrilled me only weeks earlier. I am invited to read for a lead role in *The Exorcist*. It was probably those circles under my eyes that caught the attention of the casting director who called. But the role goes to Linda Blair.

Other jobs I do get: *The New York Times* has sent me to a suburban Connecticut junior prom to write about the lives of the teenagers in attendance there. I have lunch with an editor at *Mademoiselle*, and the editor of *McCall's*, and an editor at Random House. Within a couple of weeks, I have signed a contract with Doubleday—publisher of my now-delayed dollhouse book—for more money than my father ever earned in a year of university teaching. I am going to write my memoir.

But although this represents all the kinds of success I've aspired to for so long, and everything for which my mother has groomed me, now that it lies within reach I feel an odd detachment. Partly that comes from the realization that none of this whirl of quasi-celebrity is going to deliver me from my deep sense of aloneness and isolation on the Yale campus and beyond. But the more substantial reason I am having so much difficulty focusing on all the offers now coming my way has to do with my growing attachment to a man I haven't even met.

The contents of my mailbox at Yale continues to overflow. Even my parents are getting letters. One week after the publication of my piece in the *Times*, my mother sends a report from home.

> *Dearest Joyce,*
> *I have thought of you a great deal this past week, with a mixture of feelings you can imagine: pride, love, anxiety, joy, excitement, apprehension. Also a certain startlement. I never doubted that you would achieve brilliant success, most probably in writing. I just didn't think it would happen so suddenly or so soon, and with such dramatic reverberations. Did we cast you on the tide? Were you ready to be cast? Where will the current carry you? I don't know, but the tide is moving....*

Although my correspondence with J. D. Salinger is in its very early stages, the influence of his writing voice is now visible in mine. My letters to him are full of slightly overdone run-on sentences, stuffed with capitalized words, italics, parenthetical asides, qualifiers, interior debate with myself. The stakes are getting higher now, but also, I am feeling more sure of myself.

"Dear Mr. Salinger," I write (in a letter that has crossed paths with the one in which he instructed me to call him Jerry):

> *I begin this next paragraph timidly—a Let's Make a Deal gambler (do you know the show? Probably not. My television references are almost always missed by friends with a whole other sphere of experience) who, with every new prize, has more to lose. I don't want to enter areas that are none of my business or be sent, not just out of those forbidden rooms, but exiled from the whole house.*

> *Still, if a conversation cannot be two-way, it's not worth having at all; it's a house I shouldn't be inside to begin with (forgive my mixing of metaphors—I'm tiptoeing you see, and losing my balance as tiptoers do). Besides, conversations between strangers by mail can have a kind of drunken openness that even better friends, in a living room together, can't attempt.*

> *So I'll ask. What is a day in your life like? Do you sit at a desk and write? Do you listen to music or visit or eat peanut butter sandwiches? Perhaps I've built a drama and a mystery where none exists. But surely you must know that there is a mythology....I don't mean to intrude. I am not, honestly, a scoop-seeking fan (autographs, maybe? A splinter from the fence?). Just—I hope you'll believe me—a concerned friend who has slightly, but trustingly, opened the door herself—and feels the one on the other side should do the same. In trepidation, Joyce M.*

His answer comes swiftly, as they always do. His days up in Cornish often run together, he says. A big part of them is often spent in the practice of homeopathic medicine. Today, for instance, he called his mentor in Colorado, Dr. Lacey, to discuss a diagnosis he'd made concerning his daughter. They spent a few hours on the phone.

In his letter, Jerry talks with a certain ruefulness about the way the study of homeopathy, like his studies of religion and mysticism, has taken him away from his writing for long periods. But he takes comfort from the understanding that eventually the things that interest him are likely to show up in his fiction.

He offers me a list that amounts to a roundup of the sorts of things he loves and cares about that fill his day: Jane Austen, vaudeville, his daughter's basketball playing, Hui Neng, the neighbors on *I Love Lucy, samhadi*, Bert Parks. The last item named on his list is myself.

My days now revolve around my trips to the post office to pick up my letters from J. D. Salinger. Never before have I felt the excitement or joy or anticipation to equal what I experience on those occasions when I look through the glass window of my Yale post office box and see an envelope with his handwriting, or the familiar pitch of his manual typewriter.

I always write back quickly. I adopt a tone of ever-greater world-weariness to match the one he uses when he writes to me.

"Dear Jerry," I write, in a letter dated May 17—less than three weeks after receiving his first note.

> *That last letter must have made me sound like a very grim and weary person, so I want, first of all, to amend that picture, not only because a depression is so boring but also because I am really quite cheerful; it is the people around me who seem miserable—spiritless, at least... why are they always sleeping? When I am unhappy, then it is only because I so rarely find people to be happy with. Happy? Well, not quite. Joyful. (I bet that sounds like one of those awful posters they tack up on the walls of church youth group coffeehouses, but I mean it, really.) It is the dilemma of my life that friends matter terrifically to me, that I like to like people, but find so many so unlikable. I was not raised by my parents so much as I was sharpened, schooled and burdened with a critical sense I can never turn off. I wear*

it like a pair of X-ray glasses or—do you know Andersen's
Snow Queen fairy tale?—that snow child with the chip of
glass in his heart, who sees the ugliness in everything.

At the point I write this, I have not yet read *Catcher in the Rye*. I don't know about the scene where Phoebe demands of Holden that he name one thing he likes a lot. Or that once Holden has named his dead brother, and the experience of sitting on the bed talking with Phoebe, he has a hard time coming up with anything else he likes. But I am well acquainted with the feeling of not liking most of what I see in the world.

He wonders if I am familiar with the word *landsman*—and I am. It's a word my mother used, interchangeably, with our family phrase "one of us." Literally, a landsman is a person who comes from the same place, back in the old country. A landsman is someone with whom you find a connection of the heart and soul.

Jerry tells me we are landsmen, he and I.

I write back, as always, the day his letter arrives. "Oh, yes, I know the word landsman well, the people to whom it refers very little—well, landsmen are, to me, a rare and valuable group of just a few. Finding one makes me happier than I can say."

The quality of feeling between landsmen is not about sexual passion or even, in conventional terms, love. It's more basic than that even. You *know* this person. You register what happens in similar ways. You understand each other.

For me, the list of landsmen numbers two, my mother and my father. Their conclusions and assessment of whatever situation I put forth to them—the task of writing my *New York Times Magazine* essay, or analyzing the "Nun's Priest's Tale," or the syntax of Spiro Agnew, or the inadvisability of using drugs—will always be brilliant, impeccable, and irrefutable.

But whom does that leave me with to talk to about *them?* I used to ask myself: Whom will I ever find powerful enough to take my parents' place in my life? Where can I ever go, and feel at home, besides the house in which I've grown up?

The girl I was before Jerry Salinger entered my life still hitch-hiked home from New Haven more weekends than not—choosing tea in her parents' living room and reading manuscripts out loud for critique over campus film festivals or sports events, smoking pot, late nights at Pepe's Pizza with friends her own age.

For eighteen years I have lived in terror of leaving my parents, and yet dreamed of making my escape. I have run to my mother's bed and my father's studio at the same time I kept wishing for another, safer home.

Within weeks of embarking on my correspondence with Jerry, he becomes my rescuer, my destination.

What I see in Jerry Salinger—and this is far more significant for me than his literary celebrity—is the possibility that there might be another human being on the planet in whose presence I won't need to conceal my true identity. What's the desire of a boy to kiss me or have sex with me, compared to the extraordinary sense of relief and comfort of finding a fellow human being who recognizes and embraces me like a long-lost countryman? It's not his fame as a writer that draws me to him. It's his voice. Eventually I will come to love his voice on the phone, his voice in the room with me. But what I love first is his voice on the page.

On the surface of things we can hardly seem more different. That he's thirty-five years older is just the first of a very long list of differences between us. We are both (as he has pointed out in that first note) half-Jewish, but he grew up in a family of increasing privilege in New York City in the twenties and thirties. I'm a small-town girl. He fought in World War II, landing on Utah Beach on D-day. I ran the Kids for LBJ headquarters on our tree-lined street in Durham, New Hampshire, and later handed out daisy stickers for McCarthy in the mill town of Berlin, New Hampshire. He has been married before—twice. I have kissed one boy in my whole life.

Then there's the huge matter of our attitudes toward worldly success. He was the toast of New York in his early thirties and chose to leave all that. He wants quiet and solitude, to read and meditate and study for hours every day without distraction. I want to go to parties full of famous people. I want to dress up, go out to lunch, give interviews, have my picture taken, dance at the Plaza. I want to go to Hollywood. I see myself up on the stage at the Dorothy Chandler Pavilion accepting an Oscar, see myself performing on Broadway, dining at Elaine's, posing for *Vogue*. If there were a *People* magazine at this point I would want to appear in its pages. I want to have money and worldly praise and beautiful clothes.

For me, the notion of being recognized has always represented a kind of belonging. For my sister—a more modest type—the goal used to be winning the National Spelling Bee. If she could just do that, and get her name in the paper for it, she used to think, she'd have friends. If I could just get on television, I always used to suppose, I, too, would finally fit in.

Every night of my life since I can remember, I have lain in bed before falling asleep, making up lists in my head of things I need to accomplish the next day. I have sung and danced and painted and written stories, always in a way that said, "Here I am! Look at me! Tell me you approve."

It is unfathomable to me, at eighteen, that some people actually grow up feeling reasonably content with themselves. It will be years before I understand some people go to bed every night with a sense of well-being that has nothing to do with winning prizes or publishing their stories.

There is probably no square mile in the nation, the spring of 1972, with a higher density of bright, ambitious young people than the mile or two that constitutes the epicenter of the Yale campus where I live. I don't know this at the time, but at the law school dining hall where I clear dishes away for my scholarship job, one of the students whose dishes I am clearing is Bill Clinton, and another is Hillary Rodham. Down the street at the drama school, I attend the performances of a drama student named Meryl Streep.

With the publication of my *New York Times Magazine* article, I seem at last assured of getting all the things I've wanted for myself. Just as that's happening, along comes Jerry Salinger speaking to me from the pages of the letters whose arrival I now await so anxiously that I know just when the fresh batch of afternoon mail gets sorted at the Yale post office. In a voice of exquisite understanding and sober, wise reflection, Jerry tells me things in his letters that my mother, my agent, the editors I now travel to New York to meet, never do.

He tells me to disregard money—something I care about desperately, never having had it. He says he'd hate to find himself "slowly shaking my head" for the rest of his life, as he would if I passed up the thing I do better than I know for television journalism or any activity that doesn't require of me a nearly painful degree of care and introspection. The week he writes me that, I get a call from Richard Salant, the president of CBS News, inviting me to come talk with him, and another from Osborne Elliot, editor of *Newsweek*, inviting me to write a column for a new feature beginning soon in his magazine called "My Turn."

Jerry assures me he isn't any kind of guru. He's fairly intuitive, he tells me, and an inveterate reader, and one who ponders all kinds of things. If ever he made a wise move, he says, he did so only out of a complete cynicism concerning the motives of his fellow man.

I have never known anyone besides my parents to choose words with as much precision as Jerry. He calls a paragraph "oafish" and another "prose-proud" and another "late-at-night." He speaks of my absence as my "not-here-ness." He makes wonderful, small distinctions between one word and another. He loves "permanence," not "petrification." He loves "wholeness," "lastingness." He doesn't simply think, he has "grave ruminations," "grey thoughts," "elegiac affection," "nice Jewish considerations," "little big worries."

He writes with a kind of excitement and pleasure some people would reserve for speaking of a person's hair, or eyes, or body, about the choices of words I have made in my letters to him. He tends to develop enduring affection for things I say.

It's true of Jerry, as it is of Holden Caulfield, that there are many things he despises in the world. Most things, probably. But he is also funny and observant and extraordinarily tender—sentimental, even—about things he loves. Often these things have to do with his children, or with any rare evidence he finds in the world of true innocence or simplicity.

The things he cares about are the kinds of things I care about, too. He talks about his garden and his daughter playing basketball and reading newspaper advice columns, his affection for a particular Hitchcock screenwriter, and a bit player from British films of the thirties. When he takes Matthew to see *Fiddler on the Roof,* he cares little for the elaborate production numbers, but loves a single shot of a rural train station. The glimpses I get of Jerry's life and his experiences would seem far removed from mine, but the goings-on at his house, and in his mind, come to seem more real than anything happening in my life in New Haven.

All through this spring, as I go through the motions of attending classes and carrying my tray along the line in the dining hall, performing my lines in *Measure for Measure,* I am mentally in Cornish. With Jerry, I am not engaging in the tiresome, incessant interior monologue anymore. I am taking part in a marvelous conversation.

His letters to me never carry the slightest hint of sexual feeling. Although my letters to him are full of stories, I do not recount for him my experiences earlier in the school year concerning my roommates' activities on the bunk beds, or my own agonized sense of unworthiness at the awareness that no such activities were going on in my own bunk bed. I never mention the absence of a boyfriend. He never mentions any woman in his life, past or present, including the mother of his children.

For me, there is actually some comfort and safety in the fact that Jerry is not a physical presence. I know by this point that he and I are bound to meet, but I feel surprisingly little urgency. I like having him where he is—on paper, in my mailbox. As a highly inexperienced and fearful girl, uncomfortable in her own skin, I view with relief the fact that I don't have to deal with the mechanics of bodies, kissing, or nakedness. What our physical separation offers him—why a man of his age would want to carry on what is now a correspondence of considerable intensity with a girl he's never met—is something I don't ask myself.

For all my pursuit of publication and prize money, I've never given much thought to becoming a writer, though in every letter he reminds me that I am one. Writing has always been something I did because I could. I never thought of writing as my life's work or an essential part of who I might be. Now here is this writer, revered by readers vastly more serious than I, who has chosen me, of all the people he might have written to, as the girl in whose talents he most believes.

So I am forming a new picture of myself. After one of those letters, in which his praise had seemed embarrassingly extravagant, I write back expressing my self-doubt and the panic I sometimes feel that I will never again be able to produce another piece of good writing. He tells me he doesn't see how this thing I have could ever be extinguished no matter what the future holds for me.

He tells me regularly that he doesn't believe in giving advice, and doesn't have a leg to stand on as an advice-giver. Still, he offers it.

A writer like me, he says, must pour my whole self into my writing. He tells me never to stop writing whatever it is I feel I must write about, the things I love writing about, and to pay no attention whatsoever to any voices from within myself, or from the outside world, that might cause me to question what I'm doing. All my life, I have only been as good as the *Scholastic Magazine* judges and my parents told me. Now Jerry tells me to be "cool" about things, never to let anybody's opinion worry or sadden me, or—equally important—never to let the opinions of others make me disproportionately happy.

Not surprisingly, I read and reread his letters daily. He tells me we're cut from the same cloth, he and I, and that, more than anything else, fills me with comfort and joy. Partly it's our half-Jewishness that has contributed to the keen sense of outsiderishness and observership we both possess, he says, but then he goes on to mention a long list of other half-Jewish writers, and points out he doesn't feel a similarly deep connection to any of them. The bond he has with me, he suggests, is something he has never experienced before.

On paper, all the other differences that separate us fall away, and we are simply two people with a shared vocabulary. In one of my letters, I used the word "good-sense-ish" to describe myself. Jerry tells me how he loves it that I chose that word over "sensible." I hadn't given any thought to the word when I wrote it.

Now I consider every line I send him. Knowing what he likes, I tailor my language to suit him.

"You overestimate me," I write.

Not likely, he tells me. I am a girl, he says, who will make a wonderful life for herself. A life like nobody else's. I'm a girl with the world on a string.

As I become familiar with his voice in the pages of his letters, I recognize a certain irony to the way that J. D. Salinger is worshiped by so many of my contemporaries. The actual man behind the beloved character of Holden Caulfield, and the characters of the Glass family, possesses contempt for much of what young people embrace on campuses like mine. Jerry despises what he perceives as the watered-down variety of Eastern mysticism popularized by the Beatles' visits to India with the Maharishi. He barely mentions politics or world affairs—even in this election year, with the Vietnam War still going on, and the early news of the Watergate break-in soon to hit the news. When he does speak of student activism of the kind that's going on around the country at the moment, it is largely to question the motives behind students' seemingly liberal politics, and above all else, the adherence to fashion and convention—even the adherence to the fashion of unconventionality.

"There's so much perversion all around me," I write to Jerry.

Perversions! he responds. Oh yes: *spiritual, cultural, sexual.*

Seemingly out of nowhere, he brings up Masters and Johnson, whose names are much in the news this year for their sex-therapy practices and the clinics they've set up treating couples with sexual problems. Jerry has never mentioned sex in any of his letters but now he tells me that the publication of the Masters and Johnson report is one of the most destructive things that young people could have been subjected to. The whole thing is a sham, he says, because it comes out of times absent of all "orgasmic normalcy." I don't have a clue what he means, but I hang on his words.

His references are an odd mix: Masters and Johnson, Hemingway, Ring Lardner, Lao Tse. Nineteen forties New York, nineteen seventies television; the tweedy world of the Carlyle Hotel,

The New Yorker, Westport, Connecticut, and the Biltmore, the ungentrified life of rural New Hampshire. In his early days, he hung around places like the Stork Club in New York with Eugene O'Neill's daughter Oona before she married Charlie Chaplin—a marriage that took place when she was eighteen and he was fifty-three.

Jerry doesn't go out on the town anymore. His two most frequent visitors in Cornish are a couple in their sixties, Eva and Vernon Barrett, who clean and do odd jobs for him, and a young housewife in town named Sally Kemp, who comes over to study homeopathy with him.

He's still a New Yorker. Now and then in a letter he'll mention having a telephone conversation with S. J. Perelman—Sid— or going in to Manhattan to have lunch with William Shawn, editor of *The New Yorker* magazine, or getting a visit from a couple of longtime *New Yorker* writers who stop for lunch on their way back from a visit to Cape Cod. But mostly his visits will be with Sally, to work on homeopathy, and the Barretts, with whom he discusses his compost pile, or cordwood, or his tomato plants. He talks to me a lot about writing, but never about writers, except dead ones, and never about the current literary scene, which he avoids. (Though he eventually mentions a particular loathing for John Updike, who once published a highly critical piece about his work.) He writes about his dachshund, Joey, a trip to the health food store in White River Junction, a bet with Matthew that entailed not shaving for a week, getting his car fixed.

In one of my letters I ask him, with a kind of innocence you have to be eighteen to possess, if he's been doing any writing lately. He responds that he writes every day. Always has. As our friendship develops, he speaks about his writing just in passing, as if that goes without saying, and occasionally he will speak of having had one of those weeks where most of the pages end up in the trash.

One day, near the end of the spring term, I ride my bike over to the Yale Coop and pick up a copy of *Catcher in the Rye* with its familiar red jacket. It's an odd feeling, seeing the name I know from a handwritten signature on a page, printed in yellow letters on the cover. Standing in line to buy the book, I feel almost embarrassed, as if I were buying contraceptives or *The Story of O.* I stuff the book in my bag and carry it back to my dormitory room. I spend the afternoon reading it.

Although this is my first exposure to Salinger's published work, the voice in the novel is instantly recognizable. It could be Jerry talking. It's not just that Jerry has inserted so many of his opinions—about movies, or books, or actors, or music—into *Catcher in the Rye.* What's familiar is the point of view and the eye of the young Holden Caulfield, which is very nearly the same as that of the man with whom I have been corresponding these last few weeks.

I read with particular interest the passages in *Catcher in the Rye* that involve Holden's dealings with girls. Like me, Holden Caulfield remains a virgin, maintaining that he has had plenty of opportunities to change this. In Holden's case, he just hasn't got around to it. Sex has a significance for him that makes it impossible for him to embark on in a casual way. He has to like the girl a whole lot. But in the end, the only girl he really loves is his little sister.

The portrait of Phoebe, the tenderness with which Jerry portrays her, makes all other girls in the novel seem corrupt and practically ugly by comparison. Reading his description of Phoebe makes me love her. I want Jerry to feel, about me, the way he does about Phoebe.

The next time I write to Jerry after finishing the book, I ask him only one question about it: How did Holden Caulfield ever manage to fit so many activities into a single night?

He answers back that he has no idea; we'd have to ask someone really smart. Maybe my mother's friend, the famous psychologist.

Another time, he will explain to me how he came up with the name of Holden Caulfield (names on a movie marquee: William Holden and Joan Caulfield). Once or twice over the months to come he refers to somebody or other trying to obtain movie rights to the novel—something he'll never sell. Other than this, Jerry and I don't discuss the contents of *Catcher in the Rye* again.

* * *

All through his letters are the comings and goings of his children. His daughter, Peggy, goes to boarding school but comes home a lot on weekends to see her boyfriend at Dartmouth. When Jerry speaks of his own lack of a girlfriend in his teenage days, and his fears at the time that he would never find anybody, I feel once again that the years separating our ages matter less than the similarities of our outlook and the outsider status we share.

Matthew splits his time between his mother's house up the road and his father's. Jerry writes that he takes Matthew to every Dartmouth home football game. I recognize that as a testimony of love from a man who cares nothing about football, hates to be cold or sit in uncomfortable seats in a crowded stadium, and calls himself "pantywaist."

Jerry has set up his life with privacy and freedom from interruption as central concerns. The children complicate matters. Even though they attend private schools, and stay with their mother a lot of the time when they're home, they want to go to ballgames and watch TV at his house and have friends over. I'm surprised by how much Jerry allows his days to be interrupted by all this. Peggy lives a very independent life. But when Matthew's around, Jerry suspends many of his usual rules for himself about quiet, lack of interruption, time for meditation and study.

Jerry has told me at some length in his letters about his many-years-long study of homeopathic medicine. In almost every letter there is some reference to a day spent treating one or another of his children. Now in one of my letters I mention that on a bike ride into the countryside around New Haven I've picked up a case of poison ivy. Two days later a little package arrives: a remedy he's fixed for me—spotted jewel weed saturated in high-proof vodka. I use it right away and the poison ivy's gone. No surprise. Jerry Salinger has secret powers, greater than any person I've ever known.

Chapter Four

THE CORRESPONDENCE BEGINS in late April. For the remainder of the semester—barely four weeks—letters go back and forth between us almost daily. By May he has given me his telephone number and suggests that I call, collect.

I was always nervous about calling boys. I'd practice with my mother, who would begin our rehearsals by saying "Dingalingaling." But now, with no hesitation, I pick up the phone in my Yale room and dial his number.

He has a wonderfully deep, rich voice—no discernible trace of New York, although Jewishness is there in it, maybe even half-Jewishness, and intelligence, and humor, and a sense that the person speaking is doing so with a kind of self-assurance and authority few others possess.

"Is this Jerry?" I begin, when he picks up the phone that first night. "This is Joyce Maynard calling."

"What do you know? That's terrific," he says. He's a little out of breath. "I was just down at the garden," he says. "Putting in the last of my tomato plants. Black flies are murder this year. What have I been telling you? Everybody's after your blood."

"I thought I'd call and say hello," I tell him.

"Since I'm such an *old* friend," he says. "Glad you did, kiddo. What've you been up to?"

I tell him what's going on in my life—the people in my classes, my teachers, the goings-on at Yale, the play, my parents, exciting developments in my publishing career—meaning assignments from *McCall's* and *Newsweek* and *Mademoiselle.*

"I know you didn't think it was a good idea, my taking so many jobs..." I begin.

"You'll weary of it before too long," he says. "I wrote for *The Saturday Evening Post* myself, in my day. The moment will come when you'll want to put a lid on all that. The kick of the thing will wear off soon enough."

I describe for Jerry the details of the junior prom I attended in Cheshire, Connecticut, the other night, which I'm writing about for *The New York Times.* As with the Miss Teenage America pageant that I wrote about earlier in the year, I am only a year or two older than most of the participants in this prom, but my description of the event, and the one I will ultimately publish in the *Times,* suggests the perspective of a much older person, somebody for whom things like proms and boyfriends with corsages and dancing to rock and roll bands and making out in cars afterward would be strictly *material.*

"The whole thing sounds altogether too poignant for this kid," he says.

In my letters, I have regaled Jerry with stories about my life in New Haven: A boy with an obsession about children's television, who makes sure never to miss an episode of *Mr. Rogers' Neighborhood.* The girl who sits next to me in my colonial history seminar who sucks on a pacifier every time we take an exam. Our teacher, who rolls his tie up and down the front of his shirt as he talks and looks like a person who might have been better suited to Puritan times than to the ones we currently inhabit. My friend Josh, who is trying to teach me to play the piano, not with scales or rudimentary exercise, but one Mozart measure at a time. I have described my film animation class, where, for my final project, I am drawing frames for a one-minute cartoon depicting Fred Astaire dancing.

I don't tell Jerry this part, but all semester I have had a crush on a fellow student in this class: a cartoonist (something I have thought I might like to be myself) so gifted he has already begun to enjoy a certain notoriety on campus with his newly created *Doonesbury* comic strip. My dark, handsome classmate Garry Trudeau—though he is just a few years older than I, and sits directly across from me in our small seminar—seems completely unattainable as a friend, much less a boyfriend.

In the telephone conversations we have almost nightly now, Jerry is interested in everything I have to say. He wants to know what my psychological single looks like. What I had for dinner. (A broccoli spear and a container of yogurt.) One thing I do not share with him is the story of my endless anxiety about my body. Lately, in fact, I have begun feeling insatiably hungry, and put on five pounds. This is making me terribly nervous.

"How's old Shakespeare coming along? New Haven's answer to Elia Kazan come up with any brilliant new directorial touches?" he asks. I have already told him about the trendy, gimmicky production of *Measure for Measure* in which I am performing, and how—no doubt inspired by the recent release of *The Godfather*—the director has attempted to inject a gangster milieu into the play, although none of it has anything to do with the story. In fact, I say, this guy has been anointed the current boy-wonder director at Yale.

"Prince of a man like that is bound to go far in 1972," Jerry says.

"I'm actually embarrassed to be onstage," I tell him. "Now the director's decided to set part of the production in the future," I say. "The nun is a go-go dancer and the friar sports sunglasses and says, 'I'm going to make you an offer you can't refuse.'"

Jerry laughs, then sighs. "Nothing I love more than to see Shakespeare injected with biting social commentary."

"Current drama thinking around here seems to be that the only justification for doing an old play is to inject it with all sorts of sexual perversion," I say, the cynic now more than ever, the embittered observer of a world swiftly going to hell—artistically, sexually—though unlike Jerry, I possess no direct experience of the good old days. "In this production, half the men's parts are played by women and vice versa. I actually play a female character, but I make my entrance on a pulley, for no discernible reason."

"You know, wherever I look now, that's what I see," Jerry says. "Art and true culture headed no place but maggotward."

We talk and write a lot about acting, performances he's loved, actors (many unknown British bit players) whose work he most admires. "I'm not a big fan of all those actorly types," he tells me. He likes Brando. Paul Newman irritates him. Too much ego in Dustin Hoffman.

"Laurette Taylor in *The Glass Menagerie*. There was a performance for you. The play belonged to her as much as Tennessee Williams."

I've never seen a Broadway play. I know the name of Marlon Brando, but of few others he mentions. Still, we compare notes: my high school drama club, the West End. My performance as Lady MacBeth when I was sixteen. Olivier's *Hamlet*.

"He's brilliant, of course," Jerry tells me. "Still, when you're watching him, you can't help being *aware* of how brilliant he is. Something rotten about it."

What can I say? I have never seen Laurence Olivier in anything, except maybe interviewed on the *Today* show.

"More than anything else—yogi, homeopath, two-bit actor, pea-grower, movie projectionist—what I am is a writer," he tells me. "We're a funny breed. Nobody would want to be one, if he had any choice in the matter. Miserable, embarrassing business, really."

"A guy like me," he says, "has made the choice to live his life on the page. You're doing it too, from the looks of things. Who wouldn't rather be an actor?"

Jerry once acted himself. He once pictured himself performing roles he would write for himself to play.

"Jerry Lewis tried for years to get his hands on the part of Holden," he tells me. "Wouldn't let up." This is never going to happen, we both understand. The only person who might ever have played Holden Caulfield would have been Jerry Salinger.

"The trouble is, I don't really like the theater. Capital T, I mean. That larger-than-life business. Makes me nervous. Entrances, exits, curtains, lighting design—the whole thing acts on me like small doses of arsenic. Spare me those beautiful sets that inspire an audience to burst into applause when the curtain opens. But you can have your bare sets, too. Something so terribly affected about that. Even worse, probably. All that pseudo-modernity that mistakes minimalism for truth."

"Yes," I say. "That's what I think, too. I was in *The Bald Soprano* once. . . ."

Although we're talking regularly on the phone now, the letters continue. He writes about the movies he loves best—he loves movies, not films—and how, some years back, he got himself a 16mm projector so he could watch prints of old movies he loves, right there in his living room with his children: *The Thirty-Nine Steps, The Thin Man, The Lady Vanishes, Lost Horizon.* As much contempt as Jerry conveys about nearly everything being produced in the current world of film, theater, art, and literature, he holds an attitude of tenderness and occasional reverence for what came out of the thirties—the years when he was close to the age that I am now. With the exception of a handful of movies—*From Here to Eternity, The Pink Panther*—his favorites were made long before I was born.

In my dormitory most nights, as we speak, the music playing is likely to be Led Zeppelin, James Taylor, Carole King, and the current Rolling Stones album, *Sticky Fingers*, featuring a close-up of Mick Jagger's crotch with a fly that actually unzips. When I ask Jerry what music he listens to, he mentions someone named Blossom Dearie, Glenn Miller, the Andrews Sisters, Benny Goodman.

The frame of reference we share is television—the one current medium where his otherwise-withering critical sense seems suspended. He speaks and writes with only the warmest appreciation about Mel Brooks and Johnny Carson and *The Dick Van Dyke Show.* We share a deep affection for Mary Tyler Moore, although we like Carl Reiner a lot, too, and a number of the actors who play bit parts on the show. "I could spend a lifetime not missing Morey Amsterdam, though," he tells me.

"We're both *watchers*, you and I," he tells me—though of

course I have already known this about myself for years, and recognized it in him, too, from early on. We are not just talking about television, either.

When his kids are home sick, he says, he often watches TV for a week, straight. "I could go out in the back room and write, but then my children would be all alone on the sofa and they'd have nobody there to appreciate it when Laura Petrie gets her toe stuck in the faucet."

"The worse the television—the more *American*—the more I love it," he says. We reminisce about particular episodes of *The Andy Griffith Show* that I know too: the time Andy catches Barney serenading his girlfriend, Juanita, over the phone at the diner; the time Briscoe T. Darling, offered lodging in the jailhouse for the night, replies, "Smells of charity, Sheriff. We aim to keep our standing in the community."

"Remember the time Andy explains to Opie about growing up, and the responsibilities of life, and urges Opie to just sit there and think about it?" Jerry says.

I never imagined I'd meet someone else who remembers things like this. I finish his sentence for him. "And Opie says 'Do I have to, Pa?' And Andy says yes."

"Opie says, 'It kinda makes me sad, Pa.'" Jerry continues. Our words overlap.

"You know," he goes on, "that boy Opie was on to something."

It's almost never the star he likes, it's the little guy whose name most people, except Jerry, wouldn't even know. But I do. (I, who once made it my business to recite out loud every single name as the credits rolled at the end of *Leave It to Beaver*.)

We can talk for ten minutes about the character of Barney Fife, played by Don Knotts, or the time Opie, played by Ron Howard, sold the homemade pickles Aunt Bea had planned on entering in the county fair.

That leads Jerry to the subject of child actors. "Terrible thing to do to a kid—stick him in front of a microphone or a camera like that."

In my article for *The New York Times*, I wrote about the way in which my childhood had been cut short—the premature cynicism that afflicted members of my generation. Though I am not all that far from childhood myself, I share Jerry's strong interest in children. Earlier this year, for one of my classes, I spent a Saturday morning studying cartoons on television. I tried, without success, to get into Maurice Sendak's children's literature seminar, and for my term paper in Puritan History selected the topic "The Early Colonist's Perception of Childhood"—namely, that it didn't exist.

It's not hard to see that what fascinates Jerry about children in the first place has to do with their innocence and guileless-ness—something he's always looking for in the world, and seldom finds. He loves the total lack of artifice in a child. Even though child actors represent the antithesis of all that, there is the occasional one—and we agree, Ron Howard is one—who manages to maintain this natural, open-hearted naïveté, even on a stage set in front of the camera. Mostly, though, child actors are the worst frauds of all, because they manage to *affect* this look of innocence without truly possessing anything close.

"There's a thought that could break your heart," Jerry says.

One night I tell him on the phone that *Ms.* magazine has given me an assignment to fly to the Democratic National Convention in Miami this July to write about the significance of the youth vote. "Ah, Florida," Jerry sighs. "I've put in my time there." I mention something about the Chicago Seven trial, and demonstrations going on at Yale in support of Abbie Hoffman and Bobby Seale. He remarks on the death of the Duke of Windsor. I am not sure who that is.

News in Jerry's daily life concerns small events: reports that a woodchuck has gotten into his vegetable garden, one of his children's ailments, which he is treating homeopathically. The biggest news in Jerry's life, he says, is meeting me.

I would say the same about meeting him. But in my world, there's a great deal of activity these days. I have signed my book contract—news that I might have expected to elicit expressions of concern, but he is past censure now. He expresses nothing but pleasure and encouragement to me about my upcoming assignments.

"Be sure to show me that one when you're done," he says, of

the prom article. "Send me some pages." Whatever he really thinks about my topic for *McCall's*—an article to be called "My Parents Are My Friends," all about the wonderful relationship I have with my mother and father and how well we communicate—he says nothing remotely critical. "That's *great*," he tells me. "They sound like terrific people."

He works on his fiction daily, though he hasn't published a story since 1965. Another night, sitting on my bed, eating a container of yogurt that is my dinner, I ask him why he doesn't publish his work.

"Publication is a messy business," he tells me. "You'll see what I mean one day. All those loutish, cocktail-party-going opinion-givers, so ready to pass judgment. Bad enough when they do that to a writer. But when they start in on your characters—and they do—it's murder."

"It's just more of a damned interruption than I can tolerate anymore," he tells me. This is a constant theme for him: not just the unwelcome critics, but all the well-intentioned and even likable people—old friends, his beloved children, even—who come between Jerry and his work. When he talks about interruptions, I feel complete assurance that he never means me.

A recurrent theme of his communication to me is how much he loves my writing. He says he doesn't know what kind of a writer I will be. He despises literary prizes, reviews, New York intellectuals. He hates artiness in writing, and writerliness, and writers who seem to court an image with as much calculation as movie stars—tweedy types sucking on cigars on their book jackets, or exquisitely sensitive-looking women in black turtlenecks. Jerry knows all their names and follows what they've been up to more closely than I would have supposed, and possesses little but contempt for what he sees of the literary world.

When Jerry speaks about the effect my writing has on him, he uses the words another person might about more physical, sexual experiences. There is something in the way I write and think that makes him feel good. My writing "arouses affection." It gives him satisfaction.

"I haven't had a friendship like this before, you know, kiddo," he tells me one night. "Don't quite know what to make of it, and I don't much want to worry the thing to death. God knows what's to be done about it. I'm just happy knowing you exist on this planet of aliens. Or maybe you and I are the aliens. Either way it would be a lonely world for me without you."

Jerry tells me I write the way I look. And I already know how he feels about my writing. Somewhere over the course of our correspondence, Jerry starts signing his letters "love."

I wake thinking about him. I compose letters to him in my head throughout the day. Maybe the reason it has become increasingly hard to carry on a correspondence, he tells me, on one of our now-nightly telephone conversations, is because we have the makings of such close friends.

"You make me want to break out the champagne," he says. "We have something wonderful here, you know, kiddo?"

Early on in our correspondence I track down an old issue of *Life* magazine with photographs of him in the Yale library. From those fifteen-year-old pictures I know he is a tall, lean man, with a long and handsome face. In another, earlier picture I've studied, also from the library, he is sitting on the edge of a chair with a cigarette in one hand. Almost more than his face, I study his hands in the photograph: long, elegant fingers that look as if they'd been drawn by Hirschfeld. I have gone back to the library several times since then to study these pictures.

In late May, I write him a letter about a bike ride I took "with a friend" to a wooded spot on the outskirts of New Haven, where there is a swimming hole in the middle of the woods, and a waterfall flowing down into it.

I am an unbelievable coward.
I was raised in what I take to be the great Jewish tra-
dition of don't-hurt-yourself and, in particular, watch-out-
for-your-head. So though I swim, I'm petrified of diving, also
climbing ladders and trees and passing cars, even with miles
of white dotted lines ahead, and of a hundred other things

that add up to a handicap as real as a physical deformity.
    But—back to the swimming hole—my friend, not know-
ing this, pulled me right underneath the place where the
waterfall splashed down, so that the weight of bathtubsful
of water crashed down on me. I became frantic, dazed—
convinced I was burning, drowning, dying in any case. I
have never in my life been so frightened (and that says a
lot, because mine is a life filled with magnified fears). But
when it was over I felt happier than I can ever remember.

I don't say in my letter that my friend is the boy, Steve, with
whom I danced the polka that one time—the very handsome one
I met in that first play I was in. I do not say that when I stripped
down to my leotard to swim under that waterfall, all I could think
about was how my nipples would show when my leotard got wet.

But though I don't talk about these things to Jerry, I am trying
to tell him something about myself. I'm afraid of the waterfall
and drawn to it, both. How I feel about stepping under the water
is how I feel about sex. I am terrified, but also filled with longing.

Early in June, classes at Yale end. Sometime in those last days in
New Haven I get on my bike with a copy of the classifieds in
hand and ride around New Haven in search of an off-campus
apartment to rent when I come back to school in the fall. I find
one and, with money from my book advance, put down the de-
posit.

My classmates are looking for summer jobs—waitressing at
the Cape, answering the telephone at someone's father's law office.
Several of my friends are going to hitchhike across country, or
travel around Europe, staying in youth hostels. A number of them
will be living with their boyfriends.

John Oakes, the editorial page editor at *The New York Times,*
invites me to come talk with him. I take the train to New York
again—a trip I have taken several times in the last few weeks. I
make my way to West Forty-third Street, go in the revolving
doors. I know the routine at the *Times* now—give my name to
the guard, wait for him to call upstairs and wave me through.
Although I am wearing a dress and blazer instead of my jeans—an

outfit put together to make me look grown-up for this interview—several people in the elevator evidently recognize me from my photograph a few weeks back and greet me.

I go to the tenth floor, the offices of the editorial board. John Oakes is a pleasant, gray-haired man, around the same age, probably, as Jerry Salinger. Sitting across from me in a big leather chair, he tells me that one of the members of the editorial board, Fred Hechinger, will be on leave for a couple of months this summer. He invites me to come and use Fred Hechinger's office in the position of apprentice editorial writer.

I have never read the editorial page of *The New York Times*. I have barely ever read *The New York Times* or any other paper all year. I had been thinking maybe I'd stay at my parents' house in Durham this summer, to be closer to Jerry, and to work on my book. But now I say yes, I'd like that job.

A totally unrelated invitation comes my way around the same time—also brought about by my recent *Times* story. A Manhattan psychotherapist and his wife who own a brownstone just off Central Park West will be vacating their place for the summer. They send me a letter, though we've never met, asking if I might like to come and stay there, rent free, and take care of their dogs.

So now I have a job as editorial writer, and a dog- and house-sitting position, complete with daily maid service, in the city I've dreamed of living in since that first visit to the World's Fair.

Before embarking on my summer plans, though, I want to spend a few days in New Hampshire. I have to meet Jerry Salinger.

Chapter Five

I HAVE TRIED to imagine what was going on in my parents' minds as they picked me up from the bus from Yale before I made my trip to Cornish. Nobody suggests this is a bad idea or questions what might be going on in the mind of a fifty-three-year-old man who invites an eighteen-year-old to come and spend the weekend. (But then, my parents never seem to recognize the oddness or the danger in my hitchhiking, either. And they never say much about whatever they think of my surprising loss of weight last year. In fact, my mother goes with me to the Elaine Powers exercise salon, anxious as always to slim down herself and proud of having such a skinny daughter.)

In our household, the oddest combination of attitudes exists: extreme caution and overprotectiveness surrounding things like playing sports, yet total disregard concerning the universe of possible danger and harm surrounding my father's drinking, my obsessive dieting, and now, my rapidly blossoming relationship with an obsessively private and secretive man thirty-five years older than I.

My father seems in the worst shape I've ever seen him: consumed with worries about our dog, English department politics (even though he has retired), the moral decay of society, and his arthritis. He may not be drinking more than before, but his body appears less able to take it. He's looking frail. Instead of the lyrical landscapes he has been painting for years, he is doing only abstractions now. Large works, with slashes of red and orange ripping across their centers.

My mother is very proud that I have attracted the attention of such a famous and brilliant man. And she is something else—excited. In just a few weeks my mother will turn fifty, an age that might have been appropriate for receiving the attentions of a fifty-three-year-old. At the time, her own sexual and romantic life seems finished, although certainly her interest in sex and romance is far from dormant. For years she has lived vicariously through her daughters, seldom more than she does now.

Up in my bedroom, surrounded by the bookshelves in which my Barbies were set up until just a couple of years ago, she and I lay out the pattern pieces for a dress we will make together for my trip to Cornish, just as, the fall before, we sewed a dress for my visit to the White House and my Julie Nixon Eisenhower interview. As with our last sewing project, she speaks of the outfit we're making as "a costume." This time I dress the part of the child innocent.

The dress we make is nearly exactly the same as the one I wore to my first day of first grade. The fabric we choose was probably designed for the curtains on a child's room: stiff white broadcloth, printed with ABC's in bright primary colors. The style, the same one we used when we made my dress for my first day at Yale, is so simple we don't even need to buy a pattern. It's a sleeveless A-line shift, fastened at the shoulders with oversized mother-of-pearl buttons, so all I have to do, putting it on, is raise my hands and slip it on over my head, the way a child would do. The dress is very short, with giant solid-color broadcloth pockets onto which my mother appliqués alphabet letters cut out from the printed fabric—*A* on one pocket, *Z* on the other. I am so thin and flat-chested, the dress requires no darts. I wear it with purple Mary Jane–style flats.

I have my driver's license but we've only got one car in our family, and I've been invited to visit Jerry for a whole weekend. My parents wouldn't feel it was safe for me, anyway, to be out on the highway driving the sixty miles or so from our house to Cornish on my own. I am planning to ride a bus, but then we find out that my English teacher from Exeter, our good friend

Mark, who has business that weekend at Dartmouth, can deliver me to Hanover, where Jerry will meet us.

Riding with Mark and his wife, Anna, north along Route 89, looking out the window at the New Hampshire countryside, we exchange news of other students from my class at Exeter, talk about the book I'm going to start writing, the classes I took this year at Yale, my plans for a course of study in the future. Mark was the first teacher to truly encourage my writing. A deeply intelligent, quietly perceptive man, he says nothing to indicate there might be something worrisome about this visit I'm making.

Although I know his face only from that old issue of *Life* magazine, I spot him right away. Jerry is standing on the front porch of the Hanover Inn the first time I see him. He's very tall—six foot two or three—and his height is more startling because he is so lean. He wears blue jeans and a crew-neck sweater of the sort a Dartmouth alumnus might sport coming back for a reunion or heading out to a ballgame at the old campus. His arm rests on a pillar on the porch of the inn with the debonair grace of a performer in an old musical or a soft-shoe artist.

The only photographs I've seen of him are at least ten years old. He still has the thick hair of a young man, but where in the pictures it was black, he's all gray now, clean-shaven as always, and impeccably groomed, with a very long and deeply lined face.

He told me once that on a trip to New York, a few years earlier, Lauren Bacall hailed him from across a crowded street, supposing him to be Jason Robards, her husband at the time.

There's something gangly and boyish about him—long legs, long arms, long fingers on his hands, one of which he runs through his hair as he catches sight of me, the other raised high over his head in a wave, without any sign of embarrassment at such a public gesture.

I am no longer aware of Mark and Anna's presence. I jump out of the car in my alphabet dress and purple shoes. Jerry steps over the railing of the inn as he moves toward me.

I run as if I were meeting an old friend I hadn't seen for years. He doesn't quite run, but there is a look of pure joy on his face.

He isn't conventionally handsome in that movie star way, but I love the way he looks and moves. You would know he'd be a good dancer. There's no trace of a young man's macho swagger in the way he moves—nothing approaching a display of physical strength, or speed, or athletic prowess, though I can imagine him being good at shuffling a deck of cards or shooting pool. Even if I didn't know who he was, I would notice Jerry.

Nothing about him seems old or strange. It seems to make perfect sense that I put my arms around him as he embraces me.

If he registers shock at my odd outfit, nothing in his behavior suggests it. "You're wearing the same watch you had on in the photograph," he says.

I introduce Mark and Anna. Jerry is courteous, even friendly. He looks them in the eye and shakes their hands. He tells them how much he appreciates their bringing me. "Joyce has told me so much about you," he says. "You must have taught her a great deal in that class of yours." Mark gets my bag from his car and loads it in the back of Jerry's BMW. Jerry opens the car door on my side and I get in. "I can't believe you're finally here," he says. As we drive out of town onto the highway, fast, I am thinking, I could be in this car forever. I don't ever want this to end.

We talk all the way to his house—a twenty-minute drive over a two-lane highway, followed by winding uphill roads that go from tar to dirt. I look at his hands on the gearshift—the elegant fingers I studied in the magazine photograph. My mother is a gardener, too, and has the fingernails to prove it: broken, uneven, usually with a little dirt still there from the last time she pulled weeds. Jerry's fingernails are perfectly manicured and clean.

He is talking about plans for the weekend. We'll take a walk to the top of the hill where he lives. I can choose whatever movie I want to watch. As many movies as I'd like. Have I had any more problems with poison ivy? If so, he's got some more spotted jewel weed for me.

"Matthew's over at his friend Matthew's house today," he says. I know about this other Matthew already. Peggy, who's home from boarding school, is probably off playing basketball with her boyfriend.

"Peggy's playing basketball with her boyfriend," he says.

He drives fast, and skillfully, but now and then he looks over at me sitting on the passenger side, and smiles. Finally I'm here. It's hard to know where to begin. And on the other hand, there seems no need to say anything. For the first time in as long as I can remember, I feel no need for speech.

"We are *landsmen*, all right," he says. My heart lifts.

We pass through the town of Windsor, Vermont—the kind of small town I know well, with one main street, a post office, a hardware store, a couple of convenience stores, and idle-looking teenagers sitting on front stoops watching cars go by. He points out the former house of his old friend in town, Learned Hand, an eminent judge who befriended him when he moved here to escape New York almost twenty years ago.

We're in Cornish now. We pass the elegant Augustus St.-Gaudens mansion, now a museum, and, a few miles farther up the road, he points out the house that belongs to his ex-wife, Claire, the mother of his two children. His own place lies just beyond hers, at the top of a long unmarked driveway, off a winding dirt road. A sign posted at the end of the driveway says PRIVATE, NO TRESPASSING.

The house itself is a simple one, a single-story, ranch-style place with a deck that looks out to the north, a horizon dominated by an unobstructed view of Mount Ascutney. Except for Jerry's vegetable garden, the land around the house is wild, with acres of open fields below, where Matthew rides his three-wheeler off-road bike. There's a trail behind the house that leads to the top of the hill. Jerry's dachshund, Joey, lies in the sun on the deck as we pull up. "We're home," he says.

I have spent less than an hour in the company of Jerry Salinger, but I am feeling something I have never experienced before.

"I've waited a long time for you," he says. "If I didn't know better, I'd say you belong here."

"Some people would call this an awkward situation," I say. "Actually, it's the first unawkward situation I've been in for a while."

He looks at me hard. I do not look away.

* * *

Sex is still an excruciatingly awkward subject for me. But I feel safe with this man. I know he loves me. I can't imagine any way he would ever hurt me.

We enter Jerry's house through the basement, where he keeps a giant chest freezer filled with nuts and fiddlehead ferns and vegetables from his garden. We go upstairs from there, into the living room. Inside are a couple of worn velvet down-filled couches and comfortable chairs, tables piled with books and homeopathic journals, catalogues, film reels, and newspapers. A couple of oriental rugs cover the floor. There's a TV and a record player, piles of letters, papers, old *New Yorkers* stacked high, and copies of *The New York Times*. It's a small house—a kitchen, a living room, and a bedroom each for Jerry and his two children, plus a small, cluttered room filled with books and papers where Jerry keeps his typewriter. Beyond that, though he doesn't show me this (and in all the months I live here, he never will) there is a safe—as large as another room—where he keeps his unpublished manuscripts. In spite of the French doors along one side of the main room, looking out to the mountain, the house is very dark.

He has prepared a lunch for us: whole-grain bread, a little cheddar cheese, some nuts mixed with honey. He sets two folding TV tray tables on the deck.

"I hope this is all right," he says. "I don't entertain much. Not exactly the Junior League here."

"That's a relief," I say.

He cuts himself a piece of cheese and a slice of apple. "Good combination," he says, munching.

I cut myself a slice of apple and cheese, too.

"So how's this book of yours coming?" he asks. "Those New York types had better not try to change one thing about you."

"I'm just getting started," I say. "I've been making lists of topics I want to cover. I went to the library while I was home to look through old *Life* magazines. Just to jog my memory."

"From what I could gather in that first piece of yours, you remember everything that ever happened to you," he says. "Not a whole lot gets by you."

"I wish I didn't see so much," I say. "I'd probably have a lot more fun if I wasn't *watching* all the time."

"You're a writer, that's all. I spotted it in you the minute I saw your face on that magazine cover."

"I never planned on being a writer. I still don't. It's just something my parents taught me how to do. I never have much fun doing it."

"Fun! Where'd you get the idea fun might be involved? Can't expect to join the party if you plan to write about it. There's nothing remotely enjoyable about the life of a writer, and if either of us had any choice in the matter, I have no doubt we'd be out there doing just about anything else. I'd rather play for the Yankees myself."

"I'm supposed to deliver my manuscript by October first," I tell him.

"Some marketing whiz up on the forty-ninth floor, no doubt, worried that you won't be young enough if they don't rush your work into production. I'd hate like hell to see you sell yourself short."

After lunch, we take a walk up the hill behind Jerry's house. We haven't run out of things to talk about since I got here, though it's been a few hours.

"This half-Jewish business," he says. "Where did it leave you?"

No place, I tell him. Split down the middle.

"My mother never celebrates the Jewish holidays," I say. "For years, the closest thing I ever had to a church experience was Easter Sunday, when my father and I used to sit outside the Episcopal church in town, eating fresh-roasted Spanish peanuts. All my friends complained about their parents making them attend church, but I longed to go. When I was eleven or twelve, I went over to the one house of worship in our town where I could imagine fitting in."

"Let me guess," he says. "Unitarian?"

Once again he knows me. "I volunteered to be a Sunday school teacher for a class of five-year-olds. Of course, being Unitarian, we didn't do much Bible study. We had lectures on things like 'Rare Butterflies of South America' or 'What to do about Vietnam?'

"So one Saturday, in preparation for my class the next morning, I biked to a stream I used to go to with my father, looking for tadpoles. I scooped a bunch of them into a glass jar and brought them in to my classroom the next morning. I had a project worked out where we'd follow their growth from week to week and chart their development into frogs."

"Little duffers loved that, I'll bet."

"Well, they were definitely excited. So much so, they put their hands in the bowl. Only when they took their hands out, the tadpoles were clinging to their skin so tightly I couldn't get them off. The children all started wailing. Suddenly I realized they weren't tadpoles at all. I had brought in leeches. In the end, I had to get one father to come in with a lit cigarette and burn the leeches till they dropped off the children's arms. There you have it. My spiritual education."

Jerry laughs. "An in-depth study of leeches," he says. "Good preparation for the world of publishing."

Somewhere along the path, climbing the steep hill behind his house with the dog following, he takes my hand.

I tell him about my family. "My father's drinking seems to be getting worse now that he's retired," I say. "The first night I got home from New Haven he wanted to talk to me about the human soul. He said surely it must have occurred to me that the pre-Christian world perceived the individual soul in a far different light from the Christian world. He wanted to show me a reproduction of a Donatello Madonna. In the middle of taking out the art books, he suddenly jumped up and said 'Sibelius! We must listen to Sibelius!' "

"I keep catching myself talking to you as though we're veterans of all the same sorry pieces of history," he says. "I want to ask you some dopey question like where you were on VE Day. Then I have to slap my forehead and remind myself you're a kid."

"I never really fit in with my age group," I tell him.

"That makes two of us, my friend," he says. "I can take society well enough, so long as I keep my rubber gloves on. Although lately, I have to say, I keep feeling the irrepressible urge to cut off my ear and catch the next train to Antarctica."

"Same reason I ended up in my psychological single," I say. Then I tell him about the roommates, and the bunk bed, and the noises in the night.

"I'd call that a hell of an imposition," he says.

"Maybe I'm just not cut out for collegiate life."

"Try the army," he tells me.

I tell him the story of my name. "My sister was four when I was born. She was a very sensitive, very precocious child. She was used to a lot of attention from our parents. So my mother, who had probably been reading way too many psychology books, cooked up this idea for how to make her feel more excited about getting a new baby sister or brother. She said Rona could choose my name."

"That could be dangerous," says Jerry. "No telling what a four-year-old might cook up. Thelma. Ebenezer. Howdy Doody."

"Well, my sister was always a big-time reader. Even at four. In fact, she was so taken with a book my mother had read her about Joan of Arc that she would only answer to the name of Joan."

"I assume they kept the matches out of reach?"

"Her other passion was Greek mythology. So she told our mother she wanted to name the baby after her favorite character, if it was a girl. Daphne."

"Evidently your parents went back on their word?"

"No. Daphne's the name on my birth certificate. But a couple of days after I'd come home from the hospital, Rona announced to our parents that they must under no circumstances call this baby Daphne ever again. Of course, they obeyed. Joyce is actually my middle name."

Jerry is silent for a moment. "You figure she just didn't have you pegged as the Daphne type?"

"You might suppose. But in fact, she only recently confessed to me the real reason she wanted my name changed. Once I'd been around a couple of days, it suddenly hit her that the very last name on earth she'd ever want me to have would be her *favorite*. And I hate to say it, but that's been the story of our relationship. I love her, and I actually believe she's fond of me, too. But she'd be the first to tell you, she wasn't wild about me coming on the scene. She probably would have preferred to be an only child."

"Old Charlotte Brontë probably wasn't all that hot on Emily either."

"She's just very sensitive," I say.

A little farther along the path, I ask about his own name. Jerry is short for . . .

"Jerome. Crummy moniker. Sounds like a podiatrist. Or a writer, for God's sake. Even worse."

For dinner that night, there is more bread, a plate of steamed fiddlehead ferns, and slices of apple. Afterward, Jerry pops a bowl of popcorn for us and tosses it with tamari sauce rather than butter. He clears a spot for me on the velvet couch and wraps a blanket around my feet. I have been coughing slightly, which worries him.

The first movie he screens for me is one of his favorites, an early Hitchcock, *The Thirty-Nine Steps*. After that one's over he puts another reel on the projector—*The Thin Man*. I fall asleep somewhere in the middle of the second half.

Earlier that day, Jerry had set my suitcase on the spare bed in Peggy's bedroom. I haven't met her yet. Now, as he finishes rewinding the second movie, he makes sure I have everything I need. Towels. Water. The right pillow.

He stands next to the bed, smoothing the sheets slightly. I have taken out my contact lenses, so I'm wearing my glasses now. I remove them, and set them on the nightstand.

"Now I can't even recognize you," I say. "You could be anybody."

"I'm actually Clark Gable," he says. "Make that Gomer Pyle."

Sometime in the night Peggy comes in and lies down in the single bed beside mine. It's late. She's been with her Dartmouth boyfriend. When I wake up, she's still asleep. I put on my jeans and a T-shirt and go out into the kitchen.

Jerry is already up. He serves us a breakfast of Bird's Eye Tender Tiny Peas and whole-grain bread on the deck.

"I want to teach you about this diet of mine," he says. Cooking food robs it of all the natural nutrients, he explains. Not only that: Refined foods like sugar and white flour—even whole-wheat flour, honey, and maple syrup—take a very heavy toll on the body. Although he has served me cheese, dairy products are also a bad idea, especially if they're made from pasteurized milk, which has, after all, been heated above one hundred and fifty degrees, the temperature at which crucial nutrients are destroyed, he says. Cooked meat is one of the most harmful things a person could eat, and of course, raw meat isn't safe.

Jerry has developed a particular technique for preparing meat. First he takes the special, chemical-free, organic ground lamb he buys at the health food store and forms it into patties, which he freezes. He believes this will kill whatever bacteria might be there. Then he cooks them, but only at a temperature of a hundred and fifty.

Mostly, Jerry tries to avoid cooked food altogether. His main diet consists of raw fruits and vegetables and nuts. Speaking of the food most people eat, Jerry uses the word "poison."

"You don't realize it, but your body is filled with toxins," he says. A headache is the result of toxins releasing into the system.

"Doctors!" Jerry says. "Bunch of cardigan-wearers who couldn't cut it on the PGA tour. Endlessly prescribing medicines that only mask a person's symptoms, instead of taking them as what they are, a message from the body to change the ways we live and eat. If you listen to one thing I tell you, let it be to stay away from doctors."

Jerry has been eating this way for a long time now, and except for partial deafness in one ear—result of a war injury—his health is very good. Vedantic literature tells us the natural life span of a man is one hundred twenty years. He plans to live that long. By this time, nothing Jerry tells me about what he can do would surprise me.

It's close to noon when Peggy emerges from the bedroom—tousled, a little bleary-eyed. She's not unfriendly, but neither does she exude enthusiasm.

"I want you to meet Joyce," Jerry says. "She's the one I told you about. She wrote that magazine article."

"Hi," she says. Then she picks up a magazine and flips through it. No small talk.

"What do you say we drive into town for the paper?" Jerry asks me. He gives Peggy a pat on the head on the way out the door. She looks up from her magazine for a second.

It's a ten-minute drive to town, back over the dirt roads and onto a covered bridge that spans the Connecticut River, leading into the town of Windsor, Vermont. When we pull up in front of the newsstand on Main Street, both of us hop out of Jerry's car and walk into the store together. Jerry says hello to the man behind the counter, who knows him by name. He picks up a yo-yo for Matthew.

"That was pretty unusual for me," he says, as we pull away from the store and go back over the covered bridge.

"Getting a yo-yo?"

"Bringing somebody into the newsstand like that," he says. "A guest. Except that you don't feel like a guest."

Just where we turn into his driveway, Jerry shifts the car into neutral and pauses a moment. He leans over, puts his hands on my shoulders and kisses me. I kiss him back.

Afterward, he takes a long look at me. "You know too much for your age," he says. "Either that, or I just know too little for mine."

We drive up the hill to the house and climb the steps through the basement again. He tosses the paper on the couch. Matthew is here now—also his friend, who is also named Matthew. They're watching television and reading *Tin-Tin* comics.

Matthew's a very sweet-faced boy, as tall as I am already, with an open, friendly manner from the moment I meet him. "This is Joyce," Jerry says.

Matthew smiles. "Hey," he says. Jerry tosses him the yo-yo. Joey the dog looks up but doesn't move. "Not exactly Asta here," he says.

"You had your picture in *The New York Times*, huh?" Matthew says.

* * *

Sometime in the early afternoon—after another lunch of nuts and bread and cheese—Mark and Anna come by to pick me up, having gotten directions from Jerry. The three of us sit in the living room while Jerry fixes a tray of cold drinks. He asks about Mark's work as a Dartmouth trustee, the books Mark teaches in his English classes at Exeter. He is particularly interested to hear that Anna grew up in Germany. He has spent time there, during the war and afterward.

When it's time to go, Jerry carries my overnight bag out to Mark's car. He gives me a copy of a book, *Food Is Your Best Medicine*, by Dr. Henry Bieler.

"Next time I'll pick a movie that won't put you to sleep," he says. He bends to look at me, in the backseat of the car, but doesn't kiss me. "Call me when you get to New York," he says. "You're going to set that town on its ear."

New York City feels far away now. My hometown of Durham does, too. Also New Haven.

As we head down the driveway, I look back at Jerry, standing there, waving again, the same way he did when I first caught sight of him. I feel a sense of loss and uprooting so sharp I have to look away.

When I return to my parents' house, my mother is waiting, full of questions. Normally I would tell her everything, but I feel a new distance between us. I no longer want to give my mother total access to every detail of my life. I feel a new wariness and distance, and even a certain not-wholly-disguised irritation that she would attempt to appropriate my new life.

"What was his house like?" she wants to know. She's disappointed that it isn't more lavish. "What did you eat?" I tell her about the frozen peas and unleavened bread.

"Sounds grim," she says. My mother has tended to judge people in part at least by their appreciation for good food. She has a hard time respecting or liking anyone who eats margarine rather than butter.

My mother's view of all things—including food preparation— has always been mine. Now, describing Jerry's method for cooking meat at a hundred and fifty degrees, my voice takes on a new sharpness. "More heat than that, and you kill the valuable enzymes in the protein. Cooked food is poison," I explain. So is white flour and sugar.

"What does he have for dessert?" asks my mother.

"Sunflower and pumpkin seeds, with unpasteurized honey," I tell her.

But surely when he comes to lunch at our house (an event she is already planning) she can serve him pie? I express doubt. Maybe with a whole-wheat crust (a completely unacceptable idea). Never with ice cream, that's for sure. Then I describe to my mother what happens to ice cream in your stomach.

"First you've got a pasteurized milk product—rich in fat, filled with sugar. You freeze it. Then you eat it, and it thaws, in effect, inside your intestine. So now there's all this old animal fat sitting in your intestine. *Putrefying*."

The whole thing sounds so sickening I can hardly describe it without feeling nauseous. Although the truth is, I have always loved ice cream.

Two days after I leave Cornish a letter arrives from Jerry, written and mailed the day before. He's missed me all day, he writes.

He felt particular affection for Mark and Anna, he tells me, knowing how important they are to me. After I left, he spent some time treating Peggy homeopathically for an ailment. Then he gave her my article in the *Times* to read. I can tell it matters to him to be able to tell Peggy about me. He's proud of me. I love it that he feels no need to conceal from his daughter the fact that he has taken an interest in me. Not the extent of his interest, maybe, but some of it.

I'm touched that he's concerned about my cough that weekend, and even amused that he worries he might become a nuisance with his homeopathic ministrations. He's too tired tonight to tell me all the thoughts he's had of me today; it's enough that he simply knows me. He misses me "sorely."

A couple of days after my return from Cornish I leave home again, only this time I'm headed for my job in New York City and the

Central Park West brownstone of Katja and Ray Mendelson, the couple who have invited me to use their house and watch their dogs while they're away on Long Island for the summer.

The Mendelsons' house on West Seventy-third Street, a block away from the famous Dakota apartment building, is huge, and filled with original art and very modern furnishings. I reach my bedroom on the top floor via private elevator. Most of the house goes unused, although a maid still comes in daily to look after things.

At *The New York Times*, too, my circumstances are impressive for an eighteen-year-old. I am installed in the office of a vacationing member of the editorial board, behind a huge desk, facing a wall full of books about world history and current affairs. I am supposed to sit and compose editorials. Several times a day, a copy boy a few years older than I comes into the room and delivers a fresh sheaf of wire service reports on breaking news stories meant to keep me abreast of what's going on in the world. Although I'm writing editorial opinions, the section of the paper I have always turned to first in newspapers is "Dear Abby," followed by the comics and gossip about Hollywood stars.

There is no shortage of news in the world during the summer of 1972: George McGovern is seeking the Democratic presidential nomination. Angela Davis is found not guilty of the murder, kidnapping, and conspiracy charges for which she had been tried in a California courtroom. The Supreme Court rules the death penalty unconstitutional. Less than a year from the day when boys all over my Yale campus waited anxiously for their number in the draft lottery, President Nixon announces there will be no new draftees sent to Vietnam. And—though this is not yet big news— five burglars discovered to have links with the CIA are arrested and charged with breaking into the executive offices of the Democratic National Committee in the Watergate Hotel.

In my own life, too, there would seem to be an abundance of rich and exciting experience: I have not only my job at the *Times*, and a contract for a book due for delivery in October, but all of New York City, where I have wanted to be for so long, glitters out my bedroom window. One day, walking the Mendelsons' dogs in Central Park, I pass John Lennon with his son.

Still I feel oddly depressed. I write a letter to my sister, who

keeps it, in the family tradition. Twenty-five years later, she sends
my letter back to me.

Dear Rona,

  ...I suppose Mummy has represented my life as bud-
ding writer with all of her Jewish mother pride and exag-
geration. Things are more complicated than that....

  ...Suddenly I'm having to reassess the goals I've been
pushing towards so hard, so long. I may very easily cut
myself off from school and people my own age, I may have
ulcers by nineteen, I may already have made myself un-
approachable....

Jerry Salinger has moved into my head. We talk together on the
phone every night, and sometimes in the day, from my office at
the *Times*. I think about him constantly now.

Sitting in Fred Hechinger's office now, I do not spend much
time composing editorials for *The New York Times*. Mostly what
I do is compose letters to Jerry. Wandering down Columbus Avenue, walking the dogs, I plan my next visit to New Hampshire.

Our friendship has changed since my visit to his house. Where,
before we met, our letters went on for pages—about writing, publishing, movies, acting, homeopathy—they are shorter now, but
there is a feeling of hunger in his words that wasn't present in
his earlier correspondence.

He writes about the uniqueness and intensity of our friendship.
It makes him very happy, but it's a burden, too, in the way it
occupies his mind.

"All these years you haven't been around, and it hasn't seemed
like a problem," he tells me on the phone. "But now that I've met
you, and you're gone, things seem out of balance. This morning
I found myself looking over at the chair where you sat, and it
seemed unbearably sad that you weren't in it. I keep wanting to
look over at you, and you're not there."

His letters to me in June are the happiest I'll ever hear him.
I love it when he says I make him cheerful. He describes a scene
in which he runs into Matthew and Peggy in town, and how

happy they all were to see one another. He says how good it is to have a handful of characters in your life that you can truly love. I know I am one of them.

After receiving my first letter from New York City he tells me he would have liked to annotate my whole letter with responses to every line. I can tell what he'd really like would be to show me New York City himself. He knows the name of every apartment building on Central Park West. He used to live in one.

His letter says he has just this minute got off the phone from talking to me, and now here he is writing. But he can't stop talking to me.

He writes about my writing, as usual, and his hopes for me. In my last letter I had told him writing isn't all that important to me. He tells me now he hopes I was telling him the truth. As for himself, unfortunately he loves to write, but only when it's going well. What he tells me he loves best by far is a sense of integration between his life and his work, and freedom from the feeling of disconnection that dogs him. Having a life in which all the pieces fit together is something he pursues, he tells me, with the singlemindedness and passion of a "fan."

There's less bitterness in the letters he sends me now. Where the first letters, in April and May, came from a man whose outlook is dark and cynical and finished with the world, the one who calls me nightly in June and July is filled with hopefulness and something approaching optimism.

"I was thinking I might pass through Durham on my way to see you," he says. "It's probably about time I introduced myself properly to your parents."

"The first time my old boyfriend Jim showed up on our doorstep, my father said, 'Tell me, man, what's the definition of Beauty?' " I say. Even with Jerry, I do not share the sort of questions my mother is capable of asking.

"Beats talking about the Red Sox," he says. "I can't say I won't feel a little awkward at first. Hat in hand, and all that. But it'll be good to sit down and have a nice long talk with people I can actually respect." He asks if I think they'll like him.

How could they not, I say, moved by the image of Jerry not as a legendary literary figure but a slightly shy and awkward suitor in search of approval from his sweetheart's parents.

"We will all agree on one thing," he comments. "We're all nuts about you."

There's a new tone even to the advice he gives me, a quality of tenderness and almost boyish infatuation. He got onto this whole thing, he says, because he loves "real writing" and he loves my writing. He loved my writing, he says, even before he loved me. More than that even, he says, he loves my life.

He sends me a flyer for an antiques auction taking place somewhere around White River Junction the next week, and suggests that we could go. He calls to say he picked the first peas from his garden. He calls to say he just finished reading the editorial page of the *Times*. "When are they going to run something you have to say, anyway? That page is crying out for the voice of a girl like you, if you ask me."

"It's a one-hour trip, La Guardia to the Lebanon Airport," he tells me. "You could take a cab from Times Square Friday afternoon and be here in time to catch the sunset," he writes me. He could drive me back to New York again, the following Monday. But before that letter even arrives, he has called me with another plan. He will come and pick me up for the long Fourth of July weekend and drive me to New Hampshire himself.

I feel thrilled, flattered, proud, excited, and scared.

Ten days after I've begun my job with *The New York Times*, Jerry drives five hours to New York to pick me up—me and the Mendelsons' two dogs. When he pulls up in front of the brownstone on West Seventy-third Street, I come running into his arms. He strokes my hair. "God, I've been waiting forever for this," he says.

We buy a bag of bagels and lox on the Upper West Side. Then he turns right around and drives, very fast, the full five hours straight back to New Hampshire. This time, when I walk into his house, I know where I'm headed.

Chapter Six

JERRY'S BEDROOM IS not particularly large. There is nothing much in it but a queen-size bed, a night table with homeopathic journals on it, a mirror, a dresser. The window by the bed has no need for curtains since all that lies beyond is open land and sky. It is just nightfall. There's a door leading to a bathroom, and a door leading to the room where Jerry writes and meditates every morning, and a door leading to the rest of the house, where the children's rooms are. But there are no children here this weekend. Matthew's with his mother. Peggy's with her boyfriend.

I'm standing at the foot of the bed, in another one of my short little-girl dresses. He pulls it over my head. No bra on my thin body. I have no need for one. Only cotton underpants. He takes those off.

There are no discussions of birth control, and I don't think to ask. I am less mature than most eighteen-year-olds. It is just a few years since I put away my Barbies.

I know so little about sex, and what I do know is mostly sad and odd. My trips with my mother to Calef's Country Store to buy anadama bread and read dirty jokes. Her articles in *Good House-keeping* and *Woman's Day* about premarital sex and venereal disease.

Sex is the movie they show us in seventh-grade gym class, about the miracle of menstruation, and my own terrible shame when, a couple of years later, the miracle finally happens to me, and I cannot bring myself to tell my mother. So a full year goes by, until the day she confronts me, having cleaned my closet, and found, at the very back, a brown paper bag filled with a year's worth of used sanitary napkins, now crawling with bugs. "How could you?" she says. Now I am more ashamed than ever.

Sex is my father's sad, dark little study that smells of liquor, with its single bed and half-marked student papers and blue books strewn on the floor, books of eighteenth-century literature and his funny old-man pajamas, and the way, when he emerges from his room in the morning, wearing them, he keeps his hand cupped over what he calls his private parts, and the way my mother throws back her head and laughs when he does. It is my mother's large, sunny bedroom, where I come to visit her in the mornings.

For me, sex is my mother's large, full breasts, and my own very small ones. The long silk robes she wore, entertaining students for the gatherings she held to read and analyze student manuscripts, her musical laugh and flirtatious manner with high school boys as she poured them tea and passed around plates of her wonderful homemade cookies and asked them about the first time they went all the way.

For me, coming from the place I have come from, sex is something comical and ridiculous and pathetic that mostly only other people do, something I observe happening in the dark corners of cast parties, where I sit reading record jackets.

Sex is the first-day freshman women's orientation at Yale, when they hand out the women's health brochure and a condom falls out onto my lap. Sex is lying on my top bunk on the fourth floor of Vanderbilt Hall, while, in the bunk beneath me, my roommate and the boy who has come home with her tonight writhe on the mattress, pumping faster and faster, until suddenly, in the darkness, comes a moan and a sigh. Then quiet. Sex is the waterfall, with the water pounding down on my head so hard I think I'm drowning.

Standing now in Jerry Salinger's bedroom, letting him take my clothes off me, I observe the scene as if it were one of the movies he screens for me in his living room.

The young girl unbuckles her shoes. The older man steps out of his blue jeans, and then his underwear. A naked man is in the room. The girl lies down on the bed beside him. The man puts his arms around her.

He says he loves me. I say the same to him. I feel the way I imagine a person does when she has a religious experience. *Saved.* Rescued, delivered, enlightened, touched by a divine hand.

I have never seen a naked man. Now that I do, I want to curl up on his lap. I want him to wrap his arms around me. I want him to hold me. All this he does. Then I am lying flat on the bed, his body looming over me, pushing my legs apart.

When we attempt intercourse, the muscles of my vagina simply clamp shut and will not release. After a few minutes, we have to stop. I am weeping, less from the pain in my genitals than the pain in my head, which feels ready to burst.

I get up from the bed and stagger to the bathroom to pour water on my face. I have never had a headache like this before.

"Lie down," he says quietly. "Let me do your pressure points." He has put on his bathrobe now. He sits on the side of the bed next to me and applies his fingers to a spot between the thumb and forefinger of each hand. In a few minutes the worst of the headache goes away, though it will be a few hours before it's gone entirely.

"I didn't know it would hurt like that," I tell him.

"I'll make you something to eat," he says, jumping up. He steams summer squash from his garden with tamari sauce and sets it down for me on the TV tray table, with a tall glass of water. He wraps the blanket around me. I don't know what to say. Of all the things I've ever heard about sex, the fears I've had, nobody has ever raised the possibility that you might simply not be able to do it. Now I am more deeply ashamed than I have ever been.

Of the many times in my life when my body failed me—in gym class, when I alone failed to make a basket or get a hit, when I was the last one chosen for whatever team was choosing up players, when I climbed the ladder to a diving board but stood there, unable to jump, until finally I had to climb back down again, when I rode the chair lift back down from the top of a mountain, the one time I ever tried to go skiing, because I didn't know how to get off—my body has never failed me this utterly, or left me feeling greater despair.

"I'm sorry," I whisper. "I don't know what I did wrong."

"Tomorrow I'll look up your symptoms in the *Materia Medica*," he says gently. "And maybe tomorrow you'll be better, anyway."

But the next day, when we take off our clothes again and try once more to make love, the same thing happens: I get a headache so terrible he treats me with acupressure again.

"It's all right," he says. "I'll help you with your problem."

The discovery that I can't have sex has left me feeling more outside the world than ever. Now it's confirmed: I will never live a normal life. Who ever heard of a problem like mine? Who ever had such a problem, in the history of the world?

It is my new, terrible secret, worse than the secret of my father's drinking. The fact that Jerry knows binds me more tightly to him than ever. How could I tell anyone else?

The only place I can feel safe is on this mountaintop. In the day, we take our walks and talk for hours about movies and plays, life at *The New York Times*, television, the book I'm writing. We eat our meals of barely cooked lamb and garden vegetables, and after dinner every night, he settles me in on the couch with my blanket to watch whatever movie I choose. After the movie, we retreat to Jerry's bed, where the same scene is reenacted. The attempt. The headache. The acupressure. The alternatives.

I cry. He comforts me.

"What's the matter with me?" I say.

"I'll find you a remedy," he says.

I was supposed to return to New York at the end of the weekend, but I can't face the city yet. Sitting on his deck, listening to the sound of fireworks somewhere on the other side of the hill, Jerry says, "They'll probably never run the stuff you're writing anyway. Why don't you call and tell them you're sick?" I do.

After five days, he drives me back to Manhattan, piling the Mendelsons' dogs in the backseat. I rest my head in Jerry's lap most of the way. In the front hall of the Mendelsons' brown-stone, he sets my bags down and steps into the little elevator with me.

"Exciting place, New York," he says. "A girl like you could go far in a city like this."

"It's not that great," I say.

"This bachelor business doesn't seem to be as hot an idea as it used to," he says. "You've got me impossibly distracted. I keep wanting to hear what's on your mind."

"Maybe we could get one of those wire service machines, like the ones at *The New York Times,* and I could send you hourly bulletins. Matthew could run out to the garden with the latest updates. . . ." But I'm not in a mood for joking. I'm trying not to cry.

"I'd better get going, if I want to make it home in time to get a letter in tomorrow's mail," Jerry tells me. He bends to put his arms around me.

"I couldn't have made up a character of a girl I'd love better than you," he says to me.

I resume my job with the editorial board. The phone calls and letters are constant. Jerry views our five days together a stroke of "fairness" in his life.

"I'm sure there's some marvelous reason why we aren't to-gether at this very moment," he tells me. "But damned if I know what it is."

When I first made my plan to come to New York, I pictured myself spending time with friends from Yale and Exeter who would also be living there. Maybe I'd even make new friends at the *Times,* and elsewhere, I thought. I might take a dance class.

But I can't tell my friends what's going on in my life now. So when I'm not in my office at West Forty-third Street, I am mostly alone—at the movies, or walking the dogs, on the phone, or writ-ing letters to Jerry.

His letters to me now are full of plans for how we'll see each other, offers to drive down and see me, drive me home with him for a weekend. Or maybe, he writes, he could come stay in New York for a while. He tells me that he's been thinking of reestablishing his friendship with William Shawn, editor of *The New Yorker*, and getting himself an office there part of the week while I work at the *Times*. He asks me if that sounds like a good idea.

Knowing how I love to perform in plays, he speaks often of the two of us acting scenes from Shakespeare together in his living room. *Antony and Cleopatra* maybe, for starters. In one letter he suggests that he and I write a two-character play together and take it to London to perform, ourselves, in the West End.

I believe him. *Yes*, I say. I would very much like to collaborate with him and act in our play. I see the two of us together, up onstage, holding hands and taking our bows. I see us riding in a London taxi back to the suite at the Claridge where he has suggested we'd stay. Thick towels. Hotel soaps I will stash in my suitcase. Room service. Falling asleep in his arms.

He drives to New York again to see me, staying at the Mendelsons' apartment with me for the night. Once again, we are unable to have intercourse.

"I've been doing some research on your problem in the *Materia Medica*," he tells me. "It's called vaginismus. It's a rare disorder, but not unheard of."

We don't consult a doctor, although he calls Dr. Lacey in Colorado and describes to him the problem of a friend of his. "I'm working on it," Jerry says. So is Dr. Lacey, though he's never met me.

I reveal my failure to no one. Neither, I believe, does Jerry.

We have crossed a line now. Our conversations and correspondence now assume that we have a future together. Not that I don't express concerns. One has to do with his children, and how it would be for them if I moved in with him at some point, maybe not so far in the future.

"Children like things to stay the way they are," I tell him. "No new characters."

"Not always," Jerry says, describing Matthew's agreeableness to his introduction of new plotlines and characters into the ongoing bedtime story he used to tell. He acknowledges that Peggy might have a harder time accepting me, but then moves swiftly from a consideration of that topic, focusing instead on how he loves it that I would have brought up the question in the first place.

I have mentioned, in a letter, concern about the difference in our ages. It's a topic neither of us has ever spoken about. But I have had plenty of opportunity to think about this one.

My own father is twenty years older than my mother. Of the many problems that exist in our family, I have never viewed that as the hardest. Still, thirty-five years is a lot more than twenty. In my diary, at age twelve, I had longed for a father "in a crew cut, nice and dull, who would bring home the paycheck." I had even expressed the opinion that I hoped I wouldn't marry a man who was significantly older than I, as my mother had. I wanted a normal life. A regular kind of marriage—a regular kind of dad for my children, and a life free of the strangeness and isolation that pervaded my family.

Now I ask Jerry: "Will we make each other miserable, in the end?"

He tells me my inclination to worry about bleak prospects for the future reminds Jerry of himself. But what he tells me next eases my mind: He says he can't conceive of how two people who feel for each other as we do could ever reach the point of bringing each other pain.

If the possibility that I might move in will result in my eventual departure, he tells me he would definitely rather forgo the whole thing and continue to live apart. The minute he says that, he adds that maybe he's overstating the matter. He's never felt more hopeful.

The thing is, he's not handling my comings and goings with anything that comes close to coolness. If he isn't cool now, it's because he's so attached to me. He breaks off talking about this here—as he often does, in his letters, when things are getting close to the bone—to shift into his wisecracking voice. But as he has told me himself, he adopts a carefree tone when he's feeling his least carefree about something.

* * *

I have taken the shuttle from New York to Lebanon again to spend the weekend with Jerry. In the car heading home from the airport, I recount the story of an evening I spent, a couple of days earlier, with a girl I know from Yale, Joanie, who came over to the Mendelsons' house with her boyfriend for the evening.

"Joanie is this amazing flute player," I tell Jerry. "Her boyfriend, Brock, sat down at the Mendelsons' piano. The two of them played for over an hour.

"I wish, instead of writing, that I could play an instrument," I say. "It seems so much more real than putting words on paper. So much more genuinely expressive and emotionally powerful. Nothing I've ever written could make a person feel as excited as a piece of great music. What I do seems dry by comparison."

"Listen," Jerry tells me, looking away from the road and straight into my eyes for a moment. "Don't ever suppose it's some kind of lesser art form you're engaged in because nobody's lined up outside some goddamn smoke-filled club full of people in turtlenecks waiting to hear you transport them into some other orbit of pure ecstasy.

"I don't want to put down your friends," he says. "But you know, a lot of jazz is outright fraud. Charming, even richly evocative fraud, on occasion. But don't kid yourself that these jazz musicians are in possession of some wonderful and otherworldly power beyond anything you and I can comprehend."

"It looked so free," I say. "They could actually lose themselves in their music. I never do that, writing. God, just the opposite. I go around self-conscious all the time."

"They may possess more freedom, these musician types, I'll grant you that. They get to hang out in groups, drinking and smoking, while half the audience falls in love with them for all their so-called improvisation and raw sexual energy. What they're really doing most of the time is serving up a meal of old chestnuts from some other set they played, some other night, in front of some other adoring audience of marvelous, thrillingly cool fans."

"They were inventing everything. Right on the spot," I tell him.

"And you thought they were so brilliant, right? And you were totally inferior, in what you do? These jazz types count on you to feel that way. Most of the guys who dish out this stuff are tanked up on Jack Daniel's. Take it from me, the very best jazz improviser is still only hauling out a bunch of virtuoso effects he's got in his repertoire for the specific purpose of inspiring his worshipers with something approaching religious awe. Something designed to inspire some cute little number in the corner to go home with him after the last show."

He is driving fast as he says this. Something about jazz musicians—not just the music they play, but the way they live, their celebration of disorder, their apparent sexual abandon—has set Jerry off in a way I've never seen.

"You could be right," I say, a little subdued. "I don't know all that much about jazz. I was just thinking, it looked like so much more fun than what I do."

"Fun!" he explodes. "Not much fun in writing, I'll grant you that. No notes on a page for us to fall back on. No amazing, orgasmic rhythms to make the audience melt. No heroism that anyone is likely to detect. Not one goddamn thing to do with the body, except to try wherever possible to ignore one's own cursed immobility. God, the unnaturalness of writing. And unlike performing music, it never gets any easier, no matter how much you do it. Every damned time we sit down to work, it's that same blank page again. A person could have a better time at a Doug McLure retrospective."

In late July, having made arrangements for the Mendelsons' dogs, I fly to the Democratic National Convention in Miami. In addition to writing about the Youth Vote for *Ms.* magazine, I've been invited to appear on a panel at the convention with various other youth spokespeople types—and Patrick Caddell, the boy-wonder pollster, as moderator—to discuss the issues that will decide how young people vote.

Although I am staying in a good hotel not far from the beach, I never lay eyes on the water. I stay in my room composing a ten-page-long letter to Jerry, describing everything I see.

The letter I write to Jerry is a better piece of writing than the voice-of-a-generation piece I submit to *Ms.* In a funny way, I am becoming for Jerry a kind of emissary into the world. I go places he would never think of traveling, though he watches them on television. I venture forth. Then I come back and spin him my yarns, or tell him about them in the letters I write. In this one, from Miami, I describe a politician who strikes me immediately as heading someplace, Governor Jimmy Carter, and an encounter with a group of feminists who tear into me, at one point, for a statement I make that I would like to get married and have babies someday. Don't I know a woman sets the cause of women back every time she makes a statement like that?

As always, the letter Jerry writes to me, after receiving my own long account of goings-on at the convention, begins with a warm and loving appreciation of what I have written to him, featuring my not-very-charitable portraits of certain feminists there, including Betty Friedan, whose strident style seems particularly distasteful. He calls my letter from Miami beautiful. Reading what I write about an experience I've observed firsthand, he says, revives in him a deep love of writing that he doesn't often feel these days.

He talks about a book I have sent him, *Raisins and Almonds*, written by my mother—a memoir, published in Canada, about her growing up Jewish on the Canadian prairies. He says (not only in his letter to me about it, but in the one he will eventually mail to my mother) that he loves *Raisins and Almonds*. In his letter to my mother about her memoir, he goes on for one long paragraph, apologizing for not having written sooner to thank her for the wonderful gift of her book, and spends another paragraph praising her writing and telling her how much he values the copy she has signed for him.

The issues being fought for in Miami in 1972—the Equal Rights Amendment, women's reproductive freedom—are ones in which I will come to have a passionate stake. My mother's story would have been very different had there been an Equal Rights Amendment back when she went looking for a job in 1948 with her Radcliffe Ph.D. in her pocket—back when she was told to stay home and have babies, and leave the university teaching to her husband. The day will come when I recognize Betty Friedan as a heroine for women of my mother's generation, and the generations that follow, including mine. But in the summer of 1972, I feel little connection with the feminist revolution. And so—like more and more of what I see around me in the world—the girl I am at eighteen dismisses a good part of it.

Ms. decides not to run the article I submit to the magazine about my visit to Miami.

My parents have raised me deeply isolated in the insular world of our family, and though I doubt Jerry sets out to accomplish this, he constantly reinforces my abiding sense of alienation. The theme Jerry keeps going back to in his letters is eerily familiar. I can't trust readers, AMA physicians, agents, editors, and the people at *The New York Times.* Not political leaders. Not therapists, or sex therapists. Feminists. So-called gurus. Jazz musicians. People posing as artists. People who would pretend to be my friends.

In one way or another, what Jerry is telling me all that spring and summer returns to one relentless refrain. *"You are alone in the world. Nobody else is like you. No one will understand you."* He doesn't say this yet, but the list of those who cannot be trusted—those from whom I must keep my distance, because in the end, they are not like me either—will soon include my own parents.

I'm not quite alone, of course. There is one person who understands and knows me completely: Jerry.

What he learned most clearly while I was in Miami, he writes, is that being apart from me leaves him feeling "bleedingly" adrift.

Hearing him say that the bad haircut he gave himself, in my absence, is all my fault, I register the oddest combination of responses: excitement and pride that I have such a strong effect on such a powerful man, as well as anxiety. The feeling of being responsible for a grown man's happiness and well-being is something I know well from life with my father, who became restless and depressed when my mother and I would go away. Not simply out of fear for our well-being, but out of concern for his own.

"I fall apart without you," my father would tell my mother every year when she came home from her annual trip to Princeton, marking college boards, to find out that, once again, he'd gone on a terrible bender. "I don't do well when you're gone." These are the exact words Jerry Salinger now tells me.

"I don't like to think about September, when you go off to the land of Old Blue," he tells me. "I could handle your going to night school in West Lebanon, maybe. But this bachelor's degree business seems a little extreme, if you ask me. It may not make for a pretty picture: me moping around here all winter, knowing you're diagramming sentences and dissecting frogs, or whatever they do at college these days. Getting serenaded by some heart-breaker of a Whiffenpoof, more than likely, with a V-neck sweater and a tennis racquet under his arm and a bulldog tattooed on his navel."

"I'll write," I say. "I'll call every night."

"The thing is not seeing your face," he tells me. "I suppose I could pay you visits, now and then. But I'm just not the man-on-campus type. Put me within a one-mile radius of an ivy plant, and I'm likely to break out in a strange and hideous rash. I couldn't handle college, even when I was of an age for it.

"I could rent myself a little bungalow in Westport," he says. "I could be one of those poor saps who rides the train into Manhattan. You'd get your diploma. I'd work at *The New Yorker*."

It's exhilarating to witness the effect I am having on a man as powerful as Jerry. There exists between us now an unspoken understanding that we will be together. There is a comforting sense of domesticity about the arrangement Jerry describes, with me going to classes while he, almost like a suburban husband, commutes to his job in the city. With Jerry at my side, managing every detail, I will never have to be alone anymore.

All my life I have dreamed of passionate attachment and extravagant affection. Child of a father who had pursued my mother for six years with sonnets, drawings, and telegrams across the continent, I believe in grand romantic gestures. Still, I experience a mix of emotions while reading Jerry's plan of getting a place in Connecticut to be near me. Until this moment, the vision of my return to school in the fall and the wonderful little apartment I've rented that's waiting for me there have provided a kind of safety for me in the strange, uncharted territory of my love affair with Jerry Salinger. If I get in over my head, if the moment comes when I simply don't know what to do anymore about loving this man who hates so much of the world I adore, there has always been the prospect of Yale and New Haven to provide for me, if not an exit, then at least a temporary escape or retreat. I have never pictured myself leaving Jerry permanently in the fall. But neither have I pictured myself leaving college, or giving up what it represents in my life.

He tells me regularly that he loves my mind.

I understand what he means. That's how I feel about him. I love *his* mind, too. I long to hear from him. The way readers feel about his books, I feel about *him*.

After a visit from old *New Yorker* friends on their way back to New York from Brewster, New York, he complains of feeling disheartened. Visits—even from people he professes to like—are something Jerry endures, not anything he ever delights in. He writes of how much he wished, when his *New Yorker* friends were there, that he could feel more sense of friendship and connection. The same guests who, no doubt, drive away with the impression that they have just spent an hour or a day with the most welcoming of hosts, would not guess what he would be saying to me over the phone a half hour after they leave. "Thank God it's over. I didn't think I could stand much more."

Avoiding visits with people is one of the reasons he moved up to Cornish in the first place, he says. All he really wants in his life are a handful of people. Most of the writers he loves are dead. When it comes to writers he knows who are still alive, he's more than content to admire them from a distance in the pages of their books. He never feels much desire to seek them out personally.

I am in a different category, we know. Even when he finds himself being pulled into the most insufferable literary discussions, he tells me he feels better when he thinks about his love for me.

He misses me so much that he's driving to New York the next day to see me. He will be there by the time this letter arrives.

I miss him. He misses me back. Sitting at my desk at *The New York Times*, eating my third container of yogurt for the day and staring out at West Forty-third Street, I know I am supposed to be thinking and writing about Nixon, about drugs, about women's liberation, the upcoming elections, youth culture, Vietnam. All I can think about is Jerry, same as, he says, all he thinks about is me.

My sister Rona and I have always had an odd connection—love and distance, attachment and competition. She spent her teens shut in her bedroom, listening to Janis Joplin, Bob Dylan, and Joan Baez and reading dark, existential poetry, while I sat in the TV room watching family situation comedies or, with my father, *Gilligan's Island.*

On her twenty-first birthday, Rona suddenly got married. The next year she had a baby. It has been months since I've seen or spoken to her. She's living in Toronto on very little money with her husband, Paul, and infant son, Benjamin.

I have seldom talked with my sister in an intimate or confiding way. But now, as I struggle with the question of what to do about my feelings for Jerry Salinger, she is the person I most want to talk to. I write her a letter.

> *I find even the writing of this hard, so forgive me if it comes out sounding mushy or stammering.*
>
> *I am in love with Jerry Salinger, happier with him than I've ever been with any boy my age, and I think he's very happy with me. We are really alike, and even the differences are nice—the Zen and the yoga and the homeopathic medicine and the distaste for all the Johnny Carson-ish fame that I still half love. I think he is making me a better person and would save me from the very real danger of becoming the smarty, superficial, sometimes obnoxious person that you have always seen and that I could easily become, in the right (wrong) company.*
>
> *...I find myself wishing I was thirty, looking in a new way at all the gray-haired men I pass on the street. Oh, there are endless calculations—53 and 18; 63–28; 73–38....*
>
> *I haven't moved in with him. If I did, I know I'd never leave. I've gone a couple of times to visit, and he's come to New York. I miss him a lot when he goes....But I have*

almost no other important relationship to compare this to....
Would it be the same if I'd known anything else that's real?...

I can't imagine what M and D are thinking. M, on the surface, seems pleased that I have such a nice new friend. Has she said anything to you? Daddy has now read his books, and speaks occasionally of "Salinger." Is it that the possibility of anything more than two writer friends getting together for discussions of punctuation seems too incredible for them to conceive of, or are they simply not admitting their concern? Certainly if it were 53-year-old Joe Schmoe I was visiting, they would not be so pleased....

If I'm looking for my sister to question me or try and talk me out of what I'm doing, she doesn't.

My sister writes back, "I think our parents are quite genuinely pleased about you and Jerry, and waste no time wishing he were younger."

Chapter Seven

IN JULY, TWO of the editorials I've written that have passed the scrutiny of the editorial board run in *The New York Times*. "Not bad for a girl who grew up on the wrong side of the tracks in Kalamazoo," Jerry says when he calls that afternoon after picking up his paper. "I'd hardly even know your first tongue was Lithuanian."

I start work on my memoir, with a deadline for delivery of the book set for October, shortly before my nineteenth birthday. My publisher, Doubleday, is anxious to have the book come out while I'm still in my teens so they can make the claim that I am the youngest girl since Françoise Sagan and Anne Frank to publish a book. Jerry's predictions, in his first letter to me, are beginning to come true, though neither of us brings this up.

For a girl who would once have described a book contract with a major New York publisher as one of the better things that could happen in her life, I am not really thinking about my book much anymore. All I really care about by now is being with Jerry Salinger.

"Why don't you find someone else to take care of those goofy dogs and move in here for the rest of the summer?" Jerry says. "A girl like you shouldn't have to put up with the Upper West Side in August when she could be eating fresh-picked corn and swimming in New Hampshire ponds. You've had a nice big taste of *The New*

York Times. What you really should be doing now is working on that book of yours. I'll help you."

At the beginning of August I tell John Oakes I'm leaving *The New York Times*, offering no explanation. I find a housesitting and dog-walking replacement for the Central Park West brownstone, and Jerry drives to New York again to pick me up. Then we head north to Cornish.

On our way, we stop in Brewster, New York, to visit the house of my former teacher Mark's mother, where Mark and his wife, Anna, have been staying. Jerry brings them a bottle of Scotch and, at the request of Mark's mother, signs the guest book, "Wonderful sports program."

I work on my book for the remainder of that summer—conferring with Jerry now and then—with the plan of returning to Yale in the fall. But I don't even open the course catalogue that has arrived in the mail, forwarded from my parents' house, to choose the classes I'll enroll in. I call no friends. Although soon after my arrival in Cornish I make a trip to Durham to pick up my records, I hardly ever listen anymore to Joni Mitchell and Bob Dylan—let alone the Rolling Stones. With Jerry, I listen to big band music.

I don't swim that summer, or ride my bike, or drive anywhere without Jerry, except one time, when I get to take the Blazer (never the BMW) to a Singer sewing machine store. I have to write a book in the next three months. I should be buying an electric typewriter. I spend $400 on a Singer Golden Touch 'N Sew machine instead.

"This baby would have come in handy in a foxhole," he says as he lifts it out of the back of the car and carries the machine up the cellar stairs for me. "Put one of these on your head and you wouldn't have to worry about shrapnel fire."

The day I unpack my things, Jerry comments on my habit of leaving apple cores on the arm of the sofa. A couple of peelings from a cucumber I fix myself for a snack have landed on the floor. I can't figure out how to work his washing machine. There is no place to set up my new sewing machine without disrupting Jerry's things. He finds me crying.

He puts an arm on my shoulder. "What's up?"

"It's not your fault," I say. "This just isn't my home."

I know he doesn't want me telling people where I am, but I had supposed I could give my telephone number to my agent, Emmy Jacobson, and my editor, Elsa van Bergen. Now he hears me on the phone with Elsa. "I've decided to come back to New Hampshire to work," I say. "I'm staying up north, with a friend."

"You don't understand what these people are like," he says. "They're vultures. You can't let them get a piece of you, or it won't ever stop."

"She might need to reach me," I say. "People sometimes have questions for me. . . ."

"You bet they do," he says, running his fingers through his hair.

Very simply—oversimplified—the basic principles underlying homeopathic medicine might be described like this: Homeopathic medicine makes use of a vast range of substances from nature, in infinitesimal doses, to treat a patient in a manner not unlike the one employed with inoculation, on the theory that to cure a person you give her a very small dose of precisely what ails her. There exist, in homeopathic medicine, certain ailment-specific remedies, but the truly elegant homeopath does not address a specific ailment in diagnosing his patient. He or she looks at the whole person, and attempts to locate that person's essential remedy, known as her similimum.

This requires an enormously laborious and time-consuming process that shares almost no common ground with conventional Western medicine. No blood is taken, no stethoscope or blood pressure cuff employed. But it is not unlikely that a patient consulting a homeopathic physician will encounter a question along the lines of "Do you enjoy the sensation of the wind in your face?" "Do you tend to sleep on your left side?" "Are you disgusted by cats?" "When you were a child, did you like to pull out the hair on top of your head?" A homeopath in pursuit of his patient's similimum may examine the shape of that person's earlobes, or ask if she is unusually prone to hiccups.

Now, addressing my medical problem of vaginismus, Jerry asks very little about my sexual history, or what might have taken place in my first eighteen years of life that has left me with my vaginal muscles clamped shut.

Jerry doesn't inquire into my history, or lack of history, touching my own body. He has heard enough about my family by now to know that there is considerably more to the story than what I conveyed in my article "My Parents Are My Friends," but we don't explore this. He does not appear to attach any significance to the fact that over the duration of our relationship I do not experience a single menstrual period. He doesn't inquire into the origins of my thinness, or notice, even, that I have a problem surrounding food. Of his own sexual history, he says nothing.

Instead, he begins compiling lists of my notable traits. We may be sitting in the living room—I with a magazine, he with a homeopathic text—and seemingly out of the blue he asks me, "Do you ever feel bothered by the sensation of wool against your skin?" "Do you ever experience an urge to curse?" "When you were young, did you like to hear the same lines from a story repeated over and over?"

The similimum—once arrived at—comes in the form of a crumb-sized pellet, extracted from the glass tube in which it is stored, preferably without touching the fingers. Some homeopathic physicians simply give these pellets to a patient, much as you'd give an aspirin or a vitamin tablet, and ask her to place it under her tongue. But the form of homeopathy Jerry practices, learned from his Colorado mentor, calls for him to place the remedy in a quart or even gallon-size jug of purified water, depending on the amount of dilution, or potency. He then pounds the jug very hard with his hands, and after pounding on it (an activity known as succussing), he extracts a very small quantity of the water—maybe a glass, maybe no more than a teaspoonful. This is what the patient drinks.

Over the course of the months I am with Jerry, I watch him treat not only myself but also his children, and himself—also my mother, my father, and even my Exeter teacher Mark's dog—often with dramatic, even spectacular results. Some months into our relationship, when my mother pays us a visit, she tells Jerry she has an infected toe. He studies her toe first for a minute or two, then disappears into the back room with his books. A half hour later he emerges with a remedy. After preparing it in his customary fashion, he asks her to drink the water. She drinks it, and within minutes the inflamed part on her toe swells to many times its size, then bursts. The pain is gone.

For the duration of my relationship with Jerry Salinger, he maintains a quest for the similimum that will cure me of my problem. Cure me, period. Change me. Transform me from a person who cannot let him enter her body to someone who can.

Jerry tries many remedies on me over the months I'm with him, but he never arrives at my true similimum. If I don't hold out ultimate faith that the answer to my problem lies in one of his homeopathic tomes, at least, I am enough of a believer that I consider no other alternative. Not conventional medicine, certainly. Not psychotherapy.

One time we're driving along the highway and he suddenly reaches for my hand and says, "I just had an idea. Let me see your fingernails." He notices something about the way I peel an apple, or a sound I make when I sneeze, and goes to look it up in one of his books. "Aha!" I hear him call out sometimes, from his study. "I may be onto something here. Do you tend to crave salty foods when you're sad? Does the smell of violets give you a headache? Do you ever feel the urge to take your clothes off in public?"

Maybe I do, maybe I don't. I barely know anymore what I like, what I want, except that I want to please him. If I were diagnosed with a malignant tumor at this point, I would seek no treatment but what Jerry would prescribe to me out of his drawersful of homeopathic remedies.

Every day, in the late afternoon, we take the same walk to the top of Jerry's hill. On this particular day, I am telling Jerry the story of my visit to the Miss Teenage America pageant in Fort Worth the previous fall. Along the path, I perform imitations of the talent presentations of the various contestants: a girl who twirled her baton to "Stars and Stripes Forever," a medley of songs from *The Sound of Music,* including one number in which the contestant, dressed in a nun's habit, whipped off her long black robe to reveal a sparkly leotard and then broke into a tap dance.

"The things that kept coming out of those girls' mouths!" I tell Jerry. "There was this one who told me with a straight face how you should put Vaseline on your teeth to make them shine on camera. Who could make up stuff that good?"

He looks at me hard. "I have no doubt you could go to town on a story like that, Joyce," he says. "Observers like us, we don't miss much. You'd get all kinds of hugely gratifying pats on the back while you were at it, too, as some kind of goddamn female Truman Capote, hopping from one hollow scene to the next.

"But one day, kiddo, you're going to have to ask yourself what the point would be. Does anybody actually need to open up *Esquire* magazine and take in one more hysterically amusing little exercise in assassination by typewriter? Sooner or later you need to soberly consider whether what you write is serving any purpose but to serve your own ego."

Severe as his message may be, it's not delivered unkindly. His voice is low and quiet as he says these things to me. I know what he is saying is important.

"You know I love your writing," he says. "But loving your mind as I do, it would make me terribly sad to see you sell yourself short by tripping along, however brilliantly, with some ultimately shallow form of journalistic small talk."

"I was just telling you about one magazine article," I say. "It wasn't all that important." But I know what he means.

"You could do anything, you know," he says to me. "I could see you on the television set, standing in front of the White House in a trench coat, saying, 'Now back to you, Walter.' You could get yourself one of those desks, like Johnny Carson, and a couch for celebrities to sit on, and some smarmy, pandering Ed McMahon figure to feed you straight lines, and all of the hotshots of the moment would pay you visits and tell you when they were playing Las Vegas and what their new movie was, and you'd get your mug on the cover of *TV Guide* and you'd roll in the dough while you were at it."

"No," I say. "That's not what I want."

"And I'd sit up here watching you on the screen. Only I can't pretend I wouldn't register a certain stab of regret knowing what else you might have done with yourself of more true consequence."

The life in which I would be White House Correspondent or Talk Show Hostess or Author of Blockbuster Novels would not include Jerry Salinger. This, more than anything, leads me to dismiss the possibility of the careers he warns against.

"Suppose you made your subject something you loved and admired," he says quietly. "Something you held precious and dear. *There* would be your challenge as a writer. Any hack can make fun of some muffin-baking jamboree."

For a long time, I had pictured myself accomplishing the very things Jerry has described to me: becoming a well-known television news reporter, a talk show host. I imagined making a name for myself as a writer of deliciously cutthroat celebrity profiles, or a sharp-tongued chronicler of American pop-culture phenomena. This very week, I had written a proposal to *The New York Times* suggesting that they send me to the Pillsbury Bake-Off.

"What I want for you, kid," he says, more serious than I have ever seen him, "is to write about what you truly love, and nothing, but nothing, less than that. Not beauty pageants and high school proms, or television personalities or movie stars, or interviews with daughters of Republican presidents or Democratic presidents or even the presidents themselves. Or if you do those things, what I want is for you to find a way to do them with nothing less than originality and tenderness and love."

We walk up the hill with no sound for several minutes but the one our shoes make along the path. Now and then we stop to throw a stick for Joey. I put my hand in Jerry's pocket.

"Most writers aren't in the position that you are, Jerry," I point out. "A person has to write things somebody will be willing to pay for and publish."

"That article you wrote about your wonderful, perfect relationship with your parents," he says quietly. "Skillful. Clever. Eminently publishable. And there wasn't one honest sentence in the whole damn thing. Your father's an alcoholic, for God's sake."

We have stopped walking. We have reached the top of the hill, where we always turn around and head back to the house. I study the dirt and draw breath as a terrible wave of sadness comes over me. It's as if he's showing me a picture of my own death. Or his.

"I could never write about my father's drinking," I whisper. "I can't even talk about it with my mother. She'd be so upset."

He shakes his head. "Some day, Joyce," he says to me, "there will be a story you want to tell for no better reason than because it matters to you more than any other. You'll give up this business of delivering what everybody tells you to do. You'll stop looking over your shoulder to make sure you're keeping everybody happy, and you'll simply write what's real and true. Honest writing always makes people nervous, and they'll think of all kinds of ways to make your life hell. One day a long time from now you'll cease to care anymore whom you please or what anybody has to say about you. That's when you'll finally produce the work you're capable of."

When Jerry speaks to my mother over the phone, she invariably urges him to come to Durham for lunch. He has written her a letter of praise about her memoir, *Raisins and Almonds*, expressing his keen desire to meet her and my father. But my parents don't make long drives, and though Jerry and I always say we are going to Durham one of these days, the summer passes without our paying them a visit.

Jerry also sends a note to Mark, my English teacher at Exeter, and his wife, Anna. Maybe Jerry views Mark as the one of my friends with whom it might be most possible to have some kind of relationship. Mark is a reader and a thinker, a deeply serious person and, like Jerry, an early mentor of mine. At twenty-eight, he has also been named a trustee of his alma mater, Dartmouth College, a role that brings him to Hanover now and then. Jerry and I urge Mark to come visit that August. Over the months that follow, he and Anna pay us several other visits. They are virtually the only people who do.

The visit of Mark and Anna follows the standard pattern. Lunch of salad, whole-grain bread, cheese. A walk up the hill. A movie.

Jerry is funny and charming and attentive—a listener far more than a talker on these occasions.

"Do you ever see a student anymore who simply loves to write, for the pure joy of the thing?" he asks. "Or are they all hell-bent on making a name for themselves?

"What do they read with real affection?" he wants to know. "What about Isak Dinesen? *Gatsby* still do it for them? God, how I loved Fitzgerald when I was young. Hemingway, too, of course. But Hemingway has none of Fitzgerald's intellectual power. He's all instinct."

He asks Mark about his own growing up. Mark is also the child of one Jewish parent and one Gentile.

As much as any of the human guests gathered around the table, Jerry pays attention to Mark and Anna's beloved dog, Katie, who is getting on in years and experiencing a number of health problems.

"Would you say she's more inclined to lie in the sun or the shade?" Jerry asks Anna. "Is she the kind of dog who prefers to curl up at your feet, or does she like her privacy?"

After asking a lot of questions about Katie's habits and personality, he settles on a homeopathic remedy for her. As usual, he places the chosen remedy in a gallon jug of distilled water, pounds it with his fist and feeds the water to Katie, who laps it up.

Although Mark is a teacher of students who fall in the age group most passionate about *Catcher in the Rye*, one subject we have stayed away from is Jerry's work. We do not discuss who he is as a literary figure, how he came to live here, the circumstances that find me living with him.

"Be sure Katie takes this every day," Jerry says, giving Mark a little plastic bottle with more of the homeopathic remedy for his dog's ailing hip as the two of us walk Mark and Anna to their car. "Maybe we'll take in a Dartmouth game one of these days," Jerry says. "Or Joyce and I might come down to Exeter with my son, Matthew."

Knowing this is a man who wrote a book that, more than any

other, portrayed private school life as a sickening sham, I have a hard time picturing the two of us making a field trip to the campus of Phillips Exeter.

In August, Matthew and Peggy are around much of the time.

I like Jerry's children, but I have little in common with this cheerful, friendly twelve-year-old boy and his basketball-loving sixteen-year-old sister.

Years later, I try to imagine what Matthew and Peggy must have thought that summer. I have been a divorced parent myself now. In the years following my own divorce, I have attempted to carry on a romantic relationship with someone who is not my children's parent. And because I have, it's unimaginable to the woman I am now that even the most secure and well-loved twelve-year-old and sixteen-year-old wouldn't feel dismay upon walking into their home and finding a girl just a few years older than they are, sitting on their father's lap or curled up on the couch next to him with her head on his shoulder.

Where my way of operating in the world has always called for large amounts of conciliatory behavior—cuteness and charm, dissembling for the purpose of pleasing adults—Peggy's demeanor speaks of uncompromising honesty. Peggy, though she's two years younger, seems far more self-possessed than I. Whatever insecurities she may harbor, or secretly competitive feelings she may have toward me, I watch her with a kind of awe and fear, viewing her as someone who seems far more sure of herself in the world than I am. In Peggy's presence, I feel naked and oddly silly.

Matthew's nice to his sister, nice to me. He seems to move easily between his father's house and his mother's down the road, although Jerry never mentions her name. Matthew is good humored, smart, and athletic, and adores his father. He seems to offer Jerry nothing but joy. And what Jerry offers back is a kind of pure, loving indulgence he gives to no one else. Not Peggy. Certainly not me.

There's a lightness to Jerry with his son—when they do their Peter Sellers "Birdy Num Nums" routine from the *The Party*, or when Jerry comes in after a trip to New York, taking the steps two at a time with a new *Tin-Tin* book he's bought for Matthew under his arm. Just the sight of Matthew invariably causes Jerry to break into a smile.

I never compare myself with some other old lover of Jerry's, or a former wife. I do compare his feeling for me with his feeling for his children. If I feel jealous, I don't acknowledge it. However, looking at how Jerry can be with Matthew, and not with me, I feel sorrow.

I like having Matthew around, because when Matthew's around Jerry is more carefree. Matthew can get Jerry to attend games at Dartmouth. They watch silly movies. Jerry has bought Matthew a three-wheel all-terrain vehicle. Matthew and Matthew tool around on it together daily over Jerry's fields.

Because Matthew loves pizza, Jerry will take us out for pizza, even though pizza is a forbidden food, full of cheese and oil, and greasy pepperoni, cooked at high temperatures.

We all gorge on it. Then we go to an action movie Jerry wouldn't care about, except that Matthew wants to see it.

After we get home, and Matthew goes to bed, Jerry tells me how much he hates having all that junk in his body. It's no good for him. No good for me. No good for Matthew either, of course, but Matthew is twelve.

Jerry and I are alone together again, and all the carefree joy and ease that I felt earlier in the evening disappears.

He takes me into the bathroom with him. "You can't let this junk sit around putrefying in your intestine," he says. Then he shows me how to put my finger down my throat and make myself throw up.

Jerry uses this technique when he has consumed an unhealthy food. But once I've learned how to do this, I feel compelled to do it every day.

By the end of the summer the house at the end of that long dirt driveway in Cornish has become the place I see as my true home. There has been no more talk of Jerry's getting a place in Westport, and I view the move to my New Haven apartment as temporary—a place I'll mark my time while I get my college degree. I'll come home to Jerry on weekends.

In September Jerry drives me to New Haven. He and I carry my trunk up the stairs to my apartment, along with a bag of vegetables from his garden. Jerry has brought his projector and a print of the old movie *A Night to Remember*, about the sinking of the *Titanic*. I make a plate of steamed vegetables for us, and a plate of carrot sticks. After dinner we make popcorn and lie down together on my single bed to watch the movie. *A Night to Remember* is full of magnificent obsession, rich irony, and heartbreaking tragedy: the hubris of the ships' designers, who say the *Titanic* is unsinkable; the wealthy first-class passengers and the poor people huddled below decks in steerage; the terrified crew watching the water pour in, and the oblivious rich, who continue to laugh and drink and smoke cigars long after the ship has hit the iceberg, confident no ill could ever befall them.

One part of *A Night to Remember* makes me cry. It's a scene in which the husbands and wives and lovers are separated at the moment the lifeboats are lowered. Curled up on the bed with Jerry's arms around me, I watch the brave husbands urging their beloveds into the lifeboats and the women resisting because they would rather drown than be parted.

The next morning I'm supposed to register for classes. Jerry is driving home to New Hampshire. "I'll call you tonight," I say.

"Who knows?" he tells me. "Maybe you'll meet up with some irresistible Joe College type and I'll never hear from you again."

I stand on the curb outside my new apartment with tears running down my face as I watch Jerry's BMW pull away. For more than a month we have scarcely been apart more than an hour or two. Partly, now, I am scared I won't know how to get through the days without Jerry anymore. I am also partly scared that I may get through them too well, and that if I do, Jerry will look at me as a weak and corrupted girl, seduced by the shallow attrtactions of the world. That would be worse.

All over New Haven that day, bright, curious students are returning to campus after the long summer break, stocking up on supplies at the Yale Coop, catching up on what they did over the summer, making arrangements to meet for meals or movies. Flyers have been posted announcing auditions for plays and musical performances. Though it's fall, the air is warm enough that you can still ride your bike in shorts and a sleeveless shirt. I ride mine to the supermarket and fill my basket with the foods I now live on as a result of Jerry's reeducation. I register for classes and call up a couple of people I know, who have been thinking I spent the summer in New York. When they ask what I've been up to I am vague. "Writing a book," I say. "Hanging around in New Hampshire."

That night I call Jerry. I can hear *The Thin Man* in the background. Myrna Loy must have just scooped Asta up in her arms. He's barking. "I wish I were there," I say.

"Next time I see you, I suppose you'll give me one of those secret handshakes I've heard so much about," Jerry says. "No, I guess not. They're secret."

The next day I buy a schefflera plant and an African violet. I go over to the Hadassah Thrift Shop and buy a hooked rug and an overstuffed armchair and a bunch of mismatched dishes and cooking utensils. I get a friend to help me carry the chair home, and I spend the rest of the day scrubbing the apartment and hanging posters and putting my dishes in the cupboards. By nightfall everything's in place. My little apartment looks wonderful to me. Sitting in my overstuffed chair, munching on my apple, I call Jerry, collect as usual.

"You wouldn't recognize it here, my place looks so homey," I tell him.

"Wish I could say the same about this one," he says. "Things aren't the same around here."

"I'll be back to visit soon," I remind him.

"Right," he says. "Glad you can fit me in."

The next day I buy books and notebooks, almost guilty. But I don't attend the art class I've signed up for. I ride my bike for hours through the Yale campus. I remember how excited I was when I got into this university, and how hopeful I'd been that first day I arrived, a year ago, on the bus. I pedal my blue bike over the path past the library, the gym, the Berkeley College dining hall where I performed my role in *Punks*, the theater where I sat last spring listening to Frank Capra give a lecture to my film class.

That night I call Jerry. "Come get me," I say.

"God I missed you," he says. "It's about time."

*   *   *

I don't tell most people I know that I'm leaving, though there is one girl, Jessica, I want to say good-bye to. When I call her, she says she'd like to come over before I go. I tell her I've fallen in love, but I can't talk about it. I don't give her my new phone number.

We had just started to become friends in the spring of freshman year, and I liked her a lot. I had hoped we'd get to know each other better. Now I don't expect to see her ever again.

I withdraw from Yale, forfeiting that fall's tuition, plus my scholarship and the monthly $200 check Social Security has been sending me because my father's over sixty-five. I tell another girl I know, Jean, that she and her boyfriend can have my apartment until I can find someone to sublet it; my lease commits me to paying the rent through the following June.

Jerry arrives a few hours later to pick me up. I pile my clothes in the back of his car. He's brought the BMW, not the Blazer, so I leave most of the rest of my possessions in the apartment. The blue Schwinn bicycle I've had since I was twelve is left unlocked outside the apartment building. When I finally return, on one of my trips to New York City with Jerry a few months later, it's gone.

Passing the Old Campus on our way out of town, I see students on the quadrangle, playing guitars and stretched out on the grass with their books. The day is warm enough that people have their dorm windows open. Music filters down into the street. Led Zeppelin. The Doors. Neil Young.

We head out onto the highway, north to New Hampshire.

It's lonely in Cornish. Even the telephone is largely off limits. I write a few letters. This may be the moment when I begin to develop the practice I continue for years, creating a vision of my life on paper that has less to do with the way things really are than with how I wish them to be.

Dear Rona,
    I've hung my clothes in the closet here and am having
    my mail forwarded, and I've decided that this is really the

only place I can live. I'll feel more moved in when I have a chance to drive to New Haven and get my plants and my records (though neither will fit in here very well, I'm afraid).

I feel sick about my apartment, especially on the first of every month, when I send out yet another rent check—all wasted. I tell myself that I'm living here free, so it's not costing me more than I'd expected to pay, but I've been brought up too money-conscious to take the idea of an empty apartment in stride. I'm also a little saddened because the apartment was so nice. If I do say so myself, it looked very nice, except Jerry wasn't in it.

I missed J. terribly, and came to see that living apart was not desirable or possible, so here I am. The house itself is much less a home to me than George Street was—J's taste and mine are quite different—but I think of this, unquestionably, as home now. The view all around here is so beautiful....And much more than that, I feel easier, happier, more myself with J. than I have ever felt. In spite of all the problems (and there are many—differences in taste, life-style, my not being a Reader, or giving up ego—age difference seems almost incidental), in spite of all that, I can no longer imagine being apart. For the first time in years, I feel settled.

It's not that simple. Jerry can be moody and cranky, and even his humor is tinged with a sharp, practically sneering bitterness that scares me. His assessments of most people around him are withering, even brutal. I hear him on the phone with some acquaintance, someone from his New York days. He sounds patient and concerned. Then he puts down the receiver and groans. "God, the world is full of dreary fools," he says.

Even though I never question that he loves me, he now voices criticisms of me of a sort I never used to hear from him. Though his house is cluttered with books and papers, movie reels and Matthew's sporting gear, Jerry is a much more fastidious person than I.

I bake a banana bread in his kitchen (whole-wheat flour, honey instead of sugar, but baked—there is no way around this part—at 350 degrees, with eggs). It's bad enough that I'm baking banana bread at all. But I leave the bowl in the sink. There are banana peels on the counter, and drips of batter.

I scatter clothes on the floor. (My red-and-white-checked sneakers, which he had noted in the photograph on the cover of *The New York Times*, are less charming to him in the middle of the bedroom floor.)

I can learn to pick up after myself. I could even give up baking banana bread. What I cannot do is change the hunger I still have for what Jerry calls "worldly things." This is the thing about me that inspires his sharpest criticism.

I don't buy *Seventeen* anymore. Now the magazines I look at in the supermarket are *Woman's Day* and *Family Circle.*

The division between us goes deeper. What Jerry wants is freedom from wanting. The self-denial that he practices in his diet—"abstemiousness," he calls it—is what he believes in for other areas of his life, too. His goal, in meditation, is letting go of desire, obliterating the ego. His goal is nothing less than to empty his brain of thought. The zen term he uses for it is *samadhi,* or "no-mind."

Jerry meditates daily, but not the way certain college students do, for ten or fifteen minutes on a mat, or like a follower of the form of transcendental meditation popularized by Maharishi Mahesh Yoga. "Not a pleasant thought, knowing I can take credit for getting the whole rotten, faddish thing going," he tells me.

There is a certain kind of heavy cotton broadcloth jumpsuit, of a sort generally worn by car mechanics, that Jerry favors. Every morning, after breakfast, he puts on his, which is navy blue, with a zipper down the front, and disappears into his study to write and meditate. I may not see him again until the middle of the afternoon. He wants me to meditate, too.

But every time I assume my yoga position and close my eyes and begin my breathing, worldly thoughts keep coming in. I'm counting down from twenty, breathing in, breathing out, using my diaphragm . . . and then I think about a letter that came yesterday from a documentary filmmaker, wanting to interview me for a movie he's making about the sixties—a project I would like to participate in, though I say no.

I think about Peggy, who has come home for the weekend but barely acknowledges my presence at the house. I think about my old boyfriend, Jim.

I think about my sister's baby, Benjamin, and wonder when I will have a baby of my own. I think about my father's arthritis, which is getting worse, and his drinking, which is also getting worse. My mother's magazine articles. The words to a Leonard Cohen song.

I wonder what I should wear for the photograph that will be taken shortly for the jacket of my book, and if I should get my hair cut. I think about my friend, Jean, living with her boyfriend, Tim, in my apartment on George Street in New Haven, directing a production of *Wizard of Oz*, and about my other friend, Josh, at work on a musical. I wish I were directing a play.

I think about food. The banana bread on the counter. I want to get up and cut myself a piece. Finally, just to get the thought out of my head, I do. Only then I want another piece, and another after that, until the banana bread is gone, and I feel sick and ashamed of what I have done—at which point the only thing to do is make myself throw up.

Then I have to start all over again, emptying my mind. Every time I do, like a hole dug in the sand near the ocean, water fills it up.

Perhaps because my failures as a yogi have already revealed themselves so clearly, one day Jerry tells me there's something he wants me to remember always.

He delivers this as a doctor might, to someone who could find herself needing to perform emergency first aid someday by the side of a highway.

"The time may come when you will need to summon your strength to face some particularly difficult experience," he tells me. "When you do, I want you to remember to say this word. The word is *Om*."

I am sitting on the velvet couch with a book in my hand, *The Teachings of Ramana Maharshi*. Today is not the first time I have tried to read this book. But this morning, Jerry was so particularly critical of my habit of reading *TV Guide* as I ate breakfast that I have made a vow I will finish it this time.

I am reading a chapter called "Life in the World." I have chosen this chapter because, more than the others in the book, which seem terribly abstract, this one might hold a little more connection to my daily life and the things I care about. In this chapter, Ramana Maharshi uses a term Jerry also employs when talking about the life he and I might most realistically aspire to: "householder." If I can't attain the highest form of enlightenment, in which I might renounce earthly concerns altogether, perhaps I can become a worthy householder.

In the book, Ramana Maharshi makes use of the question and answer form to explore the concepts he is setting forth.

"Why do you think you are a householder?" he asks himself.

"Whether you continue in the household or renounce it and go to live in the forest, your mind haunts you," he says.

"The ego is the source of thought. It creates the body and the world and makes you think of being a house-holder. If you renounce, it will only substitute the thought of renunciation for that of the family and the environment of the forest for that of the household. But the mental obstacles are always there for you...."

Except for the occasional trip to New York, we live a quiet life in Cornish. Even when Peggy and Matthew are home, weekends, they divide their time between their father's and their mother's house. Eva Barrett comes to clean one day a week. Our only regular visitor is his young neighbor, Sally Kemp, who studies homeopathy with Jerry.

Sally is probably around thirty, a slim woman—attractive without appearing to make any particular efforts.

Jerry has known Sally and her husband, Dan, for years, though his friendship is with Sally alone. They have an old farmhouse on a back road not far from Jerry. They are one of those couples, of whom there are many living in New Hampshire, who have chosen to live a simple life, as free from material possessions as possible. They heat their house with wood and grow most of their own vegetables. Their daughter, a little over a year old, was born at home with a midwife. They drive a very old car. Dan makes wooden bowls from the burls of trees he cuts on his property. He is a printer and a dowser, a person who seeks out underground water by walking the land with a forked stick, responding to changes he perceives in the energy around him.

It was Sally's pregnancy and impending birth that led her to pursue her study of homeopathy. She wanted to be able to care for her child's medical needs without resorting to doctors. Sally didn't seek Jerry out as a fan of his work. She's interested only in his vast knowledge of homeopathic medicine—a subject she has pursued with such singlemindedness that during her pregnancy she took a job in town for the sole purpose of earning enough money to buy the books she would need to pursue her education in the field.

There is an otherworldly abstractness about Sally. She appears to have no interest in the everyday details of daily life that consume me—*gossip,* Jerry would call it. She never asks any questions—who I am, what I'm doing here, where I was before. She doesn't appear to care about movies, or fiction of any kind.

As a student of homeopathy, Jerry tells me she has an aptitude bordering on brilliance. I have been trying to read Jerry's homeopathic texts myself, in an attempt to share more of Jerry's life with him. But every time I sit down with the books I feel as though I'm completing an assignment to pass a course. I can't keep the names of remedies straight.

When Sally comes over, as she does once a week, she and Jerry disappear into his study for long periods. I may not hear from them for a few hours. The baby, who is still breastfeeding, stays with them. I sit in the living room.

"I sense she's depressed today," he says, studying the face of the baby as Sally carries her up the steps one afternoon. "Evidently she read this morning's *Times.*"

Sally never laughs.

* * *

Once Sally's husband, Dan, comes over with her. We find ourselves alone together in the living room while Jerry and Sally work on some diagnosis.

Dan is a New Hampshire native: a friendly man, dressed in rumpled backwoods clothing, very different from Jerry's brand of immaculate L.L. Bean attire. He stands at the windows looking out at the bird feeder and the mountain. "Some view you guys have here," he says. "You're practically right up there with God."

He takes a handful of nuts and flips through the paper. The World Series is going on. "You follow baseball?" he asks me. "I'm a Red Sox fan myself. Glutton for punishment."

It's Saturday afternoon and Matthew is home from school for the weekend. Because he has a bad cough at the moment, Jerry has been treating him and supervising his diet with particular care. No mucus-producing dairy foods this weekend. No pizza.

The three of us have been watching Laurel and Hardy. Matthew is sprawled on the couch with his head on Jerry's shoulder; I'm in the chair beside the two of them. Joey, the dog, breathes heavily at Jerry's feet. Jerry is flipping through the most recent L.L. Bean catalogue, sticking paper clips on pages that feature items he wants to order. Outside it's raining.

Matthew and Jerry have seen this particular *Laurel and Hardy* reel many times before. Part of the pleasure of watching it, for them, is the anticipation of every gag and gesture. For me, the movie is unfamiliar. I laugh at Laurel and Hardy, but what I like best is watching the team of Matthew and Jerry on the couch. Matthew takes the role of Ollie—though he is a tall, lean boy, nothing like Oliver Hardy in real life. Jerry, on the other hand, does bear a certain slight resemblance to Stan Laurel. It's the long face and the melancholy expression.

Laurel and Hardy are trying to carry a piano up a flight of stairs. Matthew laughs, then bursts into a round of coughing. Jerry gets him a glass of water, and wraps a blanket around his shoulders.

"I'm okay, Dad," Matthew says, shrugging off the blanket.

"The whole glass," says Jerry. Outside the sky is gray over Mt. Ascutney. Sheets of water pour off the roof onto the deck.

On the movie screen, Stan and Ollie continue to struggle on the steps with the unwieldy piano box, Ollie cursing, Stanley shaking his head sheepishly. He looks close to tears.

The movie finishes. The loose end of film at the end of the reel makes a familiar sound, flicking against the side of the projector. Jerry turns it off. "You two feel like *The Thirty-Nine Steps*?" he asks. That would make our third movie today. Matthew says he thinks he'll head over to his mother's house. "Very good, sir. I'll bring the car around," Jerry says. British accent this time.

Matthew throws his parka on over his long underwear. Jerry sticks a wool cap on his son's head. "See you!" Matthew calls out to me. He takes the last three steps in a single whooping bound.

I stand at the window, watching the two of them climb into the front seat of the Blazer. Matthew hardly needs help buckling himself in, but Jerry leans over to do it for him.

I follow the backs of their two heads, disappearing down the driveway.

Five minutes after he's left with Matthew, Jerry's back alone. He has brought a bag of frozen summer squash up the steps from the freezer in the basement garage to steam for dinner. We'll have a little miso soup with it, and a salad. A glass of water. Some raisins.

"I don't like the sound of Matthew's cough," Jerry sighs, as he sets the squash in the steamer. "His mother's giving him white sugar. He's been drinking Coke at school."

I set up the tray tables in the living room as the squash cooks. We sit side by side on the couch, facing the television set, eating our squash in silence.

We clear the dishes. We watch *All in the Family*—an episode in which Edith Bunker announces her intention to get a job, and Archie hits the roof. When it's over, we turn off the set. Jerry steps out on the deck in the darkness, where the rain continues to fall. "This is supposed to keep up through Monday," he tells me. "I'm glad Vernon got that wood in."

I step onto the deck next to him. Somewhere in the night sky, Orion must glow above us, belt pointing to the Big Dipper, but there are no stars visible tonight. From where we stand, there's not another house in sight. We might be the last survivors of the human race for all the signs of civilization here.

"I didn't get a thing done today," Jerry sighs.

"I'll be very quiet tomorrow," I say. I bought myself a set of Rapidograph pens on our most recent trip to town. I have a new plan to begin drawing again. Although I'm supposed to be working on my book, I'm weary of it.

"I'm going to bed," he says. This means I will, too.

We step back into the house. Jerry turns off the lights and starts the dishwasher. I follow him into the bedroom. We stand together at the sink, brushing our teeth. I take off my contact lenses. I go into the bedroom and take off my jeans and underwear and put on my long flannel nightgown.

Jerry comes into the room. He undresses and puts on his night-shirt. He climbs into his side of the bed. I get into mine. I slide closer to him, so my head is pressed against his chest, and wrap my legs around his.

My hands move over his body. In the dark, I trace the furrows in his cheeks, the line of his sternum——hip bones, thigh bones, knees. I have them memorized.

His hands reach for my shoulders. He strokes my hair. He takes hold of my head then, with surprising firmness, and guides me under the covers.

Under the sheets, with their smell of laundry detergent, I close my eyes. Tears are streaming down my cheeks. Still, I don't stop. So long as I keep doing this, I know he will love me.

Chapter Eight

WE SET BACK the clocks and our life together darkens. And instead of great, broad vistas out his window, what I see is an ever-narrowing horizon. Brown leaves. Tomatoes killed by frost. The sun setting earlier each afternoon and the wind whipping against the house. The TV set glowing in the semidarkness, as the two of us fill up on too many sunflower seeds and reruns of *Dick Van Dyke* and *Andy Griffith* and *Candid Camera*.

In the morning we eat our frozen Bird's Eye peas on TV tray tables, do yoga and meditate, go off to our writing places. In the late afternoon we make our drive over the covered bridge into Windsor to pick up *The New York Times* and the *Valley News* and the mail, come home, read the papers, watch TV, make dinner. After dinner Jerry disappears into his study to write letters. I fix myself a bowl of popcorn and turn on the television. He reads Lao Tse or Vivekananda or Idries Shah.

Other nights we watch his old movies, though usually I fall asleep.

Except for the hours in the day when he retreats to his study, alone, to write or work on homeopathy, I stay very close to Jerry—sitting on his lap, resting my head on his shoulder when we watch movies, holding his hand when we walk down the street. But even in our affection there's a kind of mad, clutching desperation.

His irritation with me becomes more pronounced. I left wet laundry in the washer. My editor has raised the question: Would Jerry consider making some kind of statement about my book that could be used to promote it?—and though I should have known what he'd say, I mention her request to him. It isn't what he says that shames me. What he says is simply, "I think I'll pass." But the look on his face, when I ask him, is one of just barely concealed horror.

I put on one of my old miniskirts on a day when Peggy's over. "Don't you have something else you can wear?" he says.

"I like this skirt," I say.

"You look ridiculous," he says. I start to cry.

"Don't take it personally," he says. "It's a common failing of mankind."

We are on one of our walks up the hill, Jerry and I, with Joey panting alongside on his short dachshund legs. It's only midafternoon, but the sun is low this time of year. The leaves that had been red and golden along this path just a few weeks back are now brown and dry on the ground, swirling at our feet.

Walking with Jerry is a different thing from the walks I took so often with my father, growing up. Both men move briskly, although my father, who is just my height, could not match Jerry's long stride. And Jerry carries no walking stick, though he brings along a ball for Joey that he tosses now and then, just as my father would pick up sticks to throw for our dog, Nicky.

Whenever my father goes outdoors he is taking in the natural world, and with a painterly passion. For Jerry, the sights along the path go largely unobserved. The walk seems to be undertaken as a kind of meditative exercise whose purpose has more to do with the interior self. Although he has lived for twenty years in New Hampshire, I don't get the feeling that his being here has much to do with any particular affection for this part of the world.

Although there must be many beautiful spots here in Cornish, and certainly there are beyond (we are an hour's drive from the White Mountains), Jerry and I take this same walk every day. Because he owns the land we walk on, and NO TRESPASSING signs are posted around the property, we never run into anyone along the trail. I take his hand as we make our way up the hill. Sometimes I sing as we walk.

"I've roamed and rambled, and I followed my footsteps, to the sparkling sands of her diamond deserts. . . ." I sing.

"I will never forget seeing Pete Seeger for the first time when he came to perform at the University of New Hampshire and my parents took me to hear him," I say. "There was this moment when Pete Seeger asked everyone to join him for 'This Land Is Your Land.' For a few minutes it felt as though everybody in the room was *good*. We were all friends. I just looked around and loved everyone. It was such a relief, feeling that way."

"The song ended eventually, I imagine?" Jerry says, with a bitter edge in his voice that takes me by surprise. "There's the catch. You can only go on for so many verses before people start remembering how much everyone else actually irritates the hell out of them.

"You've got to watch that old joiner mentality," he says. "It's not always such a pretty picture, what happens when you put a bunch of enthusiasts in a room together, and they start clapping their hands in time to the music. Could be it reminds me too goddamn much of military school. Not to mention this man's army."

My birthday in November passes as just an ordinary day. Three days later Nixon is reelected. Neither of us votes.

I'm nineteen now. A thought enters my head. *What if I'm getting too old for him?*

Jerry writes for hours every day. In the years since he last published his work, he has completed at least two books, the manuscripts of which now sit in the safe.

I know, without asking, the nature of Jerry's view of publishers. "Give me two hours in the dentist chair before I'll spend another minute in a publisher's office," Jerry says. "All those insufferable literary types, thoroughly pleased with themselves, who haven't read a line of Tolstoy since college. All feverishly courting bestsellerdom.

"Not that the absence of any true original gift or insight keeps them from demanding all manner of pointless alterations to a writer's work, for the sole purpose of proving their own irreplaceable talents," he says. "They've got to offer up all these bright ideas. Unable to produce a single original line themselves, they're bound and determined to put their stamp squarely on *your* work. It happened to me plenty of times: Polite suggestions that I change this or that, put in more romance, take out more of that annoying ambiguity . . . slap some terribly clever illustration on the cover. . . ."

Jerry dealt with that one, he tells me, by insisting on the plain covers that have become the trademark of his books in paperback: the unmistakable maroon jacket, with yellow letters, for *Catcher in the Rye*. The yellow jacket for *Raise High the Roofbeam, Carpenters*. White for *Franny and Zooey*. Nine blocks of color for the *Nine Stories*.

"The minute you publish a book, you'd better understand, it's out of your hands. In come the reviewers, aiming to make a name for themselves by destroying your own. And they will. Make no mistake about it."

"It's a goddamn embarrassment, publishing," he tells me. "The poor boob who lets himself in for it might as well walk down Madison Avenue with his pants down."

Jerry doesn't show me his writing. One thing he does show me are his archives of the Glass family, who seem as real to him as the family into which he was born, and about whom he feels far greater affection. He has compiled stacks of notes and notebooks concerning the habits and backgrounds of the Glasses—music they like, places they go, episodes in their history. Even the parts of their lives that he may not write about, he needs to know. He fills in the facts as diligently as a parent, keeping up to date with the scrapbooks.

About his own family, he says nothing, except for the one time he tells me his sister, Doris, works at Bloomingdale's. Many years later, in something I come upon about him, I will read that his father, a wholesale egg dealer in New York City, died in 1971, not long before I met him. Jerry never mentions his father's death. Or anything else about his parents.

There is one other person we don't talk about: his ex-wife Claire, the mother of Matthew and Peggy, whom he married when she was nineteen. She must be in her late thirties now. She still lives in the red house less than a mile down the road, where the two of them once lived together, and Matthew and Peggy go back and forth between the two houses. Sometimes Claire drops Matthew off.

I never meet her or even see her.

On one of my trips to New York with Jerry, a photographer takes my picture for the jacket of the book I'm writing. The photograph will appear on the cover of my book, not the back jacket or the inside flap. As with my piece in the *Times* last spring, my words will come attached to an image of me, with bangs and a soulful expression.

The picture is meant to suggest a girl out in the country somewhere, but it's shot in Central Park. When I'm done, I walk over to Bloomingdale's to meet Jerry, and we pick up a package of smoked salmon to take back to New Hampshire. "Aren't we going to stop in and say hello to your sister?" I ask him, remembering that she works here as a buyer.

"A small dose of my relatives goes a long way," he says.

We will come back to Bloomingdale's on numerous occasions for smoked salmon. But we never ride the escalator to the floor where Doris Salinger works. I don't make the suggestion again.

I pay a visit to the editor in chief and the articles editor of *McCall's* magazine—two of the many editors who have contacted me since the publication of my first piece in the *Times. McCall's* is planning to run an excerpt of my book when it's published next spring. They want to know if I have any other ideas for the magazine.

I take out a notebook in which I've scribbled down ideas, a lot of which are the usual women's magazine basics. I'd like to interview Mary Tyler Moore (which I eventually do). I want to write about kids and drugs. The effects of violence on television.

Sitting in the beautiful office of the editor in chief of *McCall's*, I flip through the pages of my Ideas notebook, pitching my topics the way my mother has taught me. I pause at one, though I know very well there's no need to consult my notes. With affected casualness, I toss this suggestion out like an afterthought. "Did you know," I say, "that more and more young people on college campuses are dieting so much they don't even go to the dining halls anymore? Some of them are even making themselves throw up. I've known of several like that."

I mention the name for this dieting obsession: anorexia. (That the self-induced vomiting also has a name is something I don't learn for several years.) The editor says the whole thing sounds a little too way-out for *McCall's* readers. Who could relate?

Joe and Joan McElroy have invited Jerry and me to have dinner at their apartment on East Thirtieth Street that night.

I have known Joe longer than anybody else besides my family. I was three when he came to Durham for his first teaching job, at the University of New Hampshire, and shared office space with my father, who used to bring him home to dinner. He was a handsome young bachelor in those days; he'd bring his guitar and sing for us. My mother was always feeding him, and highly interested, as always, in reports on his social life.

Joe left Durham when I was nine or ten, with the woman he was married to then, Joan. It is with Joan whom I embarked on the plan, in the summer after my high school graduation, to write the book about making dollhouses, although by this point we both recognize that I am unlikely to finish my part of the book. The book is published, eventually, by Joan.

In the years since leaving New Hampshire, Joe has published a couple of highly acclaimed novels and become a teacher of writing at Queens College. He has a deep interest in contemporary fiction and a deep affection for Salinger's work. Riding the elevator up to Joe and Joan's apartment on the twelfth floor, I feel happy and proud to be introducing Jerry to my friends and to their daughter, Hanna, now five years old. Hanna is the first one to greet us, twirling in the hallway with a pair of fairy wings attached to her back. Jerry slaps his palm against his forehead in mock amazement. "Ah," he says. "Who would think there'd be fairies in New York City?"

As always, in social situations like this one, Jerry's behavior suggests that of a man far more comfortable than he really is. He shakes hands warmly with Joe and Joan, saying, "Joyce has told me so much about you."

Inside the book-filled apartment, Jerry asks Joe what he's been reading lately. Turgenev's *Sportsman's Sketches*, he says. "What about you?" "Kafka," Jerry says. Joe wrote his master's thesis on Kafka. "I'm reading the diaries," Jerry says.

"Kafka said he wrote best when he was feeling most miserable," Joe says, with a lighthearted air.

"I feel miserable just because I'm writing," Jerry answers, laughing.

As swiftly as possible, Jerry moves the conversation away from literary matters. His chief interest is Hanna, who is equally enthralled with him.

"I'd be so pleased if you could pay us a visit in New Hampshire," Jerry says, without condescension. "We can build snowmen and go sledding."

I am in the kitchen at this point. Although Joan is a good cook who makes fairly exotic dishes as a rule, she's acquainted with our dietary restrictions. She has procured from an organic butcher precisely the kind of ground lamb Jerry and I eat, and frozen it in patty form as specified. Now I am overseeing the 150-degree cooking.

When we finally sit down to eat, however, it turns out I have done something wrong with the meat. "You left the meat in the oven too long, Joyce," Jerry says. He leaves his patty untouched.

I spend a good portion of that fall writing my book, which is called *Looking Back: A Chronicle of Growing Up Old in the Sixties*. But although this would seem to be the very opportunity I've awaited for so long (and one so many young writers would long for), I approach the project with weariness, and something close to dread.

Every day I sit on Jerry's velvet couch with my yellow legal pad on my lap, counting and recounting the pages in much the same way that, as a babysitter caring for difficult children, I used to check the clock. I have made a list of topics I need to cover in my book: Junior high fashions. *Dr. Kildare.* Anxiety over the population explosion. High school proms. Early political zeal. Every time I finish another one, I check it off with relief.

I may not have a highly realistic view of my relationship with

Jerry and our prospects for a future together. But I recognize that the completion of the book and its publication next spring is bound to bring about a crisis between the two of us. Writing *Looking Back* represents everything Jerry has told me not to do and everything he hates: Early publication. Exploitation of my youth, my face, my name; pandering to the fickle tastes of what he calls "newsstandland," cashing in on the precocious facility with language my parents fostered from such an early age at the expense of true thoughtfulness. Delivering more of what the marketplace demands.

Knowing all this, the book I'm writing is just about what a person might expect such a book to be. Facile. Glib. Entertaining at times, and even true. But also fundamentally dishonest, in all it fails to say and all the things I leave out.

I write a 160-page book that fall, ostensibly about my life, in which I never once mention that I grew up with an alcoholic father. Or with a mother who never felt able to talk with me about my father's drinking.

I talk about Joan Baez and Jackie Kennedy, about hearing the Beatles on *The Ed Sullivan Show,* and experiencing the Cuban Missile Crisis, the assassination of JFK, the McCarthy campaign, the prevalence of pot smoking among my friends, the Women's Liberation Movement. I talk about college without mentioning that I've dropped out.

I am giving readers what I think they want to hear, the tidy version. I suppose that if I tell my real story—the one about growing up in an alcoholic family, wanting to be famous, being scared of sex—I will sound so weird and untypical nobody will read my book or (worse terror) *like me.* And so I try, instead, to make myself into a kind of Everywoman character—Everygirl, anyway, a typical American teenager, like a character on a TV show.

In *Looking Back* I talk about Twiggy and reading *Seventeen* magazine and wishing I looked like the models I still study in its pages at the supermarket. But I never tell the truth of what else I have done in my pursuit of looking like a model in *Seventeen*: that I spent one whole summer, after high school, living on a diet consisting of little besides a single apple and Baskin Robbins ice cream. I do not talk about how I get rid of the ice cream I eat by going into the bathroom and sticking my finger down my throat.

I cannot bear to reveal who I really am to a reader. More than that, I cannot reveal who I am to myself. I care more about pleasing my mother and father—to whom I dedicate my book—than I do about creating a truly honest or authentic piece of work about my growing up.

I deliver the manuscript for *Looking Back* to my publisher in the late fall. But my editor has asked me to write a final section, summing things up, to appear at the end. I write it on January 1, 1973:

It's the new year now. (I rang it in with popcorn and Guy Lombardo, sad to see that even the seemingly ageless Royal Canadians had compromised to sound contemporary, with-it.) I'm sitting by a window in New Hampshire—I have left Yale, Chaucer classes and dormitory bunk beds for the mountain—watching the evening grosbeaks crowded at the bird feeder. They are ugly-natured birds who scare away the chickadees, but nice to look at, fighting over sunflower seeds and suet, winging away at the least sound or movement from me in my chair. The wind is strong right now—just about sunset; the temperature reads eight degrees below zero. In here, though, I am warm. The fire is laid, although not burning (old *TV Guides*, this morning's *New York Times* and dripping, snowy logs), the dog wheezes in a back room (old and asthmatic, he hibernates in winter, dreaming of a badger-hunting spring) and a tangerine peel, filled up with seeds, sits on the table next to me. The television set is off—nothing but golf tournaments and football games this Sunday afternoon—so I have played Monopoly, putting hotels on every property I owned, and won. . . . I'm thinking about what I'll have for dinner, scribbling in the margins of my yellow legal pad, examining the split ends of my hair, watching the sky change colors, checking my watch, the *TV Guide*, the temperature again. The bird feeder is empty now.

I have just finished reading my manuscript. I've come here, to this chair, this window, with this yellow pad, to write the ending of this book. . . .

I read every page of the book out loud to Jerry over the course of the months I spend writing it, much in the way I used to read my work out loud to my father and mother. Certain sections Jerry typed for me. On the handwritten yellow legal pads, he made some comments in the margins.

"The plants and the animals are the telling omissions in my recollections of the decade," I write. "Too many passing fads, too little that is lasting."

After he completed reading over my manuscript that morning, Jerry had said to me, "Plants and animals are the telling omissions in your recollections. Too many passing fads here. Too little that is lasting."

This is why I mention several species of animals on the final pages of my book.

There are many more telling omissions in my teenage memoir than grosbeaks and chickadees. Among the most obvious questions left unaddressed in *Looking Back* is this: Why was a nineteen-year-old spending New Year's Eve at home watching Guy Lombardo and lamenting the fact that his band wasn't as good as it used to be?

The phrase "with-it," used to lament the downfall of Guy Lombardo's Royal Canadians (whose downfall I could hardly have lamented on my own, since I had never heard them before this year), was Jerry Salinger's contribution. Jerry danced to Guy Lombardo, in the forties, in Manhattan, before I was born. They called him "Sonny" then.

It's his bird feeders I talk about in my book, his asthmatic dog, his velvet chair, beside a fire laid by him, with logs cut on his land, high in the hills overlooking the Connecticut River, in Cornish, New Hampshire. The person with whom I was playing Monopoly that day was not Jerry but his thirteen-year-old son, who seemed to accept with astonishing grace the notion that a young woman had moved into his father's house who was just six years older than he was, and less than two years older than his sister.

As I'm sitting on the velvet chair, Jerry is sitting next to me. The dinner of summer squash I go on to talk about on the next page comes from his garden. He and I picked those squash together the summer before, shortly after I first moved to his house. We stood at his kitchen counter slicing them and putting them in freezer bags for the winter.

I can say none of this in my book. I do not say that January 1, 1973, is Jerry Salinger's fifty-fourth birthday.

Chapter Nine

I WANT TO believe that once I'm in love everything else will take care of itself. I see myself, in Cornish, baking bread and growing vegetables; sewing and drawing, and curling up on the couch at night with Jerry to read plays out loud to each other or watch movies. I will study homeopathy. Every morning and evening I'll meditate with Jerry, as he's teaching me. My body will become wonderfully lithe, not only from the daily yoga, but also the healthy diet he enforces of whole grains and vegetables, no sugar, very few dairy products. I see myself getting back to playing the guitar or maybe taking up a whole new instrument—the flute, or the violin. I believe absolutely that Jerry and I will have babies together.

"You can't even help it," Jerry says one day when I get off the phone, briefly excited at the prospect of being interviewed by a radio personality on the subject of the sixties. "These people have corrupted you. They've made you a worldly, greedy, hungry person."

I make myself sick. I hate myself for wanting worldly things, and still I want them. The wonderful un-self-consciousness and innocence of Phoebe Caulfield riding the carousel is something I no longer possess. I was never so young that I didn't hear that terrible, all-knowing voice in my head, narrating my life.

My only hope of redemption is to have a baby. To me, having a baby with Jerry would be a way of experiencing a childhood I never had but longed for. If I cannot be the child myself that he would have wanted, I will be her next of kin anyway. If I can't please him enough for who I am myself—and the indications are that I cannot—I will please him by providing him with this other person who will be perfect in all the ways I am not. I will get to watch him loving her. He will never leave me, because I am the child's mother.

I don't even say to him, "I want to have a baby." But one day I speak of "when we have a baby."

"What do you know?" he says. "We'll have a half-Jewish baby."

We talk about the baby more and more, and when we talk about the baby, it's always a girl. We don't talk about where we might live, what our days will look like, caring for a baby; we don't discuss how Matthew and Peggy might view any of this, or even where, in this small, crowded house, the baby might sleep and play, though surely these are all the kinds of questions that Jerry has had to deal with before with his wife Claire when Matthew and Peggy were born, and in the years before his divorce, when they were very small. I don't ask how we will avoid immunizing the baby, though I know Jerry will be adamant about that. Maybe she just won't go to school.

"I'll make her a dollhouse," I say. "We'll make dolls and furniture, and play food out of cornstarch and salt dough with food coloring." I tell him about the pies my mother used to make for my Barbies, using fluted pop-bottle caps.

"I'll tell you one of the worst things you can do to a child," Jerry says. "Falsely accuse him of something. It's one of the most sickening things, when some authority type nails a kid for one offense or the other, with nothing more substantial than a hunch." Of all the child-raising issues a person could think about, I register this as an odd one to have taken on such significance to Jerry. But I nod. "That would be terrible all right," I say.

"Another thing," he says. "No military school."

Of the many secrets that exist between us and the rest of the world, the fact that Jerry and I plan on having a child (more than one, eventually) is not one. My mother seems to endorse the plan, when I inform her. "I see all the little Salingers coming to visit," she writes to her friend Marion, "piling out of the car with their organic lunches of whole-wheat bread and sprouts...."

Peggy comes home only occasionally from boarding school, and when she does, she is mostly at her mother's house down the road or with her Dartmouth boyfriend. Sometimes they hang out together in Jerry's living room. They come over on Sunday afternoons to watch sports. They bring their basketballs. Peggy carries hers in a case. They do not abide by Jerry's dietary rules, that I can see. The boyfriend even drinks Coke.

I couldn't imagine lying on the couch at my parents' house this way, with my bare feet in the lap of a boyfriend, his hand resting on my thigh. Peggy's boyfriend's my age—a big, good-looking, not particularly talkative guy, who would almost certainly be more in awe at the prospect of meeting Bill Walton than J. D. Salinger. For Jerry's part, he doesn't appear to think much of the boyfriend—speaks of him as a "lug" and a "boob" when we're alone, expresses contempt that the boyfriend chooses cartoons on TV over wonderful old movies. But when Peggy and the boy are over at the house, Jerry is always polite and even solicitous, though I detect an edge the boy probably doesn't pick up in the way Jerry calls him "sport."

I've known my editor at Doubleday, Elsa van Bergen, for almost two years now, ever since, shortly after my graduation from Exeter, I sent her the proposal for the book about making dollhouses. We have shared a number of happy, friendly meetings since then. Even back in the days when I was hardly a hot property on the Doubleday list, she has always been kind, supportive, and encouraging. She knows I am living with Jerry Salinger now, and after the one time she asked whether he might consider offering a comment for the jacket of my book, she has not brought up his name with me again. She also knows not to call his house. We communicate exclusively through the mail.

In late fall of 1972, I write her a letter. I've recently delivered the nearly completed manuscript of my memoir. Now I tell Elsa that I have been thinking about the questions surrounding promotion of *Looking Back*. I have been reassessing some of my original notions.

Years later, at forty-four, reflecting on the letter I wrote to Elsa that fall, I can only shake my head at the sanctimonious tone I adopted.

I no longer feel it's appropriate or desirable to engage in the kind of publicity we have talked about in the past, I tell my editor. Particularly in light of my current circumstances, I feel that to do so would only open me up to all kinds of crass and undesirable exploitation. My book should stand on its own. I shouldn't have to parade around on the talk show circuit as some kind of Girl Celebrity, promoting it for the purpose of protecting a publisher's investment in me. Why should anybody have to see my face? My words are enough. Or should be.

"The merit of writing has nothing to do with fame," I tell her, with language heavily influenced by Jerry. "I have no interest in becoming a personality, and I am alarmed and concerned by the current trend that requires writers to engage in activities that have nothing whatsoever to do with writing, only with protecting the commercial investments of publishers."

I will not be available for talk show interviews, I say. I do not plan on exposing myself by going on a book tour.

Elsa writes back:

Dear Joyce,

Where to start? One thing you should give yourself an opportunity to find out is that wanting to promote one's own work does not necessarily make one less of a writer. Writers have long recognized the need to get people to want to read their work in order for that work to have meaning. You know, I know, writers who are on both extremes of "fame." Few are in the position of not having to do a single thing to share their personalities with the world....

The experiences of other writers aren't going to help you much. It is because of what you are that your writing is so important. We cannot try to ignore the fact that your age and place in time is an intrinsic part of LOOKING BACK; on one level, the book would not, for many people, have the same appeal, or even be what it is, if you were not nineteen, but you make a mistake to think of yourself as "Girl Celebrity." You belittle yourself, in terms of what you are now and what you are going to grow to be....

If this letter's predominant tone is of concern and dismay it is not...fear of what the lack of your help in promoting will do to sales and to your future. It would have an adverse effect. But the concern behind my lines here is honestly friend to friend. I cannot put my finger on it but something in the communication of your new feeling disturbs me. It doesn't seem to naturally evolve out of what has gone before....

As a wise friend said to you, you have to safeguard your talent, but that comes from many things...and not from a restriction imposed upon a book which by its very nature makes that restriction inappropriate....

What Elsa says in her letter makes sense to me, and for a moment, reading it, I feel a small surge of hopefulness. Maybe I don't have to close myself off from the world altogether after all. Perhaps my continued interest in things like bookstore appearances and interviews is not unforgivable after all. I bring the letter to Jerry.

He reads it only partway through, then folds it neatly and hands it back to me with a sigh. "Perhaps you're like the rest of them after all," he says.

Jerry and I establish a small tradition. Saturday nights, after we clear away the tray tables, we watch *The Lawrence Welk Show* together. We dance along with the show.

I look forward to this event all week. Sometimes I will take a shower and put on a dress and a little makeup before the show.

The program opens with Mr. Welk inserting a finger in his cheek and pulling it out in such a way as to suggest the popping of a champagne cork. It's a long way from Joan Baez and Joni Mitchell to Norma Zimmer, the Champagne Lady, singing "I Love Paris," or the duo of Guy and Ralna, in color-coordinated tux and evening gown, staring into each other's eyes and holding hands as they sing "True Love," with bubbles drifting around their laquered-looking heads.

Tonight the theme of the program is the music of Cole Porter. "It takes a guy like Welk to massacre Cole Porter," Jerry says, as the orchestra launches into their version of "I Get a Kick Out of You." The ballroom dancers, Bobby and Cissy, flash their white teeth at the camera as they spin across the floor.

Jerry and I know all the regulars now: Henry Cuesta, the clarinet virtuoso. Mr. Welk's daughter-in-law, Tanya, and the "pretty little Mexican girl," Ana Cani. Bob Ralston, the organ player. Myron Florin, the accordion player. I can recite the commercials, most of them for laxatives and antacid products.

The next number is "Begin the Beguine," played by Henry Cuesta. On the screen, the camera pans the crowd of couples— middle-aged and older—as they fill the dance floor, the women standing in line for turns with Mr. Welk.

Jerry is an expert ballroom dancer. As little as he's told me about his own teenage years, I know he attended dancing classes in his Upper West Side and (later) Park Avenue adolescence. There was a time when he was a young man about town in Manhattan, taking Eugene O'Neill's beautiful daughter, Oona, to places like the Stork Club, smoking cigarettes. "Begin the Beguine" is as much a part of his musical history as "Sergeant Pepper's Lonely Heart's Club Band" is for me.

Last year at this time, I stood against the wall at the Plaza hotel ballroom, watching my friend Marguey and eleven other girls introduced to New York society at the Junior League ball. "Someday, I will spin out onto a dance floor with a strong, romantic partner of my own," I told myself at the time.

Jerry is so tall, I only come up to just above his chest, but he's the kind of dancer who can make even an inexperienced partner like me feel graceful. He teaches me to fox-trot in the blue glow of the television set. With no sound in the room but the snoring of the dog and that almost synthetic clarinet, Jerry steers me around the room, past the television, over to the fireplace, the kitchen, back again. There's a smell of woodsmoke in the air. I feel the pressure of his hand on my back and his long fingers wrapped around mine. "I love you so much," I whisper. "You're the only one in the world for me."

"Funny thing, attachment," he says. "It makes a person do all kinds of nutty things, when he should know better."

"Thank you boys and girls," Mr. Welk says. "And thank you, Henry. That was just wunnerful. And now, for you folks at home, here's a word about a product that can help you get your day off to a dancing start, from our good friends at Ex Lax. . . .'"

I know from stories Jerry tells me of trips to Vienna and nights in Manhattan in the forties and fifties that there was a time in his life when he ate chocolate cake and hamburgers and steak and drank martinis.

He gives me a copy of a four-page article concerning the proper elements of a healthy diet.

In cooking, we must distinguish between vegetable and animal foods. The cooking heat does not have the same effect on the vegetables as on the animal foods. . . .

If in cooking the animal foods are heated so much that they reach the heat of boiling water, they lose their food value and become useless. Milk if boiled has lost its nourishing properties and a calf fed on boiled milk exclusively, that is if given no other nourishing food along with the boiled milk, dies usually in 15 days. Also many children have died when fed boiled or canned milk exclusively. . . .

A list headed "Forbidden" includes (among many other items) the following:

All well-done meats, well-done fish, well-done chicken, turkey, canned meats, meat soups, consommé. . . .

Hard-boiled eggs, custards, cakes, pancakes, scrambled eggs and all such foods that contain eggs. . . .

Boiled milk and all foods which contain milk and any other milk product. . . .

Refined industrial white sugar and all foods and drinks containing such sugar. Brown sugar and what is called raw sugar, maple sugar and maple syrup and molasses are also bad. . . .

All canned foods. . . .

All vegetable fats. . . .

Noodles, macaroni and spaghetti. . . .

Store mayonnaise and all foods prepared with baking powder, soda, saccharin or iodized salt. . . .

Dried fruits if sulphured. . . .

Some cereals, among them Cream of Wheat, Quaker Oats, Shredded Wheat, Wheaties, and all other cereals if steamed, roasted or dried up. . . .

Baked potatoes, baked yams, baked apples, because the mineral salts in them are overheated and cannot be assimilated so that they get settled down in the gall bladder, kidneys, joints and blood vessel walls and thus cause gall stones and kidney stones and contribute to the development of arthritis and hardening of the arteries. . . .

Tomatoes, whether raw or cooked, rhubarb and pineapple. . . .

Store-frozen vegetables and fruits. . . . Peas, string beans and asparagus are often treated with a beautifully green copper arsenite which is a violent poison. . . .

Chewing gum, toothpastes. . . . coffee, whiskey, punch and toasted bread. For cleaning teeth it is better to use brush and water alone, or brush and water and powdered wood charcoal. . . .

The list of foods we are allowed to eat is short. Nuts and raisins. Fruits, preferably indigenous to the area. Popcorn. Fresh vegetables. Lamb burgers. Strictly speaking, bread is not on the list, but we sometimes get a variety of unleavened bread from the health food store, made with whole-wheat flour and sunflower seeds. This comes to represent a treat. Similarly, dairy foods are off-limits, but now and then he'll buy a hunk of cheddar cheese. The one big exception to the diet is the smoked salmon Jerry brings back with him every time he makes a trip to New York—the very best Bloomingdale's has to offer. I've never eaten smoked salmon before. Now I long for it.

In fact, smoked salmon becomes so much of a preoccupation, Jerry gets the idea that maybe we can make it ourselves. Then we won't even have to make those trips to Bloomingdale's anymore.

We drive to the hardware store together. Jerry finds a small metal basket there, of a sort intended to be used by fishermen.

We stop at Purity Supreme—"Puberty Supreme," he calls it. We pick up a couple of pounds of fresh salmon fillets.

Home again, he takes out a ladder and, while I stand on the ground below watching, he climbs onto the roof with the salmon in the basket. Jerry is not particularly comfortable on ladders or rooftops, wearing his jumpsuit, clambering uneasily over the shingles as he makes his way to the chimney. He lowers the basket with the salmon down the chimney. He climbs down off the roof, cursing slightly when he almost loses his footing. "Imagine the headlines," I say. "Famous writer killed in attempt to drop salmon down chimney." Jerry laughs.

Back in the house, he builds a fire, using special wood he's bought, designed to give the fish a smoky hickory flavor. By now we're thinking big. "We'll try various woods," he says. "See which we like best." I am envisioning smoked salmon for breakfast every morning instead of sunflower seeds.

He sticks his head into the fireplace opening one more time to adjust the flue and make sure the basket with the salmon is in the right place. His face, when he emerges, is covered with soot and his hair, normally so neatly combed, goes in all directions. I put my head on his shoulder. He puts an arm around me.

Jerry lights the fire. Within seconds, the living room fills with so much smoke we're overcome with coughing. Tears come to our eyes. I fling open the french doors to the deck. With his fireplace tongs, Jerry tries to reposition the basket of salmon, but the smoke is only getting thicker.

He runs outside. He climbs back up the ladder onto the roof again. He makes his way to the chimney and yanks on the chain from which the basket is suspended A minute later, he has hauled up the piece of soot-blackened fish. "Come to think of it, the $15.99 a pound they charge at Bloomingdale's is a bargain," he says.

*　*　*

When I met Jerry, I had just begun eating in something close to a normal fashion—attending meals at the dining hall, no longer bingeing on my secret stash of granola in my dormitory room and following that episode with a day in which I would eat nothing at all. I had actually regained a few of the pounds I'd lost during the height of my anorexic period. I was still skinny, and conscious of every pound and calorie, but no longer skeletal.

Now, even with my new practice of self-induced vomiting, I have begun to gain weight. Never feeling satisfied at the end of a meal, craving something sweet or salty, I fill myself up with nuts and seeds, and still crave something more. Or simply something else. When there's cheese in the house, or when, for a treat, I bake a loaf of whole-wheat banana bread, the forbidden food beckons to me from the kitchen until I've eaten it all—sometimes in a single sitting. There's a censoriousness to Jerry's tone when he opens the refrigerator and observes, "I thought we had a half pound of cheddar cheese. I guess you ate it."

I begin sneaking food. On the rare occasions when I go out by myself in the car, I stop and buy a container of yogurt or a box of granola. In fact, this stop is probably the reason why I have gone out in the first place. I consume the whole thing in the supermarket parking lot, in secret, and then destroy the evidence in a Dumpster, and stop in at a gas station ladies' room to stick my finger down my throat. Sometimes when Jerry goes out and leaves me alone in the house—with no car but the BMW, which I'm not allowed to drive—I eat sunflower seeds and raisins until my stomach is bloated.

I draw. Years ago, with my father, I'd work on figure studies and contour drawings. We'd study hands and feet. "You're being *automatic* in the way you draw that earlobe," he'd say. "You aren't really *looking*." Now I try to do better.

My main drawing subject is Jerry. He lends himself to my kind of comical caricature, with his long, lean frame and his long, lined face, his faintly sorrowful eyes and bemused expression. I draw him in the garden, hoeing, and bent over his desk beside a pile of homeopathic texts, working on the search for a remedy for some ailment from which his children or I may be suffering. I draw us together in the bed. He's reading a book on Sufism. I'm reading "Dear Abby." He is looking over at me with less disapproval than disappointment.

In another picture, we're dancing. He's even taller in my picture than in real life. I stand on tiptoes, looking up at him adoringly. The dog lies on the rug by the fire, and on the TV set, the face of Lawrence Welk can be seen, holding up his ever-present baton. Out of Jerry's mouth, the words, "Who needs the Rainbow Room?"

There's a therapist Jerry travels to New York to see every two weeks, a practitioner of Wilhelm Reich's theories of orgonomy. Jerry never goes into it much with me, except to say that this therapy involves working with a person's muscles, and using one's voice in a certain way that releases deep energy. This is not the kind of therapist with whom you talk about your childhood, or the kind with whom you might discuss the fact that the young woman you are living with is unable to have intercourse.

That problem remains unchanged and increasingly, unaddressed, even though the baby plan has continued to the point where a name has been selected for our future child. It's an odd name—not a name at all.

"I dreamed you and I had a baby," he tells me one morning. "I saw her face clearly. Her name was *Bint*."

He looks the word up in the dictionary. "What do you know?" Jerry says. "It's archaic British, for little girl." From this point on, we refer to our future child by the name from Jerry's dream.

Generally, when Jerry goes to see the orgonomist he makes the whole trip in a single day—five hours down, two hours of therapy, one hour to buy smoked salmon and bagels at the Bloomingdale's gourmet shop, five hours back. I have accompanied Jerry on a few of these trips, but increasingly, he says there's no point. "You won't have enough time to do anything," he says. I remain in the house, watching vast amounts of television, eating popcorn, making myself throw up, and working on my book.

But one time in the fall he takes me with him. We check into the Plaza.

The next morning Jerry goes to see his orgonomist. I have an appointment to see my editor. Jerry and I have arranged to meet for lunch at the Algonquin Hotel, where we are to be joined by William Shawn and Lillian Ross—old friends of Jerry's from his days at *The New Yorker* in the fifties. Jerry has explained to me that Ross and Shawn have been lovers for years, although Shawn continues to maintain a household with his wife. "Everybody at *The New Yorker* knows," Jerry tells me. "But it's not a topic anyone discusses with them."

In 1972, William Shawn is still editor of the magazine, though it has been months since Jerry referred to the plan he had raised to me earlier, that the two of us might come live in New York one day, maybe get an apartment on the Upper West Side, and he would go to *The New Yorker* offices during the day to write.

Jerry tells me Lillian Ross and William Shawn—and his friends S. J. Perelman, William Maxwell and Peter DeVries, and Janet and Donald Malcolm—are lone holdouts of what he sees as the fine old *New Yorker* tradition begun with Harold Ross.

William Shawn is a small person—all the more so next to Jerry—and he seems extremely old. Lillian Ross is a trim, tastefully dressed woman around my mother's age, probably.

Shawn and Jerry shake hands when they greet. Jerry kisses Lillian Ross on the cheek. We take our seats in a booth.

Jerry introduces me, reminding them of my *Times* article. "Joyce has just finished a book," he says. "A memoir."

"Oh, really," says Lillian Ross. "I wouldn't have known a person could do that at your stage."

They order drinks. I ask for water.

William Shawn—"Shawn," as Jerry speaks of him—is a man of exquisite courtliness, correctness, precision, and formality; polite, restrained, and dignified. Lillian Ross is wearing an understated suit; so is the man I will address as "Mr. Shawn." I am wearing a navy blue jumper and a bright purple turtleneck with matching tights.

"I have a collection of your early profiles from *The New Yorker*," I tell her. "My mother gave it to me when I was a little girl."

"How very gratifying," she says. "I suppose it must have been terribly exciting for you to have work published in the *Times*?" she says. "Oh," I say, "I've been writing for magazines for years." I tell her about *Seventeen* magazine—the articles about Julie Nixon Eisenhower and Miss Teenage America. When she asks about writers I admire, I mention Jane Austen and Carl Reiner. I ask her about interesting people she's interviewed lately. She shoots Shawn a look across the table. "Nobody who would interest you," she says. "Nobody nearly as interesting as Julie Eisenhower or Miss Teenage America."

Throughout our lunch, William Shawn sits quietly in the booth across from me, nodding. A less mannerly person might have shot Lillian Ross a knowing look back. If he conveys something to her, it is no more than the faint raising of an eyebrow or a nearly imperceptible twitch. I register no look of disdain on his face as I do on hers.

We say good-bye to William Shawn and Lillian Ross. Jerry hails a cab. In the cab, he says nothing about our lunch. He takes me straight from the Algonquin to Saks.

"I want to buy you a coat," he says. But he doesn't steer me to the kind of coat girls at Yale are wearing this fall.

I try on several he's picked out for me. One has a shawl collar of real fur. One looks exactly like a coat I will see in a photograph that appears in *Time* magazine a short while later, worn by Pat Nixon.

The coat he chooses for me is black cashmere, a kind of coat I could imagine Lillian Ross might wear. It costs $425, even in 1972.

Exquisitely tailored but slightly too big for me, it is appropriate for members of a ladies' auxiliary in Darien, Connecticut but ill-suited to life in Cornish, and even more ill-suited to me.

I wear the coat every day after that, whether it's cold or not.

Chapter Ten

MY PARENTS COME to visit. I'm not so young that I don't recognize that at age fifty my mother might find Jerry Salinger an enormously appealing and attractive partner for herself. She is a woman who crackles with artistic, intellectual, creative, and sexual frustration. For twenty years she has lived a substantial part of her life through the accomplishments and experiences of her daughters, never more so than she does right now. She is oddly accepting of my apparent choice, at eighteen, to leave behind everything I ever said I cared about for life on the mountaintop with Jerry. She chooses her words carefully, and has chosen the word "enchanted" to describe her feeling about him.

Although our family lives just sixty miles south of Cornish, my parents almost never make a drive this long or far. Our annual trip to Ogunquit Beach, in Maine, involved a journey of some thirty miles each way, but produced so much anxiety about traffic, highways, and dangerous drivers on the roads that my father would get us up even earlier than usual so we could "beat the traffic."

I want desperately for the three adults I love best in the world to like and respect one another. I want Jerry to see how funny and smart my parents are. I want my mother to like Jerry's house, although I can't imagine showing my parents the bedroom where I sleep with Jerry.

My father emerges from the car like an astronaut from a space capsule after an exceedingly trying orbit. He and my mother set out over two hours earlier, as I knew they would, to beat the traffic heading to Cornish. They arrive a few minutes before noon. My father is wearing corduroy pants and a Viyella shirt, with an ascot and a fedora hat. My mother wears a red suit and high heels, and a matching felt hat with a feather.

For the first time I see my parents through Jerry's eyes. They look faintly pathetic—my father in his shabby oxfords, my mother overdressed in her too-tight suit. Jerry, in blue jeans and an L. L. Bean sweater, betrays no sign of condescension. He greets my parents with the grace and courtliness of the leader of a major world power. He kisses my mother and shakes my father's hand.

"You must be very proud of Joyce," he says warmly. "You could just sit back and rest on your laurels for the rest of your lives after producing a daughter like this one."

"Joyce was always a brilliant girl," my father says.

"Rona, too," says my mother. "In fact, Rona talked at nine months. We thought Joyce was a little slow, by comparison. . . . I made a tape of Rona singing in French when she was just eighteen months old. I suppose Joyce has told you that a story of Rona's was mentioned in *Best American Short Stories* of 1964."

We show them into the house. My father studies a landscape hanging on Jerry's living room wall that I know he will regard as second rate, or worse. I pray he won't say anything. He doesn't.

"I don't suppose the Fuller Brush man bothers you too often, up here," my mother comments.

"If visitors were all like you, Fredelle, I might have a different attitude toward the whole thing," Jerry says.

"You should have seen Jerry's garden before the frost hit, Mummy," I say.

We sit at tray tables Jerry has set in the living room, looking out to the deck. He has made a salad, and there is smoked salmon, and cheese, and good bread, and—this makes me nervous—wine.

"Ah, nothing hits the spot like a good piece of cheese," says my father, who has been unusually quiet.

*   *   *

Jerry asks my mother about her writing. She discusses the book she published recently, *Guiding Your Child to a Creative Life*, filled with stories about techniques she employed with my sister and me.

"Aha. So if a mother buys this book and follows the instructions, she can end up with someone like Joyce?" Jerry asks.

My mother laughs. "Ah, Jerry," she says, "it's not difficult to see why my daughter adores you."

At the moment she's writing about male midlife crises and keeping children off drugs. A far cry from Shakespeare and the British Restoration comedy that she studied at Radcliffe, she says. My father has poured himself a second glass of wine.

"What are you up to these days, Max?" Jerry asks. "Now that you've retired?"

My father says he has just recently been talking with an old friend who lives in Ottawa. "This chap's in charge of all Canada's Board of Weights and Measures," he says. "We've known each other since we were young. Just last week, Harry flew from Ottawa to Paris to weigh the gold brick that is used as the standard throughout the provinces."

"Fascinating," says Jerry.

"Oh, I've got quite a distinguished circle of associates, let me assure you," my father tells him. "My great-nephew, Derek, holds the position of Dominion Archivist for British Columbia. I have met a great many people, going up the escalator."

In a letter she writes to her friend Marion soon after this visit, my mother describes the conversation over lunch this way:

> *Jerry's presence drives Max into what I can only describe as a panic of desperate vanity. Jerry listened patiently but with some mystification, evidently thinking Max's reference was to a real escalator. Joyce was clearly mortified, and I felt simply terrible sorrow. That Max, so much a person in his own right, should offer such credentials! When Joyce realized the escalator was metaphorical, she said, playfully but with edge, "Now tell us who you have met going down on the slide," and Jerry said "Fresh!"*

"Daddy," I say. "Tell Jerry about your arthritis. If he can just locate your similimum, he could help you."

"Sorry excuse for a set of knuckles, these," my father says, showing Jerry his hands, which are sufficiently twisted that he's having difficulty holding a paintbrush. His doctor has recently prescribed gold injections, he says, with a certain pleasure. "But I suspect I'm a hopeless case. Disheartening business, growing old, isn't it, Bub?"

"Is there any chance you might be traveling to London at any point, Max?" Jerry asks him. He knows of a terrific acupuncturist there who could be of great help. "If I'm not mistaken, he's worked on the queen," Jerry says.

"The queen, eh?" says my father. He has a fondness for aristocracy. "As a matter of fact, I had just been thinking I needed to take a look at the Turners at the Tate."

"Let me give this some thought, Max," Jerry says. "I may come up with a remedy for you to try myself." My father says that would be splendid.

"So, Jerry. I suppose Joyce has been showing her book to you as she writes," my mother says. "Tell us what you think."

"It's better than it has any right to be," he says.

As always, on the rare occasions when visitors come, Jerry offers to show a movie.

"Not possible, old chap," says my father. "Got to head back to avoid the traffic in Concord, and the night driving."

Jerry displays no sign of amusement or shock over my parents' visit. After they leave, we say surprisingly little about my father and mother. In her letter to her friend about the visit, my mother quotes me as having said to her, afterward, of my father, "Sometimes I wonder what I used to see in him."

Reading that, years later, I feel shame at how I betrayed my father. I pray that he did not register my abandonment of him that day.

Some months back, I had suggested a story to my editor at *The New York Times Magazine*. I had heard about a twelve-year-old violin prodigy, Lilit Gampel, living in Los Angeles. I suggested that I write a profile of her, and the *Times* gave me the assignment.

In early summer I had flown to Los Angeles and met with Lilit and her parents and her young brother, Alan, age eight, a pianist. It didn't occur to me at the time, but the choice of Lilit Gampel, out of the whole world of potential subjects, was an interesting and significant one. It would be hard to find a family more singlemindedly focused on the accomplishments and success of the children than the one in which my sister and I were raised, but the Gampels were such a family. Except for school and her required afternoon nap, and times when her mother instructed her to "go outside and run around the yard," Lilit spent virtually all her time practicing the violin. She and Alan got up as early as six to begin playing.

Once, she tells me, when her violin was being repaired, she spent two days without her instrument. "I was so bored," she says. Then she speaks words that could have been lifted out of my own diary from the year I was twelve. "When I went to bed I had this awful feeling I hadn't done anything all day."

Although I had spent time with the Gampel family in the summer, I want to watch Lilit perform. Just before Thanksgiving, she's scheduled to give a concert with cellist Pierre Fournier and the Phoenix Symphony. I arrange to fly there to see her. Oddly enough, Jerry decides to accompany me on the trip. He seems fascinated by Lilit.

Often, when we go places out in the world, Jerry uses the name "John Boletus"—"boletus" being a Latin word for "mushroom." For meeting Lilit and Alan Gampel and their parents, however, he is Jerry Salinger, my friend and traveling companion. If the Gampels are surprised by this, nobody says anything about it. They are far more focused on their daughter's success and fame.

Lilit has a small, pinched face and wears little-girlish jumpers and knee socks that make her look younger than her age. Her room is lined with great books and art reproductions. For movies, she says, she favors filmed versions of great operas or Chaplin. She's unfamiliar with the Beatles' music.

Lilit never watches television, except for the occasional educational program. But the extraordinary drive to be the best, and the best at the youngest age, and to please her parents, and to perform flawlessly, is a story I know. Although she is thin, she worries about her weight, and agonizes over whether or not she should eat a chocolate bar. She doesn't have many friends. She feels twelve-year-olds wouldn't understand her. Her main companion is her younger brother, a boy who loves telling corny jokes and reading the almanac.

Jerry and I attend Lilit's concert and visit with her and her family briefly backstage, after the performance. Back at the hotel, he shakes his head ruefully about what the Gampels are doing to Lilit. "It's a terrible thing to see a child trained to perform like that," he says.

Lilit could be one of the Glass children, appearing on the radio quiz program "It's a Wise Child."

The next night we fly home to New Hampshire, where he will take off for Thanksgiving weekend at Matthew's school with Matthew and Peggy and their mother, Claire. I travel to Durham, where my parents and I have Thanksgiving dinner at the home of a family friend, Helen. Helen's daughter, Judith, has evidently become involved with an eminent Russian poet many years older than she is, her teacher at the Ivy League university where she's a freshman. Helen is worried about this.

"A dashing man with a Russian accent and a pipe, reciting poetry?" my mother says. "Who's to say you and I wouldn't have fallen head over heels ourselves?"

For all the talk that has passed between us about my mind and—though he says less about this than he used to—my writing, Jerry says nothing, ever, about me as a physical person. Sometimes, when we are at work on the search for my similimum, he'll consider some physical trait of mine—the dark circles under my eyes, my dark skin, the odd indentation on the top of my head—for its possible significance homeopathically. Otherwise, no words are spoken about either of our physical bodies.

He never uses four-letter words. He virtually never mentions sex. I can think of only one time he ever referred to sexual body parts.

He is talking about a woman he doesn't like, a shopkeeper in the town of Windsor whom he regards as a nosy busybody. A physically unattractive woman. Downright ugly. This woman has, Jerry says, "a mouth like a cunt."

He makes the remark in the most offhand way, only I can't stop thinking about it. Is my mouth like that word I cannot say? And if my mouth is like my vagina—my *cunt*—what kind of a mouth would that be? A closed mouth. Clenched teeth. A mouth wired shut like the mouths of those obese women I have read about, for whom there is no other way to keep from eating.

My mouth has been put on a permanent diet of nuts, seeds, frozen peas, cucumber slices, and barely cooked, unseasoned lamb burgers. Food is a bad thing. Eating is something we do as little of as possible.

Mouth like a cunt. I want to ask him, "What does that mean? What kind of mouth is that?"

But I keep my mouth shut. Either way you look at it.

Chapter Eleven

Dear Rona,

However much I love Jerry's company, I often long for a friend around here, and I have none. My New Haven friends belong to a whole other world now, and even if I could see them regularly, I wouldn't have much to talk to them about. When I do see them, in fact (as I saw Jean and her boyfriend over Thanksgiving), it seems to jeopardize my life in Cornish. Talk of classes, gossip about old Exeter friends, discussion of the play Jean's directing—they seemed all to distance me from Jerry, so that I came back home (to Cornish, I mean) speaking differently, in my old, Mummy-ish, anecdotal, fakey way. It is a great worry.

I remember how I used to say, looking at M and D's virtually friendless situation in Durham, that I would NEVER isolate myself like that, or depend on my children to fill my life. And here I am now, five miles from the nearest town, with not a single friend or even acquaintance any closer than Durham.

J hates and is depressed by Christmas. We've just got back from New York—J had business to do in the city, and I had to clear out the last of my stuff from the New Haven apartment. Normally I love to shop and carry shopping bags and even listen to Salvation Army bands. This time, seeing it all through J's eyes, I wanted only to leave as soon as possible.... I will buy us a tree and decorate it, but cele-

brating all by yourself, with the other person smiling weakly
and trying to look chipper, isn't much fun. So I will flee to
Durham for Xmas itself and leave J. to eat his 150-degree
Christmas dinner by himself....

I don't put up a Christmas tree at Jerry's house, or play my Christmas carol records, or bake cookies. I shop for presents for my family, and I spend more money than I have ever spent on a single gift to buy Jerry a sea captain's wooden lap desk. It's made of fine cherry wood with inlaid veneer, and a green felt top that lifts up so you can store your pens and notebook inside. I picture Jerry sitting in his leather chair by the window overlooking the mountains, writing at this little desk. Now he won't have to be off in his study all the time, away from me.

His present to me is a leatherette briefcase of a design I eventually learn is meant for lawyers to carry cumbersome legal briefs. Although I feel a little deflated when Jerry presents me with my suitcase, I throw my arms around his neck. "I love it," I tell him. About the captain's desk, he pats my head and comments, "Thank you. This will come in handy next time I head out to sea." He never uses it.

A day or two before Christmas, Jerry drives me to Concord, where my sister's husband, Paul, picks me up to drive me the rest of the way to my parents' house. At our meeting spot, an odd thing happens. I collapse on the floor, blacking out entirely. The managers of the store evidently get the impression I must be on drugs, and hustle us out the door as soon as I'm able to stand up. But I'm not on drugs. I just haven't eaten in a while.

Christmas in our family is a highly ritualized experience. We always play the Joan Baez album of carols and the *Messiah*. My mother bakes four or five kinds of cookies: meringues, shortbread, Swedish kanella, miniature tarts. My father has kippered herring Christmas morning. He always gets very melancholy that day, and by the end of the day, he's drunk.

This is the first year my nephew—Rona and Paul's son, Benjamin, not quite one year old—will be with us. This part should make us all very happy. But the tension in our household this Christmas goes beyond what my sister and I remember of other years.

At Christmas dinner, my brother-in-law's first with our family, my father mentions the new Milton scholar recently hired by the University of New Hampshire. "A splendid chap," says my father, pouring another glass of wine.

"What on earth do you mean, Max?" my mother says, putting down her fork. "The man's a charlatan. He holds some kind of degree from a college in, I don't know, Florida or someplace like that. The day I met him at the Byrons' cocktail party, I said something about a fellow having 'catholic tastes' and he actually thought that meant the man was Catholic."

My father defends his colleague. Though for all the years he was on the faculty he was a withering critic of "second raters" at the university, since his retirement he has adopted an odd brand of loyalty and partisanship. "Come, come, Fredelle," he says. "The new Miltonist's a fine fellow."

"Fine fellow!" my mother explodes. "He's mediocrity itself!" She, of course, would have loved to have been hired by the university to teach Milton, or virtually any aspect of English literature. Only, as our whole family knows, they never gave her a job.

My sister and I look at each other across the table anxiously. My brother-in-law and his year-old son look equally baffled. My mother gets up from her chair. She disappears into the kitchen. We hear a pot lid clanging.

"Your mother's being ridiculous," Daddy says. He pours himself another glass of wine. "Splendid fellow, the Miltonist."

Now I am holding my father's arm. "Apologize to her, Daddy," I say. "Please."

"What should I apologize for?" he says. He lurches up from the table. Wine spills everywhere. Benjy laughs.

Rona has taken Paul away from the table now. I'm sitting alone with the baby. My father is climbing the stairs to the attic, his gait unsteady.

Several hours later, my mother brings out the Christmas pudding that she made months ago so the fruit has had time to age in the brandy. She sets the pudding on fire. We marvel as flames leap around the platter. My father has not returned.

It is the last time my family will ever be together at Christmas.

The day after Christmas Jerry drives to Durham to pick me up. This time he barely stops to say hello to my family, except to play for a minute with Benjy. I have never felt happier to be back with Jerry and heading to the place I now think of as my home.

"God, how I missed you," I say as I climb into the car. I wait until we have pulled away from the house to kiss him.

"You sound like your mother when you talk," he says sharply. "Something happens to you every time you see her. You get this false, theatrical tone to your voice. You don't even seem like yourself anymore."

I would say something in response, but I'm afraid if I do, I'll sound like my mother.

It's not just my mother's speaking voice that is the problem, either. In the last couple of months there have been intimations that Jerry holds my mother in less regard than I had once supposed. Now he tells me what he really thinks of her writing, including her book, *Raisins and Almonds*, about which he wrote to me, and to her, words of such praise back in the summer. Back then, he'd written in his letter to my mother that he would treasure his copy of her book always.

"What she writes is shallow and inauthentic," he says now. "She worships at the temple of fashion, convention, and gossip. Good writing has got to be unblinkingly honest. Your mother's is fraudulent. She cares more about making a sentence sound good than she does about writing sentences that speak the truth."

Mummy knows everything, I wrote at twelve. *She's so wonderful. I'm so proud of her. What would I ever do without her?*

Now the one person I have ever met who is strong enough to challenge my mother's place in my life is saying terrible things about her.

When he speaks of her dishonesty—the falseness of her voice, and the danger that mine has a tendency to ring similarly false—I know what he means. I think about all those articles she wrote for the famous psychologist. I think about "My Problem and How I Solved It." The made-up quotations. The words of advice my mother published in magazines—on child rearing, and marriage, and dealing with family problems, and of everything that remained unaddressed in our own family as she was writing those articles. I think about my grandmother: the rage and frustration I know my mother feels about her own mother for the way she tries to appropriate her life. And the tender, worshipful way she wrote about her in *Raisins and Almonds*. So far from the whole story.

"She's a silly, vain woman," Jerry tells me. "What's lousy is: You could so easily grow to be just like her."

"Daddy has sunk into the worst depression I've ever seen him in," my mother calls to tell me.

All those years my father had been waiting for this time, when he could once again paint full-time. Now that he's retired and that day is here, he's frantic. He goes to the English department office nearly every day for no particular reason. Some days he says his paintings are worthless. Other days he believes them to be brilliant, which only makes his complete lack of recognition as a painter all the more unbearable. His arthritis has gotten much worse. Always, by day, a fastidious man who cared a great deal about his dress and appearance, I hear from my mother that he is now going out into the world unshaven and unkempt. He's drinking in the daytime now, not just at night anymore. He's begun to experience blackouts.

My mother tells me that a student by the name of Laura Ferris, who took a couple of classes from my father in the year or two before his retirement, has become infatuated with him. We all knew Laura was sending my father notes, leaving odd little gifts of candles and incense at his office. Sometimes she cut reproductions of angels out of art books and mailed them to him. It was strange behavior, but not completely without precedent. My father was always the kind of teacher who inspired strong feeling in students. Even at the age of seventy, drinking, and somewhat disheveled as he has been recently, he is still an exceedingly handsome man, with a powerful and commanding presence in the classroom and outside of it.

So when my mother originally regaled me with the story of Laura Ferris's crush on my father, it seemed like nothing new. Over lunch with Jerry, she had made a comical reference to a letter Laura had written my father earlier that fall, telling him he was the most brilliant and wise man she'd ever met. A true sage. A poet. My father did not laugh.

Now my mother calls in tears to tell me she has found a letter on the dining room table. It's a letter written by my father to Laura, in which he says he cannot be parted from her any longer and promises to leave my mother soon. The two of them will go away together to England, he writes. His marriage is a misery, a sham.

I am stunned, hearing this. As incomplete as I knew my parents' marriage was, I have never contemplated the possibility that they wouldn't be together always, drinking their tea, discussing English department politics, listening to me read my work out loud to them in our living room.

My mother confronts my father. He is horrified and remorseful. He swears to her that he didn't mean what he wrote. Laura means nothing to him. He couldn't live without my mother.

My mother has borne enormous disappointments in her marriage, but she cannot accept this betrayal. She tells him to leave.

A week after the discovery of Laura's letter, my father has moved out of our house on Madbury Road and into a rooming house in Durham. His health continues to decline. "I have lost everything dearest to my heart," he says. "Thou hast it now: King, Cawdor, Glamis, all. . . .

"I am a ruined man."

My mother writes:

The story of Laura is pretty dreadful. And her attraction to Daddy is textbook classic. Her father was an alcoholic (and her mother a lesbian). She ran away from home at 16, had a complete breakdown and landed in a hospital. When she got out of the hospital, she married a man 20 years older, a religious sage. She now claims he threatened to kill her. She came here the summer she left him, entered Daddy's class and, she says, fell in love at once. She is religious and superstitious. She believes in many forms of life after death, reads the Bible literally, thinks the Holy Grail is a real cup Our Boy drank from. At Christmas she prepares for a real coming. She meditates and hears angelic voices. She doesn't eat meat or use lipstick or smoke or drink. Daddy describes her as intelligent in strange flashes, completely naive, "strange," dowdy ("she could be good looking, but has no idea how to dress and I wouldn't know how to tell her"). He says she does nothing well ("unlike us, she has no gift..."); her cooking is frightful, her knitting lumpy.

O, she is also something called an anthroposophist. I asked what that was and D. said, laughing, he didn't know, had never been able to understand. But she adores him— and she needs him. Daddy says, "It would be easy to underrate Laura. Everything I say sounds disparaging. But she is good and decent and eager to learn—and she is really sweet. I feel like her father, or her grandfather."

He said, "You are so formidable, I have always felt a need to struggle with you. With Laura, when she talks rubbish, I just pat her on the head."

My mother drives to Cornish. I have never seen her looking so unhinged.

Jerry puts an arm over her shoulder and leads her to the sofa. "This had to be a rotten shock, Fredelle," he says, setting a glass of water beside her.

The story pours out. She is rageful and weeping. All the things she never said out loud about my father, she is saying now: about his sexual rejection of her years ago, his arrogance and selfishness, his drunkenness.

"I'm tired of looking after him," she says. "All those years of checking my watch wherever I am, afternoons, to make sure I'm back in time for six o'clock dinner, knowing six-fifteen may be too late. Phoning from other cities evenings to see if he's drunk, and knowing I can do nothing whatsoever if he is. Wondering if he left a burner on, if Nicky would bark if he smelled flames. Has Max been making terrible phone calls to members of the English department? Coming home to a mess of phonograph records and empty vodka bottles and burnt meals in the sink."

"It was getting unbearable," she says. "He is not a man to go gentle into that good night. He rages at the prospect of old age, infirmity, death. He despairs over the waste of his talent and what he has come to see as the emptiness of his life. Just a few weeks ago he said to me, 'You don't need me anymore. The girls don't need me. Nobody needs me.' "

Bending forward to hear better, Jerry listens quietly in his leather chair. He talks as if he were a country doctor—calm, steady, kind, and wise.

"Perhaps this will eventually reveal itself to be a good thing for you, Fredelle," he says. "Your life with Max has not been easy. You're a strong, resilient woman. Haven't you ever wished for something different and better than the life you've been leading in Durham? You have ambitions of your own, surely?"

In fact, Jerry has spoken scathingly to me of my mother's huge ambitions, her infatuation with the accolades of the magazine and publishing world. But now he speaks to her with enormous gentleness. Perhaps this crisis, jarring as it must be for her, will make possible good new changes in her own life? She agrees that for years she hesitated to travel as she might have liked, out of fear that my father couldn't manage on his own without her. If he leaves, she can venture out into the world herself.

"You must take care of yourself, Fredelle," he says. "I'm going to fix you a remedy that might help you to steady your mind. And tell me, do you suppose you could give up coffee for a few days? I've been thinking about it, and I believe that would help you a great deal."

She writes to Marion about her visit that day. "Jerry gave me a potent dose of something which really did pull me together, working not as I imagine a tranquilizer would—blanking one out—but making it possible for me to be in touch with my own center, summon my strength."

* * *

The phone, always so silent, rings regularly in Cornish over the days that follow. For thirty years, my parents have been playing out the painful, very nearly tragic drama of their courtship, love affair, and quietly disastrous marriage. Now that this is over, my mother calls several times a day now, wanting to talk to Jerry. I watch him—his body bent over the phone, his long fingers pressing the receiver close to his good ear, patiently taking in that day's details.

My father calls, in tears, wanting to talk to me. "If she would only take me back," he weeps. "I had forgotten how desperately I love her."

My mother calls, wanting to know what my father said. Things have been set in motion. There is no turning back. "Will all great Neptune's ocean wash this blood/Clean from my hand? No, this my hand will rather/The multitudinous seas in carnadine,/Making the green one red."

My father's arthritis is unbearable, and he can't sleep. He has no money. "She is turning me out into the cold," he says. "I am old and weak. I am in every sense a pauper. My sole hope is that she will take me back."

"He can either go to Laura, the madwoman, or stay in some little rental room in Durham, drinking harder and more desperately than ever, having added a new intolerable guilt to his already overwhelming pack," she says. "He might as well be in Sibera."

"I understand the pain of Job," my father tells me. My mother tells Jerry she is experiencing double vision now. My sister finds the whole thing too awful to talk about.

When the phone finally stops ringing, I throw myself on the bed with my own tears of grief.

To hear Jerry speaking to my parents on the phone you would never know that his own life with their daughter is rapidly unraveling. I cry a lot now, for my parents, and for Jerry and me. I don't forget: He is the man who used to wrap my shoulders with a blanket at the least indication of chill in the house, who knelt to tie my sneakers, and brushed my hair while I sat on a bed at the Plaza Hotel. Now he is increasingly silent and grim. Except for these conversations with my mother, he spends most of the time in his study, writing and meditating. At six-thirty, when I wake up he is already out of bed and at his desk.

Months earlier, before I severed the last of my ties with Yale, I'd raised with Jerry my fear that we could break each other's hearts.

"How could a girl who can make me as happy as you ever bring me unhappiness?" Jerry answered.

"I haven't figured out how we'll manage this life of ours," he said to me back in the fall. "but you and I are such clever people, we're sure to come up with some way of being together."

It is still true, I love him more than I've ever loved anybody. I believe without question that he loves me back.

In the middle of my parents' disaster, my sister announces that she's separating from her husband. She and their one-year-old son, Benjamin, move back to my mother's house. Shortly after her arrival there, I invite my sister to spend a weekend with Jerry and me.

For many reasons, I look forward to Jerry's meeting Rona. Even in the middle of her own marital trouble, she seems like the one member of my family in possession of some semblance of calm and stability. I know that unlike my mother, Rona is not likely to burden Jerry with her problems.

My sister is the one who loved *Catcher in the Rye* and reread it many times throughout her adolescence. Where, all through our growing up, I was viewed as the family lightweight, my sister has maintained a serious, deeply contemplative nature from the age of three. I want Jerry to witness her honesty. It has always been said in our family that Rona never says or writes anything that isn't true.

There's another reason I look forward to my sister's visit, even though we often fought when we were growing up and, except for the recent, surprising spate of letters, have not been particularly close in the years since she left home: I need someone to talk to.

We drive to Durham—fast, over snowy roads—to pick Rona up. At my mother's house, Jerry moves immediately toward Benjy. He gets down low, so he's on Benjy's level, and speaks to him in a quiet, slow voice. I would love Benjy to come with us to Cornish.

But I know Rona longs for a break. Our mother has agreed to take care of Benjy and let Rona have a night on her own with us, up north.

In the car on the way back to Jerry's house, he makes a comment that takes my sister by surprise. "I suppose you always looked up to Joyce, as younger sisters do," he says.

This is odd. Rona is not only four years older, but married, with a baby. And I have just recently turned nineteen. I have even told Jerry the story of my sister's sense of displacement at my birth.

"Joyce is four years younger than I am, actually," she tells him quietly. "I'm twenty-three."

"Oh well," Jerry says, taking the BMW into fifth gear. "You're both little girls to me."

Back in Cornish we entertain Rona in the usual fashion: a dinner of salad, peas, and lamb burgers, followed by popcorn and a double feature of *Foreign Correspondent* and *Knight Without Armor*.

As usual I fall asleep before the end of *Knight Without Armor*. Jerry takes off my shoes and helps me to bed, and gives Rona a towel and a glass of filtered water as he points her to Peggy's vacant bedroom.

My sister tells me later she was depressed by the darkness and dreariness of Jerry's house, the absence of any object that would seem to have been put there for any reason besides utilitarian function. A lover of good food, even as a nearly penniless young mother, she is also disheartened by the way Jerry and I have chosen to eat.

"I guess one thing about the menu up here is one seldom feels an impulse to overindulge," she says quietly, as I clear away our dishes from breakfast the next morning. Jerry is already off in his study at work.

My sister and I take a walk up the hill alone together, keeping our respective sorrows well hidden. We talk about what's going on between our parents, but she tells me very little about the reasons for her own separation. I don't confide my worries about my relationship with Jerry.

Jerry and I drive Rona home again. Jerry tells my mother, with an appearance of regret, that he and I can't stay for dinner as she had hoped. "My son's expecting me back," he says, though Matthew's not staying with us this weekend.

Before we leave, my mother fills us in on the most recent news involving my father and Laura: They are moving to England, where Laura will teach at a Waldorf school and learn to play the cello. They want to have a child by artificial insemination.

Returning alone with Jerry to Cornish, I talk about Benjamin and my own longing to have a baby. "I'd want to have one of those front packs that lets you carry the baby everywhere you go," I say. "I know you have to put them down sometimes, but I would just want to hold her all the time."

"That could get difficult, when she reaches eleven or twelve," he says. "Not to mention at the dentist."

For all his charm and solicitousness while my sister was around, Jerry's mood is now the darkest I have seen it. Though he's been sharp with me over the months, I've never been an object of his wrath, only a witness to the chill force of his disdain. Now, in the frigid gloom of January, with snow piled high on the deck outside the French doors, and only a few chickadees left picking at the bird feeder, it is no longer inconceivable to me that I could become one of the people Jerry speaks of with bitterness and contempt.

My book has undergone its final editing now and is heading toward the galley stage. My original editor, Elsa van Bergen, leaves Doubleday. I tell my new editor, as I told my agent, Emmy, to use Jerry's phone number only in the case of an emergency. Almost every day now I receive a letter from one of them, discussing some aspect of the book's promotion. Sale of the paperback rights. Foreign translations. Radio interviews. I tell my editor I'll have to pass on those.

"Nobody sells books anymore purely on the strength of what she writes," Emmy tells me. "You have to go out and sell yourself, too. Why do you think they put your photograph on the book jacket? And on the cover of the *Times*? People are going to want to see you."

Jerry and I argue daily about this. "A writer's face should never be known," he says.

"If you hadn't seen my face, would you have written to me?" I ask him. He doesn't answer.

One day that January the phone rings. When Jerry answers it, his voice turns icy. "Yes. No. No. No. I have nothing more to say to you. Don't call me again. Good-bye."

He hangs up. "That was a reporter from *Time* magazine," he says. "Asking about you. He said he heard from some friends of yours that you were living here with me."

"No," I say. "Who? I hardly have any friends anymore."

"All these years I've done everything I could to maintain my privacy," he says to me. "Now *Time* has my phone number."

We were in the bedroom when the call came. He paces the floor. He looks out at the mountain, his back to me.

"I'm sorry," I weep. "Forgive me. I'll do better."

He seems barely to hear me. He has sunk onto the edge of the bed, staring at the floor, talking to himself more than to me.

"How could you have done this? How did I let this happen? What have I brought on myself?"

I climb onto the bed behind him. I put my arms around him. I pat his shoulders, his hair, the face that I love. I trace my fingers over his cheeks, wrap my fingers around his long fingers. He still won't look at me.

"Maybe it's hopeless," he says. "This book of yours could be the end of us."

"No," I say, crying now. "I can't let that happen. I can't live without you."

We still find moments of sweetness and tenderness. In the car together, driving over the covered bridge, we sing old songs from the forties. Watching movies, I put my head on his shoulder and sleep. I whisper to him the name of the child he has said we'll have.

"One book I do not plan to follow, raising her," he says grimly, "is *Guiding Your Child to a Creative Life* by Fredelle Maynard, Ph.D."

In some ways, as the months have passed, I've found myself less restless, more accustomed to the slow, quiet pace of our time together. The memory of college life has receded, and the taste for things I used to love is growing fainter. It's been months since I listened to rock and roll music, though I know the words now to "Begin the Beguine," "Sentimental Journey," and "The White Cliffs of Dover." I don't buy makeup anymore. I don't shop for clothes. When I receive an unexpected check for selling a reprint of my *New York Times* article, I use the money to buy a 16 mm print of the Hitchcock movie *Rebecca*. It costs $325.

Once in a while Jerry takes me to a movie in Hanover at the Nugget Theater, where the Dartmouth students go. I wear my cashmere coat; he wears his old leather bomber jacket. We sit together with me on the side of his good ear.

Filing out of the darkened theater after the movie, I watch the Dartmouth students, just my age or a year or two older, heading out for beers or back to their dormitory rooms and off-campus apartments. This time last year, I was in New Haven. Not happy, I remind myself.

One night, when we come home from the movies, I throw myself on the bed and cry. I can't imagine anywhere on earth I could go and be content anymore. As lonely as it is on top of the mountain with Jerry, enough time has passed since I moved here that I can no longer imagine making my home anywhere else.

It is when I catch glimpses of another life that I often end up feeling most restless and fighting with Jerry. "I might like a bowl of ice cream after the movie," I say. He notices me stopping to read a poster advertising open tryouts for a local production of *The Misanthrope*.

"You love the marvelous, exciting things the world has to offer," he says, more weary than bitter, though there is definitely bitterness in his voice. "I'm holding you back. You're not ready for this."

*   *   *

Every afternoon we still make the trip over the covered bridge into Windsor to pick up Jerry's *New York Times* and the mail, which may include galleys of my article about Lilit Gampel, or a piece of business having to do with my book. Once a week, we go to White River Junction, to the health food store.

At the end of the day, if it's not too cold or snowy, we take our walk up the hill with Joey. We cook our lamb burgers and squash, set out our meals on our tray tables to watch the news. The first POW's return from Vietnam. Evel Knievel jumps on his motorcycle over fifty-two cars. American Indian activists occupy the Pine Ridge Sioux reservation in Wounded Knee, South Dakota. The federal prosecutor orders further investigation into the Watergate break-in.

Chapter Twelve

~

IN MARCH, PEGGY and Matthew are on a week's vacation from school, and the four of us travel to Daytona Beach, Florida. Jerry has chosen Daytona Beach in part, at least, on the recommendation of Dr. Lacey, who knows of a homeopathic physician there who favors the high potencies he and Jerry believe in.

Jerry says this Florida doctor can address my sexual problem. I don't question his choice to combine this mission with a family vacation.

It has been a particularly brutal winter in New Hampshire, one storm after another, day after day where the temperature fails to rise above zero. I have longed for the warmth of Florida. But Daytona is a depressing place.

Our hotel sits right on the ocean, and Matthew is happy, as always, because there's a game room in the hotel, and a vibrating bed, and a shoe-shine kit in the bathroom. Peggy is disgruntled. She misses her boyfriend. As Jerry has already explained to me, she and I are sharing a room, while next door to us, Matthew and Jerry are bunking in together. This seems odd to me, knowing that the children have observed the two of us sharing a bedroom since July.

"Let's take a dip," he says. We head to the beach.

Even before we've spread our towels on the sand, we learn a disturbing thing about Daytona. Cars are allowed to drive up and down the beach—fast and loud. Matthew says something, but the sound is drowned out by V-8 engines speeding past, drag racing.

Still, we spend the afternoon on the beach. Jerry warns Peggy to protect herself from the sun, but she's anxious to get a tan. Matthew jumps in the waves. Jerry is trying to read his homeopathic journal. "Come on in the water, Dad," Matthew calls to him. Jerry looks reluctant, but he gets up to join Matthew. I open my book of the *Teachings of Ramana Maharshi,* turning to a random page.

That night we eat in the hotel dining room. The kids order spaghetti and garlic bread. Jerry and I get a salad, no dressing.

Other patrons of the hotel, surveying our table, would suppose what they are seeing is a single father vacationing with his three children. But my behavior is very different from that of his children. I am careful and anxious.

Our waiter brings Jerry's salad with dressing. The people at the next table have a toddler who is very unhappy, and the wife is complaining because the husband plans to take off and play golf for the afternoon. Peggy mentions a game she's missing because we came here. Worried that all the aggravating details of being away from home will get on Jerry's nerves, I keep quiet.

Not Matthew. He stabs his fork into his meatball and holds it aloft, like an Olympic athlete, holding up his medal. "Ta-da!" he says. "Mark Spitz!"

"Quit it, okay, Matt?" Peggy says.

"Guess what, Dad?" Matthew says. "In the lobby, they had all these brochures of neat places you can go see. There's this amusement park, with a really great-looking roller coaster."

"I need to get a new bathing suit," Peggy says. "The one I brought makes me look fat."

The next morning, Jerry and I have arranged to see the naturopathic practitioner Dr. Lacey has recommended. Jerry has made the appointment under the name of John Boletus and his friend Joyce. We take a cab to her office, leaving Matthew and Peggy back at the hotel. Jerry has given Matthew change for the game room. Peggy has a bad sunburn and wants to sleep.

Over the phone from New Hampshire, Jerry had told this doctor only that he is a student of homeopathy, interested in consulting with her on a number of matters. She ushers the two of us into her office.

He tells the doctor he lives in New Hampshire and is engaged in various varieties of research. He has an abiding interest in Eastern medicine—acupuncture, acupressure. In the last ten years, the primary focus of his study has been homeopathic medicine. He himself favors the high-potency approach employed by Dr. Lacey, among others. He understands that this tends to be the approach she favors as well.

Sitting here saying nothing, I wait for Jerry to begin describing the particular reason why we are here. But now he and the woman physician are talking about differing schools of thought concerning potencies. The issue of succussing a remedy in water versus taking it in pellet form, under the tongue. He is mentioning the names of particular remedies he has been working with lately. Their names sound like potions from a fairy tale: *Sanguinaria. Aconitum napellus. Drosera rotundifolia. Gelsemium. Passiflora incarnata.* . . . Bloodroot. Monkshood. Sundew. Yellow jasmine. Passion flower.

Lately Jerry has been studying the uses of pulsatilla in the treatment of headache, he tells the doctor. She takes a homeopathic journal off the shelf. "I wonder if you're familiar with this article on the subject," she says. "I myself was tremendously excited when I read the findings here."

"I would have favored a potency of 200x," Jerry says. "Having experimented with a similar form of treatment myself on several occasions . . ."

I look out the window. Palm trees. Cement. I think about swimming. I am roused by the sound of my name.

"My friend here, Joyce, is anxious to consult you about a problem she's experiencing that I have been trying to assist her with," Jerry is saying. For the first time, the doctor turns to me. She studies the single sheet of paper, attached to a clipboard, that I filled out when I arrived. *Female. Nineteen years old. 110 pounds. Five foot six inches. Experiencing difficulty having intercourse. Frequent headaches. Amenorrhea.*

"So," she says. "You suffer from a tightness of the muscles surrounding the vagina? How long has this situation existed?"

"Eight months," I say.

"And the remedies you've considered . . . ?" She turns to Jerry. He lists several.

"Has she experienced acupuncture before?" she asks Jerry.

"Only acupressure," Jerry says. "I've worked with her pressure points, but strictly for the headaches."

"I want to perform a physical examination," she says. Jerry leaves the room as she instructs me to remove my underpants and shows me where to put my feet up on her table.

Her physical examination of me is very brief. No sign of physiological abnormality, she says, as I'm putting my underpants back on.

"You're very tense," the physician says. "I'd like to try a little acupuncture on you." Then she instructs me to take my dress off and lie on her table in my underwear.

She washes her hands, and takes out a little tray of needles. She places one on my abdomen and begins to spin it in place, until it breaks through the skin. There is no pain.

Then she places a group of needles around my nose, and another on my abdomen, and one near each of my ears. I concentrate on the buzzing sound of the fluorescent light and close my eyes.

In my most hopeful moments of anticipation of this doctor visit, I pictured this doctor presenting me with a tiny crumb of some magical remedy I would place under my tongue that would open me like a flower. Jerry and I would return to our hotel, return to New Hampshire, suddenly, gloriously able to make love. By the time we leave her office, I no longer hold out any hope of having been cured. I feel exactly the same as I did before, only horribly humiliated.

Grim-faced, Jerry pays the bill. We hurry out the door. In the cab I cry a little. I have never undergone a pelvic exam before. Jerry puts his arm around me. We say nothing about the experience.

When we get back to the hotel, we meet Matthew out by the pool and then go to the room, where Peggy is just getting up. We put on our bathing suits and take our towels and books down to the beach. Peggy has to lie under a beach umbrella. Matthew sprints toward the water, calling for his dad. Jerry has bought him a kite and he wants Jerry to fly it.

Jerry and I sit on our folding beach chairs alone together for a moment. He stares out at the water, the children, the hungover college students on spring break, the cars racing up and down across the sand. He looks very old. His shoulders are hunched. He rests his forehead in his hand.

"You know," he says, "I can never have any more children. I'm finished with all this."

One of those crazy Daytona Beach drivers has just driven by, making so much noise with his souped-up engine that for a moment I am not sure I heard it right, what Jerry just said to me.

"What did you say?" I ask him.

I see Matthew splashing in the waves, his new orange kite lying on the white sand. Jerry's bag of bananas and sunflower seeds. The homeopathic journal and the Ramana Maharshi book. The towels, with their hotel insignia. The music from somebody's portable radio—Neil Young singing "Heart of Gold." The sun at high noon. Sand flies on my legs. The smell of suntan lotion.

I see Jerry's face, as familiar to me as my own, and dearer than anything. His long lean body, in old-fashioned swim trunks. His hands raking through his silver hair. My hands reaching for my beach towel and my book and my room key. The sound of my own voice, as if what I were hearing were dialogue from a movie and not my own self speaking.

"I can never have any more children," he says again, staring out at the ocean. "I'm finished with this."

Then he turns to me and speaks, with a coldness I have never known before from him, though we have certainly fought. Here is the chill wind I have always feared.

"You'd better go home now," he says. "You need to clear your things out of my house. If you go now you can have everything gone before the children and I get back. I don't want them upset, having to witness all this."

*   *   *

I get up from the sand. I must be breathing, but it feels as though the air has left my lungs. My vision blurs. I walk back to the hotel.

Back in the room, I peel off my bathing suit and put on my dress. I take my clothes out of the drawers and begin packing. I take my ticket off the bureau where Jerry has left it and dial the number of the airline. "When is the next flight to Boston?" I ask. There's a blizzard going on up north. No planes are expected to fly into Boston until the next day at the earliest. New York is no better.

Sometime late that afternoon Jerry and the children return to our two adjoining rooms. Jerry has taken Matthew and Peggy shopping. If the children have noticed anything strange about my sudden disappearance, they don't mention it.

"When you've seen one Stradivarius, you've seen them all," Jerry says to Matthew in his Inspector Clouseau accent, putting an arm around his son's shoulder.

"Take your filthy hands off my asp!" Matthew says, also in character.

"I got a flight back tomorrow," I tell Jerry.

"Joyce's father is sick," Jerry tells Matthew and Peggy. Matthew looks momentarily concerned. "But he'll be okay, right?" he says. I say *sure*.

The four of us go out to dinner. I don't eat. Afterward we go to see *The Heartbreak Kid*, an Elaine May comedy featuring Cybill Shepherd and Charles Grodin as a couple who meet during Grodin's disastrous honeymoon in Florida. I watch the movie more intently than any I've seen all year.

All this time I have been hoping for the moment when Jerry will take me away alone to talk, and we will reenter the familiar space we occupy, when it's just the two of us *landsmen*. I wait for him to signal me, but he doesn't.

We prepare for bed—I in my room with Peggy, he in his, with Matthew. He says good night, barely looking at me. I say good night back to him.

Lying there in the darkness while she sleeps, all I want is to be able to cry freely. But I know I mustn't wake Peggy. So I go into the bathroom.

The sound of my crying wakes Jerry. He stands in the doorway in his pajamas. "You've got to be more quiet," he whispers. I let my knees give way. He catches me. He sighs deeply.

He sits down on the closed toilet seat. I sit on his lap. His pajama top is wet with my tears.

"I don't think I can live without you anymore," I say. "Don't send me away."

"You know the story, Joyce," he says. "We've been through all this before. Let's not make it harder."

We sit there a long time, saying nothing. Finally, sometime before dawn, I make my way back to bed, although I don't fall asleep. In the morning, before Matthew and Peggy get up, Jerry goes down to the lobby with me. Because he has always paid for everything, I haven't even brought money on this trip. Now he stuffs a couple of fifty-dollar bills in my hand. We walk out in front of the hotel, where a row of taxis is lined up. "This girl needs to go to the airport," he says, easing me into the backseat as one would a very frail elderly person. I am looking into his eyes, still hoping he's about to hit his palm against his forehead in that way he has and say "Christ! What was I thinking of?" and pull me out of the taxi.

"Don't forget to turn the heat down and lock the door after you, once you leave the house," he says. "I'll give you a call." He pats my shoulder and kisses my cheek.

I watch out the window as the taxi pulls away. He looks at his watch and runs his hand through his hair. He turns and walks back into the hotel.

I have no memory of the trip back from Florida.

My friend Jean, to whom I'd given my apartment, tells me that I showed up in New Haven that same day, or the next. She remembers the sight of me on the steps of some dormitory.

I tell her she must be wrong. I have no memory of getting myself to New Haven. Maybe it was later—the next month.

"No," she tells me. "You had a tan. You told me Jerry was

still in Florida with his children. You said something about cars on the beach. You weren't making a lot of sense."

I make my way to Hanover. From there I take a taxi over the same stretch of highway Jerry drove with me that first day he picked me up. It's a half-hour ride to Jerry's house.

A lot of snow has fallen since we left, just two days earlier, and Vernon Barrett has not been by yet with his plow. I am barelegged and wearing sneakers as I make my way up the hill, up the steps, and let myself in the door. The house is so cold I see my breath.

I clean my things out of the closet. I set my records and typewriter by the door, along with the sewing machine I bought, still in its box. I have surprisingly few possessions or clothes. I take with me a couple of books Jerry has wanted me to read— the meditations of Lao Tse, an old novel he picked up for me in a used bookstore called *The Dolly Dialogues*, and a mystery written by Josephine Tey. An introduction to homeopathy. The Xeroxed copy of his dietary regime. I wish I had a photograph of Jerry and me, but for all the months we spent together, there are no pictures of the two of us.

I'm packed and ready to go within an hour. I call my mother. Just hearing her voice, I begin to cry so hard she can't understand what I'm saying, except the one part that's clear. *Come get me.*

"I'll come right away," she says.

She arrives a few hours later, leaving her car at the foot of Jerry's unplowed driveway. Standing in the cold living room, I see her trudging up the last snowy stretch of road on foot, in a white rabbit fur hat and red suede boots. When she gets to the door, I fall into her arms, though I also know, as we stand there, that I will no longer find the kind of comfort in her arms I once would have.

The two of us make just a couple of trips in the nearly knee-deep snow to haul my possessions down the driveway. I can't bear to look at the pain on my mother's face.

After *everything* is loaded in the trunk, I go back in the

alone just one more time before leaving for good, to make sure the heat is turned down again and to turn out the lights. On the window of Jerry's bedroom, where the glass is dusty, I write, with my finger, the name of the child we had talked about: BINT.

Chapter Thirteen

IT'S OVER THAT quickly.

One day Jerry Salinger is the only man in my universe. I look to him to tell me what to write, what to think, what to wear, to read, to eat. He tells me who I am, who I should be. The next day he's gone.

He had described to me the path toward enlightenment. It had required a kind of discipline and self-denial I did not possess, an ability to let go of ego, and lay down desire for worldly pleasures. I had always stumbled on that path. But I have never questioned the belief that his path is the right one. Not having Jerry to lead me, I feel left behind and lost, not simply alone physically, but spiritually stranded. I've been well acquainted with the sensation of loneliness all my life. Never like this.

One of the movies Jerry and I watched a few times was *Lost Horizon*—the original 1937 version. *Lost Horizon* is a romantic story about a planeload of travelers whose airplane crashes somewhere in the mountains of Tibet, with snow all around, and no civilization within a thousand miles.

Just when they've virtually given up hope of survival, the travelers are rescued by a tiny band of guides who lead them to a warm, sunny, and magical place called Shangri-la, where they are treated with great kindness. They are given robes to wear and foods to eat unlike anything they've tasted before. Two of them— the leader of the group, played by Ronald Colman, and his younger brother—fall in love with a couple of beautiful young women living here, played by Jane Wyatt and an actress named Margo.

Except for the character played by Margo, the inhabitants of Shangri-la are very contented. They possess the secret to immortality. As long as the new immigrants stay in this kingdom, they will never grow old or sick.

But as wonderful as life is in the new land, the brother of the Ronald Colman character becomes restless. He hungers for the city, and the excitement of the world that lies beyond. When he tells Ronald Colman that he and his lover, Margo, are leaving, Ronald Colman is distraught. He wants to stay with Jane Wyatt, but he can't let his brother make the treacherous journey through the mountains alone.

Finally, after much inner struggle, Ronald Colman agrees to accompany his brother and Margo across the mountains, out of Shangri-la, though he knows his decision is irrevocable. As they make their way through the snow, away from paradise, a terrible thing happens. As Ronald Colman and his brother watch in horror, the beautiful face of Margo shrivels up before their eyes. She becomes a hideous old woman.

The day I unpack my belongings in my old bedroom, I feel similarly exiled. Twenty-four hours after saying good-bye to Jerry and getting on the plane in Daytona Beach, I can think of nothing but how I will get back to him.

I call Jerry at his hotel in Daytona Beach. With no vestige of pride remaining I beg him to give me another chance.

"Matthew and Peggy are here," he says flatly. "This is not a good time to talk."

I call him again the next day, and a few days later once he's returned to Cornish. "Take me back," I weep. "I have no home but with you. I don't need anything except to stay with you."

His voice is cold. "This isn't going to work, Joyce," he says. "It's finished."

Over the course of the months we spent together I had heard him on the phone speaking with distant friends who thought they were better friends of his than they actually were. I sat with Jerry when he got calls like that, and I know about the heavy sigh he makes after he puts down the receiver from such a call. "Thank God that's done. I wish they wouldn't call," he'd tell me. "If I never heard from them again, I'd never miss them."

The tone he used to speak with those people is the one he now uses with me. I would prefer it if he'd hit me. Instead, he's calm and reasonable and detached.

On the other end of the phone I'm too upset to speak. This makes him firm, stern even. It's the voice he might use speaking to an inept hotel clerk, or to his dog if he'd been caught relieving himself on one of the oriental rugs.

"You need to pull yourself together, Joyce," he says. "I have to go now. Matthew's calling me."

It is April 1973, two weeks from the publication date of my book. I'm staying in my old room at my mother's house.

My throat is sore from making myself throw up. I write Jerry daily. *Whatever it was I did, I'm sorry. Whatever it is you want me to change, I will.*

Every night, during the two or three weeks I stay at my mother's house, I go downtown to call Jerry from a pay phone. I don't want my mother and sister to hear. After a few days of this he becomes impatient, irritated, and then simply weary of me.

"Why don't you just get on with your life?" he sighs. "Go out and flog that book of yours. Get all that glorious publicity you always wanted so much."

One night when I'm crying too hard to speak, he hangs up on me. I lean against the glass walls of the phone booth, looking at my own image in the silver base of the pay phone. Then I put another dime in and dial him back. This time he doesn't pick up.

Sometime during the first weeks after I've returned to my former home a package arrives containing the first copies of my autobiography. The cover shows me sitting on a rock in Central Park.

"I'm basically an optimist," I have written in my book. "Somehow . . . I feel everything will work out—just like on TV."

Advance reviews of *Looking Back* are encouraging, my editor tells me. Orders of the book are strong. The book is being serialized in the *New York Post*. The *Today Show* has booked me to be interviewed by Barbara Walters and Edwin Newman. The editor of *Newsweek* wants me to write a piece for the magazine about youth in America, and invites me to travel to address a conference of its most important corporate advertisers, to be held in Florida. "Arnold Palmer will be there to provide golf instruction," they tell me. "And Yvonne Goolagong, for tennis."

None of this holds any appeal for me. With Jerry no longer around to say the things he always said, I adopt his attitudes as my own. I tell my editor I don't want to speak at the American Booksellers' Association convention. The only person whose opinion of me matters now is the one who is no longer watching.

I fly to New York for my *Today Show* interview, my face looking puffy from making myself throw up. True to Jerry's predictions, *Vogue* magazine has commissioned Richard Avedon to take a full-page photograph of me to run as one of a group selected to represent "The American Woman Today."

The Avedon portrait conveys a sense of defeat and weariness strikingly different from my picture in the *Times*, taken a year earlier. I had a hopefulness and lightness at eighteen. The nineteen-year-old who looks out from the pages of *Vogue* conveys nothing so much as an air of bleakness and profound sorrow.

My father's in England now with Laura. My sister and Benjy are living with my mother, who has filed for divorce and, for the first time in her life, entered into therapy.

The few people my age whom I consider to be friends are at college. My family's old house now feels unbearably sad.

In my first article in *The New York Times* I had written, "I feel a sudden desire to buy land—not a lot, not as a business investment, but just a small plot of earth so that whatever they do to the country I'll have a place where I can go—a kind of fallout shelter, I guess. As some people prepare for their old age, so I prepare for my twenties. A little house, a comfortable chair, peace and quiet—retirement sounds tempting."

Back when I wrote those words, I had not read the passage in

Catcher in the Rye in which Holden Caulfield talks about leaving the world.

> ...I'd build me a little cabin somewhere with the dough
> I made and live there for the rest of my life. I'd build it
> right near the woods, but not right in them, because I'd
> want it to be sunny as hell all the time. I'd cook all my
> own food, and later on, if I wanted to get married or
> something, I'd meet this beautiful girl that was also a deaf
> mute and we'd get married. She'd come and live in my
> cabin with me, and if she wanted to say anything to me,
> she'd have to write it on a goddamn piece of paper, like
> everybody else.

I have twenty thousand dollars in the bank from the sale of my book. I decide to use it to get myself a cabin in the woods.

I buy a new car for three thousand dollars' cash. I don't even know what state my cabin will be in, so I try a few: Upstate New York. Vermont. Massachusetts. Connecticut. Maine. I buy real estate guides and maps and keep driving. I stay in motels where I watch TV at night, eat yogurt, and call Jerry.

"Today the realtor took me to a stone house in the woods where I could keep bees," I tell him. "There was a pump in the kitchen for water."

"Sounds great," Jerry says.

"You won't believe this," I tell him. "Some little old man had built a bunch of tree houses, with bridges connecting them. There's a pond with a rowboat."

"Terrific."

Every morning, I pick up the newspaper in whatever little town I'm in and check the real estate listings. Over the next three weeks I put more than a thousand miles on my new car.

One day I find myself back in New Hampshire, stopping at a real estate office in a very small town called Hillsboro, just sixty miles west of where I grew up, and about fifty miles from where Jerry lives.

Many real estate agents don't take me seriously when I say I want to look at houses, but this one seems unfazed to have a nineteen-year-old walk into his office, telling him she wants to buy a house in the country. He knows the perfect place.

We drive five miles out of town, down a dirt road that dead-ends at a farmhouse. More than two hundred years old, the place has been occupied only in summer for years; it isn't insulated, and there's no central heat. But the house sits on fifty acres with no other houses in sight. There's a waterfall down the road that you can hear when you stand out on the back porch. The property has blackberries and wild roses growing on the stone wall, and five or six acres of cleared fields, perfect for a vegetable garden. The house, an antique cape, comes furnished with old mismatched upholstered chairs and rag rugs and standing lamps, and single beds with mended spreads, and two rocking chairs and a big old trestle table on the porch. There are three fireplaces, and a Dutch oven for baking bread. There's a crib upstairs in the sleeping loft, and a pantry full of pots and pans and dishes, and a fully outfitted old picnic basket with tin plates and silverware.

I don't spend any time asking about the roof or the septic system. But I take my time inspecting the picnic basket.

"I want to buy this house," I tell the realtor. The asking price is $65,000—high for 1973, but I offer full price. We go back to his office and fill out an application for financing. I write a check for a thousand dollars on the spot, binding my offer. It's accepted that night. Two weeks later—Memorial Day—I sign papers and move in. It is the beginning of black-fly season.

I have no job and my book money's gone. I have never built a fire by myself or shoveled snow or operated a sump pump. I don't know how much wood is in a cord or how to start a lawn mower. I have no plan for what I will do with my life in this little town where I know no one.

The day after I move in, driving along Main Street, I see a sign advertising free puppies. I take home two of them. I plant flowers and tomatoes and peas. I buy oil lamps and candles, a hammock, a teapot, a health food cookbook, an autoharp, a basket for flowers and a Victrola. I set vases of lilacs in every room.

I make a schedule for myself that I post on the refrigerator, accounting for every moment of my waking hours.

> 6 A.M.: *Get up. Do sit-ups. Jog.*
>
> 7 A.M.: *Eat banana. Meditate. Take shower.*
>
> 8 A.M. to noon: *Write.*
>
> Noon to 1 P.M.: *Free time. Take a walk with dogs.*
>
> 1 P.M. to 3 P.M.: *Write.*
>
> 3 P.M. to 4 P.M.: *Walk to Gleason Falls. Swim.*
>
> 4 P.M.: *Work in garden. Read good books. Draw.*
>
> 5:30 P.M.: *Drive to town. Buy groceries.*
>
> 6:30 P.M.: *Dinner, and watch news.*
>
> 7 P.M. to 9 P.M.: *Read. Write letters.*
>
> 9 P.M. to 9:30 P.M.: *Sit-ups. Bed.*

Sometime in mid-June I finally call Jerry. "I just thought you might want to have my number," I say. "I see," he says. It doesn't sound as if he's writing it down.

My mother writes to her friend Marion that summer.

> *Joyce is encountering every disaster I had sketched when I tried to persuade her not to sink her last penny into that house. This past week she drove her car into a field. (She was having a picnic, and though this was no more than a couple hundred yards from the house, she thought she'd drive there.) The car was impaled on a rock; she tore out the transmission. No parts available locally. She's marooned.*
>
> *She has alienated the local plumber by canceling an agreement to have him install heat. Too expensive. Last week she discovered that her water supply has failed totally—no taps, no toilet. Must find new plumber, maybe well digger.*
>
> *Now it turns out the septic tank leaks. Believe me, none of this gives me any told-you-so satisfaction. My therapist tells me to leave her alone....*

Bills are mounting.

Since leaving Jerry I have lost all ability to control my eating. I don't know how to eat three regular meals a day anymore. Any food I buy I have to finish. If it's something high in calories, I make myself throw up after I eat it. An hour later, I'm likely to eat something else.

Like my father, who maintained his job as a teacher for all the years of his active alcoholism, I manage to work in spite of having become increasingly controlled by my diet. Shortly after buying the Hillsboro house, I accept a job offered to me by CBS Radio to become one of a group of political and social commentators on a series known as *Spectrum*.

My job calls for me to record a broadcast twice a week, in which I will be featured, along with Murray Kempton and Jeff Greenfield, to represent the liberal point of view on a range of political and cultural subjects of the moment. I record the pieces on cassette tape and mail them to New York. Once a month I travel to New York to tape a debate for the *CBS Morning News*, in which I will be pitted against one of the network's conservative commentators, often Phyllis Schlafly. One week we argue the merits of the B-1 bomber. Another time, it's premarital sex. In the commentaries I produce on my own, at home, I write about cutting back on gas consumption in light of the fuel crisis, capital punishment, Watergate, the birthday of Fred Astaire.

One week in July, I choose ice cream for my subject, which gives me the opportunity to convey, over the national airwaves, what Jerry Salinger has taught me about its lethal properties. I spend my two-minute broadcast quoting from a book he gave me, Dr. Henry Bieler's *Food Is Your Best Medicine*:

" 'The freezing process,' " I say, quoting Bieler, " 'gives to the cream its last and finishing touches of physiological corruption. Like the melting glaciers of the past, which in releasing from their frigid storages the long preserved tissues of animal life, surrenders them to dissolution and decay, so the ice cream melting in the body of the individual sets free the carcasses of the cream and milk cells, to lay them open to the relentless attacks of swarming and festering material, though the evidence of putrefaction escapes the taste by being masked into unrecognizability by the great deceiver, sugar. In this physiological interment, the ice holds the function of the embalmer, and the sugar, the embalming fluid.' I'm Joyce Maynard for *Spectrum*."

My agent, Emmy, gets me magazine assignments. I write an article about Barbie dolls, a reminiscence about the first time I heard the Beatles, reflections on *Leave It to Beaver*. In the year 1973, if a magazine wants someone to write an article about what young people are doing or thinking, very often I will be the person editors call. I become Spokesperson for my Generation—the first and by no means the last time in which I will create an identity on the page that bears little resemblance to my own. With the money I earn I manage to make enough extra to put in central heating, storm windows, new electrical wiring.

All through that first summer I live alone in Hillsboro I keep calling and writing Jerry. Sometimes it will be with a question. "Do you think I should put in Big Boy tomatoes or Jet Star?" But what I really want is for him to come see my house.

"We could have a picnic in the field," I say. This time I won't try driving there. "You'd love my dogs."

"I'm pretty busy, kid," he says. "Matthew's home. Dentist appointments. Car trouble."

"It's not that far," I say. "We could take a walk." When he remains noncommittal, I abandon my casual tone.

"I have to see you," I say. "I don't know what to do."

"All right," he says finally. "I guess I could stop by."

He shows up with Matthew. I've spent the morning fixing us lunch—cucumber slices arranged in the pattern of a flower, soup and salad, whole-wheat bread, a hunk of cheese made from unpasteurized milk. The table was set long before his car pulled up.

"We've already eaten," he says. "I'm taking Matthew into Concord to pick up a part for the car."

We sit on my porch. "I want to make a path down to the field," I tell him. "And I was thinking I'd hang a swing in that tree."

"Cool," Matthew says. I ask him what he's up to this summer. "Hanging around," he tells me.

"I'll show you my garden," I say to Jerry—having pulled weeds all afternoon the day before so it would look good.

"I'd love to, but we've got to hit the road," he says. "What do you say, Matt?" Matthew bounds up from his chair.

"You've got yourself a great setup here, kiddo." Jerry tells me, as they head out to the car.

"I was going to show you Loon Pond, and the waterfall down the road, where I swim," I say. "I bet you'd be brave enough to jump off the rocks, Matthew."

"Some other time," Jerry says. They are gone within a half hour of their arrival.

In August I send Jerry a letter asking for information about homeopathic medicine: What remedies I should purchase to have around my house, and in what potencies; what homeopathic journal to subscribe to. I enclose a self-made multiple choice form, with blanks and boxes to check off to make answering easier. *Look how little I ask for,* I'm telling him.

He doesn't take my bait.

"Dear Joyce," he begins, going straight to business. He says he'll forego the multiple-choice pages I sent. Homeopathy's more complicated than that, he tells me, with faint reproachfulness.

Then he goes on to tell me where I can buy a *Materia Medica* (India).

Because so many homeopathic publications come from England, I'd asked him in my letter for the current value, in American dollars, of the British pound. He tells me the value of the pound is $2.44 that day.

In response to a question I asked concerning the advisability of getting distemper shots for my two dogs, he tells me that if a person were feeding her dog anything other than the special health food variety he favors, he might opt for getting the shots.

He lists fifteen remedies that are, in his opinion, the most essential.

That's about it, he writes.

I come to the last paragraph, hoping this will be where he has something to say to me about the two of us. I want him to tell me how much he loves me, how much he misses me, how sad he is that we can't be together, if it's true we can't. I want him to tell me again about his bright hopes for me, because I can no longer imagine them myself. There are just three more sentences:

He says it's late; he's tired. He's been answering letters since his return from New York that day. He dropped Matthew off, on the way back, at a friend's house in Connecticut. Says the two of them got lost driving home. He signs the letter "love, J."

Because it's the only word in the letter that speaks of his connection to me, I spend a long time thinking about that word, "love." I remember the first time he signed a letter to me that way, and all the possibilities his choice of that word had signified then. Now there would appear to be none. This is the last letter I ever receive from him.

I have not been keeping to the schedule posted on my refrigerator. I'm writing magazine articles and radio broadcasts, but with little enthusiasm. My father calls often, wanting to talk about my mother. My tomato plants are strangled by weeds. My squash plants have been eaten by deer or woodchucks, and my corn is stunted. I take long walks with my dogs. I have made one friend, Jan, a born-again Christian woman a few years older than I, who lives up the road with her husband and two young children. We are both hooked on the soap opera *All My Children*. Every day we discuss what the character of Erica is up to.

One time, when I'm rearranging furniture in my upstairs loft, I open the door to the crawl space and a bat flies out at me. Then another. In a minute, the room is swarming with bats. They're banging against the walls and windows, making a high-pitched shriek. I sit on the floor unable to move. Finally I make my way down the stairs and call a neighbor, who says he will help me get rid of the bats and does. For nights afterward I keep an oil lamp burning next to me and stare at the ceiling, waiting for another bat to swoop down.

* * *

My mother writes, urging me to see her therapist. She has suggested I have myself hospitalized for the eating disorders that have
taken control of me to the point that I can no longer keep food
in the refrigerator.

In this letter, I reject my mother's offer of money for psychotherapy. It's just not possible, I say.

"I cannot do this," I write back. "Whatever truth there may
be to the powers of a therapist to help, he can do so only if he is
trusted, believed in, respected—and I feel none of these things.
Arguing this is pointless. Believe if you will that I'm deluded, but
as long as these delusions exist for me, they are more real than
any perception of reality that you might entertain. It does no good
to tell a man with the DT's that he doesn't really have ants crawling all over his skin. . . ."

Recognizing that my life is desperately in need of structure, I talk
to my old English teacher, Mark, about the possibility of taking
a class or two at Dartmouth. He arranges it. I sign up for a class
in the modern novel, making the hour-long drive to Hanover
twice a week. Every time I drive to Hanover, I watch for Jerry
on the street but I never see him.

A writer for *Esquire* magazine calls to say she'd like to write
an article about me.

Maybe I suppose I will actually be able to show Jerry, in this
article, how well I'm abiding by his rules, with my organic garden
and my diet of raw vegetables. The only rule of Jerry's I have
seriously disregarded is the one about agreeing to be interviewed
for magazine articles in the first place.

The interviewer arrives on a chilly November morning, my
twentieth birthday. I pick her up at the airport in Lebanon—the
airport I used to fly in to when I came to visit Jerry during that
brief period I worked at *The New York Times*. She accompanies
me to my Dartmouth class and sits with me in the car while I
make a tape of one of my *Spectrum* broadcasts that I need to
express-mail from Hanover that afternoon. Then the two of us
drive back to Hillsboro, where she spends the night at my house.
The next day I drive her to the airport.

In her article, which will run a few months later, the writer has no difficulty conveying the portrait of me as an unhappy and neurotic young woman.

"Every hour or so a shutter bangs against the side of the house," she writes. "Joyce Maynard, wrapped in a quilt, rocks back and forth in her rocking chair in front of the fire. Makeup covers the dark circles under her eyes. . . ."

In a way that makes the scene sound very sinister, she describes my house as being filled with unused toys and an empty crib. There's a jar of salamanders on the table, gathered after a rainstorm, and cats jumping up on the table. My bathroom "is a slob's bathroom," with hair clogging the hairbrush.

"She sleeps in a flannel nightgown in a bed filled with hot water bottles. Yes, all the grandmotherly virtues—maidenly, demure, sensible, boots by the fireplace. But taut, raked inside. At times she's six. At times a dowdy sixty. Even her body system is pure. She eats only once a day—yogurt, vegetables, fruit, a few grains of wheat germ. Raw foods. Never two foods mixed. . . ."

My parents, she writes, have forgotten my birthday.

The subject of J. D. Salinger comes up.

"Joyce says: 'If I had a relationship with a famous person it would be the last name I'd mention.' Very pure and moral, her tone; very full of soft-voiced rebuke and downcasting of eyes."

" 'Please . . .' " I am quoted as saying. " 'If you have any respect for certain great books that might once have meant something to you. . . .' She speaks about the sacred privacy that genius deserves. This is her trust. She says she will never talk to anyone about Salinger. Her purity blows through the room like a draft. . . . She hugs her sides and sits by the fire, rocking. . . ."

Months pass, whole seasons. Young as I am, the life that lies before me looks like a seemingly endless expanse of icy water without borders, more fathoms deep than any diver ventures. The space Jerry's departure has left feels bigger than any land mass remaining.

I have begun to understand that Jerry is gone forever from my life. Now that this has sunk in, I am left believing I will never love any other man again the way I loved him. I will marry and have children one day, but nobody will ever again know me the way Jerry did.

I also hold to the unshakable conviction that Jerry will never love anyone else the way he loved me once. I take my remaining comfort from the assurance that what existed between us—irretrievable though it may be—will never be duplicated. The place I occupied in his heart could not be filled by any other girl.

It's the winter of 1974. It has been six months since I last saw or heard from Jerry and almost a year since the day I left Daytona Beach. It's late at night. I am sitting by the light of an oil lamp in the living room of my house in Hillsboro, my dogs breathing heavily on the rug by the fire. I'm listening to sad country music—the music I now listen to more than any other because it seems to hold most reference to my life. Tonight the record is George Jones, as it often is. "Today I Started Loving Her Again." "Just Someone I Used to Know." "The Grand Tour." I'm reading Salinger's *Nine Stories*, published in 1953, the year I was born.

The sixth story is "For Esmé—with Love and Squalor." It's the story of a soldier taking a top-secret pre-invasion training course and stationed in Devon, England, near the end of the war, just as Jerry was.

The story begins on a rainy afternoon. The soldier's off-duty. He stops into a church where a children's choir is rehearsing. He sits there for a while listening to them. One child in particular attracts his attention.

She's thirteen—ash-blond hair, "exquisite" forehead. Her "blasé" eyes look as if they "might very possibly have counted the house." But it's her voice that draws him to her—a voice that is, he writes, "distinctly separate from the other children's voices." She has "the best upper register." Her voice is "the sweetest sounding, the surest, and it automatically led the way." The young girl, he says, "seemed slightly bored with her own singing ability." Once or twice she actually yawns, "although she conceals it well."

Later that afternoon the young soldier stops in a tea shop in the little town. This same girl comes in with her younger brother—a boy who loves to tell the same one corny joke and sounds to me startlingly like Lilit Gampel's little brother, Alan.

The girl smiles at the soldier—an "oddly radiant" smile. The soldier smiles back. The girl comes over to his table.

The girl tells the soldier about her parents, who have died. Her mother, she says, was "quite sensuous," inquiring of the soldier whether he finds her cold. It's an odd comment for a girl to make. But Esmé is a girl like no other—the oddest combination of child and woman.

She apologizes for how bad her hair must look, on account of being wet, and asks the soldier if he's married, which he is. She asks the soldier what he did before joining the army. He says he was a writer. She says she would be "extremely flattered" if he would write a story about her someday. She prefers "stories about squalor."

"For Esmé—with Love and Squalor" is a love story, although nothing sexual happens between the soldier and the girl. Nothing inappropriate in any way. It is an encounter of exquisite tenderness and correctness, ending with a handshake. The girl asks if the soldier would like her to write to him. She says she writes "extremely articulate letters for a person my—"

Age, she was going to say. A person her age. But he interrupts her. He says he would love a letter, and gives her his address.

By the time the letter from Esmé arrives it is "several weeks after V-E day," and the soldier is in a hospital in Bavaria, having suffered a mental breakdown at the front. What Esmé says in her letter conveys the most disarming combination of attempted sophistication and innocence. She is trying hard to be a woman of the world. But she is nothing like a woman of the world. She is simply the most perfect, irresistible, magical child a tormented soldier could possibly get a letter from at a moment in his life when the world seems most dark and hopeless.

One detail about the young girl Esmé so startles me that I have to put the book down for a moment before continuing with the story:

Esmé wears an oversized man's watch "much too large for her slender wrist"—the watch of her dead father. It is an "enormous-faced wristwatch," the soldier notes, that might fit better around her waist than around her wrist. It's a watch like the one Jerry

Salinger himself commented on that I wore in the photograph on the cover of *The New York Times Magazine*.

I live alone in my house at the end of the dead-end road for two years.

My sister and her husband have gotten back together, and are raising their son together in Toronto. My parents are divorced— my father back from England now, and living with Laura in the town of Wilton, New Hampshire. My mother has struck up a love affair with a British-born businessman, Sydney Bacon, who wrote her a series of letters after reading her book *Raisins and Almonds*. Now she has begun to talk about moving to Toronto, where he lives.

My relationship with my mother has been strained in recent years. She says I blame her for the dissolution of my relationship with Jerry. Now that her therapist has pointed out to her the unhealthiness of those many years she endured, sacrificing her own needs on my behalf and my sister's, she has become sensitive to every perceived instance of my selfishness and thoughtlessness to her, and is angry and accusatory when they occur. Her therapist has a theory that my mother should "cut Joyce loose." For a girl raised to believe her mother would always adore and praise her, it's baffling and frightening to hear my mother tell me now, in language that no longer even sounds like her, all the ways I have abused and hurt her.

She writes of me, to my sister.

Joyce is heavier than she has ever been. She would die if she knew how many people have commented on that. Emmy even spoke of it. (Market value of product affected?) Marilyn Hapgood, who had seen her on TV, thought it must be the camera. That round face wasn't elfin Joyce.... I drove up to Hillsboro last Sunday. The amount of work needing to be done there is overwhelming—house very dirty and cluttered with treasures like quilts from the last auction, grounds ragged and overgrown. She says she would like to go to New York if she could afford it, and I wish she could. But I am not weak and foolish enough to think I should give her money.

I see my father regularly. He is painting again and attending Alcoholics Anonymous meetings. He speaks regularly of leaving Laura, who flies into rages at him, he says, and sometimes becomes physically violent with him. He speaks of "making an escape" from New Hampshire. But he would never leave his dog, Nicky, who's old and fragile and depressed—all the things that are true of himself.

He calls me, drunk, late at night, or in the middle of the day— weeping, sometimes, and other times rageful as he recounts yet another aspect of my mother's abandonment of him. "Please come over," he says. And I do.

One day, in the fall of 1974—November, hunting season—I hear a car pulling up in my driveway.

There is a dark, official-looking vehicle parked in front of my house, with an animal's body tied to the roof, a single stream of blood dripping onto the windshield. It's my dog Sammy. The game warden faces me, with his fingers in his belt. "He was chasing deer in the woods," he says. "I had to shoot him."

I don't think I can survive another winter in this house. I am not in good shape, and I know it.

My producer at CBS announces that they're revising the *Spectrum* lineup, and I am no longer part of it. The same week, I get a call from my old friend Josh, who's a senior at Yale now. He's directing a production of the Sondheim's *A Little Night Music*.

"Why don't you come and take a part in the show?" he asks.

The character I am to play is twelve or thirteen years old. I have only a few lines, and one verse of a song. I used to say I had no interest in playing bit parts, but this time I don't care.

"Yes," I say.

Chapter Fourteen

MY FRIEND JOSH, the director, has made an arrangement with the dean of his residential college, allowing me to live on campus for the duration of rehearsals for *A Little Night Music*. I am staying in one of the cement cubicles of the Ezra Stiles dormitory. Because the bathrooms here are shared, it would be difficult for me to continue my daily practice of making myself throw up. I tell myself I am finished with that, and post a new schedule on the wall of my tiny single room:

> *6:00—Wake up. Do sit-ups. Go for a run. Draw.*
> *7:30—Go to dining hall. Eat fruit and cereal.*
> *8:00—Library. Read.*
> *9:00—Sit in on classes. Ride bike. Write.*

Every evening I attend rehearsals. Afterward I often go with members of the cast to the coffee shop in the cross-campus library, where we talk about Sondheim, classes, and other plays we'd like to perform.

One night, early in my time in New Haven, a friend of Josh's who is not in the play joins us. Glenn is a pre-med student who grew up in Scarsdale. The son of a successful doctor, Glenn is a handsome, confident young man and just a year older than I am.

"I'll walk you back to your dorm," he says, when the library closes and our group disbands. On the dark path, he puts an arm around me. When we get to the dormitory he kisses me.

The next night Glenn stops by our table at the coffee shop again. The night after that, neither of us joins the group of cast members. He has invited me to have dinner with him at a Chinese restaurant in New Haven.

I haven't eaten at a restaurant in years, and seldom eat whole meals. For me, a dinner might be a head of lettuce or a container of ice cream or a bowl of popcorn. Looking at the menu, I feel my stomach clench.

"I have a problem," I tell him. I sense, already, about this young man a certain air that indicates he will be a good and sympathetic caregiver. He listens very closely, and I tell him more than I'd supposed I could. I confide in him the story of my years of denying myself food. Then I tell him about my sexual problem.

In the three and a half years that I have been unable to have intercourse, I have only told the doctor in Daytona Beach, and even then it was Jerry who spoke.

"So, tell me about it," he says, handing me his plate so I can try the shrimp in lobster sauce.

For the next four weeks, while I rehearse my play and he prepares for finals, Glenn feeds me. We have dinner together almost every night, often in restaurants around New Haven. We spend a lot of time in his room, kissing and touching each other.

One weekend he announces he's taking me to New York. He wants me to see Tavern on the Green.

Walking down Fifth Avenue that Saturday Glenn says that he wants to buy me a dress. We go into a department store where I try on many and he studies them, analyzing which style looks best on me.

That night we dine on Dover sole and coquilles St.-Jacques with escargots—all foods I've never tasted before. We have wine and chocolate mousse. Although we haven't made love, we are able to talk comfortably about subjects I would once have regarded as unmentionable. There is none of my mother's amused prurience about sex when Glenn discusses it.

The final week of rehearsals for *A Little Night Music* leaves me little time for seeing Glenn. That weekend, there are four performances.

The night of the last performance, Glenn asks me to come back to his dormitory room with him. "I'm going to make love with you now," he says.

We climb the steps to the top floor, and he opens the door for me. He has set candles out. He puts a record on the stereo—the soundtrack to his favorite Broadway musical, *Pippin.*

We have already spent many hours necking in this room, but this time he undresses me and lays me on the narrow single bed and touches my whole body. He talks to me very softly, and when he enters my body, I feel a single moment of sharp pain. But it is not the old terrible agony of the locked door and the banging crowbar.

"I knew you'd be fine," Glenn says afterward, wiping my tears away. I fall asleep.

Having found a man with whom I can have a happy, relaxed time—not a landsman, but a man with whom I can make love, at last—I suppose that we will be together forever. A few days later, when I go back to New Hampshire, I expect that Glenn will be coming to join me soon. I know he has plans to take a summer school course in New York and work in a lab. But I assume we will figure out a way to be together.

This is a good deal more than Glenn feels prepared to take on at twenty-two, on the verge of heading off to medical school. He calls every night in New Hampshire, but when I ask him, as I always do, when he's coming to visit, he says he's not sure. Finally one night, he tells me he can't see me anymore. "I just don't know what to tell you, Joyce," he says. "There are all these things I'm supposed to do right now."

I'm crushed. I had pictured a summer of swimming at the waterfall with Glenn and cooking wonderful meals together that we'd eat on the trestle table on my porch by candlelight. I am alone again in my single bed.

At the end of the summer of 1975, I decide to move to New York City and rent out my house in Hillsboro. I get a studio apartment on Nineteenth Street and Irving Place and begin doing the rounds of magazine editors' offices, picking up assignments.

The first months in Manhattan are lonely and hard. When I was with Glenn I had thought my struggle with eating disorders was behind me, but I find out that, once again, I am controlled by food. I vacillate between bingeing and starving myself. I am living in the city I had longed to explore since I was twelve, but I am too preoccupied with my struggle to venture beyond the deli and the gym. Twice I check myself into a fasting retreat upstate, where I take in nothing but water for a week and feel briefly elated. Within days of my return, I'm back to my old routine.

Although my music listening began with Bob Dylan and Joan Baez, and eventually moved toward rock and roll, for the last several years now the music I have listened to most has been country—hard-core heartbreak music. My favorite singers are Tammy Wynette, Merle Haggard, Dolly Parton, and George Jones.

In November of 1975, I decide to go to Nashville. I want to meet the people whose songs have formed the soundtrack for the last two years of my life.

I check into the Hall of Fame Motel, on Music Row. I start calling record company offices, identifying myself as a journalist who'd like to interview some of the major artists they represent. I have a vague notion that I'll write something about Nashville, but no assignment.

It's amazingly easy, getting people to talk with me. Within a day, I'm sitting in the office of Mae Boren Axton, the woman who wrote "Heartbreak Hotel." Twenty minutes after meeting me, she's on the phone to friends all over town, telling them there's this nice little girl sitting in her office who'd like to come over and say hey.

I walk down the street to see Porter Wagoner, who spends a couple of hours with me, reminiscing about his days with Dolly Parton. Tammy Wynette invites me to her house, where we sit on a plush white couch as she discusses the breakup of her marriage to George Jones. Dolly Parton says she's just heading out on the road to perform up north someplace in the Smokies. "Why don't you hop on my bus?" she says. So I do. Before she starts singing the song "Jolene," Dolly looks out in the audience and says, "I'd like to dedicate this next one to a friend of mine named Joyce."

The next night I go to a little club on Music Row called Possum Holler, owned by George Jones. He's performing here tonight.

I sit alone at my table, against the wall, listening to George Jones. Something in the way he sings moves me like nobody else. I believe I understand the kind of pain he sings about.

Out of nowhere, a drink is set down in front of me. "I didn't order that," I say to the waitress.

"He did," she says. She points to a very tall man standing in the corner, wearing a cowboy hat and dressed in black. He nods at me when I look his way.

I take a sip of the drink. I don't look at the man again. When I finish the drink, another just like it appears in front of me. I finish my second drink.

At some point the man sits down next to me. He stares straight ahead at the stage and takes my hand. I don't hold it back, but neither do I push him away.

When George Jones finishes his set, I get up, holding on to the table to steady myself. For the first time, I speak to the man. "Thank you for the drinks," I say. "I'm going now."

Without saying anything, he follows me outside to the street, where I have been planning to get a cab. "I'll drive you," says the man. "That's not necessary," I say, but he takes my arm and steers me to an enormous Cadillac. I get into the front seat. He pops an eight-track tape with his photograph on the front into the tape player. His voice has a tinny, plastic feel to it, nothing like the singers I love.

"I'm staying at the Hall of Fame Motel," I say. I have that feeling that I'm standing a few feet away watching my life.

When we reach my motel, I get out of the car, thanking him once more. But he's getting out too. He follows me into the lobby, and into the elevator.

I'm still in a dream state, numb.

I push the button of a floor that isn't mine. Then I push another button for a different floor. But I don't know what to do when I get to those floors. I push the button for the floor where my room is, and I walk to the door. I put my key in the lock. I turn to him to say "I'm going to bed now."

The man places his hand over mine on the doorknob and

pushes the door open and pushes me inside. He unzips his pants and grabs my head and presses my face against his groin.

When he's done, he walks slowly to the bathroom, fixes his contact lenses and puts his cowboy hat back on. He leaves in silence.

The next morning I take a taxi to the airport and fly back to New York. I say nothing about this to anybody.

My one-room studio in New York City lies just below street level with a window looking out at the sidewalk, giving me a good view of people's feet as they walk past. The place is so dark I have to turn on the lights even on a sunny day.

Just after Christmas I find a much better place. It's a small one-bedroom apartment, almost like a ship's cabin, on the top floor of a wonderful old building facing Gramercy Park. The apartment has a terrace on three sides, with a view of the park and the Manhattan skyline, including the Empire State Building, which is now lit in red, white, and blue for the bicentennial.

In January I send a letter to *The New York Times* again—this time to Abe Rosenthal, the managing editor of the daily paper. I ask whether he'd consider me for a job as a reporter at the paper. A couple of days later he calls and invites me to come for an interview.

I have never gone for a job interview, which may explain how it could be that upon meeting Seymour Topping, an assistant editor at the paper, I begin our crucial interview by remarking, "You are the *topping* to my day. I hope to *see more* of you."

They hire me anyway.

The job I have gotten is a journalist's dream. It's hard to imagine a more exciting place to be working than the third floor at 229 West Forty-third Street. Never more so than this year, 1976, when the paper launches the special sections *Home, Living, Sports,* and *Weekend,* under the direction of the assistant managing editor, Arthur Gelb.

My desk sits in the middle of the newsroom. In later years when I visit the paper, reporters will have cubicles with partitions separating them, and computer terminals. But in 1976, we are all still stationed at desks with old manual typewriters, surrounded by ringing telephones and rushing copy boys. Sometimes, at the end of the day, I ride the elevator down to the basement, where I can watch the typesetters at work setting my stories in lead, one letter at a time. The first time I watch the presses roll I call my mother, holding the first edition in my hand. "My story's actually in the paper," I tell her. "All over the city tomorrow morning, people having their coffee will open their paper and see words I wrote, just a few hours before."

"You're going to have a wonderful career," she says.

The New York Times becomes my whole world. I am one of the first reporters at her desk in the morning, and often I am still there at nine or ten that night. Even when I'm not in the *Times* building, I feel as though I'm on the job. I make my way around the city, looking for a story wherever I go.

My greatest difficulty as a reporter concerns my inability to write at a typewriter, or even in a room where activity is taking place. My old pattern, learned in the home of my parents, of sitting on my bed with a yellow legal pad and writing in long-hand, is still the only way I know to write. As a reporter on deadline, I have to adjust my routine. Most days I spend the morning collecting the information for my story. In the early afternoon, I check in with the assistant metropolitan editor about what I'll be writing. Then I take a taxi back to Gramercy Park, run up to my apartment, pull out my legal pad and produce the story. I race back down the elevator, hail a second cab, return to the *Times* building to type my story and turn it in. When I have to, I can accomplish the whole thing in just over an hour.

I have never worked so hard. I work on weekends, too, covering feature stories and interviewing celebrities. Sometimes the paper even runs my line drawings to illustrate my lighter stories. I begin to make a name for myself as an up-and-coming reporter.

Shortly after a story of mine runs about the suicide of the comedian Freddie Prinze, Abe Rosenthal calls me into his office. "I've been keeping an eye on your work," he tells me. "I think you've got a terrific future as a journalist. Foreign correspondent.

Critic. Columnist. There's no telling what you could do. I'd like to hear what direction you've been thinking about for yourself."

Approval and praise from the managing editor of *The New York Times* is an intoxicating thing. But what I really want is to have a normal, regular life with children, a garden, and a dog. I want to live in my house in New Hampshire, eating three meals a day and sleeping in the arms of a man who will not leave. There is so much I believed in once that I don't believe in anymore.

"I don't know what I want yet," I say.

Chapter Fifteen

IN SPITE OF my workload at *The New York Times*, I continue to meet with magazine editors, picking up freelance work on the side.

One is an editor at *Cosmopolitan*, to whom I propose a piece about the difficulty of finding a good man in New York City—a difficulty that probably has more to do with who I am at the time than it does with the men in New York City. She assigns me the story. Then she asks if she can give my phone number to her nephew. He recently moved to New York to pursue his career as an artist. He's renting a loft on Duane Street, picking up house-painting jobs and taking slides around to galleries. "Maybe you remember Steve from Yale," she says.

It has been nearly five years since the time Steve and I danced the polka and swam together under the waterfall. The next Sunday he's standing at the door to my Gramercy Park penthouse.

I remembered Steve as a very handsome young man. Still, the look of him when I open my door that afternoon takes me by surprise. He has smooth skin and chiseled features and the body and natural grace of an athlete or a dancer. Maybe it's his astonishing good looks that have given him this air of un-self-conscious effortlessness. He smiles at me. "I thought we could go see some art," he says.

Listening to Steve talk about Jackson Pollock (a painter he reveres—and one whose work Jerry dismissed, as he did all modern art), it's plain that paintings are alive to him. A look comes over him when he talks about paintings. There's a heat and intensity to what he says. For a person who seems to measure out his words almost as if it costs money using them, he possesses a surprising fluency when he gets to the subject of art.

After the museum, we walk the forty blocks back to my apartment. Steve's hungry. He opens the refrigerator. Finding nothing but three eggs, he cooks us an omelet while I light candles and put a record on the stereo. We eat sitting on pillows on the living room floor while Doc Watson sings "If I Needed You."

"If I needed you, would you...come to me and ease my pain?" In the years I lived alone in Hillsboro I played this record every night. At a time when no love had appeared, Townes Van Zandt's lyrics took on the power of a hymn.

Steve tells me his upstairs neighbors, above the loft he shares on Duane Street, have a baby. He was over there the other night playing with her.

I don't tell him I have a crib already waiting in my house in New Hampshire. "I don't even know anybody who has a baby in this city," I say. "Everyone's too busy with their careers."

He reaches over to kiss me. I lie back on the pillows.

Sometime in the middle of the night, Steve asks me to marry him. I say yes.

He has to leave early the next morning for a housepainting job. Over coffee in my kitchen, I tell him about my house in New Hampshire. "We could drive up there this weekend," I say. "The house is just sitting empty. It's so quiet there."

"Great. I haven't seen the stars in months," he says.

This is a Monday. That night I am surprised when he doesn't call. The next day there is still no word from Steve, and I realize I don't even have his phone number. Wednesday, silence. I eat a whole container of ice cream and throw up.

On Thursday he calls me. "What time are we heading north?" he says.

"Whenever you want," I say with relief.

It's normally a four-and-a-half-hour drive from Manhattan to Hillsboro, but the last half mile is very slow because of a recent snowfall. My dead-end road has been plowed, but there are drifts against the door to the house. When we get inside, it's very cold. I turn on the heat. Steve builds a fire.

We had stopped for groceries in town, but I was so eager to get here I picked up only a handful of items. As Steve walks through the rooms, I put water on to boil for asparagus. In a separate saucepan, I melt butter and whisk in flour and milk. I grate in some cheese and pour it in a bowl. We sit on pillows by the fireplace, sharing a single plate of asparagus, dipping the spears in the sauce.

"I'd call this the sauce of life," he says.

"I don't even have a recipe," I say. "I hope I know how to make it again."

"Why don't we have a baby?" he says.

Steve invites me to his loft to show me his artwork. He constructs very large three-dimensional works, creating wooden skeletons a little like kite frames, onto which he attaches stretched canvas. Some of them are painted bold, often jarring colors, but the ones I like best are more subdued and subtle. They billow out from the wall like sails catching the wind. They are unlike any work anybody else seems to be showing in the galleries of SoHo at the time.

Nineteen seventy-seven is a time filled with promise for young painters in SoHo. Julian Schnabel and David Salle, both still in their twenties, have only recently been discovered, and already their work is being sold for huge amounts in the galleries we walk past. Just the week before this, Steve got a call from O. K. Harris, a prominent gallery owner, who says he'll stop by and take a look at his work. Paula Cooper has also expressed interest in him. Although at this point Steve is supporting himself with house-painting jobs, his energy and confidence and total conviction about the art he's making allow me to believe it will only be a matter of time, and probably not much time, before a gallery decides to represent him and he begins selling his work. Even though I grew up in a household profoundly overshadowed by my father's inability to live as a painter, I cannot imagine this golden young man not finding success and approval for his art.

* * *

We are walking down a street in lower Manhattan one night. Something possesses me to say to him, "Show me something to prove you love me." Barely hesitating, Steve stops in the middle of the street. He picks one foot off the ground, so he is standing on just his right leg, and holds his left foot in front of him, with his right hand. He balances that way for a moment, on one leg. Then the one foot that was still standing on the ground lifts into the air. He is still forming a hoop of his other foot and his hand. He brings his right foot through the hoop and lands again, one-legged, as cleanly as a cat.

Steve comes over one day with a present. It's a two-volume dictionary from a used bookstore with old engravings in it to illustrate the more interesting words. A night we sit together with colored pencils and color the pictures in, listening to an old record of Stephan Grapelli. One day we make a scratchboard drawing of ourselves entwined in each other's arms over a meal and a bottle of wine, surrounded by pillows.

I would never say of Steve that he is my *landsman*. He is a deeply private, even elusive person. Where so often the ways Jerry looked at the world had struck an affinity with me, what Steve says almost invariably takes me by surprise.

"What are you thinking about?" I would ask him during one of our frequent silences.

"The concept of negative space," he might say. Or it may be something very basic. "I was thinking about what kind of drawing pencil to get."

He is not effusive or romantic with me. He doesn't tell me he thinks I'm beautiful, or that he thinks about my body, craves to make love with me, imagines the two of us in some exotic setting together. There is a matter-of-factness to his attitude. He has told me he loves me. He has asked me to marry him. We have agreed that we both want a baby. It seems settled and uncomplicated.

It's only a good sign to me that we're so unlike each other. He seems to love his family, but to feel no particular need to discuss them, and he asks me almost no questions about my own family and past. After my brief mention of my year with J. D. Salinger, he asks no further questions, and never brings the subject up again. He is a person more concerned with abstractions than with human detail or stories. He doesn't ask to read what I write or to look at pictures of me growing up. One night I spend a long time telling him the story of my father's drinking.

"Too bad. Sounds rough," he says.

Years before, as a child, there was an ad I used to study in comic books featuring an offer that always fascinated me: "One Hundred Little Dolls for a Dollar." But the idea of actually sending in the money and getting the dolls, wonderful as that would be, always seemed impossible. Now I send away for them, though the price has risen to $2.98.

When the dolls arrive, they're very small and made of garish pink molded plastic, like something out of a Cracker Jack box. Some are clowns. Some look like Carmen Miranda. Some are ballerinas. Steve takes two of the dolls back to Duane Street with him one night: a pink plastic cowboy and cowgirl. He brings them back the next day, hand-painted with every detail down to the decorations on the boots and the belt buckles. To paint the eyes and the fringe on the cowgirl's skirt, he used a single hair of his paintbrush. I have no further doubt I will marry him.

One day, a few weeks after I meet Steve, *The New York Times* sends me to Berrien Springs, Michigan, to interview Muhammad Ali and his wife. Originally I was to be granted just an hour for my interview, but Ali takes a shine to me, and suggests I stay on for a few days with his family. This is something of a coup.

I tell Muhammad Ali I have to get back to New York. By this point, Steve and I are spending every night together. I can't bear to be away from him. This feeling is sufficiently strong that the next week, when I am scheduled to interview the hot young star John Travolta, I cancel. To the understandable disgust of a number of women at the paper, I quit my job at *The New York Times*, break the lease on my apartment with a key to Gramercy Park, pile my possessions into a U-Haul truck, and move with Steve back to New Hampshire.

Less than three months from the day Steve and I met again, I am pregnant. The day we find out, we throw our arms around each other and waltz around the bedroom, though no music is playing.

Looking back, I realize there was never a time I felt more hope than I did during those first few months with Steve. I was finally going to be part of a happy family.

We travel to Ohio to meet his parents, who seem very happy at the prospect of having me for a daughter-in-law. We get a puppy—a big-pawed mutt, half retriever, half lab. I scatter flower seed everywhere, supposing that's all it will take to have a glorious garden in time for our summer wedding, and plant rows of tomatoes, beans, squash, peas, and carrots. I bake pies. Steve draws nude portraits of me with the puppy. At night we eat dinner by candlelight on our porch, looking out over the apple trees in our back field and the woods beyond. One time I spend a whole afternoon making potato chips from scratch—a process so laborious I end up with little more than a dozen.

In my family, growing up, mealtimes were always a time for conversation and storytelling—so much so that on numerous occasions, my parents set a reel-to-reel tape recorder under the table. With Jerry, meals were conducted without ceremony on TV trays, seemingly for the sole purpose of taking in healthy sustenance. Then came those years of out-of-control eating, in which I ate no true meals at all.

Now with Steve I long to re-create the ritual of a meal around the table. I set out special plates I find at yard sales—different each night—and put on music, and a dress, before we sit down, and when we do, we say grace.

But Steve doesn't talk much. I develop the habit of saving up conversational topics over the course of the day to bring up over dinner, but his answers often seem to me painfully terse. Eventually, to keep the conversation going, I revert to my habitual question with him, "What are you thinking about?"

"Paint," he says. Or "the hardware store." He mentions some property of physics, or cell theory, or his new running shoes.

From the day I find out I'm pregnant, I am poring over in-utero photographs of a developing fetus by the photographer

Lennart Nilsson, but my favorite pregnancy book is *Spiritual Midwifery*, a collection of first-person birthing tales published by a commune in Tennessee that practices home birth. With my distrust of doctors acquired from Jerry, I tell Steve I want a home birth.

We have set our wedding for July 2. My mother and Sydney arrive from Toronto a couple of days before the ceremony, which is to be held at an old country church a mile down the road from our house. There will be a picnic supper for friends back at our house after our wedding, with Steve's sculptures set up in the field. We make no provision for the possibility of rain.

My mother, who has embraced Judaism in a new way since embarking on her love affair with Sydney, has evidently been hoping that Steve and I will invite Sydney to be the cantor, but we have already chosen hymns. Never having set foot in a temple, I can't imagine holding a traditional Jewish wedding. As a compromise, I suggest that we adopt the traditional Jewish practice of having both the bride's mother and her father walk her down the aisle. When my father shows up later that afternoon, I explain this to him.

The rehearsal the night before the wedding is the first time since my parents' divorce that I have seen them together. The tension between them is terrible from the beginning. When we get to the point of practicing my walk down the aisle, with one of them on each side of me, the scene turns almost comically uncomfortable. The aisle of the little New England church would be narrow, even for two people. For three, it's virtually impassable, even if the three could be in step, which my mother, my father, and I seem incapable of accomplishing. My mother yanks at me from one side. My father grips me tightly from the other.

I accept my sister's suggestion that perhaps having our mother walk down the aisle with our father and me isn't a good idea. Our mother is wounded.

That night, at the rehearsal dinner with Steve's family, my father gets drunk. In front of everyone, as the gathering is breaking up, he confronts my mother. "Ah, yes, Fredelle," he says, his speech slurred and his eyes moist. "There can be little doubt of your wit and brilliance and your matchless energy. I marveled at you thirty years ago, and marvel at you still. But in the end, what have you made of yourself? A great mind without a moral core, a rudderless ship. What do you know of God? What do you understand of Beauty?"

My mother is fuming. My sister disappears as quickly as possible. Steve's parents, looking startled, make their way back to their car. "When our children get married," I say to Steve, "this won't happen."

Our wedding day dawns clear and sunny. Steve and I get up very early and head out of town to pick buckets of daisies growing by the side of the road to decorate the church. Later that morning, we walk to the end of our driveway and replace the sign I'd put up four years earlier, which said MAYNARD, with one bearing his name.

We are married by a retired minister and pewter-maker whose wife plays the recorder while a friend plays the ancient pump organ in the church. Surrounded by daisies in the sunlit chapel, Steve faces me and reads the lines selected by my mother.

> "Let me not to the marriage of true minds
> Admit impediments: Love is not love
> Which alters when it alteration finds
> Or bends with the remover to remove.
> Oh no! It is an ever-fixed mark
> That looks on tempests, and is never shaken
> It is the star to every wandering bark
> Whose worth's unknown, although his height be taken.
> Love's not time's fool, though rosy lips and cheeks
> Within his bending sickle's compass come;
> Love alters not with his brief hours and weeks
> But bears it out even to the edge of doom."

My vow comes from Shakespeare too. Also provided by my mother.

> "My true love hath my heart, and I have his,
> By just exchange one for the other given:

I hold his dear, and mine he cannot miss,
There never was a better bargain driven...."

Sobered up, my father has brought a contingent of a dozen AA friends to keep an eye out for him this morning. Steve's two handsome brothers usher in my mother. She's wearing a low-cut Mexican lace dress and no bra. Steve's parents are conservatively dressed.

A very elderly eminent German photographer who has retired to this town takes black-and-white snapshots with her camera, mostly of my father's AA friends. There are no formal portraits taken of Steve and me. But friends' photographs show the two of us whirling around the dance floor. I study the pictures now in search of traces of the trouble that would come so soon, but I find none. In the photographs, I'm beaming, barefoot in my white Mexican wedding dress, which is looking tight already from my pregnancy.

Steve takes several housepainting jobs that summer and I write the treatment for a made-for-TV movie that never gets past the development stage. Every few weeks he travels to New York for a day or two to make the rounds of galleries and leave his slides. A wealthy collector has expressed an interest in commissioning a large piece for the lobby of his offices. "Have you called him back?" I ask Steve. "I'll get around to it soon," he says. He has misplaced the number. "How could you?" I demand. "Take it easy," he says. "If the guy wants me, he'll track me down again."

One time when he comes back from New York, and I ask him how his appointment went, he says the woman didn't show up. "You drive two hundred and fifty miles and she doesn't show up?" I say. "Didn't you call? Didn't you check before you left?"

"It's not as easy as you think," he says quietly.

My mother has given us a washing machine, but there's no money to hire a plumber to come hook it up. "We need more money," I tell Steve. "If you don't do something about this, I'll have to."

"Will you get off my back?" he says. "I'm *trying*."

*   *   *

Within the first weeks after our marriage Steve begins to suffer terrible, paralyzing migraine headaches. When one comes, there is nothing I can do for him, or anything he can do for himself, but sit alone in a dark room, waiting for it to be over.

"Do you want something to eat?" I ask him. "Let me give you a back rub."

"No thanks," he says. "Please go away."

Having reached the stage of pregnancy where I look thick and heavy without being obviously pregnant, I feel matronly and unattractive. I burst into tears. I want him to reassure me, but this isn't Steve's style. "I think I'll go for a run," he says.

I tell him a little about my eating disorders, and the compulsion that still comes over me sometimes to finish three containers of yogurt in a single sitting. Steve offers this advice: "Eat whatever I eat," he tells me. "Do whatever I do."

For years I have counted every calorie and worked to keep my intake to a minimum. I've watched my body so closely, I could always tell when I gained a pound. I have only had to put my hand on my stomach or my ribs to know how successful I have been.

Now that I'm pregnant, all this is changed. I am supposed to be gaining weight every week, and I am. For the first time in years I am having regular meals again.

One day I feel a deep, interior fluttering. At first the sensation is so slight I'm not sure what it was, but before long I recognize it's our baby moving. One day—some weeks later—I feel a small, firm pummeling from within. When I lift my shirt, I can see a foot or a fist pressing on a place on my belly. "Come here!" I call to Steve.

There is another thing I love about pregnancy. For as long as I can remember, I have awakened every morning with an oppressive awareness of my obligation to create something worthwhile. As young as age six or seven, I have gone to sleep every night with the question, "What did I write today? What did I make that will matter?"

Now I am making a baby. I don't need to write a word, and still I'm accomplishing the most important thing.

* * *

I do need to write, though, because we have no money. Steve continues to travel to New York every few weeks to leave his slides at galleries, but no one has agreed to represent him. He looks for housepainting jobs in New Hampshire, but there's very little work. He and his younger brother build a beautiful studio in our field with money we get from refinancing our house, but money is so tight there's only just enough to pay the mortgage. We barter a painting with the midwife who will be delivering our baby, and a neighbor agrees to provide us with fresh eggs forever in exchange for an erotic drawing by Steve of the man's wife.

Every Sunday afternoon, all that fall, I stand at a folding card table along the side of the highway passing through Hillsboro, with our wedding presents spread out on display. We sell a crystal bowl for fifteen dollars. A set of wineglasses goes for five. I sell my black pantsuit bought for a hundred dollars at Bloomingdale's the year before, and my Diane von Furstenberg wrap dresses, for three dollars apiece. At the end of the day, when I come home, I spread my earnings on the kitchen table to show Steve. "Great," he says.

"Couldn't you say something more than that?"

"I don't know what you want from me, Joyce."

I freeze huge quantities of food—vegetables from our garden, berries for pies, spaghetti sauce made from our tomatoes. One of the few photographs I have of myself from my first pregnancy shows me standing next to our open freezer pointing proudly at the stacks and stacks of frozen meals I've prepared. In the other photograph—this one taken at the very end of that pregnancy—it's clear I've been crying.

"You've hardly taken my photograph the whole time I've been pregnant," I was saying, through my tears.

"Okay then," he said. *Snap.*

I had hoped, when Steve and I married, that I would get to take a little time off during my pregnancy to fix up the house and get ready for the baby. I pictured that once the baby was born, I would spend my days for a while rocking and nursing and walking to the waterfall or sitting on the shores of Loon Pond. I figured Steve would be selling paintings by this point. If not, he would have figured out another way to make some money.

By October all of our bills are overdue, and I'm feeling desperate. We fight about money. Steve retreats into his studio. Many nights we eat our meals in silence. I no longer ask him what he's thinking about.

One time we pull into the gas station in Hillsboro, where we have taken to buying gas just a few dollars' worth at a time. A man approaches my side of the car and asks if I'm Joyce Maynard. Yes, I say, although I go by my married name now.

He hands me a piece of paper: Having broken my lease on my New York apartment months before, I am being sued for all the back rent, plus damages, which now totals several thousand dollars. In the end, Steve and I find a lawyer in town who settles the suit for a thousand dollars, but even that is more money than we have.

By my twenty-fourth birthday, in November, I am on the telephone to editors at women's magazines in New York, proposing articles I will write. I haul out my old, youth-spokesperson mantle for an article on my generation's attitudes about marriage. I write a story for one of *The New York Times* special sections about the time Steve and I had the mistaken impression that we were in possession of a winning ticket in a lottery run by our local supermarket chain. It turned out we were wrong.

In my retelling, I make this story into a comical event. This is the first of many occasions when I take devastating experiences and turn them into funny stories.

In recent years, I had said I was done writing for the women's magazines. I have voiced Jerry Salinger's scathing views of the kinds of work my mother pursued in the pages of *Woman's Day* and *Good Housekeeping*. I have called my mother's writing dishonest, inauthentic, a terrible compromise of commerce over art. Now I'm on the phone to all my mother's old contacts, pitching ideas for stories about keeping the romance alive in marriage, having fun in lean times, encouraging your husband to communicate. More than once over the course of these months,

I fling myself on the bed in tears. "Where is the money going to come from?" I ask Steve. "What are we going to do about this?"

One day, after one of these explosions, he disappears quietly into his studio. He comes back in the house a few minutes later, with a stack of pieces of paper cut to the size of dollar bills and painted with a face meant to look like George Washington. He stands over me where I lie, pregnant and weeping on the bed, and scatters the pretend money over me and walks away.

Sometime near the end of January, I set out alone in our Renault to see the midwife in Concord. It's snowing and the road is slick. The car skids into a tree. I'm unhurt, but the car is totaled.

We have no money for another car, or even a rental, until our insurance check comes through. For two weeks, we're stranded at the house. Now and then a neighbor stops by with groceries. Then comes the worst snowstorm to hit New England in a hundred years. It's days before the power is restored and snow plows reach our road. The snow's so deep we can't see out the windows on the ground floor. Steve skis out to the mailbox everyday, looking for the insurance check. It finally comes on Valentine's Day. With only days to my due date, we locate a 1966 Valiant sedan. We head straight to the mall, where Steve helps me pick out a bright pink chenille bathrobe and three sleeper suits for the baby. Two days later, I go into labor.

Years before, with Jerry Salinger, the muscles of the most intimate, private part of my body had clamped shut when I tried to open them. All through my pregnancy, I have had a secret fear that when the moment comes to give birth, my body will fail me again.

The contractions, when they begin, are the most powerful feeling I've ever known, but I know how to handle them. The image that comes to me, as I lie on our bed, breathing, is of myself surfing—though I never have. I ride every wave perfectly. I wait out the currents. I catch the next one, and I ride that one, too, always managing to keep just ahead of the point where the water would break over my head and pull me under.

Then I'm pushing. Steve kneels beside me on one side, while the midwife kneels between my legs at the foot of the bed. With one more roaring scream, I feel our daughter burst into the world.

From the moment of her birth, Audrey is a beautiful baby—dark as a gypsy, with a full head of black hair and large eyes. I put her to my breast. Seeing her mouth on my nipple, her tiny fist wrapping around my finger, the soft little snuffling noises she makes as she sucks for the first time, the world falls away. I am so elated and amazed, I barely notice the searing pain that accompanied that last, explosive moment when her head emerged from inside of me, followed, a few moments later, by the placenta. Now I realize my body is torn and ragged. I feel so tender that when the midwife suggests stitching me I scream, "No!" She doesn't repeat her suggestion.

The next morning Steve buries the placenta in the snow beside the cherry tree in our field. It is a year, almost to the day, since he first showed up on my doorstep in Gramercy Park, but those days now feel like part of somebody else's life, not mine.

I have wanted to be a mother since I was a little girl. Now that I am one, I say I have everything I've wanted most.

But there are times when I put Audrey to my breast that I feel a sinking so profound it almost crushes me. For nine months, all my energies have gone into making this baby. Now she is no longer inside me, and I experience a terrifying sense of my own emptiness. I had so totally given myself over to her, for all those months, I no longer knew who I was, separate from her.

I let myself gain fifty pounds during my pregnancy with Audrey. I imagined the day after she was born, I'd step on the scale and find myself with most of them gone. But the day after giving birth to my seven-pound baby, I still have over forty pounds to lose. A year before this, I was living in New York City, working at *The New York Times*, riding in taxis, and charging my clothes at Bloomingdale's. Now I have no career, no money. I'm living at the end of a dead-end road five miles from a very small town where I barely know anyone.

I am also experiencing such severe pain from the birth that every time I go to the bathroom, I weep. I have no friends here with babies of their own, so there is nobody to ask, Is this normal? When the midwife checks me out she says, again, that she'd like to do a little stitching. I can't bear the thought of being touched.

Three days after Audrey's birth, my mother comes to see us. There is no one in the world I want to see more than my mother, stepping off the plane in her big hat, shopping bags in each hand, carrying soup and cookies and baby blankets she's been sewing out of old cut-up nightgowns. She's the one person who will be as interested as I am in every detail of my baby's existence, and my own. The first thing she says as she greets us at the airport is, "Well, I guess now there can be no doubt about it. You two definitely *did it*."

Steve is stunned to learn that my mother plans to stay for at least ten days, and that she will be staying at our house instead of a motel.

Within an hour of my mother's arrival he is suffering from a massive migraine. The next day he's worse. For my mother's part, she seems to ignore Steve almost totally, commenting to Sydney over the phone about how much Audrey looks like me, and calling her "Joyce's baby."

With Steve still suffering, I make tea, and with Audrey in my arms, suggest that the three of us sit down to talk. I tell my mother that I feel she's ignoring my husband. I tell my husband that in Jewish families, there's a different attitude from the one he's used to. More emotional. I tell my mother I think the distrust she shows my husband may have to do with her tendency to associate him with my father—and with her distrust of men, in general. I tell Steve how much I love my mother, and that I want her here to take care of me.

When I'm finished talking, I feel I've done a good job of communicating how I feel in a way that shows them both my love. My mother unexpectedly announces, shortly after this, that she needs to return to Toronto immediately. Sydney needs her, she says. I'm disappointed, but too caught up in our baby to give much thought to my mother's abrupt departure.

Three days after my mother's return to Toronto, I call her collect, as I always do. I hear her voice say to the operator, "No, I don't accept the charges."

"Mum," I say. "You must've heard wrong. It's *Joyce*."

In a very cold voice this time, she says again, "I don't accept the charges." Then she hangs up. Hearing this, I fall to the floor.

Steve calls her back to ask what's going on. "I think it's better that Joyce and I discontinue our relationship," she tells him. "Clearly she doesn't want me in her life anymore."

Over the course of the months that follow, my sister attempts to sort out what has happened. She reports that my mother has said I made anti-Semitic comments to her. My mother relays her deep sense of betrayal at hearing Christian hymns played at my wedding the summer before. "How could Joyce do such a thing? There were Holocaust survivors in the congregation."

It's very cold in our house that winter. I partly blame Steve for leaving me to make the impossible choice between my husband and my mother. I ache to talk to her. I see my father, who is renting a small apartment with Laura in a nearby town, but my father has never been a person to offer support or care, least of all now. He reports that Laura is trying to kill him. He would like to "make an escape," but he cannot leave Nicky, his dog. He tells me his hands are so twisted he can barely drive, let alone paint. He needs to borrow money or he will be evicted from his apartment, and though we have very little ourselves, I give him three hundred dollars.

One day he calls in tears. My mother has sent him a letter in response to one of the dozens he has written to her. Now he reads it over the phone.

She doesn't want to hear from him, she tells him. She has nothing to say. She signs off with Drayton's "Sonnet on Parting," one of the first poems she and my father read together.

> *Nay, I have done, you get no more of me,*
> *And I am glad, yea glad with all my heart*
> *That thus so cleanly I myself can free.*
> *Shake hands forever, cancel all our vows,*

And when we meet at any time again
Be it not seen in either of our brows
That we one jot of former love retain....

She does not sign her letter "love," or even sign her name.

Audrey becomes the great joy of my life. After I have my daughter, I feel connected at last. At the supermarket, strangers come up and admire my baby. We talk about feeding and sleeping, teething and rashes, when the baby will smile, when she will stand, her long eyelashes.

The person I really want to show my daughter to is my mother, and she's not speaking to me, or sending me her wonderful typewritten letters full of funny stories. I send her letters, though. My letters are not about me, or the terrible rift that has taken place between us. Now, when I write to my mother, I simply give news of my daughter, and enclose snapshots. These she will be unable to resist, I know, even as she's resisting me.

Six months after she disowned me, my mother calls to say she'll be in New York visiting Joe and Joan. "I was thinking perhaps you'd feel like bringing the baby into the city," she says.

Of course I feel like it. I put on Audrey's red dress for the trip, with white lace tights and little knitted booties. Steve and I set out on the highway.

I am not sure how this happens, but just as we're approaching Manhattan, with me at the wheel to give Steve a break, the car goes into a 180-degree spin. I can see the car that's about to hit us, and even the horrified face of the driver as he slams into us. Miraculously, no one is hurt. We are even able to drive the Valiant the rest of the way into the city. When we get there, my mother is waiting for us.

"You brought her," she says.

Chapter Sixteen

OUR MARRIAGE CHANGES after Audrey's birth. We are parents, but less and less are we lovers. We also argue more about money, about who cares for the baby, about my wish that Steve would talk to me more, and his that I'd leave him alone.

He is spending long days in his studio. He also adores Audrey. He draws beautiful pictures of her, and when he goes for his run he bundles her up and puts her in the front pack on his chest, and cradles her head so she won't be too jostled.

But he was also raised in a family where child care fell to his mother. Steve burns to paint. He says he needs time alone. He wants to go running, and play sports, and do things a man can't do with a baby. Particularly since I am the only one who can feed her.

From the first, the roles we establish as parents are very different. I am just so happy to have a baby, I figure I can handle anything. I will care for her and write magazine articles and be a loving wife and lose the extra forty pounds.

But the effort leaves me weary. In my dream picture of motherhood, I see myself rocking by the fire with my infant in my arms, not propping her up on a pillow in the crook of my arm so I can simultaneously nurse her and type. In my dream picture, my husband comes home with a paycheck.

Several months before Audrey's birth, I had been approached by a small college in Southern California to deliver a talk about writing. The pay wasn't that much—five hundred dollars plus airfare—but I accepted. Now, with Audrey less than four weeks old, I board a plane bound for San Diego with my infant in my arms.

The flight makes her cranky. The time change disrupts her sleep. When the hour comes to deliver my speech, Audrey is wide awake and wailing. Accustomed to being fed on demand, she will be comforted by nothing but my breast. As the head of the English department concludes her introductory remarks, I unbutton my shirt and drape a borrowed blanket over me like a poncho. With Audrey concealed under the blanket and my arms around her wriggling body, I step out onto the stage to begin my remarks.

Twenty years later, I will meet a woman who was among the students in the audience that day. "At first we didn't understand," she tells me. "It just looked as if you were wearing some kind of shawl. But then there started to be all this movement under that blanket, as if something was alive under there, and you could see this little foot kicking. Then you explained."

When Audrey is six weeks old I get an assignment from *New York* magazine to do a story on houses of prostitution on the Upper East Side of Manhattan. Because I am a nursing mother, I take Audrey with me to New York, strapping her into her infant seat beside me when I drive into the city to conduct my research. Through an old contact, a detective I'd interviewed back in my reporting days, I get the name of the proprietor of an escort service who can only be reached by telephone so late at night it's almost time for my daughter's first feeding. He gives me the address of an East Side town house where one of the women he employs has agreed to talk to me at midnight the next day.

Audrey cries when I'm supposed to be taking notes. She doesn't want to be bundled into her front pack at an hour when she's accustomed to lying next to me in bed. By the second day of my trip, I realize that completing my assignment is impossible. Driving home with Audrey once again placid in her car seat, I have no idea how I will earn a living now. I am filled with despair.

When Steve first moved to New York City after college, he'd promised himself two years to become established in the city. He left before the two years were up. Now, the winter after Audrey's birth, we agree to leave the house in Hillsboro again and return to Manhattan. We sublet a loft space on West Twentieth Street and find a day-care situation for Audrey that will allow me to work half-days. In addition to spending more time taking his slides to galleries, Steve can get work as a housepainter again.

Shortly after our move—the week of Audrey's first birthday—I discover I'm pregnant again.

We have no money. We are also arguing a lot about all the old themes of money, child care, what Steve sees as my excessive need for intimacy and affection, and what I see as his distance and aloofness. Still, I cannot help feeling elated when I get the results of the pregnancy test, and I give Steve the news the minute he comes home from his painting job that night.

"There's no way we can have another baby," he says.

"It will hardly cost anything," I tell him. "We'll have a home birth again. We're already set up for babies. Taking care of two won't be that much different from taking care of one."

"I had other things I wanted to do with my life besides being a father," he says. His voice is flat. "I'm going for a walk," he tells me. When he returns, he says, "You know what we've got to do."

All that week, the prospect of my having an abortion hangs in the air. Steve says very little to me about this or anything else. He gets another of his paralyzing headaches. Audrey spends all of one night screaming with pain from an ear infection.

I remember how happy Steve was when we found out I was pregnant with Audrey. I picture the loneliness of a pregnancy he could not celebrate. I have never seen his mood so dark.

A week after getting the news of my pregnancy, I agree to the abortion. We are so broke we have to borrow money from Steve's housepainting partner to pay for it.

Steve is working, so I take a taxi alone to the Upper East Side for the procedure, after explaining to Audrey's babysitter, when I drop her off, that she'll be staying longer than usual.

In the waiting room, I study the faces of the other women. Most are very young, teenagers. A couple of them have come with their boyfriends. One rests her head on her mother's shoulder.

When it's my turn, I am led into a room and given a hospital gown. A nurse comes in to explain the procedure and gives me a mild sedative. I lie down on the table and put my feet in the stirrups.

It has not been a full year since I gave birth to Audrey, on our bed, with a double-wedding-ring quilt made by Steve's grandmother folded at the foot, snowdrifts against the window, and the smell of woodsmoke in the air. Now a fluorescent light flickers overhead as a tube is inserted into me. A moment later, the machine is turned on, and there is a terrible roar and a gurgling like water down the drain. Then it's over.

A few hours later, I come home. I wrap myself in blankets on the couch of the loft, but I can't stop shivering.

A couple of weeks later I write an article for *Redbook* magazine about having an abortion, in which I discuss my sorrow and ambivalence about the choice I made, but never address the terrible arguments Steve and I had leading up to it.

With the money from my magazine article, we are able to pay back Steve's friend, and some of our other outstanding bills. *The New York Times* invites me to write a series of six "Hers" columns to run over the course of the next month and a half. It is one of the best jobs a woman writer could ask for. But I continue to be haunted by a bone-deep sense of regret and loss. I feel myself becoming bitter toward Steve for persuading me to do something that felt so wrong.

From the day I have the abortion, I feel I am one child short. An obsession to have another takes hold.

Four months after we sublet the place in Manhattan, we return to New Hampshire. Every month now—whatever is happening in our lives, however badly we're getting along, however overworked, no matter how little money we have—I ask my husband again: "Can't we conceive a child?" I see a pregnant stranger and I turn to Steve. "Look," I say. "She gets to have a baby."

"Why don't you just appreciate the daughter you have, instead of harping on another one?" he says. I do adore her. But as she grows older, and I see her extraordinarily outgoing nature, and her longing to be with other children, I hold Audrey up to him, too.

"She should have a brother or sister," I say. "I'm the one taking care of her most of the time anyway. I could be taking care of two, instead of driving all over the countryside looking for friends for her to play with."

The night we visit our friends Laurie and Dave, and they announce that Laurie's pregnant again, just fifteen months after delivering their first child, I cry in the car all the way home. The more I talk about the subject, the more Steve resists. "You're going crazy, Joyce," he says. "I'm sick of hearing about this."

Because Steve has said we don't have enough money for a baby, I try to earn more. With no clue where I'm going, I write the first sentence of a novel I decide to call *Baby Love*. The novel I write is an invention, but at its center is the character of a young woman who is going through some of the same things I experienced in the desolate-feeling months after coming home from Daytona Beach and buying the house in Hillsboro. This character, too, has said good-bye to the great love of her life on a beach in Florida.

In the novel, I sketch out the bare outlines of a broken love affair between a young woman and her much older lover. Fueled with my obsession with having a child, I fill the book with young women who are pregnant or raising babies.

The novel I write deals with the experience of great, overwhelming love and attachment and a crippling sense of loss on the one hand, and sets those feelings in direct contrast with the experience of parenthood.

I write in a white heat of excitement. I finish the novel in a state of more pure happiness than I've known since the birth of my daughter.

I send the manuscript to my agent. The next week I receive a substantial offer from Knopf to publish the novel. I receive notes of praise from Joseph Heller and Raymond Carver. Flushed with pride, I send Jerry a copy of *Baby Love*.

Four days later the telephone rings.

"This is Jerry Salinger calling," he says. Knife in my heart. As if I wouldn't know. "I read this book you sent . . . this thing you call . . . your *novel*. . . . Though why you thought I'd want to see it I can't imagine." His speaks as if he were handling a piece of rotten meat.

"I thought you might like it," I say.

"I'm sickened and disgusted," he says. "What you sent me here is a piece of junk."

"What was wrong?" I ask him. "You told me to write about what I loved."

"*Love?* You have to be joking. Do you have no shame at all? This is nothing more than a tawdry, cheap-shot piece of perversion."

I am swooning. It's not just that I've written a novel Jerry doesn't respect, or that I bake with white flour, or that I had my daughter immunized.

There had been a time when I supposed the day might come that I could once again drive up to Cornish and sit with my baby on Jerry's deck. After I write *Baby Love,* I know there is no hope of ever finding my way back to him. In his eyes, I am one who has been shown the path and actively left it.

Shortly after the death of his dog, Nicky, my father announces that he's moving to British Columbia. He needs me to help him move out of his apartment in the middle of the night, he tells me, so Laura, who's away for the weekend, won't find out. He says she attacked him with a rolling pin recently. He's afraid of what she will do if she finds out he is leaving for good.

Although my father lived in Victoria as a young painter, except for a few brief visits, he hasn't been there in almost fifty years. His brothers and sisters are all long dead. He has one niece who lives in Victoria with her husband. Her son, Derek, who works for the Provincial Archives, has expressed an interest in my father's paintings. But Derek's promise to take my father's paintings to galleries hardly seems sufficient basis for a frail and nearly impoverished seventy-five-year-old man to make a several-thousand-mile move.

My father is adamant, however. In the end, I put him on the

plane. The only belongings he brings west with him are his books, his paints, and his lifetime's collection of paintings.

The first reports I receive from British Columbia after my father's departure from New Hampshire are surprisingly promising. Derek has helped him settle into a little one-room studio at a senior citizen's residence hotel in Victoria. Several old friends have come to visit. He is attending AA meetings, where he is already establishing himself as a rousing speaker on the subject of the ruination brought about by liquor. Several attractive women from his various AA groups, my father reports, now stop by to take him for drives along the ocean and out for tea.

"I don't intend to lead them on, chum," he tells me. "I'm finished with all that. Still, they're charming women. Delightful."

Within six months of his arrival in Victoria, paintings by Max Maynard are selling for several thousand dollars apiece. Not only has Derek kept his promise to show my father's work to art dealers in Victoria, my father has received an offer of gallery representation. He is invited to have a one-man show in Vancouver.

After I get the big check for *Baby Love*, Steve agrees we can have another baby. I get pregnant almost immediately.

When I was pregnant the first time, with Audrey, my excitement was all about the nearly magical event of watching a fetus develop into a baby, and awaiting my transformation into the role I had wanted for so long, that of *mother*. Now that I've been a mother for three years, what thrills me most about this pregnancy is the prospect of presenting our daughter with a sibling. Everything I didn't have with my own sister is everything I want for Audrey to have. The brother or sister is due just after her fourth birthday. I am barely six weeks pregnant when I give her the news that we're going to have a baby, and from the moment she learns it, she begins preparing for sisterhood.

I tell her she can take care of the baby. One day, to prepare her for her responsibilities, I buy a seven-pound ham and let Audrey carry it around the house. She ties a bonnet around the ham, and calls it Hamhead. By the time her baby sister or brother is born, she says, she will be strong enough to carry him wherever she goes.

* * *

Sometime in my second trimester of pregnancy, my father calls from British Columbia. He is taking a cruise to Alaska for the purpose of sketching the wildlife and glaciers along the route. He invites me to come. He is also proud that for the first time in his life, he might actually pay for such a trip. He would love to show me off to his friends in British Columbia—his sprightly daughter who knows so well just what to say to please and charm gentlemen of advancing age.

All those years when my father was living in New Hampshire following his divorce from my mother, drinking heavily and calling me up at night, I had lived with daily worry over what might happen to him. But now that he's three thousand miles away, and seemingly secure with his newfound artistic success and his redis-covered family, I have made the choice to distance myself from my father.

I know there is not much he would like more than to take me to Alaska and relive, again, our old days of sketching together, studying birds and wildlife and the way the light falls on a land-scape. But I am a mother now, more than a daughter. I have someone else to take care of besides him: my own child. And the baby on the way.

My father travels alone to Alaska. Onboard the cruise ship, he produces a wonderful group of paintings and drawings. He comes home with tales of ravishing and brilliant women who fell in love with him, whose advances he had to spurn. Even now, at close to eighty, he is courtly and dapper and charming.

But he also caught a cold onboard ship. A few weeks later, it turns to pneumonia. Bedridden in his residence hotel, my father sends out for a bottle of vodka. Then he orders another.

A friend finds him a few days later in a state combining pneu-monia with severe intoxication. He is hospitalized.

In January I travel to British Columbia to see him. I am seven months pregnant and have gained forty pounds. My face is round and full, my ankles swollen, my breasts filled out. I am dressed in a hand-me-down maternity jumper, and my skin is pale. With little time for vanity, I have cut my hair short.

Walking heavily into the hospital, on my way to see my father the evening of my arrival in Victoria, I catch sight of myself in a window and feel shame. I am embarrassed to have my father see me this way: so large, so visibly and undeniably a *woman*, as opposed to the skinny girl in whom he had delighted, and for whom he believed such wonderful promise lay ahead.

"Ah, chum," he says, as he catches sight of me, leaning over the bed. *"Look at you."*

I put my arms around him. I have brought English marmalade and cashews and tinned oysters. I pull up a chair, and he tells me the story of a nurse who has evidently taken a shine to him. "Charming girl," he says. "Nothing will come of it, of course. But I gave her a drawing."

On the dresser beside the bed, I see a stack of sketches made on paper place mats. The line is less steady than usual, but still identifiable as his.

He asks about Steve's artwork. I show him pictures of Audrey and a drawing she made of the three of us and her imaginary baby brother or sister. Unlike my sister at this age, and possibly even me, my daughter cannot recognize a Caravaggio or point out the difference between Monet and Manet. But my father puts on his glasses to examine her stick figures. "Take a twenty-dollar bill out of my wallet, would you, my dear?" he says. "I want you to buy her a box of Cray Pas. We can't have her doing without art supplies."

I stay in Victoria three days. We reminisce about his days as a young painter in Canada, talk of his hopes for my sister and me— and about my mother, for whom he expresses the oddest combination of bitterness and extreme admiration. "What a brilliant, marvelous woman," he sighs. "Never met another like her. What a waste."

On the day I'm due to leave Victoria, I stop by the hospital one last time. My father wants to take a walk to the sun room with me. When I arrive, he has shaved and combed his hair, and though he's dressed in pajamas and a bathrobe, he's tucked an ascot around his neck.

With some effort, he sits up and swings his legs over the side of the bed. His legs are thin and white. He asks me to take a pair of socks out of the drawer for him.

They are good wool argyle socks. Unlike my mother, my father has never shopped for bargains. There's a hole in the toe that my mother would have darned.

"I want to teach you something, chum," he says to me. In the past, at moments like this, he has reminded me to work on my crawl stroke, or (his perennial theme) to read the Old Testament. But what he does now is show me his method for putting on socks. His mother taught him this when he was just a little boy, he says, but now, with the arthritis so bad in his fingers, it has come in handy. "You never know. Your children might find this useful sometime," he says.

Instead of putting one's foot into the whole sock, he tells me, and having to work the toes around, a fellow can begin by turning the sock partially inside out, in such a way that all he needs to do is stick his toe into the toe portion of the sock, and then peel the rest of the inside-out sock down onto the foot. "Look," he says. I watch him slowly demonstrate with his pale white foot, first one, then the other.

"I'll remember that," I say and kiss him. Later, in the hallway, as I'm running out the door to my waiting taxi, a nurse stops me. "Your father," she says. "You know, we're all in love with him."

It's late March, the end of another long New Hampshire winter. My husband is stretched out on our living room couch watching the Celtics. Larry Bird is at the top of his game. Every now and then I hear Steve's voice from the other room, celebrating another two points or cursing a failed foul shot. Boston's winning tonight.

Nine months pregnant, I'm in the kitchen by the woodstove, baking. My long history of eating disorders, coupled with frequent periods of financial anxiety in our marriage, has left me with a strong desire to hoard food for the future. A notebook hanging by a string from the freezer door lists its contents: Six lasagnas. Four chicken casseroles. Spanokopita. Four apple pies and three blueberry. Thirteen quarts of raspberries. A half dozen loaves of poppy seed cake.

By this time of night the brownies I've just baked to freeze are cooling on the counter and I'm cleaning up the kitchen. It's ten-thirty and I'll be going to bed soon. My husband will stay up to watch the end of the game.

The phone rings. It's a woman calling from British Columbia, an AA friend of my father's whom I met back in January when I flew to Victoria to visit him in the hospital. She tells me that my father has taken a turn for the worse. He's in an oxygen tent and his blood pressure is dropping. He's not expected to live through the night.

There's nothing to be done. He's not conscious. I can't talk to him. I could call my mother in Toronto, or my sister. But every time the subject of my father comes up between my mother and me there is tension between us. For my sister, our father's death will be a deeply complicated and upsetting event, but I know enough about her darkly critical assessment of him and how profoundly she believes he failed her to know that even his impending death is unlikely to arouse tender or sentimental feeling. So at the moment of my father's approaching death, there is no one to call.

My longing for closeness with a sibling colors my thoughts about the baby on the way. Like me, this child will be born four years and a month after its older sister. I don't speak of this out loud, but I hope for a boy. The only story I know of two sisters, four years apart, is about distance and separateness—a sorrowful collusion of silence. If the phone rings in the night for one of my children one day, telling her that a parent is dying, I hope the first person she calls is her brother or sister.

I put down the receiver. My hand is trembling. I cry out to Steve, who doesn't hear me right away. "My father's dying," I say, leaning against the counter, crying. Steve comes into the room and puts an arm around me.

My body's shaking. I am feeling more violently ill than I can ever remember. I feel as though my insides are being twisted and wrung out. Steve helps me into the bedroom. By this time I'm shaking so violently that Steve has to lie down on top of me to steady me.

Moaning and weeping, I pace between the bathroom and the bed. A searing pain overtakes me. Then comes a deep, low groan that I've known only one other time in my life. I am lying down and holding my belly. I lift up my nightgown. Our baby's head is crowning.

Steve runs into the kitchen to call the midwife, although there's no way she could make the twenty-five-mile trip to our house in time. I scream. *Come here. Come here.* When he does, I grip his hand so tightly my fingernails leave a mark.

"I'll be right back," he says. "I need to go outside and have a smoke."

Clutching him harder, I cry out, "Don't leave me!"

"I'll only be gone a couple of minutes," he says.

"You don't understand," I say, calling out as he's leaving. "I need you. Don't go."

I follow him, bent over, one hand between my legs.

Steve turns and looks at me. "You're losing control, Joyce," he says. "I just need to collect my thoughts."

I am on the floor, holding on to his leg as he reaches for the door handle. "Get a grip, Joyce," he says. "You're hysterical."

My hands grab at his boot. He shakes me off. He steps out the door and I crawl after him. From where I kneel on the floor of our porch, I can see Steve standing in our snowy driveway. I'm screaming as he lights his cigarette.

Flooded with a sense of pure desolation, I drag myself back into the house and onto the bed. Steve returns. He kneels between my legs and slips a couple of fingers inside. In one explosive burst, our new baby is in his hands. "It's a boy," he shouts.

Some time after we put the baby on my breast, the midwife arrives. I can hear the sound of her shaking the snow off her boots and the voice of my husband, asking about her drive and the condition of the roads.

We have waited for her arrival before cutting the cord. Now she lifts the baby to clean him off. He's pink and fat and responsive, a ten on the Apgar scale. She estimates he's a ten-pounder.

"I guess you two didn't really need me," she jokes.

Steve says, "Lucky for us I was just looking over my Fireman's

Emergency Preparedness Manual yesterday. That's how I remembered to check around the baby's neck for the cord." His voice is relaxed and celebratory.

I get off the bed so the midwife can put on fresh sheets. She hands me our baby.

After the midwife leaves, Steve turns off the television set, which has been on the whole time. The basketball game has just ended. He climbs into bed. "So, we'll name him Charles?" he says. His father's name. Also his older brother's.

Some time around six or seven, Audrey comes into our room. Before I have a chance to tell her the news, she spots the dark tuft of still-damp hair on the baby's head.

"My dream came true," she says as she climbs in next to us.

Until this moment, I hadn't faced the realization that it's morning now, and my father wasn't supposed to make it through the night. I rush to the phone.

He has taken a surprising turn for the better, and I am able to describe his new grandson to him. In a few weeks, my father is attending the opening of the show of his Alaska paintings.

But a death has occurred here. I feel it that morning, and try as I will to obliterate it, the memory stays with me. It is the memory of Steve's boot. I see my hands grasping his ankle. He shakes me off and disappears out the door.

My father dies six months later. I fly to British Columbia for the funeral. In the coffin my father looks very small in a tweed jacket, with a blue ascot and his hands folded in front of him holding a fedora. The rug we had woven in Mexico years ago, made from his drawing of the horse, hangs at the front of the church as friends come forward with their memories. One old friend reminisces about my father's performance, at seventeen, in a production of *Richard III*. Another, who was a student long ago in a class of elementary school children my father taught in the rural British Columbian territory of the Okanagan, tells about the day my father introduced the children to the work of Cézanne and Van Gogh, and another time when he read the children the entire poem of "The Lady of Shalott," and even though they were very young, and tired, and hungry for lunch, nobody had wanted him to stop. Jack Shadbolt, my father's painter friend, stands at the podium and demonstrates my father's strong, rhythmic crawl stroke.

Someone else tells the story of a time when, as a young man, my father spent all night outside the apartment of a woman he was in love with, painting a mural on her wall of the two of them dancing half-clothed in a forest like characters in a bacchanalia.

"I have never known anyone to fuse himself so passionately with what he was doing," another friend says. "He possessed an astonishing capacity for ecstasy. I never knew a man to love art the way Max Maynard did."

Chapter Seventeen

NOTHING I'VE EVER done has suited me as well as raising my children. Not that I don't experience exhaustion and frustration and impatience and, sometimes, outbursts of anger that remind me alarmingly of my father. But I feel a kind of peace and comfort I have never known before.

As my daughter grows, and when her brother joins her, my children bring me into the world. Because I want them not to know the fears I grew up with, I take them to a ski mountain where I can barely stand up myself. At six, Audrey rides with me on the chairlift that I haven't dared get on since that one time when I was a child myself. She, who has no fear, tells me when to lift the bar and when to lower my skis in the snow.

In certain ways, I approach the raising of our children as my parents did: Every night, Audrey and Charlie and I pile into the bed with a stack of books. Even during times when we have very little money, we always have art supplies and ice skates and bicycles. When spring comes and the ice thaws, my children and I make little boats the way I did with my father when I was young. We launch our boats in Beard Brook, running beside them on shore as they bob along, until we lose sight of them. In the summers, we catch frogs and swim every day in the pond we've dug beside our house. In the winter, Steve clears the pond for skating and builds a sled run in back of our house. He brings the children into the studio and paints murals with them. We tap our trees for maple syrup and make apple cider and dollhouses and rocket ships and Barbie clothes and sculptures and forts.

Over the years, I go to the kinds of lengths that my mother would have to provide our children with magical experiences and educational enrichment. When Audrey's four, I send her to a preschool thirty miles from home. Because it takes an hour to get there, her baby brother and I spend the day in the nearby town of Keene, swimming at the Y and going to the library until it's time to pick her up. Hearing that the Ramses Egyptian exhibition is at the Boston Science Museum and won't be back on this continent within our lifetimes, I haul my children and a few of their friends to Boston—a trip in which I lose my toddler son while tending to my daughter, who has just thrown up from carsickness. Observing my two-year-old son's passion for the Michael Jackson *Thriller* video, I get an assignment from the *Times* to write about taking Charlie to see Michael Jackson perform at the Meadowlands in New Jersey. Needing to be home the next morning, we drive back to New Hampshire that night, after the show.

When Audrey's less than six, I start bringing her to New York City a couple of times a year. We ride buses, subways, and escalators, and I walk her through revolving doors. I take her to see the Calder circus, which my mother brought me to see on my own first trip to Manhattan when I was twelve. There's so much I want Audrey to take in: the whale at the Museum of Natural History and the *Water Lilies* room at the Museum of Modern Art, and the stretch of shops in midtown, on the West Side, that sell beads and interesting hat trimmings, which we buy to sew onto her overalls and dresses. When we need a bathroom, I take her to the one at the Plaza.

I take her to plays, and to hear Pete Seeger and Arlo Guthrie sing at Carnegie Hall, and to the offices of *The New York Times*, and to Gramercy Park, where I point out the terraces of my old apartment. We drive to the city to see *The Nutcracker* at Lincoln Center, where she studies the outfits of the other children as closely as the ballerinas. Later, back home, in the art classes she conducts for Charlie, though he's just two, I hear her instructing him, "Today's lesson is how to draw a rich girl."

Our children register the tension that exists between their father and me. Still, I believe we are managing to give them a secure home life and the assurance that their well-being does not depend on what they achieve. I don't teach my children to write at an early age.

I am haunted by the abortion and by what happened on the night of Charlie's birth. I begin to believe I can erase the memories if we have another baby.

This time I don't discuss it with Steve. Our third child is conceived.

That winter, Steve decides to rent a part-share in a studio space in New York City to use as a base when he takes his slides around to galleries. I stay home with Audrey and Charlie. During the long afternoons, when the sun sets at three thirty, and the temperature outside is below zero, Charlie takes his nap and Audrey and I snuggle together on the couch watching reruns of *The Loveboat*.

There's something alluring about the vision of life on the cruise ship—the endless carefree limbo onboard the boat, where everyone falls in love and problems are always resolved. "Wouldn't it be great if we could sail away on the *Loveboat*?" Audrey says.

I get the address of the Cunard Lines. Seven months pregnant, I write the company a letter, offering my services as a shipboard lecturer on the subject of writing. I hear nothing back.

Steve is invited to show his paintings in Savannah, the best opportunity he's had since our marriage. The date they've scheduled for the opening is the day our baby's due to be born.

Steve points out that my friend Laurie can be with me for the baby's birth.

"You're an old pro by this time," he says. "It'll be a piece of cake."

Neither of our children has been born early, but with Steve due to leave for Georgia in five days, I buy a bottle of castor oil and drink the whole thing in one sitting. I get sick and go into labor.

Willy's birth goes well. This time the contractions are manageable enough that I can breathe my way through them and rest before the next one. He is also a ten-pound baby, but his entry into the world is less sudden and violent than his brother's.

During my pregnancy, I had told Steve I didn't want to give the baby his first name, if it should be a boy. But now that the baby's here he says, again, "Let's name him Stephen." I agree. But only if we call him by his middle name.

Audrey's at school when he's born, and Charlie has been sent to our town's day-care center for the morning. He's been told he was going to be a big brother, but at twenty-three months old, he hasn't grasped the idea, until he gets home that afternoon, and finds Willy in our bed, nursing.

I can still see Charlie as he was that day: a little stunned, sucking the thumb of one hand and resting his other hand on top of Willy's head. For years after that, whenever the two of them sit together in the car, or on the couch beside me, reading, Charlie arranges himself with his thumb in his mouth and a particular blue ribbon he likes wrapped around his middle finger, and his other hand resting on top of Willy's head as if he's maintaining an electrical connection. If he's playing with a friend, his baby brother sits watching in his infant seat. Charlie never passes through the room without touching the top of his brother's head.

Audrey's birthday falls two days after Willy's birth. We give her a pair of roller skates, and Steve takes her out to his studio to try them out. Five minutes later he carries her back to the house. She's fallen on the skates and broken her arm.

The next day Steve flies to Savannah for the opening of his show. More snow falls.

Steve comes back five days later. We have scheduled Audrey's birthday party for that weekend, with twenty children coming to our house. "You get hysterical when you're getting ready for a birthday party," Steve says, as he leaves for a day of skiing. Late that afternoon I get a call from the ski slope informing me that my husband has taken a bad fall and I'd better come pick him up.

I buckle the children in and drive to the ski area, arriving in darkness to find Steve barely conscious and in great pain. We have no medical insurance. It will be months before Steve can work again. The doctor says his wrist is shattered and he may not have full use of his left hand. He will need orthopedic surgery, but not until the swelling goes down.

The next day twenty children arrive for Audrey's party. We play the usual round of games. When everyone's gone, I go to find Steve in his studio. He's lying on a mat with his jaw clenched.

I take him to the hospital a few days later. In a five-hour surgery, the orthopedic surgeon inserts a metal plate in his wrist, then puts him in a cast, prescribes more painkillers, and tells us to seek good physical therapy once he's well enough. Instead, Steve chooses to become a sheetrocker, the most grueling and punishing of the carpentry trades. He eventually regains full use of his wrist.

With close to ten thousand dollars' worth of uninsured medical expense racked up from Steve's and Audrey's accidents, I lie awake thinking about how to earn money, making lists of articles I'll write. Willy learns to hold his head up and crawl. He holds a bottle younger than any baby I have ever seen.

When Willy's less than three months old, a call comes from the Cunard Lines, to whom I'd written my *Loveboat* letter months before. They want to know if we can be ready to sail on the Queen Elizabeth 2, from New York to Southampton and back—a ten-day, round-trip voyage—the following Monday. They will provide me with expense-paid, first-class passage for two in exchange for two shipboard lectures about writing.

Our infant son is still breastfeeding, and our older son has just turned two. Our daughter is just getting out of her cast. Steve is still experiencing a lot of pain and feels that the rest of a cruise might help his recovery.

A young single mother we know agrees to stay at our house and care for our children while we're gone. I buy a breast pump in the hopes of keeping my milk from drying up while I'm away from Willy. Steve borrows a beautiful white dinner jacket from Laurie's father for formal dining onboard ship, and a tux. Not having lost all of my pregnancy weight, I borrow a couple of loose-fitting evening gowns.

In the photographs taken by the roaming ship's photographer and posted each day on a board outside the shuffleboard courts, Steve could be a senator or a diplomat. In one, he is shaking the hand of the ship's captain. His arm was still giving him a lot of pain, but he is no longer wearing his sling. His handshake appears vigorous and his smile is open and friendly.

I look rougher around the edges. Three months after Willy's birth, I still have dark circles under my eyes and the full breasts and rounded stomach of a nursing mother.

During the day we sit on our deck chairs and read or talk with other passengers. Three times a day I retreat to our cabin and put the breast pump to my breasts to keep my milk flowing. One time I carry it above deck and pour it into the Atlantic Ocean.

Nights onboard ship, there is ballroom dancing. I love to dance, and Steve is a good dancer. But we do not take to the floor. We sit at our table, sipping our drinks, watching the dancing couples swirl around the room.

The ship's comedian stops by our table. "Try this out on your kids," he says. He folds a dollar bill so it forms the shape of a C and places it in my palm.

"Say 'wing' three times."

"Wing. Wing. Wing," I say.

He picks up the dollar bill as if it were a telephone receiver and speaks into it. "Hewo? Hewo? Hewo."

"I think I'll call it a night," says Steve.

Chapter Eighteen

NOW AND THEN, some reporter writing a Salinger story calls me, looking for a comment, as one or two did when Mark David Chapman was discovered to have had a copy of *Catcher in the Rye* with him when he shot John Lennon outside the Dakota apartment building. When Jerry Salinger's name comes up I have a set response. "I knew him a long time ago," I say. "I don't talk about him."

I am invited to a party in New York City, celebrating the publication of a collection of essays by women writers, in which several *New York Times* "Hers" columns I'd written were reprinted. The party is held on the top floor of a lavish apartment building overlooking Central Park West, and there are many women writers present.

The writer Phyllis Theroux approaches me. "I was hoping to meet you," she tells me. "A couple of years ago I hired an au pair to help with my children. She was unpacking when I happened to walk past her room and saw this packet of letters on her bed. I asked her what they were. 'Oh, those,' she said. 'Those are my letters from Jerry Salinger.' I asked if she meant J. D. Salinger. She did."

If there was going to be more to the story, I never hear it. My knees buckle and I feel sick. I walk away, unable to speak.

My encounter with Phyllis Theroux lasts no more than three minutes. But the world looks different afterward. I finished grieving the loss of Jerry Salinger years ago. A few years after that, I grieved a second loss when I recognized his contempt for the writer I'd become. Now, when I thought I had no more to lose, comes a fresh devastation.

All these years, I had believed I held a singular place in Jerry Salinger's life. He didn't love me anymore, but I never questioned that how he had loved me once was different from how he had ever loved anybody else. I held on to the belief—like something from a country song—that just as I would never again feel the connection and attachment I'd once known with him, neither would he feel it for anybody else. I carried that belief all those years, like a pearl tucked in my pocket. I fingered it now and then. I might not have grown into a woman Jerry Salinger could adore. But I never questioned that he had adored the girl I once was as he had never adored any other.

Now, standing in that roomful of successful women writers, with my drink in my hand, and the lights of Manhattan glittering below, I feel excommunicated. My letters from J. D. Salinger were my secret treasure, proof of my specialness. It had never occurred to me that some other girl elsewhere might be in possession of letters, too.

I am given the job of writing the monthly book review column for *Mademoiselle* magazine. Every day now, the UPS truck pulls up to our house with packages of books and book galleys for me to read. One day a galley arrives of a biography of J. D. Salinger by Ian Hamilton.

I read the title, *In Search of J. D. Salinger*. There was a time when just the mention of his name filled me with a sense of loss. I told myself long ago I was done with that.

I flip through the galley only briefly. Although it's clear that Hamilton is a serious and respectful literary biographer, Salinger did not cooperate in any way with the preparation of this book. The Hamilton biography relies to a great degree on excerpts from letters Jerry Salinger had written to various friends and editors between the years 1939 and the early sixties. These were letters whose recipients had given or sold them to university libraries, where Hamilton had tracked them down.

I put the book down. Some time later, I receive word from Hamilton's publishers, Random House, explaining that the galleys

I originally received have now been blocked from publication. Having learned about the extensive quotations from his letters in the Hamilton biography, Salinger has registered copyrights for his unpublished letters, and is now charging Hamilton and his publishers with violation of copyright.

The original ruling in the case finds in favor of Ian Hamilton and his publishers. Although the ruling recognizes Salinger as the copyright owner of letters he wrote, the judge finds that the portions of letters Hamilton quoted or paraphrased are sufficiently slight as to fall under the category of fair use.

That decision is later overturned by a stunning decision of the higher Court of Appeals, which rules that there can be virtually no fair use of unpublished material such as letters, and that Hamilton's quotations and paraphrasings are sufficiently extensive to constitute copyright infringement.

I take in the saga of Ian Hamilton's attempts to publish his Salinger biography with no more than fleeting attention, and in all the months it takes to play out, I never again pick up the galleys. When Ian Hamilton's biography of J. D. Salinger is finally published in a vastly altered form, I can't bear to read it.

Steve is working as a sheetrocker now. He comes home exhausted, pours himself a beer, roughhouses with the children before dinner, watches a game, and goes to bed early.

He has an idea about a kind of painting he wants to do. Bodyprints, he calls them. He will cover a naked body with paint and lay the body like a human rubber stamp on a piece of canvas. The body he uses is mine.

It's winter and the uninsulated wood-heated studio never gets that warm. Steve heats the paint on the stove for me. Standing close to the stove, I strip away my clothes. He slathers my body with vaseline and applies the warm paint with a roller.

Pieces of canvas are already laid out on the floor. I lower myself onto them one at a time, and press my body against the surface to make a strong impression. Steve helps me get up in such a way that I won't smear the paint.

There's no water in the studio so I run back into the house naked, covered in paint, and step into the shower. I stand there a long time, scrubbing carefully to get every bit of paint off my breasts because I'm still nursing my son.

We're out of money again, and the difficulty of earning a living goes beyond the problem of finding time to get to my desk. Once I get there, I can no longer imagine a story.

After the publication of *Baby Love*, my editor at Knopf has succeeded in getting me an advance for an untitled second novel. For months now I've been receiving checks that are supposed to be supporting me while I write the novel. Instead, I had a baby. The money's gone.

I tell my editor I can't deliver a novel. I don't know how to be a serious writer and a mother.

Of the fairy tales I read to my children at night, one that has always held a particular power for me is the story of the miller's daughter who spins straw into gold. Every night she is shut into a room with a pile of straw. Every morning, when they let her out, a pile of gold sits in its place.

I have always said I know how to fix bad writing. I learned how from all those gatherings of my mother's students in our living room while I was growing up. I can put a red pen on someone else's sentences.

I call up an old editor friend of my mother's from *Good House-keeping* whom I first met on that trip to New York when I was ten. She's working at *Family Circle* now. With the image of the miller's daughter and her spinning in my mind, I make her an offer.

"I will come to New York for two days a month," I say. "Put me in an office at the magazine. Pile manuscripts on my desk. I don't care what they're about or who wrote them. I'll make them publishable. I don't need my name in the magazine. I have no interest in a byline. I want a check for a thousand dollars every month."

So once a month I leave our children with Steve and a babysitter, and drive to New York City. Some months before, when my "Hers" columns were appearing in the *Times*, I got a letter from a mother of four, Vicky, saying she liked my writing, and would like to be my friend. Now, on my trips to *Family Circle*, I spend the night at Vicky and her husband's house in Brooklyn Heights. My days are much as I'd promised the editor they would be. She gives me manuscripts in need of attention and I tidy them up. The magazine has also retained the services of an eminent baby doctor who knows more about babies than about magazine writing. I am enlisted to help.

In many ways, I am replaying my mother's story. Not just with the writing for women's magazines—ghostwriting, even—but also in the compromises I've made in my marriage.

Trying to maintain the appearance of well-being, I become obsessed with keeping my children's possessions in order. I tiptoe into their rooms at night, like a crazy person, to sort their Legos into bins: red, blue, yellow, white. I line up Charlie's Smurfs in neat rows along the windowsill. One day, when Audrey loses the shoe from her new Crystal Barbie, I spend hours tearing up every room in our house, searching for it. Another time, Charlie drops an inch-long plastic pirate sword out the window of our station wagon, the very thing I had warned him would happen. I circle that stretch of highway eight times with my high-beam lights on, looking for the sword in the road until I find it.

I write an article for *Family Circle* called "Motherhood Burnout." The piece is filled with quotations from many overwhelmed mothers. Everything said in that article actually came from me.

As my life increasingly resembles my mother's, I find myself resenting her so deeply that it's now almost impossible for us to be together. My sister tells me stories of our mother's life in Canada—the party she throws for a hundred men, and no women; the one in which she hires a troupe of Shakespearean actors to mill through the rooms, periodically breaking into the performance of a scene in which my mother will take the leading female role each time.

Hearing the stories, I feel my usual odd mix of responses: mortification and pride. Love and dismay. Longing and fear to see her. I want to go to Toronto but I'm also afraid she'll reject me again.

I send a substitute: my daughter.

From the age of four, Audrey flies alone from Boston to Toronto to visit her grandmother, whom she calls Grandma Del. I know my mother will be exciting company for Audrey. I know she will do all the things a little girl would love—take her out for milk shakes at a fancy restaurant, bake cookies, cut out paper dolls, let her dress up in many fancy outfits and hats. She will tell Audrey stories that might or might not be true, better than any show she could watch on TV. She will let her fingerpaint with chocolate pudding, and take her to a ribbon factory, where she can fill up a shopping bag with scraps of any kind of ribbon she wants, and when they come home, she and Audrey will sew doll clothes and bake pies and get manicures. My mother will be, for Audrey, a very nearly magical person.

My daughter will love my mother, and my mother will not be critical or judgmental about my daughter when she visits in Toronto. And later, when I pick her up at the airport and gather her in my arms, I can imagine the times my mother and my daughter shared, and remember how it used to be with her when I myself was young. That night I call my mother and we talk about what a wonderful little girl Audrey is. She tells me all the things they did on their visit.

"Did she tell you about the other day, when I let her take down all my silk scarves?" my mother says. "She pushed all these chairs together and draped the scarves over them to make a playhouse. We had baked a miniature pie, just the size for her dolls. She arranged them on a little table in the tent. Then Joyce said . . ."

"*Audrey*," I tell my mother.

"Right," she corrects herself. "I meant Audrey."

Chapter Nineteen

IN THE SPRING of 1984, not long after Willy's birth, I'm invited by *The New York Times* newspaper syndicate to launch a weekly column about family life. More than twenty papers sign up to run "Domestic Affairs."

Through my weekly column, readers come to know that Charlie sucks his thumb and has a deeply contemplative, philosophical bent; that Audrey possesses a virtually unquenchable optimism and love of friends, strangers, her brothers; that if someone in our family gets into trouble, odds are high it'll be Willy, but he'll be so funny, it's hard not to laugh even if we're scolding him. About my marriage, I remain vague. My stories have made it plain that Steve is a man of few words, that I'm a woman of many. "Cut to the chase," he tells me when I take too long recounting my experiences.

I learned storytelling from my mother, a woman who talked herself into her life by using the most powerful tool in her possession, her own words. Like my mother, I practice revisionist storytelling, creating a family mythology more comfortable than the real one that I can't bear to acknowledge. A dazzlingly skillful writer, my mother used words to protect herself from discomfiting truths as much as to reveal them. "Write the way you speak," she used to tell me. Often, I spoke like my mother, too—the very thing Jerry Salinger told me he hated about me.

I know that Steve is not entirely comfortable with my writing about our family as I do, though there are areas I recognize as off-limits. When people ask me what my husband thinks about the column, I always tell them the truth: He doesn't read it.

In the early days of "Domestic Affairs," I tended to focus on the humorous aspects of family life and child-raising. I am Lucy, Steve is Desi. We disagree, we fight, but in the end, our names are always intertwined within a big valentine heart, and I end up reminding myself how lucky I am and how good our life is. Often, too, I reveal myself to have been foolish and impetuous. I cast my husband in the role of the strong and silent type, reeling me in when my emotional nature gets the better of me.

I tell the story about a time I take an unexpected windfall check and use it for an impulse purchase of a two-thousand-dollar oriental rug at a time when we have little money to spare and live in a house furnished with yard-sale purchases. We argue, and Steve makes me return the rug. In the column, I end up acknowledging the good sense of his firm actions, and my own foolishness for buying the rug. I do not say that the windfall check was, like most checks that come our way, earned by me. I do not allow myself to examine fully the yearning and frustration, and the absence of autonomy I felt that had led me to buy the rug in the first place without consulting my husband.

Although I say in the column that I lose my temper, I do not tell the whole story of my rages, or the times I say to Steve in the middle of an argument, "I'm going to jump out of this car." I tell about my disappointment when he gives me a pressure cooker for my birthday, but not about his own when I fail to acknowledge what it meant that he had replastered our bedroom for our tenth anniversary. The knife cuts both ways. I do not quote his remark to me, justifying why I should perform more household tasks than he, because "I expend more calories sheetrocking." But neither do I fully examine what it means for a man longing to be a painter to pack a lunchbox every morning and head off to construction sites to hang drywall.

In the column I write about the night of Charlie's birth, I tell only the part in which Steve singlehandedly delivers our son, after first checking to make sure the cord's not wrapped around his neck. I don't tell the other part, about the cigarette and the boot, or the time when I felt such frustration at his seeming indifference to me that I stood with a pair of scissors poised open over one of my braids and told him, "I'm cutting off my hair."

"It's your hair," he said.

My inability to speak honestly leaves a bitter taste in my mouth. But in spite of my selective retelling of my family's story, I have come a long way from my old *Looking Back* days. In small ways, I try to make it clear in my writing that the family living at the end of this particular dead-end road in New Hampshire, like the families of most people reading the column, is struggling every day and falling far short of perfection. I also mean to honor the unglamorous and uncelebrated work of people raising children and maintaining a home.

For the second time in my writing life, I hear back from large numbers of readers. Every week now a big envelope arrives from my syndicate in New York filled with long, heartfelt letters from all over the country.

The relationship that I develop with readers after I've been writing the column for a while is unlike any I have ever found. People write to say they feel they know me. They make it part of their routine, Saturday mornings, to check in and see what I've been thinking about, and what's been happening at our house. I come to know the look of their handwriting on the envelope, and the names of their husbands and children. I put their photographs on my bulletin board, and soon it's covered with the images of women I've never met. These voices of strangers in my mailbox— the very kinds of voices Jerry Salinger once warned me about— become a sort of lifeline.

The reason why so many women send me letters is that, in a quiet and cautious way, I have been talking about the conflicted side of motherhood and marriage in the pages of their newspaper. Some people may suppose that all I'm doing here is telling funny little stories about kids' high jinks and comical husband-and-wife tiffs, but the women who write to me know better. They sense my sadness and loneliness, and go through their days feeling some of the same longing.

These letters have a powerful effect on me over the eight years I write "Domestic Affairs." The columns I write in the later years still contain funny stories, but they are less likely to conclude with tidy endings.

Some years later, when I announce in my newspaper column that my husband and I are separating, many readers write to express shock and dismay, or even sharp criticism. They knew things weren't perfect, they write. Things never are. But we had such a loving marriage.

Other people write to say they saw it all the time. It was always there between the lines. It was even in the oddly melancholy, tense-looking photograph on the cover of my book of collected "Domestic Affairs" columns—a picture of me with our three children at my side, standing in front of our house in New Hampshire. My eyes look red for good reason: I was crying before the photographer arrived because Steve didn't want to appear in the photograph.

Perceptive readers could see my marriage was falling apart. One, a columnist in the Portland *Oregonian*, even wrote a column herself, speculating that "Joyce and Steve are in trouble" and pointed to a poll I had recently conducted in which I'd invited readers to write to me with their views concerning marital fidelity. When I traveled to one city to address an audience of column readers, I was amazed at the size of the crowd that showed up to hear me. The first thing one of them wanted to know when I opened the discussion for questions was "Did you ever get another oriental rug?"

"No," I said, smiling.

"*Do it,*" she told me. "It's cheaper than a divorce."

That night I called my husband, home in New Hampshire with our children. "You wouldn't believe it," I told him. "A thousand people turned up to hear me speak."

"Just don't come home with a swelled head," he said.

Later, when people would ask me how I knew my marriage was falling apart, I say, "I read my columns in the paper."

* * *

One day the surveyor drives up. "We're making new maps of town," he says. "Since you and your family are the only ones that live on this road, you can pick the name."

I save the announcement about naming the road as a treat to lay out for the family over dinner. "Imagine," I say. "From here on out, every map they make of Hillsboro will show the name we choose printed for everyone to see."

Willy, who is three, wants to name it Dead-End Road. Charlie's choice is Happy Road. Audrey wants to call it Fifth Avenue. Steve wants the road to bear his own last name.

Giving Steve's family name to this piece of property feels like an eradication of me. I wouldn't want to name the road *Maynard* either. I want a name that represents all of us.

We don't argue so much. Our disagreement leaves us, as they often do, with silence.

Charlie has sucked his thumb since he was a baby. As he approaches kindergarten, he decides he wants to quit. I take him to an orthodontist, who for $150 fits him with a retainer that will make thumbsucking so uncomfortable he'll give it up. The first night he gets the retainer he cries softly in his bed. When I can't stand his sorrow and suggest that he take the retainer out, just this first night, he shakes his head and says, "I'm going to stick it out."

The next day I drive Audrey and two of her friends to the city of Keene, thirty miles from Hillsboro, where they take a gymnastics class. I always take my sons along, and afterward we all go out for hamburgers.

It's close to eight o'clock by the time we leave the restaurant. We're halfway home and everyone is exhausted when Charlie lets out a small gasp. He has left his retainer on the table at the restaurant.

I turn my station wagon around and make the drive back to Keene. Friendly's is just closing as we pull up. Our waitress didn't find any retainer when she cleaned off our table. "Maybe it's in the trash."

"Where's the trash?" I say. She points to a large Dumpster on the side of the building.

I rearrange the children's backpacks and gymnastics clothes to make room for four enormous bags of garbage.

When we get back to our house, I put the children to bed and lay newspaper over our entire kitchen floor. I drag in the trash and, bag by bag, spread it all out on the newspaper and pick through french fries and bits of burger buns and pickles. The next morning, hearing that I didn't find the retainer, Charlie tells me he will give up sucking his thumb, and he does.

I am patient and tender with my children most of the time. But I'm exhausted and depleted and lonely and frustrated. Now and then—more frequently, as the years pass—I explode. Sometimes at my husband. Sometimes our children.

It happens once on Christmas morning. For the last two weeks, I've stayed up late, baking and sewing, shopping at three A.M. one night when a local department store announced it would stay open for twenty-four hours to help busy shoppers. We've thrown a party for fifty people, for which I felt the need to prepare a dozen gourmet dishes—the most elaborate being one from a Julia Child cookbook that called for me to hold an uncooked chicken to my lips and blow so forcefully that I am able to separate the skin from the meat, which I throw in a food processor with an assortment of expensive ingredients. Then I stuff it all back into a casing hand-sewn by me, made out of the chicken skin in the shape of a basketball. "Chicken Melon" is the name of the dish.

I have driven several hours in search of the child-size store mannequin Audrey has her heart set on and a Caribbean steel drum for Steve. I've mailed out a hundred Christmas cards, with a photograph of the five of us, taken with an automatic timer, sitting on our couch beside the tree, looking happy.

I'm in the kitchen Christmas morning after the presents have been opened, and wrapping paper is all around the house. Having just finished making a chocolate sheet cake and a bowl of mocha cream, I'm trying to prepare meringue mushrooms for a *bûche de Noël*, while Steve and his brother watch a football game. Willy is crying.

I ask Steve to help. "Just a minute," he says.

I look into the living room, with its perfectly constructed scene of family happiness, and it begins to spin. I watch the scene unfold with horrible fascination.

Now Joyce picks up the yule log she's just assembled. Now she stuffs it down the garbage disposal. She's grabbing a garbage bag. She tears into the living room. She's not just throwing wrapping paper into the bag, though. She gathers up the new stuffed animals, her husband's Christmas sweater, her daughter's Christmas Barbie and ski parka.

"Christmas is over!" I scream. My family watches in shock. Audrey tries to hold me back. "Sit down a minute, Mom." Charlie begins to suck his thumb again. Willy is yelling. Steve says "Get a hold of yourself, Joyce," and leaves the room. His brother is already outside.

I end up crying and apologizing to everyone. I take the toys back out of the garbage bag. I make another cake.

"If you could see yourself, Joyce," my husband says, shaking his head. I'm gasping for breath. His voice is icy calm as he points the video camera at me. The red light goes on.

Chapter Twenty

IN DECEMBER OF 1988—married eleven years, our children now aged nine, five, and three—I make a videotape of our family. I begin taping at the start of the Christmas season. There is footage of Steve carrying in our snow-covered Christmas tree, and our children hanging up the ornaments. I tape them decorating our gingerbread house, and Audrey with her friends singing carols at her annual cookie party. I capture my son Charlie dressed up as Santa Claus, Willy wearing nothing but one of Steve's T-shirts, dancing around our kitchen as he sings every verse of "The Twelve Days of Christmas," and Audrey singing "Go Tell It on the Mountain."

I tape Christmas Eve, and Christmas morning: Steve, holding up his new sweater and the encyclopedias his parents sent. Audrey and Charlie putting together a Lego set. Willy, hugging his new stuffed animal, with a hand-sewn outfit made by me, like the kind my mother used to make for my stuffed animals. Later that night I walk through our house with the video camera, taping my children asleep in their beds. The next day Audrey takes the camera and records me skating around our pond, working on my ice-dancing routine, while the song I've chosen as my accompaniment blasts from a portable tape player.

I send our Christmas video to my mother in Toronto. I want her to see how happy we all are. I hear nothing from her.

Finally I call. Her voice on the phone is flat. When I ask about the videotape I sent, she's vague. "I can't talk now," she says. I hear her calling out my cousin's name while the phone clatters onto the table.

Speaking in a hushed voice, my cousin tells me she has come over because my mother appears to have sunk into a strange and terrible depression. For days now she's been unable to stop crying. Three weeks ago she was in Mexico with Sydney. Two months ago, out promoting her new volume of memoirs, *The Tree of Life*, and appearing on the television talk show she's been hosting, offering parenting advice. Now she can't get out of bed.

"What started this?" I ask my cousin.

"Your videotape," she says.

Gail was visiting my mother when the tape arrived in the mail. Watching the tape, my mother became increasingly agitated and upset. It started when Audrey sings "Go Tell It on the Mountain" and mentions Jesus Christ. She got worse when Steve opens the box of encyclopedias given to us by his parents and we all say something about how much we wish they were here. When they got to the part on the tape where I'm skating, my mother became so upset she rose from the couch, walked over to the television set and yanked the tape out of the VCR with so much force she broke the case.

"Joyce is in trouble," she said to Gail. "She is desperately unhappy. Her marriage is falling apart."

The psychiatrist my mother consults in the aftermath of what I will come to refer to as The Fatal Tape Episode offers the opinion that she's suffering from a depression stemming from her relationship with me. During this period, my mother becomes so disoriented that she has a hard time finding her way home when she goes on errands. When my sister takes her swimming at the Y our mother keeps bumping into the walls of the pool.

At Passover, when she attends a friend's seder, she will take her turn reading from the Hebrew Hagaddah. She delivers the words with her usual clear diction and elocutionist's capacity to make her voice heard in the farthest corners of the room. But the words she speaks so musically are neither Hebrew nor English. They are gibberish.

The psychiatrist continues to treat my mother for depression.

On Mother's Day she collapses on the floor and is taken to the hospital. The MRI they give her, finally, reveals a massive, inoperable tumor—lodged in the portion of her brain that controls language. The doctors tell us she will probably die within weeks.

The day I get the call I leave for Toronto. I go straight to the hospital. Outside my mother's room I encounter Sydney, my mother's companion, who has told her that she appears to have suffered some kind of minor stroke. "She'd want to know what's really wrong," I tell him.

I walk into the room and approach my mother's bed. I lay my face beside hers and stroke her astonishingly smooth cheek. At sixty-six, my mother is a beautiful woman.

"Joyce," she says. There's terrible fear in her face, not a look I can ever remember seeing on her. I know what she's been worrying about: Alzheimer's disease.

"What's the matter with me?" she says.

"You have cancer," I tell her, bending low over the bed, with my arms around her. "A brain tumor."

"Aha," she says, her eyes very steady on my face. The look of panic is gone. "And what exactly do they plan to do about it?"

"There are things they can try," I tell her. "But it seems to be inoperable."

"You mean I'm going to die?" she says. Afternoons in our living room, teaching writing, she always told her students use the real words for things. *Die*, not *pass away*.

"It looks that way," I tell her.

"Hmm," she says, looking more perplexed than frightened. "Isn't life *interesting*?"

I stay in Toronto at my mother's house most of that summer while Steve cares for our children with the help of babysitters.

Although my mother is dying, and the tumor has affected her speech and her movement, she is in no pain and can remain at home. She is also lucid, and able to engage in conversations. Oddly enough, though the tumor that is killing her has affected language, and muddles her ability to summon any word, the things she says now feel more real to me. Although my mother has always had the capacity for frankness, she was not always honest. The doctor has explained that one effect of this kind of tumor is the way it suppresses inhibitions.

"You girls are my trousers," she tells Rona and me. She means *treasures*.

"Sydney and I were having such a good time with sex until this tumor slithered in," she says, dreamily.

A minister friend of hers pays a visit. Before he leaves, he bends to kiss her. "I'll see you again, Fredelle," he says.

"Not necessarily, Bob," says my mother. "I could kick the bucket any day now."

"I'll see you again," he repeats, calmly.

This time there's almost an edge of impatience to my mother's voice as she tells him, "Not *necessarily*, Bob."

"Oh, no, Fredelle," says Bob. "You don't understand. I *will* see you again."

This time, my mother breaks into an affectionate and amused smile. "Come, come, Bob," she says. "Don't tell me you still believe that stuff?"

Weeks go by in which my mother continues to function well. She and Sydney decide to get married, and we throw a wedding in her garden, with a *chuppa* among the flowers.

As I dress for the wedding in her room, she comments, "Did your breasts always look like that? Or just lately?" Now, as my mother makes her way through the crowd of friends assembled in her garden on her grandson Benjamin's arm, she greets each one as she passes.

"Oh, Tony," she sighs. "I would have married you myself, if you weren't gay!"

"And you, Joe, having another child, at your age. What a magnificent accomplishment!"

"Margaret! How I wish I'd had as many lovers as you!"

The rabbi performs the service. "Fredelle Bruser and Sydney Bacon, long life to you both," he finishes, as Sydney breaks the glass. My mother looks out ruefully and says, still able to fill the garden with her voice, "Would that it were true."

*   *   *

Steve brings our children to Toronto to see their grandmother. To Charlie and Willy, who are six and four years old, my mother's illness is a sad event but not one that they fully grasp. They never had the long visits with their grandmother that meant so much to their sister.

Audrey is eleven. Before my mother got sick, she and Audrey had been planning a trip to Mexico the summer after Audrey's twelfth birthday. Ever since Audrey was very small, my mother has been sending her postcards from her travels with Sydney and packages of glitter and fabric, hotel soaps and perfume samples and funny poems. The last time they got together, she and my mother picked out a pattern and spent the day sewing Audrey a dress, with rick-rack trim and appliqués on the pockets. Then they made one for her doll.

On her eighth birthday, after she blew out the candles and Charlie asked her what she'd wished for, she told him, "I wished Grandma Del would live forever."

Audrey knows her grandmother is dying. Now, as she arrives for her visit, with her long braids and her horn-rimmed glasses and her dark skin, her sturdy little body and a pink velvet hat, she moves without hesitation to my mother's bedside and bends to embrace her. She stands there that way for a long time. Audrey settles into a chair next to the bed as if the two of them were having one of their tea parties.

"You got married!" she says to her grandmother. "That means your name is Mrs. Bacon now!"

My daughter has recently performed the role of Koko in *The Mikado*—though it is a male part. If she had been well, my mother would never have missed this performance. She asks Audrey to sing her song, "Tit-Willow." Audrey does, in a pure, clear soprano. Tears stream down my mother's cheeks, but she is smiling.

"How I will miss her!" my mother says, when the song is over.

While I'm staying in Toronto, I take out my mother's files of her old letters, hundreds of pages dating from the forties to just a few months ago. I come upon one in which she talks about a perennial subject of hers, her constant struggle with her weight. "If I ever get a brain tumor," she wrote, in 1962, "I can tell you I'll stop counting calories."

Now I cook for her. Every day I bake a poppy seed cake or a pie for the many people who come by to see her. My mother made the best pies and taught me all her secrets. I teach a number of her friends how to bake pies like hers.

She and her friends sit in the garden eating the poppy seed cake and drinking tea. She always asks a great many questions about the work they're up to and their future plans. She remembers if someone has recently embarked on a promising-looking love affair, or if somebody's child has been having problems at school. As always, she is consumingly interested in sex. To nearly every visitor who stops by over the course of the summer she puts the question, "How many lovers have you had? Who was the best?" When the time comes for my mother's friend to go home, she asks her to choose a hat from her vast collection.

We talk a lot that summer, more than we have in years.

My mother can still make it down the stairs from her bedroom, although as the weeks pass she gets shakier. She loves to sit in her garden, and once a day I take her out in the wheelchair through the park, where she comments on whatever flower will be coming into bloom next. When I arrived it was hyacinth and tulips. We're into marigolds and zinnias now.

My sister and Sydney have been saying we need to hire someone to care for my mother, since they're both working, but I don't want a stranger in the house. It seems to me she should be cared for by someone who loves her, and I am willing.

As the weeks pass, this becomes more of an issue between us. Rona tells me "You're overinvolved, Joyce." She calls me obsessed and clinging.

I am very thin, with my hair pulled into tight braids, wearing the same shapeless shift day after day. I make daily trips to three different fruit stands to see which one has the best raspberries, and ride the bus to my mother's favorite bakery for her favorite challah bread.

It's late July, and I am alone at the house with my mother.

While taking her, very weak now, downstairs for our walk, she collapses in my arms halfway down the stairs. When she falls, I can't lift her. I run for help, and after we've got her into bed, I hear the voices of my sister and Sydney and one of Sydney's friends, conferring downstairs. "It was pure lunacy trying to take her to the park," Sydney says. "She doesn't always think," Rona says quietly.

"The kitchen's a mess. This girl never heard of a Brillo pad," says Sydney's friend.

My sister comes to me in the next room. "You're losing perspective, Joyce," she says. "This isn't healthy."

I go home to New Hampshire for a couple of days to see Steve and our children with the plan of returning after the weekend. I tell Steve on the phone that I'd like to go away with him alone for a night to Vermont.

As we finish our meal at the Four Columns Inn in Newfane, Vermont, a few days later, our waiter approaches the table. "There's a telegram for you," he says, directing me to the phone.

The telegram is from Sydney. I suppose I'm about to hear that my mother's dead. But no. He's telling me that he and my sister have hired a nurse and housekeeper. I may return to Toronto if I choose, but only if I'm willing to abide by the terms he sets down.

"You may see your mother twice a day, for visits not to exceed an hour in duration. You are no longer to prepare food in the kitchen. In your future visits to Toronto, you will not be staying at our house. Tony and Eddie have agreed to let you stay in their spare bedroom."

When the operator is done reading the telegram, I hang up the phone and make my way back to Steve. The meal has just been set at my place, but I can't eat. I don't care that I'm weeping in the middle of the restaurant.

Across from me at the table, Steve chews his meat and looks at me. "I don't have anything for you, Joyce," he says.

When the weekend's over I return to Toronto and move into Tony and Eddie's house. Twice a day I visit my mother.

Among her last remaining pleasures is good food. The new housekeeper is serving foods I know she wouldn't like—Jell-O and store-bought cake with colored frosting. I notice these things with the eye of an obsessive. I am the daughter of a woman who loved butter so much she buttered our toast on both sides when I was little—always careful to spread the butter right out to the crust while it's still hot enough for it to sink in. The housekeeper draws a single swipe of margarine across the toast when it's already cold.

On my way out one morning after my ten-thirty visit, I ask the housekeeper if she'd mind letting me show her how to make the poppy seed cake my mother loves. She's most agreeable, and I tell her I'll come over early the next day with the ingredients.

The next morning, as I approach the doorstep, Sydney comes out to the sidewalk. "It's not time for your visit yet, Joyce," he says.

"I've come to make a cake for my mother," I say. "I'm teaching the housekeeper."

"No, you're not."

I set my bag on the ground. Eggs, butter, brown sugar, poppy seeds, and sour cream tumble out onto the sidewalk. I moan.

I know when I go to see my mother later that day, I have to tell her good-bye.

I lie down beside her on the bed. "I have to go back to New Hampshire, Mum," I tell her.

"I know, dear," she says.

"You have been an extraordinary mother," I say.

"I know," she says.

"I love you," I tell her.

"You girls," she says. "My finest accomplishment."

I will not hear her voice again except one time, after I'm home and we all know she will die soon. My sister puts her on the phone for a minute. My mother can barely speak. She says only one word, over and over, into my ear. *Love. Love. Love. Love.*

Chapter Twenty-one

JUST BEFORE MY mother's diagnosis, Steve told me our marriage was beyond repair. We went to a counselor together, less to fix the marriage this time than to cope with our sorrow over its imminent ending. One day the counselor put a question to us: What did each of us want out of a marriage? I wanted, I said, to be in love, and to be greatly loved myself. Steve shook his head. "I was in love once," he said, and I knew he meant me. "I'm glad I'm past that now. I have other things I want to accomplish in my life besides loving someone."

Now that my mother's about to die, I can't bear to lose my husband too. I come home that August to tell him I want to save our marriage, and maybe even have another baby.

"It was calmer when you were in Toronto," he says. "This summer showed me we're better off apart."

I am devastated. This is not my home anymore. A road sign made in my absence and listed with the town surveyor bears my husband's name.

I do what I did the last time a man I loved told me we were finished. I start looking at real estate.

My mother dies on October 3, 1989. I have known this moment was coming for five months, and still, when I receive the call telling me she's gone, the most terrible loneliness comes over me. I go outside beside our pond. "I'm an orphan!" I cry out.

Five days later, I move out to a big old Victorian house I've bought for my children and me, thirty miles away.

I do not fly to Toronto for the brief service following my mother's cremation. The only person in Toronto I want to see won't be there.

I'm thirty-five years old when Steve and I separate. Except for the eighteen months I spent in New York City, I had lived in that house in Hillsboro since I was nineteen, almost half my life. Now I wake in the night, forgetting where I am, and bump into the wall, expecting to be in our old bedroom. The town where I've moved—Keene, New Hampshire, with a population of twenty thousand people—is hardly a metropolis, but I'm not used to the sound of cars driving past the house, or streetlights.

The children, hearing the news of our separation, each respond with their particular expression of sorrow. Willy lets out an animal wail, pounds the wall, and explodes, "Now you're going to be divorced for the rest of my life." He is angry for a long time.

Charlie leaves the room quietly and takes out a set of colored pencils. Without saying anything to either Steve or me, he begins to draw. The picture he makes is of a heart—not the cookie-cutter variety of valentine heart, but one that seems to be drawn, a centimeter at a time, in blood.

When he's finished making his heart, he forms a small dot on the paper just above it, meant to represent a nail on the wall. He draws a couple of lines connecting the heart to the nail, as if this were a painting hanging there. Underneath this he writes, "Love is the best art of all."

Audrey behaves as if nothing is terribly wrong. She is quiet, agreeable, and appears cheerful, although her smile is tighter than usual. For several weeks—weeks in which her grandmother dies and her mother begins moving belongings out of the house—Audrey tells none of her friends what has happened.

Not long after this Audrey begins to suffer a sore throat that doesn't get better. Within a few weeks she has lost her voice. The diagnosis by the throat specialist is a severe case of vocal nodules, requiring surgery, to be followed by six weeks of total silence.

Believing it's too much to ask an eleven-year-old not to talk for over a month and a half, I find Audrey a vocal therapist. For two years we make weekly trips to see the therapist, and very slowly, Audrey regains a voice, but it's different. Her old voice was high and girlish. Her new voice is lower, and strangely sultry for someone so young.

All summer I wrote about the experience of watching my mother die. The week of her death, I announce the news in the column. One week later, I have to tell the rest: I tell my readers that Steve and I are separating, and I'm moving out of our house. I will keep writing "Domestic Affairs."

For the first time, I can speak to the many women and men whose marriages have failed. I am able to address the experience of single parents—many of whom write to say that my old columns depicting my family life with my husband and children had sometimes left them feeling excluded.

But of the forty newspapers that have been carrying "Domestic Affairs," more than a dozen drop it after the announcement of my separation. One, the *Minneapolis Star*, doesn't even run the column in which I announce my separation, leaving many readers in the Twin Cities under the impression (as I later learn from concerned letters) that I must have been so grief-stricken by my mother's death I simply couldn't work anymore. *The Sacramento Bee* receives such an outcry after dropping the column that it is reinstated.

My newspaper syndicate reports to me that a family page editor told her "Joyce Maynard isn't qualified to write about family matters anymore." The fact that I would leave my marriage serves as indication that I place my own personal needs over those of my children. I never say in the column that it wasn't my choice to leave.

In the weeks following my separation I receive nearly as much mail as I did following the publication of my first article in *The New York Times*, seventeen years earlier. I hear from several men who accuse me of bringing about the ends of their own marriages. "My wife and I had a highly successful relationship until you announced your separation," one of them writes. One woman wrote that when she read about our separation on the bus to work, she burst into tears.

Many of these women are angry with me.

* * *

In the two years after the separation, my son Charlie adopts the role of mediator and peacemaker in our household. Often Willy is funny and affectionate and excited about things. But he is also troubled enough that I take him to a therapist. It's never his wildness or disobedience that's hardest for me to take. What leaves me in despair are the times when he shuts me out and refuses to speak to me. What I can't handle is that impassive expression, the blank, hooded eyes, his jaw set.

He is playing music very loudly in his room. I have asked him three times to pick up the dishes he left in the living room. Now I tear over to him, where he's lying on the bed, arranging baseball cards.

"Come downstairs right now," I say.

"In a minute." He keeps on looking at the cards.

"Now," I say. Charlie comes in the room.

"Mom's going crazy," Willy says.

I walk over to his boom box and rip the plug out of the wall. "This is history," I say as I carry it out of the room.

Willy is only six, but he's a strong and powerful boy. He faces me. "That's mine," he yells. "Give it back! I'm calling my dad!"

I take him by the shoulders. "It's going to be okay, Mom," Charlie says. "You know Willy."

"Look at me," I say. Willy turns his face away.

"Look at me," I say again. "Don't you dare shut me out!" My son is frozen, eyes to the wall. His face is filled with defiance and terrible sadness.

I want to put my arms around him. I think about last week, when he hit a home run in the playoffs with the bases loaded, and how, after rounding third and tagging home, he didn't even break stride, but kept right on running straight into my lap.

"I hate you!" he says.

I know I will regret this, and I still can't stop myself. I raise my hand and slap his cheek.

By the spring of 1991, our divorce proceedings have turned ugly. My husband has filed a motion to have our children removed from my home, charging that I am an emotionally unfit mother. Because of this, they and I are being evaluated by a court-appointed guardian ad litem, who asks me many questions about my having come from an alcoholic family. Steve's lawyer will eventually cite passages from my own writings in "Domestic Affairs," as examples of my unstable nature and her client's superior abilities to care for our children. A crucial piece of her case has to do with the time I hit Willy. The therapist Willy has been seeing has been asked to testify that I committed child abuse, but he has refused.

In the courtroom, I sit and listen to my husband telling about a conversation he had with our son, following the slapping episode.

"And the next weekend, when the children came for their visitation, what did you say to Willy about what his mother had done?" she asks. "How did you comfort him?"

"I took out a magazine article we had about Michael Jackson, where he talks about his father abusing him, and says how he forgave his father. I told Willy I hoped the day would come when he could forgive his mother like that. I told him she was getting help for her problem."

Up until now I have kept writing my newspaper column. But I can no longer write about what's going on in my life. I am no longer able to pretend, as I used to, that things are better than they are. After eight years, I tell my newspaper syndicate I'm ending "Domestic Affairs."

It is the week before the final column is due and I haven't begun to write it.

I don't know how to say good-bye to the readers of my column. Their letters were a deep source of comfort in the loneliest years of my marriage. For the first time in eight years I call my editor to tell her I'm going to be late. She tells me she can hold off the deadline for an hour, or two at the most.

"Write the way you speak," my mother told me. At one thirty, I finally begin to speak. At three I'm finished.

Mothers of my generation grew up with a lot of ideas from television. A man I know—still single at the age of forty-

three—says he has spent his whole life trying to locate Donna Reed. Join the crowd, I told him.

...I came into my own motherhood at the forefront of a revolution. The message society conveyed to my friends and me, as we entered womanhood, was that we could have it all. Marriages and babies, and careers too. No more bridge clubs for us. We would find career fulfillment. And then come home to bake the cookies and give the birthday parties, same as our mothers did, without ever dropping a stitch. Mothers could do anything. Mothers were perfect.

...I thought I would fall in love, get married, have babies, and live happily ever after. I was right that having children was the best experience of my life. I just didn't know that in addition to providing me with the greatest riches I have ever known, it would also leave me feeling bankrupt, overdrawn, wiped out. I didn't know that I would often find myself standing in my kitchen, with this infant in my arms more precious to me than breath, whose tears I couldn't stop, feeling more loneliness and isolation and pure panic than I'd ever known before....

For thirteen years now, I've been trying to figure out what it is that mothers are supposed to do.... I thought it was a mother's job to make her children's lives as perfect as her own had failed to be.

...When your children are very little they think those things too. At three or four, my sons would say, "You made me do it," if they spilled their milk or lost their toy. If a person makes herself responsible for her children's happiness, she must also be accountable for whatever sorrow comes their way.

I will always remember a day I found myself driving with my son Charlie, headed directly into the sun. Charlie was two. He was squinting, covering his eyes, and then he started to cry. "The sun's in your eyes," I told him.

"Take it out!" he said. He really believed I could do that.

When I left my marriage two years ago a lot of people offered up their ideas to me, once again, about what mothers

*were and were not supposed to do. Mothers were supposed
to stay married to fathers....Mothers were supposed to meet
the needs of their family first, whatever their own might
be....*

*...It's not only children who grow. Parents do, too. As
much as we watch to see what our children do with their
lives, they are watching us to see what we do with ours. I
can't tell my children to reach for the sun. All I can do is
reach for it, myself.*

Chapter Twenty-two

THE DIVORCE IS made final. The children will stay with me, traveling every other weekend and vacations to our old house in Hillsboro, which is their father's now. We might have gotten past the bitterness of our marriage, but the wounds of the divorce have left me in a state of so much anger, I have taken to spending hours in the pool at the Y. The water is one of the few places I feel calm.

I still don't feel at home in my body. I am haunted by the memory of my mother's voice, as she was dying, when the brain tumor seemed to have an effect on her not unlike truth serum, and she asked me, "Did your breasts always look like that?" I remember how I loved breast-feeding my children. I was in my glory then. I felt ripe and fertile and bountiful and—after all those years of inhabiting a child's body—*womanly*.

For $3000, I undergo cosmetic surgery—the insertion of silicone implants in my breasts. In my conference with the doctor, I had asked how large my breasts would be after the surgery. "It depends how much tissue we have to fill," he told me. I wake up with size 40 breasts, upright as a pair of headlights.

The operation leaves me with a cartoon body. Some time later, after the surgery, when I will encounter my mother's husband, Sydney, in Toronto, he will say to me approvingly that I look like my mother now.

I sell an article to *Self* magazine about my surgery. One reason I publish this article has to do with my constant anxiety about money. My custody battle with my husband has left me owing my lawyer more than $50,000, and he has put a lien on my house. But though I approach my magazine writing as a way of supporting my family and getting out of debt, I also approach the task with a sense of relief. I haven't freed myself from all my secret-keeping obligations, but I have come a long way from the days when I couldn't name the parts of my body in my own diary.

For over thirty years, Jerry Salinger has sought his protection in privacy and silence. I have come to believe that my greatest protection comes in self-disclosure. It's shame, not exposure, that I can't endure; I've lived with so much of it. It's the things people don't talk about that scare me.

If I tell what I do, nobody else can expose me. If I live my life in a way I'm not ashamed of, why shouldn't I be able to talk about it? I am surely not the only woman who made herself throw up everyday, or flew into a rage at her children, or who felt abandoned by love. I am not the only woman who ever looked at her postchildbearing breasts in the mirror and burst into tears. I know now—finally—that I'm not the only one who had an alcoholic father. That was my first experience with shame, the one that made all the others intolerable.

For all the years I lived in that house at the end of the dead-end road in Hillsboro—on my own for three years, with Steve for twelve—there was a ritual I never failed to perform. Every time I rounded the last bend in the road, where the house came into view, I'd say under my breath, "I'm home." If I ever neglected to speak the words, I used to think, something terrible might happen. Who knew what? I took no chances.

More than once, during particularly bad times in our marriage, my husband said, "We can't get a divorce. You could never bring yourself to leave this house." I could have pointed out that maybe he'd be the one to leave, but he loved the place too—the pond we'd dug, the studio he'd built with his brother.

We were at an impasse. For me, there was always the knowledge that our three children were born under this roof. The house was also the refuge I had found for myself in the very lowest moment of my life—the place I made my home at a time when I thought I would never have a home again.

But I left the house in Hillsboro after all—left it to Steve. I left the house, knowing it would simply be too lonely and isolated a place for my children and me now. When I moved my things out, I believed, as I did when I left Jerry Salinger's house, that I might never feel completely at home anyplace ever again. The big old Victorian house on School Street was chosen for its easy bike access to school and ball fields and all the things that always seemed to me to speak of a normal, happy, all-American childhood. "It's a *Leave It to Beaver* kind of neighborhood," I say.

Our mother's house in Toronto is sold. Unpacking boxes of my mother's belongings, I come upon a plaster life mask of my father, made when he was around thirty-five. When I hang it on the wall of our new house, Charlie says to me, with some surprise, "What's that mask of Dad doing on the wall?"

Studying my father's image on the wall, I realize how much these two men looked like each other. Both are heartbreakingly handsome men—strong jaw and cheekbones and eyes that burn into you. Both are of a nearly identical height and build. I had never acknowledged the resemblance until now.

Gradually, we make our new place into a good home. I dig flower beds around the bare yard. Our friend Geoff builds us a patio so we can barbecue outside in summer, and another friend makes a goldfish pond with a waterfall. We put a swing on the porch, and a big trampoline in the yard. I paint the house pink, and the walls of our front room red, and put a dollhouse in the window. At Halloween, with a bunch of kids from the neighborhood, and the contribution of ripped-up sheets from half a dozen neighbors, we build a fifteen-foot-tall chicken-wire mummy—arms extended in front of him—and hang it from the tree out front, lit with a spotlight. Trick-or-treaters come from all over town to see. Each year now at Thanksgiving, when my children go to their father's house, I have a party to bake pies for the soup kitchen in town, teaching friends my mother's technique for making pie crust. For the whole month our dining room is given over to making valentines—glitter and doilies everywhere.

We get a Boston terrier puppy we name Opie. My sons play baseball in spring and soccer in the fall. My daughter runs cross-country. Wednesday afternoons, my sons' music teacher, Frank, who plays piano at the Unitarian church in town, rides over on the Harley he bought for his fiftieth birthday, with a baritone horn and a trumpet attached on the back with a bungee cord, to give Charlie and Willy their lessons. Charlie performs the role of the Artful Dodger in *Oliver*. Willy plays Ben Franklin in *1776*. Audrey gets a car, a '67 Valiant very similar to the one Steve and I bought, sixteen years earlier, the week before her birth, only this one is decorated with stickers, silk roses, and pom-pom fringe.

Our house is full of kids playing air hockey in the basement, jumping on the trampoline, listening to music in Audrey's room. On her ceiling Audrey has hung over one hundred dried roses she's been given over the years.

My main job these days is writing a column for *Parenting* magazine about raising children. I take on a lot of other work besides that, which gives our family more financial stability than we've known for a while. One summer, while my children are away with Steve, I write a black comic novel called *To Die For*.

I am not free from struggle, but I have relaxed my old manic standards for myself. I take up tennis, a game I had always wanted to play. For the next several years—until he so far surpasses me there's not much fun left in it for him—I play tennis with Willy. At the worst moments between us, when he's his angriest or most troubled about what goes on between his father and me, the tennis court will sometimes be the place we work things out. Summer nights we get on our bikes as late as ten o'clock and head to the night-lit courts at the college, where we hit a ball until close to midnight.

I make friends in this town. One, the newly divorced mother of a friend of Audrey's, mentions shortly after we meet that she and her family moved here from Cornish, New Hampshire.

"Oh, really?" I say. "I lived there myself once, a long time ago. Where was your house?"

"Just down the road from J. D. Salinger," she says.

"Did you ever meet him?"

"Not me," she says. "But my younger daughter, Mary, got to be good friends with him. He was crazy about her."

I am having an argument with Audrey. She's thirteen or fourteen. She brought our big set of felt-tip pens over to her father's house and left them there. Now, when I want markers, there are none. "It's not enough that I provide this family with every kind of art supply there is!" I yell. "I'm providing them for him, too!"

Audrey's voice is very soft now as a result of the vocal nodules, but there's a firmness as she answers me. "You shouldn't put us in the middle, Mom," she says, "I'm sorry you have to pay for so much stuff. But it's not my fault, or the boys' either."

Looking at my daughter's face, so much like mine at that age, I am struck by how unlike me she is—wiser, in so many ways, than when I was thirteen, or even twenty or thirty. It has not occurred to me until this moment that in all the years of my growing up, I cannot remember a single occasion when I looked my mother in the eye as Audrey is looking at me now and told her she was wrong.

"You're right, Audrey," I say. "I'm sorry."

My sister and I have slowly established a relationship of wary affection. We speak on the phone now every month.

For many years after leaving home, Rona maintained a career as a freelance writer, covering subjects having to do with business, medicine, or education. She wrote without calling attention to herself.

After our mother's death, she became a columnist for a Canadian magazine in which, for the first time, she addressed issues in her own life. "It took me all that time to write like *me*," she says now. "All those years of Mother's training, I didn't know where my voice had gone."

She is named editor of *Chatelaine*, Canada's largest magazine for women, an accomplishment our mother would have loved. In the letter she writes at the front of every issue, she often speaks with warmth and pride of our mother and our mother's continuing and powerful influence on herself and many others who knew her.

There is still so much bitterness between Steve and me that just sitting on the same bench at a Little League game is awkward. Friday nights, when the children pack their belongings into brown paper grocery bags and head to Hillsboro, and Sundays, when I pick them up, are filled with tension and fights, mostly about stupid things. In spite of this, our children manage to negotiate the gulf between their father and me.

Back when *To Die For* was published, a producer optioned the book for a movie. For several years I have held out the hope that the film might be made, knowing if that happens, I'll make a lot of money. "If our ship comes in, I'll take everyone on a trip," I say. "If our ship comes in, we'll put up a basketball hoop and tar the driveway." "Everyone gets a new bike if our ship comes in."

In the winter of 1995, the call comes telling me our ship has come in. Nicole Kidman has agreed to star in Buck Henry's adaptation of *To Die For*, with Gus Van Sant directing. I can finally pay my lawyer's bill, and all the other bills that have hung over me since my divorce, and still put money away for my children's college education. I take the three of them out to dinner at the best Italian restaurant in Keene. We take a trip to Hawaii. We put up a basketball hoop and tar our driveway.

I lobby for a part in the movie, sending the producers a videotape of myself reading lines from the script. They agree to give me a small speaking part as Nicole Kidman's lawyer. The movie is filming in Toronto. Production begins in May, the month when my mother had traditionally held her annual garden party.

All her life, from the grange halls of her elocution days to her late-life career as a television talk show hostess moderating discussions of child care, my mother sought a stage to perform on. She loved an audience. She was a larger-than-life character, I always said. She should have been in the movies.

I tell the producers of *To Die For* I won't be needing a hotel room because I'll be staying at my sister's house. This is the first time I've visited her home since our mother's death.

The night I arrive Rona says she has something to give me. She returns to the room with a small plastic bag containing what look like stones and sand—our mother's ashes.

"I've had these in my drawer for ages," she says as she hands them to me. "Ashes aren't my thing."

The next morning a car picks me up very early and brings me to the location where they'll be shooting my scene. Since I'll go directly to the airport from the set, I have brought my suitcase containing my mother's ashes.

The car deposits me at a trailer where the wardrobe mistress outfits me with my costume, a beautifully tailored suit my mother would have appreciated, high heels, and a briefcase. My hair is styled in a bun. Nicole Kidman sits in the chair next to me, more beautiful in real life than she is in the movies. I ask her to sign an autograph for my children. Then I go to my trailer to dress.

We spend all morning shooting the three-minute scene in which I appear so that the director can record the action from every possible angle. Nicole and I make our way through the crowd of extras playing reporters at least thirty times while I deliver my lines, holding tight to my briefcase. Finally, the director says, "It's a wrap." I go back to my trailer and take off the beautiful suit and the high heels and return the briefcase.

First, though, I remove from it the small bag that I'd put inside earlier that morning containing my mother's ashes. I knew my mother would have been amused that she finally got to be in the movies.

One day Audrey and I will scatter my mother's ashes in Mexico.

I still can't let my mother go. I'll see a woman in her mid-sixties walking down the street, wearing a big, colorful hat, with the kind of purposefulness to her stride that my mother always had. For a minute I will follow this woman, pretending it's her.

In the bathroom of a friend's house, I see a bottle of the perfume my mother wore and I open it and breathe it in. I'll reach into the pocket of a coat that used to be hers, and find some little list to herself with the name of a book or a record or a movie. *Bagels. Sour cream. Rhinestones.* Those would be for Audrey.

In the wake of so many losses, I find myself wishing, again, that I could make some kind of connection with my long-ago landsman. So once again, I write Jerry Salinger a letter. "Can I come and take a walk with you one day?" I write. He doesn't answer.

I long to make peace with Steve, too.

The idea comes to me that maybe I could create a fictional character, a woman like me, living in circumstances similar to mine, in the aftermath of a divorce with a similar amount of bitterness to mine. If I wrote a novel about this woman maybe I could explain to Steve how I feel. I could bring my character to a point of forgiveness that I have been unable to achieve, myself.

In the spring of 1994, when my children go to their father's house for spring vacation, I pack my computer in the car and drive ten miles to the Brookside Motel. I stay there two weeks, working on the first draft of the novel, *Where Love Goes.*

In the novel, the woman recognizes, finally, that she loved her husband once. In some ways, she probably always will. "How can you look at your child and not see in his face the part of him that comes from his father?" she thinks. "How can you not love that part?"

At the end of *Where Love Goes,* the divorced mother has forgiven her husband. They're not friends but they can sit and talk together on the bench at soccer games the way my children long to see their father and me do.

The movie of *To Die For* is chosen to open the Toronto Film Festival. I decide to bring all three of my children to the gala premiere. I call my sister to give her the news.

"I hope we can manage to get tickets," she says. "These things tend to sell out."

"Rona," I tell her. "Of course I'll get tickets for you."

"So I guess you'll be needing a hotel?" she says.

My sister and her husband have a large, beautiful house. Benjamin is out on his own now. "I was thinking we could stay with you," I say.

"Oh," she says.

The next day she calls back. "I've been thinking about the problem of your visit," she says. "You and the children can stay at the house."

"That's great," I say.

"Paul and I will stay at a hotel."

So they do. But every morning, before work, they leave their hotel and return to their house to have an enjoyable breakfast with us.

"You know, Rona," I say, "sometimes I get the feeling you don't even *like* me."

"No," she says slowly, in a way that makes me understand how hard it has been for her.

"It's not that at all," she says. "It's just that you ... take ... up ... so ... much ... space."

It's Sunday in mid-January in the winter of 1995, and my night to pick up our children at our old house in Hillsboro. Tonight in particular, I dread the drive, and not just because it's snowing.

Steve and Charlie have gone out for dinner with friends tonight, and Audrey didn't come to Hillsboro this weekend, so the only one I'm picking up is Willy. Normally I stay in the car with the motor running, waiting for the children to bring their stuff out. But because Steve isn't here, Willy suggests that I come in the house.

I haven't been inside the place for years, and I'm not prepared for what happens to me when I step into my old kitchen. A bitter taste rises in my throat. I step into the hallway and glance at the bed where all three of our babies were born. Light from the full moon shines in the window. I go back in the kitchen, run my hand over the wood of the kitchen counter, where I must have prepared thousands of meals, and look out the window to an eerie and beautiful streak of light slashing across newfallen snow. I remember another full moon when Steve and I had fought so bitterly I paced the rooms of this house until dawn, lying down next to first one of my sleeping children, and then another, unable to find peace.

This isn't the first time I feel that bitter taste: I had it the day seven years ago that I drove a U-Haul filled with my belongings down this driveway, the day I sat in a courtroom hearing a guardian ad litem evaluate my performance as a mother. The surprise comes from discovering that years later, standing in my old kitchen for the first time in years, the wild rage I supposed I had put aside flares up again.

Willy's excited to have the chance to show me all the new things in his room. I admire the pictures he's put up on the walls of his room and a rock he found in the woods, a carved wooden horse from a yard sale, a picture Steve made him of a space alien. But my head's pounding.

On the kitchen counter lies a screw gun that Steve uses in his work as a sheetrocker. I pick it up and palm it as if it were a .45. I put it down again and then pick it up. I look to see where my son is now. In the bathroom.

I tuck the screw gun under my jacket and walk out the door. I stand in the driveway, looking up at the moon, big as a plate and hanging right over my head, lighting the apple trees, the lilacs, and the skating pond. The snow's falling hard.

I raise my arm the way my sons have taught me when we're playing catch, and let the screw gun fly. I watch it land in a clump of snow-covered bushes and walk back into the house and call Willy.

By the time we get back to our house in Keene I feel sick with shame and embarrassment. In the morning I try to work, but all I can think about is Steve looking for his screw gun and realizing it disappeared the same night I came to pick up Willy.

I put on my jacket and go to my car. With so much fresh snow on the roads, it takes me nearly an hour to reach our old house.

As I turn the final bend in the road leading up to the house I see with relief that Steve's car isn't there. I pull up alongside the porch and walk over to the clump of bushes where I threw the gun. At first I can't spot it.

Then I see the handle, just barely sticking up out of the snow. I dry the gun off on my shirt and carry it onto the porch, where I set it on a table. I get back in the car and drive away.

Chapter Twenty-three

IT COMES TO me that winter, 1996: I have to leave New Hampshire. So long as I live here, I will be haunted by my history. Audrey's leaving home herself in a few months. My sons still have a few years left before they head out into the world, but they are old enough, too, that I believe they could handle living farther away from one of their parents now.

My friend Shirley, a realtor, sticks a FOR SALE sign in our front yard, under the tree where we hung the mummy. That afternoon, she brings the first of many families of strangers to walk through our house.

Our lives are going to change. I don't know how. I don't even know where we're going, only that it's time to go.

The next few months are among the hardest times we've known. Walking through the rooms of this house I've come to love, I look out the window at the kids jumping on the trampoline in the yard—boys in pants so big they sometimes fall down as the boy goes up—and wonder what I was thinking of to set this whole terrible, wrenching change into motion. Our house is crammed with stuff, every toy my children owned that I could never bear to part with. Drawers full of my children's old school papers and letters and art supplies, junk jewelry, fabric, buttons, photographs, my mother's sewing machine, her mixer, her hats. Friends ask me how I'll ever manage to vacate this house, it's so full of things. "You'd better just light a match," one says.

"Why don't you move to New York?" one friend suggests. My friend Vicky, the reader with whom I used to stay in my *Family Circle* days, suggests Brooklyn Heights. Another reader friend suggests Denver. Somebody else, Portland, Oregon.

I travel to Northern California for a weekend and look at houses. Three weeks later, on a second trip—this time with Charlie—I stop in at a real estate open house in a town just north of San Francisco. The house costs more than I have any business spending, but because I have one good tax return, from the year of the movie sale, I qualify for a mortgage. I ask myself "What's the worst that can happen?" and make an offer.

The day my offer is accepted, I get a call from Audrey, back home in Keene, to say our house has just been burglarized. Gone: our bicycles, snowboards, stereo equipment, guitar, VCR, camera, computers—including the one I work on, with hundreds of pages of work on it, not backed up on any disk.

When I come home, I spend hours with the police and the insurance investigators. It turns out my daughter had a party at our house the night before the burglary, and noise complaints were filed with the police. Two days later, when she called to report the burglary, she and her friends became the chief suspects. "In a majority of cases like this," the detective tells me, "it turns out to be someone in the family."

Now detectives are interviewing all of Audrey's friends. One day I look out my window to see a detective talking to one of the boys who comes and jumps on our trampoline every day after school. Soon nobody is jumping on the trampoline anymore. Every kid in our yard is under suspicion. I look at them differently, too. What if it was this boy that I used to invite in for cookies, or that one?

My daughter and I, who have been at odds all year, argue bitterly now. "You know you weren't supposed to have a party while I was away," I say. *Now look.*

With the approval of the police, I send a letter to the local paper. "The hard drive to my computer was stolen," I say. "I earn my living as a writer. If anybody knows where it is, please return it. Just leave it on our doorstep. No questions asked."

Two days later, at ten o'clock at night, I get a phone call from a woman in town. "Come to my house right away," she says. No need to ask why.

When I get there, she and her ex-husband, who lives in my neighborhood, are sitting in the living room with my computer hard drive, which they got from their twenty-year-old son, a boy Audrey knew slightly in junior high but isn't friendly with. The father found my hard drive in a storage building out in back of his apartment. But he swears his son didn't burglarize my house. "He met a student from the college at a party who asked him to hold on to it for him for a few weeks," the father says. "He was just doing the guy a favor."

"Our son's never been in any kind of trouble before," his mother tells me.

I wish they had just left the computer on my doorstep, but mostly I'm just so happy to have my hard drive back. I tell the father to bring it to my house and leave it on my step tomorrow morning, and I'll simply tell the police that part, keeping their son's name out of it.

The next morning, the hard drive is returned. But it turns out the young man also had another item his parents had not mentioned before: my portable computer, which is damaged and no longer usable.

I know if I tell the police and the insurance company about the damaged portable computer, too, my story will sound implausible and they won't reimburse me. The police have already spent hours grilling Audrey, who, I am clear, is guilty of nothing but having a party against my wishes.

I call the ex-husband back. "Just take the portable computer away," I say. "I can't deal with it." He tells me his ex-father-in-law has a backhoe. I ask no more.

I call the police and the insurance company to say someone has returned my hard drive, but I don't mention the portable computer. The police send a detective over to dust the hard drive for fingerprints.

I replace the stolen items, putting thousands of dollars' worth of purchases on my charge card. I believe the whole thing is over.

Three weeks later, when I call the insurance adjustor to say I need the check to pay my charge card bill, he says, "The company can't reimburse you yet. The case has been reopened for investigation." My charge card is frozen, and beginning to rack up penalties and interest.

Another detective shows up at our door—much tougher looking than the last one. "Something smells rotten and we think it's your daughter," he says. "I'm not letting this go until I find out the real story."

One minute after he leaves, I'm on the phone to one of the few lawyers in Keene I haven't already encountered in my divorce—a criminal lawyer, who is also the ex-husband of my ex-husband's divorce lawyer. He's in the middle of a family barbecue, but I say I need to talk to him right away. "I'll meet you at the office," he says.

Half an hour later I'm sitting across from him, telling the whole story. I think he's going to tell me he can make everything all right.

He tells me the kid who had my computer is currently under indictment for another crime. Then he tells me I've committed two felony offenses: obstruction of justice and insurance fraud. I could go to jail.

He gives me my options. "You can tell the police the truth yourself. Or I can try to smooth things out for you. Whatever you do don't confess to anything without talking to me."

The next morning, the police detective calls. My lawyer has been in touch and told him the whole story. Five minutes later he's at my house.

The last time I'd seen this detective, he was very tough and scary. Now his manner is completely changed. "Listen," he says, putting an arm on my shoulder. "I can understand how a thing like this happens. You're a single mother. Moving. Under a lot of stress, I bet. Here's what I want. Just write everything down that happened. From the beginning."

I'm so relieved. Of course I will tell him. Writing, I can do. How soon does he want it?

Now.

I go to my desk. While the detective waits in the next room, I type my story. It's six pages long. I leave nothing out.

I print it and hand it to him. "Boy, this is terrific," he says. "You sure type fast."

I'm still so grateful, I take a copy of *To Die For* off the shelf and give it to him.

Half an hour later, my attorney calls. Evidently the police detective took my account of what happened with our burglary and turned it in, as a confession, to the district attorney's office, which has charged me with two felonies. The twenty-year-old who appears to have burglarized my house is charged with nothing.

"You told them way too much," my lawyer says. "I'll go talk to the D.A."

My criminal lawyer gets me off the hook with an apology and a slap on the wrist.

In late May, Audrey graduates from high school. Charlie and Willy finish seventh and eighth grade. They end the year with a production of *West Side Story*. Willy plays Ace, one of the white gang. Charlie, in dark makeup, with his hair dyed black, is Bernardo, head of the Puerto Ricans.

Sitting in the darkened theater—one of the last nights I'll spend in New Hampshire—I look over at Steve, a few rows away, the person in this audience to whom I am both most connected and most estranged.

Our sons look so much like him. Charlie in particular, whirling across the stage now, in the big dancing scene right before the rumble, could be Steve that night we danced the polka. Same athletic grace. A face that could break a woman's heart.

There will not be a lot of moments, in my life as a parent, more glorious than this one, watching our two sons sharing the same stage this way: Willy belting out "When You're a Jet," Charlie dancing. I know his character is going to die. Still, when the knife is thrust into my son's chest, I let out a scream.

After the show, waiting in our separate corners of the room for our children to take their makeup and costumes off, Steve and I face each other.

"They were something, huh?" I say warily.

"They sure were," he tells me.

"I might not see you again," I tell him. "We leave next week."

"I know," he says. "Safe trip. Good luck."

Charlie and Willy and I dismantle our trampoline. We spend every day now packing. But I have also made the decision that I will bring very few of our belongings to California. My children can bring their things, and I give each of them a trunk to fill with whatever they want of our household possessions. I pack our favorite children's books, Audrey's dollhouse, my records and CDs. A few pieces of furniture, my collection of old souvenir plates from most of the fifty states. I'll bring my father's paintings, and some boxes of old family letters I brought from my mother's house after she died, but haven't opened.

I hang a giant sign on the front of our house announcing a yard sale the last weekend of June. One reader who has heard about the yard sale travels from Florida to attend, and several come from New York. Two longtime column-readers I've never met come from Indiana to help with the sale. One of them has not been on a plane since she was a teenager. One former football player friend sleeps over the night before to guard the door from the antique and junk dealers who begin trying to muscle their way in at sunrise. By nine o'clock, there are so many cars outside our house the police have to close off the street.

All weekend people troop through our house picking through the piles of clothes and dishes and old toys and furniture in the yard.

I decide to look at our yard sale as a party, our biggest ever. Everyone we know in our town comes. They all go home with something that used to be ours—my children's toys, Audrey's rhinestone jewelry and hats, my salt shakers and teapots, Willy's Charlie McCarthy ventriloquist puppet, my mother's precious teak dining-room table, the cashmere coat Jerry Salinger had bought me. By the end of the day our house is stripped clean.

On July 2, on what would have been my nineteenth wedding anniversary, I close the door to our big pink house for the last time. Audrey, Charlie, Willy, and I stand on the sidewalk and shoot off a Chinese rocket. As we're heading out of town, I see tractors in all the fields and breathe a smell I know well. All over New Hampshire this weekend, farmers are cutting their hay.

Chapter Twenty-four

OUR NEW HOUSE is less than half the size of the one we left. There's no place for a garden here, or a trampoline. With no room for an office, I set up my computer in our living room. Over the fireplace, I hang my father's painting, *The Woman in the Red Hat*. Another painting that I hang in my bedroom, a New Hampshire landscape, still has one of my father's three-by-five cards taped on the back, from a time long ago when he entered it in a local art show. He has marked the price $25.

Our house is halfway up a mountain. From my desk I can see hawks circling below and the peak of Mt. Tamalpais. Often when I get up in the morning the mountain will be totally obscured by clouds and fog. As the hours pass, the mountain slowly begins to emerge, like the image in a Polaroid photograph developing before my eyes. By noon, its green and craggy form stands squarely in front of me from where I sit.

Everything looks different from here. My family, my marriage, my divorce. Things that seemed huge on School Street in Keene, or my kitchen table in Hillsboro, or Jerry's velvet couch, or my old bedroom in Durham, are now three thousand miles away. Back in New Hampshire, there seemed no stretch of road I hadn't traveled. There were ghosts everywhere.

My first weeks in Northern California are mostly solitary. My sons are spending the summer with their father in New Hampshire, as they will spend most vacations now. Audrey has a job on Cape Cod.

I spend my days hiking the mountain and walking along the coast and exploring the unfamiliar streets of San Francisco. I never run into anybody I know.

There is a kind of euphoria that I experience for the first few months in California. There is huge relief that the terrible ordeal of moving, the burglary, the battles with Steve, are over. As Willy says when he comes back at the end of the summer to enroll in his new school, "We can be anyone we want out here."

I'm not sorry I pulled up stakes. My children are adjusting well. They've made new friends. I have, too. In the fall my daughter drives west and gets a job at a ski resort in Lake Tahoe. We're getting along.

By late fall, though, a sense of melancholy begins to overtake me.

A line comes to me in a dream one night. It stirs me so deeply I wake from my sleep. It's the first line from Isak Dinesen's *Out of Africa*, a book I haven't looked at for twenty years. "I had a farm in Africa, at the foot of the Ngong Hills."

It's such a simple, ordinary sentence. And that one word, *had*, speaks of such loss and longing. The farm is gone. The woman won't be back.

Just before moving to the West Coast, I made a trip to New York to talk with an editor about a book I wanted to write. It will be a memoir, I said. For the first time, I told her, I am able to talk about some things I could never say before. I believe I am ready to tell the story of Jerry Salinger and me.

I have signed a contract to write this book. I receive an advance that will support my family for about a year if I'm careful. I keep the contents of this book secret, for fear of Jerry's response. Although I finally want to explore this story, the thought of incurring his wrath still terrifies me. I tell almost nobody what I'm writing.

The problem is I'm not writing it. For twenty-five years I've gone to my desk almost every morning and done my work, no matter what was going on in the rest of my life. I went to my desk the day after my babies were born and the day my mother died. Now I sit there looking out at the mountain, unable to get beyond my own great sadness. I take magazine assignments to postpone starting the book. I am still struggling to make sense of my story.

All the years I was married, and even after, when I was divorced and living in Keene, I never reread my letters from Jerry. For a while I even lost track of where I'd put them. When it suddenly occurred to me a few years back that I hadn't seen them in a very long time, I started looking for the letters, and couldn't locate them for days. They were scattered in several different places. Some I never did find, and of the ones I located, pages were missing.

As I was searching for the letters I realized how much they meant to me. Contemplating the possibility that they might be gone forever, I felt a level of loss greater than what I would have felt if I'd misplaced almost any other possession in our house.

When I found the letters at last, I did not read them. I knew well enough what they contained, and the opinions of the man who had written them.

Now, at the age of forty-three, I take the packet of letters out again. I choose a night when my children are visiting friends. I spread the letters on my bed and take in the sight of the familiar handwriting and the typewriter font that used to make my heart lift.

I begin to read. This time, Jerry Salinger's words—familiar as they are—strike me differently.

Over the Christmas vacation of 1996, while my children are in New Hampshire, six months after moving to California, I finally get to work. I spend a week writing what I think will be the single chapter of my story that has anything to do with Jerry Salinger. I write forty pages—a brisk and detached-sounding summary that one friend who reads it describes as sounding like the narration to a PBS documentary—and say I'm done. I put it away for six months, not looking at it again during this time.

In July of 1997, when the children leave again, I rent out our house to bring in extra money, and because I feel a need to get away from home to write the things that come hardest. I'm going to spend the month in San Francisco, taking care of the house and dog of a family going on vacation.

Once again, I take out the story of my time with Jerry Salinger.

I call my old English teacher from Exeter, Mark—a friend for all of my adult life, though we've been out of touch in recent years. I tell him what I'm doing. "What do you remember of those visits you paid to Jerry's house that year?" I ask him. I am looking for some other witness besides my own eighteen-year-old self, who can give me the perspective of an observer, one of only a handful, who saw a little of what went on between Jerry and me that year.

My old friend's response takes me by surprise. His voice on the other end of the phone is reserved and distant. "I will have to think about that," he says.

When, having heard nothing, I write to him to ask again, he writes back to say he cannot support what I am doing. He views the book I'm writing as a violation of Jerry Salinger's privacy. He doesn't use the word *exploitation*, though in the months to come, many others will. He and his wife have nothing more to say.

I knew when I embarked on this book that it would offend some people. But the words of my old and trusted friend stun me. I put down his letter and look out the window, feeling sick.

I write a hundred and fifty pages over the course of the next few weeks—pages that span the period from the publication of my first article in *The New York Times* to my return from Daytona Beach.

I am unsettled. I begin to write with more emotion.

While I'm staying in the house in San Francisco, my sister tells me that for all these years she's kept the letters I wrote her when I was young. Opening the envelope full of them that she sends me now, I feel as though I'm hearing a voice, not from the grave, but from a person who no longer exists. The experience leaves me shaken. There's so much this girl doesn't know.

I have been writing for my living twenty-five years now, but no story has ever been as difficult and even physically painful in the telling as this one. Every few hours I have to get up from the table where I'm working. I snap on the leash of the dog I'm caring for and walk with him down Fillmore Street, buy myself a cup of coffee and take a long time drinking it.

For four weeks I'm alone in the room. I'm grateful for the dog, and for my telephone conversations with my cool, reserved, and painfully honest sister. Now and then, to break the silence, I call up a reader I've come to know over the years, from letters, and read something to her over the phone. I hear from my cheerful, wisecracking children, on a camping trip in Idaho with their father. Sometimes, sitting alone in the room, I picture Jerry Salinger's face. I imagine him looking over my shoulder reading what I write. I get up to walk the dog.

For a while, there is a man I spend time with. But as I get deeper into my story, I no longer want to be with him or any man. I am restless and edgy and troubled. I've lost my appetite. I no longer want to play music.

One of the many enduring influences of Jerry Salinger on my life has been a distrust and avoidance of doctors. My children's births were attended by midwives. I sought out pediatricians for them now and then for checkups and immunizations, and I have made the occasional trip to the emergency room with one of them for a broken bone, and a few years ago I located a homeopath in New Hampshire to whom I brought my children. But I never went to doctors myself.

Since the summer, though, I have been experiencing gynecological problems of a sort that have plagued me, intermittently, over the years. Now, for the first time in my life, I make an appointment with a gynecologist.

What she tells me after the examination leaves me shaken.

"Clearly, you experienced severe tearing, peripherally as well as internally, during one of your deliveries," she says.

"You must have had a lot of pain over the years. You should have had surgery a long time ago."

Looking through the names of doctors in the yellow pages, I had come upon one I recognized. My old boyfriend Glenn, the man to whom I finally relinquished my long-held virginity, is evidently a physician now practicing in San Francisco. I call him.

He's married, with two young children, living just a few miles from me. Although it's been two decades since we've spoken, I still feel comfortable with him. I tell him about the book I'm writing. I ask what he remembers about my sexual problem.

"I knew we could work it out," he says. "All I had to do was pay attention."

When the day comes to pick up my children at the airport, it's a huge relief to put the manuscript away again.

I catch sight of my sons coming through the doorway of the plane—taller than the last time I saw them, brown and grinning; Charlie with his skateboard under his arm, Willy with his tennis bag. I throw my arms around them. They've given themselves buzz cuts. As we head to the baggage claim to pick up the rest of their stuff, I can't stop rubbing the tops of their heads.

In the fall I make myself busy with other things: Audrey has started college at Santa Cruz. I write a screenplay for *Where Love Goes*. Charlie and Willy are playing junior varsity soccer on the same team, and I love watching their games. In the last game of the season, it is Willy who scores the tying goal, followed by another. In the last minutes of the game, the coach tells Charlie, who has been playing defense all season and longing to be an offensive player, to substitute for his brother in the position of striker. Charlie says he'd rather stay where he is and finish the season playing with his brother.

Audrey calls to say she's giving a presentation in front of her Introduction to Feminism class, displaying a quilt she's made and talking about the significance of quilts and sewing in the lives of women. I take the day off and drive two hours south to Santa Cruz to hear her.

Watching my daughter as she holds up her quilt in front of the large lecture course, speaking in a voice filled with self-assurance, I think, as I have so often over the years, how my mother would have loved to see this. When we held our moving sale back in New Hampshire, we got rid of the boxes of fabrics we'd collected over the years, many from my mother. But one square in Audrey's quilt, orange and red Chinese silk, comes from one of the full-length home-sewn gowns my mother used to wear to greet me when I came home from school.

After the class, Audrey brings me back to the dormitory suite she shares with six other young women. They are cooking a meal of tofu and organic vegetables. They are all deeply concerned with being healthy and strong.

On the wall in the living room they share is an artwork Audrey and her roommates have created. They have made plaster casts of their own naked torsos and painted them silver. As we sit down to eat, I study the seven bellies and the fourteen breasts. "They're all beautiful, aren't they?" my daughter says.

I am thinking about my book every day, although I haven't looked at the manuscript since August. Hiking along the trails to the top of Mount Tam, or over the mountain to Stinson Beach, I think about Jerry Salinger, the letters, my marriage.

I reread all of Salinger's work. More than ten years after it was first published, I go to the library and check out Ian Hamilton's biography of Salinger I had avoided reading before. Without the letters, and with so few sources willing to speak of Salinger and so little information available, Hamilton has little to work with.

A single line in the book stands out for me. It's a comment made to Ian Hamilton by a writer named Leila Hadley, who knew Jerry Salinger in the early fifties. Speaking of Salinger, she says, "It wasn't a sexual power, it was a mental power. You felt he had the power to imprison someone mentally. It was as if one's mind were at risk, rather than one's virtue."

Briefly, I consider researching World War II actions in which the young Jerry Salinger was known to be involved as an intelligence officer. One of the more significant of these was known as Slapton Sands. A rehearsal for D day, conducted on beaches off the coast of Devon in April of 1944, Slapton Sands proved to be one of the most terrible Allied failures of the war. Through a series of communication mistakes, the Germans got wind of the Allied forces' plan and attacked in a way the Allied troops were totally unprepared for. Seven hundred and forty-five Allied soldiers were lost on a single day. News of what had happened was covered up (a job that would have fallen to Army intelligence officers). Not until after the end of the Eisenhower administration was the story finally told.

In Salinger's story, "For Esmé—with Love and Squalor," the date of the young soldier's meeting in a town just off the coast of Devon with the little girl, Esmé, is given as April 30, 1944, three days after the battle of Slapton Sands. Some months later, when we meet the soldier again at the end of the story, he has evidently suffered a mental breakdown.

I consider launching full-steam into a study of Slapton Sands as a way of possibly revealing to myself some key to the mystery of Jerry Salinger's secrecy and his choice to remove himself from the world. I come to recognize that understanding my experience with Jerry won't be revealed from studying distant battlefronts.

From a magazine editor friend, I get the telephone number of Phyllis Theroux.

"We met years ago at a party in New York," I begin. "I don't know if you'll remember——"

"Of course I do," she says. "I've always felt badly about that. I told you the story of our au pair girl's letters because I had this vague idea I'd heard something about you knowing Salinger at some point, and I thought you might be interested. I had no idea it would upset you. One look at your face and I knew it had hit you hard."

I also had a correspondence with J. D. Salinger, I tell her. Until that day, I had supposed I was the only one.

The au pair girl's name was Colleen O., Phyllis tells me. She was twenty-one when Phyllis hired her to take care of her household and her children in the summer of 1980.

Colleen came from an Irish Catholic family. Some time before she came to work for Phyllis, she had taken a bus to the Dartmouth Winter Carnival to visit a friend there, maybe a boyfriend. The year was 1977 or 1978.

On the long bus ride north, she struck up a conversation with a very charming gray-haired man sitting next to her. When the bus reached White River Junction, she still had to get to Hanover, another five miles over the river. She asked the man where she might find a bus or a taxi. He offered to give her a ride. He looked "harmless," she told Phyllis. So she got in his car.

He told her his name was Jerry Salinger. "Do you mean J. D. Salinger?" she asked.

They exchanged addresses and began to correspond.

The exchange of letters continued for a few months. It wasn't any kind of romance, Phyllis was certain. Colleen had no problem showing Phyllis the letters. Mostly, Phyllis recalls, they were mildly amusing reports of household goings-on with his son, his garden, his house. Nothing an au pair girl couldn't show her employer. "Colleen was impressed to be receiving letters from a famous writer.

"When she told me the story, she said something about how she owed him a letter, but in an offhand way," says Phyllis. "Almost as if it were a chore. You know: 'Do nails. Wash hair. Write J. D. Salinger.' It didn't seem to be a very big thing in Colleen's life."

The big thing in her life at the time was a young man whom she'd met shortly before taking the job with Phyllis, who was now calling her every night after the long-distance rates went down. It became clear within a few months of Colleen's arrival that she was in love with him.

In the end, Colleen O. left her job as au pair to Phyllis Theroux and moved back to Maryland to be close to Mike D., the young man who had been courting her by telephone all that summer.

They got married. Phyllis thinks she still has a wedding snapshot Colleen sent her. Colleen was the subject of an essay that Phyllis published. It had nothing to do with J. D. Salinger. She says she'll send me a copy.

A few days later the envelope comes with the essay. It's a

tenderly written story of a young girl so organized and efficient she showed up at Phyllis Theroux's house at the age of twenty-one with her own pressure cooker. The young Colleen had a job at an art gallery and ambitions to go back to school and travel, have adventures, get to know the city away from her hometown of Belair, Maryland. But every night, she got a call from the young man who wanted her to come and be with him. She was terribly torn.

In the envelope she sends me, Phyllis has also enclosed a photograph of Colleen and Mike on their wedding day. He has a kind and handsome face—dark hair, blue eyes. He is leaning toward Colleen and smiling. It's a picture of a young man in love.

The girl in the picture also looks wonderfully happy and singularly without conflict on her wedding day. She wears a modest blue taffetta dress with short sleeves and a white Peter Pan collar with a blue taffeta rose pinned on the front.

She's very pretty, with curly, sandy-colored hair and brown eyes, and a wide, trusting smile. Her cheeks look naturally pink, without a trace of makeup.

I am driven to know more of Colleen O.'s story. If I can understand what happened to someone else, I may be able, finally, to understand what happened to me, and the curious hold that Jerry Salinger has had all these years when I supposed he'd never loved anybody else the way he had loved me.

I want to know what he said to her in those letters. Did he tell her they were landsmen, too, and hold up to her a picture of herself as a girl unlike any other, who might discover with him, and no one else, the meaning of enlightenment?

Phyllis Theroux has told me that she heard Colleen and Mike got a divorce a while back. She's long since lost touch with Colleen. But I track down the phone number of her former husband, who lives in a small town in southern Pennsylvania.

It's an odd way to introduce myself to a stranger, to tell him about my love affair with J. D. Salinger, twenty-five years ago. "I'm trying to understand what it meant," I tell him. "I have the impression your ex-wife also had a correspondence with J. D.

Salinger," I say. I tell him I'll understand if he'd rather not talk to me.

But he wants to talk. His voice on the other end of the line sounds shaken but eager, almost hungry, to talk with me. "J. D. Salinger?" he says, as though it's the first time he's uttered that name in years. When he speaks to me, he calls me "ma'am."

"I can't believe you've called me like this," he says. "After all these years, finally there might be some kind of explanation."

When Mike D. met Colleen O., he had a nine-month-old son, also named Mike, whose mother had abandoned the baby. He was a nursing student. So was Colleen.

"She was the sweetest, most innocent girl," he says. "Very trusting. Old-fashioned in some ways. She had high values. She wanted so badly to make something of herself. She was a very loving, generous person. How could I help but fall in love with her? She was the love of my life."

He courted her all that summer she worked for Phyllis Theroux. She had earned a college scholarship, but when she decided to leave her job and marry Mike, she left school. "I told her she didn't have to, but she wanted to work, and dedicate herself to being a mother to Mike, Jr.," he says. She adopted the baby.

"We had a good life together," he tells me. "A little boy we treasured, and we were planning on having more children." Hearing him say this, I recognize, as a person who's gone through a divorce of my own, how one person's vision of their marriage can differ from another's. The woman whose husband says they had a wonderful life—the same thing Mike is telling me now about himself and Colleen—might have a very different story to tell.

Mike had suffered from kidney disease, and when he was with Colleen he was on dialysis three times a week. But his health was always good. He was waiting until Mike, Jr., got older before he had a kidney transplant. Meanwhile, he was strong and well enough that he and Colleen led an active life. They took weekend trips with their son. He played sports. There was no shortage of physical affection.

She had told him she had some letters from J. D. Salinger. She was very proud of these letters. She spoke of J. D. Salinger as her good friend. "It just goes to show that you never know whom you might run into," she told her husband.

Now and then she'd get a letter from this Jerry Salinger. "I'd never read any of the gentleman's books, but if my wife wanted to be friends with the man, that was fine with me," he said.

He and Colleen bought a farm with space for horses and chickens. On their kitchen counter they kept a journal, open to record their daily entries about their lives.

Colleen had been a devout Catholic when Mike met her, but over the years, she developed an interest in Christian Science.

"Out of the blue one day, on Thanksgiving, with all the relatives coming over later, she called me at work to say she was leaving us. She took all her things and went to her sister's house. Mike, Jr., was four years old. We were heartbroken."

He got this feeling that in another week or two, she wouldn't speak to him at all, so he went to see her while he still could. "Forget that I'm your husband. Pretend I'm just some person, and try and tell me why you're leaving," he said. She had no answer for him.

Shortly after moving to her sister's, she moved again. He never had a street address or phone number, just a post office box in Windsor, Vermont. "I wrote to her every day for two years," he says. "I felt maybe she'd had some kind of breakdown. I didn't understand what she needed, but I wanted her to always know back at home we still loved her. I gave her a gold necklace with a cross and told her to wear it every day, to protect her. I didn't understand what was happening."

In the twelve years since Colleen has left—"Col," he calls her—she has never explained what happened. "I'd be watching some show like *Unsolved Mysteries*, and I'd half expect to see her face on the TV set," Mike says.

He never filed for divorce, but when the papers came, he signed them. He wasn't going to get in her way if that was what she wanted. For years, his son carried a photograph of Colleen because nobody believed he had a mother and he wanted to prove he did.

Mike D. has never remarried. A few years back, in preparation for the kidney transplant, he sold the farm and gave away the chickens, knowing it would be too hard for his son to keep up with the chores on his own. When he finally got his new kidney, four years ago, there were complications, and he had to stay in the hospital longer than he'd planned. He made sure his son got a bank card, and taught him how to make simple meals. Twelve years old at the time, Mike, Jr., took care of himself at home for six months.

Mike, Sr., is healthy now. He's opened up a dialysis center, which he manages along with holding down his regular nursing job. He coaches Little League.

Colleen visits them one or two times a year. Once when she came to visit, they noticed she was wearing a very plain gold band on her ring finger. "She told our son she would never take it off."

The last time she came to visit, last summer, Mike, Jr., asked if he could come to Vermont to visit for a week. She said it wasn't possible. He and his father asked no further questions. "She's a very private person," he says.

If they even knew what had happened, it would be better, he says. "For twelve years, I've lived with this mystery."

Their son's in the tenth grade now, at Catholic school. (The reason, maybe, why he's never read *Catcher in the Rye*.) He's a good student, his father says. He plays baseball. He has lots of friends. They still keep Colleen's picture up.

Every month she sends $50 for child support, with the return address of a post office box in Windsor, Vermont. For Christmas last year, she sent her son a scarf and $25. On his birthday every year comes an envelope with the number of dollar bills to match his age. This year it was sixteen.

A year and a half has gone by now since I left New Hampshire. I have not been back. Now, in November, weeks after the moment when the leaves are in their glory, I feel a powerful need to return to my home state.

I know the writing of this book is part of it, too. I keep raking my memory for the piece of my story that I haven't uncovered yet. I know it's there. I think if I return to New Hampshire, where nearly everything that ever happened to me took place, I'll arrive at a point of clarity and understanding. Three days before my forty-fourth birthday, I board a plane and fly east.

Chapter Twenty-five

I MAKE A stop in Washington, D.C. There are more than two hundred pages of Salinger letters at the Library of Congress that can only be read there. I think that maybe if I read them, the voice of Jerry Salinger will tell me something. Somewhere in those pages, I might find part of my answer.

I arrive in Washington at eight A.M. and take a taxi in the pouring rain from the airport to the Library of Congress. I find the special documents room, where the Salinger letters are kept under lock and key. Nobody can make copies, and even the notes a person takes while looking at them will be inspected before leaving. But for ten dollars, anyone can read them.

The earliest letters, from the forties, are written to Whit Burnett, editor of *Story* magazine and a former Columbia writing teacher of Jerry Salinger's, from a class he took in his early twenties. The letters to Burnett reveal a young man of wild ambition and desire to publish his work—cocky, self-promoting, posturing at times, and surprisingly obsequious. The young Jerry Salinger is deeply concerned with the opinions of editors and reviewers and he compares himself regularly to other writers—Fitzgerald, Lardner, Hemingway—concluding that he is more talented than all three, as well as younger. He places a high priority on making money, and tells Burnett he plans to hit the jackpot.

He writes from Europe, where he's stationed with the army, that he's deeply unhappy, but adds that all that matters is he's never written better. He's got some stories in the works, about a terrific kid named Holden. Jerry Salinger says there's a novel in him, but not one he's ready to tackle until he's sure he can pull it off. Some magazine editor type has evidently referred to him as "a craftsman," when he would have preferred to be one who has taken the short story to a new level of honesty and simplicity. Nobody understands who he really is.

Another set of letters was written to a woman named Elizabeth Murray, the sister of an old classmate, but not a girlfriend. The letters to Elizabeth Murray, as well as those to Whit Burnett, contain passing references to one girl or another with whom Jerry's briefly involved, although their names seldom come up.

One definitely stands out, though: Oona O'Neill, an early flame, who appears to have spurned his advances. One of these letters contains a bizarre passage in which Jerry describes his fantasy of a scene filled with dark sexual overtones between Oona, age eighteen, and the pathetically geriatric Charlie Chaplin, age fifty-three, whom she married, to Jerry's obvious disgust. Jerry Salinger must have been proud of this passage: The same language concerning Chaplin and O'Neill appears in a letter to Whit Burnett written several months later.

There's a sense of profound despair in these letters, covered up with humor. Talking about what's going on at the front, he can be funny and wry, and frequently sarcastic. He makes a joke about one occasion in which he dove for a ditch to avoid enemy fire, but the reader is left with the impression that he has been deeply shaken by what he's seen in the war. He's trying hard not to lose his mind. He speculates that he should get married, if only to steady his nerves. Girls frequently accept his proposals, but he loses interest.

Reading these letters from the front, one gets a sense that the young Jerry Salinger has witnessed terrible and profoundly upsetting things here. He muses on the notion of firing a slug into his own palm, and considers the effects the injury might have on his ability to type.

He makes one brief mention of a stay in a hospital, apparently for psychiatric reasons. Most of what he talks about, though, even from the front, is his writing, which clearly obscures everything else that's going on. In a letter written just days after the Japanese bombing of Pearl Harbor, it is not until somewhere at the end that he gets around to mentioning the disaster in the Pacific. In another letter to Elizabeth Murray, Jerry Salinger spends several paragraphs discussing stories he's working on or publishing before telling her he's getting married in a week or two, to a "fine" girl whose name he neglects to mention.

A letter to Ernest Hemingway, whom he met briefly during the war, reveals his concern about his place in literary history. He'd give a lot to get out of the army, but he mustn't risk the possibility that when he publishes the novel he intends to write, after the war, he could be ostracized for having had a psychiatric discharge.

To Hemingway, he writes he's working on a play involving a character named Holden Caulfield. He'd like to play the role himself after the war's over, opposite Margaret O'Brien.

With the exception of one line in one letter, in which he makes a joke about his mother, Jerry hardly ever mentions any member of his family—his parents or his sister. He refers only briefly, in a single letter, to having just terminated the marriage he made after the war, explaining to Elizabeth Murray that he and his young wife made each other miserable, and that he was unable to write the whole time he was with her. Reading this letter, I experience a momentary chill. Dated June 13, 1946, it's written from Daytona Beach, Florida.

The letters that seem the most genuine are the ones written during the fifties, when he was married to Claire and living with her in the red house in Cornish.

These letters are written to Judge Learned Hand, his older, much-admired friend, who spent the summers with his wife in Cornish during this period. The voice in these letters is not affected with sarcasm. It is often melancholic and yearning and filled with respect.

In these letters, Jerry expresses concern about the possibility that Claire may become restless during the long, lonely winters with their baby, Peggy. In one passage, he describes a scene in which his young wife is trying to make the best of things, dreamily flipping through magazines while he sequesters himself day after day, writing.

She's only twenty-six, he writes. She should be having more fun.

Chapter Twenty-six

NOVEMBER 1997. NEW Hampshire is bleak. There is no snow on the ground yet, but the air always seems coldest to me this time of year.

Almost all the leaves are off the trees now, and even the ones that haven't fallen are brown rather than orange or red. People's vegetable gardens look defeated, with the shriveled remains of plants killed by frost and old rotten pumpkins and squash lying on the crusty soil. The sun goes down early these days; it's dark before five.

I stay at a friend's house in the little town of Harrisville, next door to the preschool Audrey went to when she was four. I visit my old neighbors from our street in Keene. I knock at the door to our old house, and the new owners, a family with three children, take me through the rooms.

Driving through the streets, I see my lawyer, my postman, kids who used to jump on our trampoline. I wave to the parents of Audrey's old boyfriend.

I take a walk with my friend Peggy around the perimeter of Dublin Lake. I have been telling her about what I'm writing. I come to the part about how I couldn't have intercourse with Jerry Salinger. In the past, I've always regarded my inability to consummate my relationship with Jerry as a terrible and even tragic event in my youth. For the first time, as I'm telling Peggy about this, I understand something new.

My body was sending me a message. Nobody around me——

not my mother, my friends, my teacher—told me to be careful, that this was not right. But my own body would allow no trespass.

"I don't know how I can lay this to rest," I say to Peggy.

"What would you ask Jerry Salinger now, if you could talk to him?" she wants to know.

I ask Peggy if I can borrow her husband's truck.

The next day, November 4, is cloudy. Rain threatens. It's a sixty-mile drive to Cornish. I play music the whole time I'm driving.

I go first to Windsor, Vermont, the little town just over the Connecticut River from New Hampshire, where Jerry always kept his post office box. I walk into the post office and run my hand over the post office boxes. This is where he came to pick up my letters, and where he dropped his in the mail to me.

I lived in this town many months, but the only people here I ever knew by name were Sally and Dan Kemp. Yesterday I called Dan to ask if I could come to see him "What do you know?" he said. "I haven't spoken to you in a quarter of a century."

When I get to Dan's house he's outside moving a woodpile with his backhoe. In his late fifties, he is an open-faced man, wearing a worn flannel shirt and jeans. He takes me in the house and puts on water for tea.

It's the kind of house I have been inside often in my New Hampshire days, especially in the early days of my marriage, in the seventies. Herbs drying over the woodstove and the smoky smell of wood heat. Plants hanging in macramé holders and oil lamps and hand-woven rugs and back issues of *Mother Jones* and *Mother Earth News* and wood burl bowls he's made in his shop.

He is a jovial, instantly friendly man. You would think, to hear him talking to me now, that we were old friends.

We talk about many things. His marriage to Sally, their divorce, and the woman he's with now. He shows me pictures of his daughters. The older one was the baby Sally used to bring along for her homeopathy study sessions with Jerry Salinger.

"Jerry probably paid a lot of attention to your children," I say.

"To tell you the truth, they didn't think much of him," Dan says. "They said he was always kissing them."

I remember Jerry never thought much of Dan Kemp. This didn't keep him from asking Dan to do him a favor now and then.

Dan says Jerry calls him once in a while when he has wanted to sell his car, to avoid dealing with the public. Back in the sixties they used to throw around a baseball and talk about the teams they favored—the Yankees for Jerry; for Dan, a native New Hampshire man, the Red Sox.

These days when they run into each other, they talk about their vegetable gardens. Jerry has asked Dan about Sally, who moved back to town not long ago, and lives just down the road, but she has not gone over to see her former mentor.

"A long time ago, Jerry asked Sally to leave me and move in with him," Dan says. "She told him no and it never came to anything."

"Did Jerry ever say anything about me?" I ask him. "Didn't you think it was odd that I was there? Did Sally ever ask anything?"

"He told Sally some story about your publisher sending you up here to work with him on a book you were writing."

"Were there other girls?" I ask.

"There were always girls in one way or another. There's a woman living with him now. She's been around a few years. Before that, others came and went.

"He had a way of writing letters. One time there was this young woman over in England he took a shine to. He flew over there to meet her. He took one look at her and got right back on the next plane."

There was another one. "She was a college girl from California. Nineteen seventy-seven, probably. Maybe seventy-eight. Jerry would've been around sixty. The two of them exchanged letters for a while. Then this girl got the idea that she should come here. She shows up one day in downtown Windsor, and calls him up.

"So Jerry calls Sally. He needs her to come right over. He wants her to pose as his girlfriend, and go with him to deal with this girl.

"They met her at the diner. Jerry tells the girl he's with Sally. They keep it brief and send her away."

"How did this young woman take it?" I ask him.

"Pretty bad, according to Sally. The girl was totally out of it. She fell apart completely, you could say."

A month or so later, Dan tells me, he ran an ad looking for a printer's assistant for the printshop he ran in those days. Who should answer his ad but this girl? He recognized her name from Sally's story.

She was a beautiful girl, too. Smart. Well spoken. She even knew a fair amount about printing, since that had been her father's business.

"I couldn't hire her," he says. "Jerry would have been furious. When I told her I knew him, she started to cry. She kept talking about how she had to see him again. She had to get to him. That's why she needed this job, so she could stay in Hanover and be near him."

Later, Dan tells me, the young woman had some kind of breakdown. She went to the state hospital in Concord for a while. She's back in Hanover now.

Now? I say. She must be . . .

"Around your age," he says. "Sometimes I see her in the street, talking to herself, not that she recognizes me. She spends a lot of time in the Dartmouth Library. There's a policeman in town who has coffee with her sometimes. He says she's still writing letters to Salinger. When Jerry gets one, he turns it over to the cops."

"I have to go," I tell Dan. I have another stop to make. He walks me out to my car and says good-bye.

By the time I get to Jerry Salinger's house, it's four o'clock. The last light of day is closing in. Dark clouds fill the sky. Dry leaves swirl around the wheels of my truck.

I recognize the spot, though the only marker is the NO TRES-PASSING sign still posted at the foot of the driveway leading up the steep hill to his house.

When people made their pilgrimages to see him in the days when I lived here, they would park their car on the side of the dirt road and walk up the hill. Usually these visitors would be young people. I know, when I reach this spot, that I am not going to park. I'm driving up the hill.

As I come over the crest, the house comes into view. A few years ago I read that there was a bad fire here, but he must have taken great care to rebuild the place. It looks exactly as I remember. The deck looks out to the mountain and the garage is underneath, though there is a second garage now, too, with bays for three more cars. The satellite dish is also new.

I turn off the ignition and get out of the truck. I look out at Mt. Ascutney, watching the clouds building and the way the shadows fall over the field. His garden has been cleaned for winter.

I walk up the last stretch of hill to the house. I go around the back, to the door by the kitchen. My heartbeat is surprisingly steady.

I'm standing at the door now, next to the bird feeder. Through the window, overlooking the doorstep, a woman stands at the sink, washing dishes. She's a sweet-faced person with a no-nonsense haircut, dressed in turtleneck and neat blue jeans. It takes me a moment to realize I've seen this face before, in a blue taffeta dress with a Peter Pan collar: Colleen O., the love of Mike D.'s life, and the woman whose photograph Mike, Jr., used to keep in his wallet when he was little to prove he had a mother.

I ring the bell.

Colleen moves back and forth in and out of view for a moment or two, then calls out through the window, not unpleasantly, "What do you want?"

"I've come to see Jerry," I say. "Could you tell him Joyce Maynard's here?" The steadiness of my voice surprises me. A flicker of a smile crosses her face.

She goes into one of the back rooms. "Someday, you may find yourself in a situation where it may help you to say this word," he told me once. *Om.*

There are certain moments in your life when all the senses seem to enter a state of intensified acuity, and you notice every single thing. Your eyes take in more, and what they take in, they take in with a sharpness they didn't possess ten minutes earlier, and will not possess ten minutes later—a cloud formation, a stick on the ground that looks chewed by a dog. You hear the sound your boot heel makes touching the rubber mat on the doorstep, and the pecking of a bird picking up a single grain of birdseed. You can feel your own blood moving through your veins.

Childbirth was one of those times for me. Holding a baby for a few hours at a time, watching her nurse. So was sitting beside my mother while she lay dying, and all I had to do was watch the breath come in and out of her.

It's hard to say how long I stand on this doorstep. Five minutes maybe. More likely ten. There is no reason in the world why he would come out of that room. Only I know he will, and he does.

All these years I have thought of him as such a tall man. Now, as Jerry emerges slowly from the bedroom and stands in front of me in the doorway, he seems shrunken. He is a little bent over.

He's wearing a very fine bathrobe and slippers. He is thinner than ever. At seventy-eight, he still has all his hair. It is pure white now. He is clean-shaven, and his face is deeply lined.

He does not invite me in. I remain standing on the step. I have never looked a man in the eye before who looked back at me with an expression of greater bitterness or rage.

"What are you doing here?" he says. The words come at me. *Spitting*. "Why didn't you write me a letter?"

"I wrote you many letters, Jerry," I say. "You never answered them."

"What are you doing here?" he says. His voice comes from that place deep in the diaphragm the orgonomist taught him to use. It's a voice that doesn't have to be loud to make itself heard.

"I came to ask you a question, Jerry," I say. "What was my purpose in your life?"

I would not have believed that a person could ever look more angry than he did the moment he first laid eyes on me. But now his mouth, which doesn't speak yet, curls as if he has bitten into a piece of fruit, and found it to be filled with maggots.

"What was my purpose in your life?" I say again. The image that comes to me is of Rumpelstiltskin, as I always imagined him, and even acted him out, there on my bed all those years ago with my sons and daughter snuggled up beside me—that moment when the miller's daughter has one chance left to guess his name, or her baby will be lost to her forever. And she guesses right. That is how Jerry Salinger looks now, when I put my question to him.

"That question—" he says, almost too angry to speak. "That question—that question—that question is *too profound*. You don't deserve an answer to that question."

"Oh yes I do," I say.

I am still calm. I can feel warm water washing over me. I am swimming my crawl stroke, and my breathing is steady. I am skating on black ice over Loon Pond on a moonlit night with Steve's arm around my waist. I am cutting up apples for pie, with a baby propped in an infant seat on the counter next to me. I am hitting a tennis ball with my son, under the lights at the Keene State courts, at midnight. I am riding with my daughter on the chair lift, and I know just when to lift the bar and lower the tips of my skis.

"You're writing something, aren't you?" he says.

"I'm always writing," I say. "I'm a *writer*." I have never called myself that, before. I have always left it that I write.

"You're writing a *book*, aren't you?" he says. He says it as if it were a pornographic act. "I've heard you're writing some kind of . . . *reminiscence*."

"Yes," I say. "I am writing a book."

"You have spent your career writing gossip," he says. "You write empty, meaningless, offensive, putrid gossip. You live your life as a pathetic, parasitic gossip."

I am looking at his hands, his fingers wrapped around the belt of his bathrobe. The same long, elegant fingers that I loved— fingers that touched my naked skin before any other man had, before so many other things happened.

"I'm not ashamed of the work I've done," I say. "I've worked hard to be an honest writer."

He throws back his head as if to laugh, only no laughter comes out of him—only the stifled sound of the syllable *"Ha."* "You always did have an inflated notion of yourself and your so-called talents," he says.

"You know," I tell him, "I never took myself seriously as a writer until you told me I was one."

He stands there for a moment. Then, taking a step backward, he raises his long thin finger so it's pointing directly at my heart.

"You, Joyce—" he says, finger still pointing. "You. You. *You*."

His whole body is quaking, and his eyes stare out at me as if he were beholding a sight of unspeakable horror.

"The problem with you, Joyce, is . . . *you—love—the—world.*"

"*Yes,*" I say, smiling. "Yes, I *do* love the world. And I've raised three children who love the world, too."

"I knew you would amount to this," he says. *"Nothing."* He, the man who told me that if there was anything he knew at all, it was that I would be a true writer no matter what. Nobody, ever, could take that away from me, he told me once. Never forget that, he said. Let no one ever tell you what to say. *Trust nothing but your own strong voice.*

"I want to say good-bye to you, Jerry," I say.

"I don't hear well," he says. His voice seems less powerful than it was a few minutes ago. I can no longer smile. I feel nothing but a wave of sorrow. This was a wonderful man one time. I loved him more than anything on earth. I danced with him in the living room to the magic accordion of Myron Florin, Lawrence Welk's finest. I have no desire to hurt him. Only to let him go at last.

"You mean to exploit your relationship with me, I suppose?" he says.

"It may be true that someone standing in this doorway has exploited someone else who's standing in this doorway. I will leave it to you to meditate on which one of us is which."

As I walk away he calls out one more thing: the last words I am ever likely to hear from the first man I loved.

"I didn't exploit you!" he calls out. *"I don't even know you."*

Slowly, I walk back to Chris's truck. I don't get in right away. I stand there a moment, taking in the view of Mt. Ascutney one more time. The last light of day is disappearing.

I climb into the cab. Turn on the ignition. I head very slowly down the hill. When I get to the main road, I pull the truck over and take out my notebook. I write down everything that just happened.

Just as I start the engine again, the storm finally breaks. The combination of the rain and my own clouded eyes makes it so I can barely see out the windshield. I crash Chris's truck into a stop sign a minute later, badly enough to bang up the muffler a little, but not so much I can't head down the highway.

The CD I've been playing over and over, all day, comes on again, and I begin to sing. And for this one moment—even an hour from now, it won't be so anymore—I am in possession of the most beautiful singing voice. I feel my lungs expand. It's Paul Simon's song about going to Graceland.

"The Mississippi Delta was shining like a National Guitar," I sing. I'm passing the Connecticut River now. I'm on the highway, heading home.

Someplace between Lebanon, New Hampshire, and Keene, with the darkness closing in, a lost memory hits me so strongly I pull over to the side of the highway.

It's not true that I had never seen a face that angry before. I *had* seen such a face.

It is the day the call comes from Time *magazine. We're in his bedroom.*

"My work," he says, sinking onto the bed. Head in his hands. His fingers raking through his hair. "Everything I've ever cared about. You are destroying them. What was I thinking of?"

"I'll disappear," I say. "I'll tell them I won't say anything when my book comes out. I don't want any of that. I just want to be with you."

"Oh, but you do care," he says, turning to look at me now with an awful imitation of a smile. "And how! You want so much."

"Only you," I say. "All I want is for you to love me."

Now is when the image comes to me, like a scene in a movie I had slept through long ago that I'm seeing now as if for the first time.

What I see is his face, as I had never before allowed myself to remember it. It's the very same face I saw today, and his voice terrifies me with its coldness.

"You talk about love," he says. "You love so much, don't you? You are greedy and hungry and grasping. You can't stop loving all the

foolish, empty, hollow attractions the world has to offer you—all the things your mother loves, all those meaningless prizes about which you care so inordinately much. She did this to you. You have chosen your mother's way. I hope it makes you happy. I doubt it will."

"No," I scream. "I don't choose that. I choose you. Not her. You."

"There's no hope for you, Joyce," he says. His voice is very quiet, hissing, barely audible. "Just look at you." He shakes his head with something like pity as he gets up to leave. He goes into the kitchen. I can hear him taking out a pot. He's fixing himself something to eat. I am having trouble breathing.

I don't want him to see me like this. I open the door to his closet and climb in. I close the door and sit there, crouched on the floor, for a long time. Hours.

It's nighttime when he comes back into the room and gets into bed. Now I come out, take off my clothes, put on my nightgown, and climb in next to him.

"I'm sorry," I whisper. "I'll never speak of you to anyone again."

"You foolish little girl," he says. "You foolish, foolish little girl. Do you have any idea how weary I have grown of you?"

I have driven thousands of miles of New Hampshire roads, mostly with children. Looking in the rearview mirror I could always see their faces: Willy with a bagel on a string around his neck, making truck sounds. Audrey singing to herself, a made-up song about princesses, or reading to her brothers, Charlie sucking his thumb. Now and then my children would fight, and I'd pull over by the side of the highway and turn off the ignition, close my eyes, count to ten. I might even tell one of them to step outside the car and do jumping jacks or sit in the tall grass for a minute until whatever problem it was that had seemed so terrible looked different. Once or twice I got out of the car myself and sat on a rock while they called to me, "Come back, Mom. We're ready to be good."

I have known wild frustration, exhaustion, impatience, loneliness, and anxiety as a parent. But never pure despair. I always believed that things would eventually be good again, and they were.

Alone in the truck now, I speak the names of my children— three words that, more than any others, conjure up hopefulness and joy. I seldom have to drive them to their destinations any-more. They drive themselves, and when they do they sometimes get speeding tickets. They are launched in the world, like the little paper boats we used to build and sail together in the brook down the road from our old farmhouse in Hillsboro, whose progress we'd follow for a while, racing along the shore, till the current carried them away. Only a handful of years remains in which a child of mine will live under the same roof with me. This is a fact that alternately evokes a sense of loss and possibility.

"You don't need to worry about me anymore, Mama," my daughter told me recently. "You did a good job with me. I'm not always going to do the things you'd want, and I'm probably going to make some hard mistakes. But when I do I'll be strong enough to cope with them. I'm still growing, but I'm very sturdy at my center."

Route 89 South takes me to the exit for Bradford, New Hampshire, where I stop to see my friend Laurie and her husband, Dave, Steve's sheetrocking partner, who are just sitting down to dinner with their daughters. We have a bowl of soup. I drive from there to Hillsboro. I come to the sign at the end of our old road, with Steve's last name that he painted there the day of our wedding.

He's not home, but I get out of the truck and stand in the field in the darkness. Only for a moment. I leave a note on the door for him. *I stopped by. Sorry you weren't here.*

I stop by Geoff and Leslie's house. Geoff has brought home a pizza. Leslie makes coffee. They tell me what's going on with their children. I tell them what's happening with mine.

It's late when I get back to Keene. I will sleep at my friends Shirley and Bill's. When I walk in the door, close to midnight, there are streamers up and cake waiting. Bill says he'll put on water for pasta; there's homemade marinara in the pot. In ten minutes it will be my birthday.

Afterword

I WANT TO say something about letters, because they have played a profoundly significant role in my life.

For more than four decades my mother documented her life and the experiences of our family in letters to her parents and her friends. I regard the carbon copies of the many hundreds of type-written pages she left as her most precious legacy to my sister and me, and to anyone else lucky enough to read them. My mother's letters—quoted throughout this story—were an invaluable re-source in the writing of this book, as was my father's correspon-dence with my mother during the six years of their courtship—a correspondence that included drawings and original verse as well as extravagant expressions of love. No doubt the fact that I was the product of a love affair that knew its finest hours on paper contributed to my forming such a relationship myself, years later.

After growing up and leaving home, my sister and I main-tained to some degree our family tradition of letter writing. I am deeply grateful to Rona Maynard for having kept the letters I wrote to her during the year I spent with J. D. Salinger and after-ward. Rereading them from a distance of more than two decades, I felt as if a message in a bottle had washed up on my shore. The words and feelings of myself at eighteen years old came back to me in one powerful wave.

One set of letters that make up a crucial piece of my history are the forty or so pages of my correspondence with J. D. Salinger, from April 1972 to August 1973. Long before I met the author of the letters, I fell in love with his voice on the page. Sometimes funny, other moments tender, and frequently wise, knowing, and scarily prescient, Jerry Salinger's words formed the basis of my powerful and enduring attachment to him, and haunted me for years after he left my life.

I understood, when I approached the task of telling this story, that while the physical pages of J. D. Salinger's letters are mine, the language of those letters belong to the man who wrote them to me, and that he would never allow his words to be quoted at length here or elsewhere.

Faced with the prospect of telling this story without the ability to reproduce fully the contents of the letters, I initially felt at a loss. While I continue to regret my inability to share with readers the precise and inimitable language contained in those letters, I have worked painstakingly to suggest the sense of them, and the feeling they engendered in the girl who received them. Conveying the feeling brought about by language without the language itself was one of the most challenging tasks I have ever faced as a writer, and one that, in the end, I felt equipped to handle. While it remains a loss for every reader not to have access to the letters themselves, I believe I have remained true to the spirit of the author.

Another large challenge that faced me as I moved deeper into this project was the task of recounting events and conversations that had taken place a quarter-century ago or more.

I was raised from my very earliest youth to be an *observer*. My parents encouraged me to take in the particulars of my surroundings with a reportorial ear and eye. Like it or not, all my life I have been taking mental notes. The fact that I lived this way is not only part of the story I tell here; it is also the reason why I am able to recount what I experienced as precisely as I have. The dialogue recounted from my past has been reconstructed to the best of my ability, as are the details of what happened. While I could not swear to the exact veracity of every syllable quoted in these pages, I believe if film footage or tape existed documenting the stories re-created here, it would possess a startling similarity to what's reported here.

Some names have been changed. In a few instances, I have

rearranged the chronology of events or left out details that seemed unnecessary and would in no way enlighten a reader's understanding of my journey through life. While I have no doubt that some will view my choice to tell this story honestly as an invasion of others' privacy, I have tried hard to describe only those events and experiences that had a direct effect on the one story I believe I have a right to tell completely: my own.

This book contains stories some people will regard as inappropriate for a parent to tell when she has teenaged children. As for me, I see no way I can ask my children to be honest people themselves if I don't honor them with truthfulness. Every sentence was written with an awareness of their eyes on the page someday, and an assurance firm as granite that there is no story I could tell—no story that exists—that would change my children's love and acceptance of their parents, their sense of themselves, or their knowledge of how treasured they are. No marriage that created our three children could be called a failure. That our family has also known its struggles and pain will not come as news to anyone who inhabits it. I pray what my children take from my telling of this story is freedom from the kind of shame I experienced as a young person, and the lesson that every child, woman, and man should possess license to speak or sing in his or her true voice.

Raised myself in a household in which painful experience was not freely discussed, I believe that a person's best source of strength and protection resides in her ability to speak openly and without shame about the real events of her life. I believe my children have learned that lesson. So far only one of them—my fifteen-year-old son, Willy—has read this book, my older son and daughter having made the choice to wait for a while. But they are well acquainted with the stories in these pages, and will find no large surprises when the day comes that they read my story.

Recently a woman posted an indignant message to me on the discussion forum of my Web site, asking how I could live with myself, knowing that one day my children were likely to read *At Home in the World*. Willy was in the room at the time, so I read her question out loud to him. "Mind if I answer that?" he said.

Word for word, here is the note he dashed off to her:

Oh Kathe,

I have read my mother's most recent book and though parts were hard to hear, I was glad to read every page of it. I am sure that in your own life you have been faced with adversity and pain that affected you profoundly, as has my mother. The fact that she chose to express hers in writ-ing is—I believe—a sign of her strength and an expression of the faith she has in her children. I am the youngest of my siblings and possibly the 'least mature,' however, not for a moment do I suspect any conflicting feeling from my fellow siblings when I say that we all love and support our mother despite her zany stories of despair and woe. I think that we can all relate and learn from these tales if they are approached with an open mind (and in my case, a little love).

Sincerely,
Stephen Wilson Bethel

Many people supported me during the writing of this book.

Jim Dicke, II, a longtime reader from New Bremen, Ohio, underwrote the last crucial months of work on this book in a way that allowed me to set aside worries and other jobs as I have never been able to before. In doing so, he offered not only the financial wherewithal to work in a new way, but the gift of one reader's great and deeply heartening faith in me.

Lee Larson, longtime reader from Portland, Oregon, gave me the use of his house in Cannon Beach, Oregon, to go away alone and write for a good part of one long and rainy winter.

My sons, Charlie and Willy Bethel, encouraged me to go away to Oregon to write this book, broke no bones while I was gone, and gave me a hero's welcome when I walked back in the door. I could not do what I do without the gift of their acceptance and understanding, as well as that of their sister.

My agent and friend, Gail Hochman, has challenged me when I needed it, advocated for me relentlessly, and supported me without fail. More times than I could count, Gail has shepherded me through the hardest kinds of decisions a writer has to make—not simply business decisions but editorial ones as well—with her extraordinary gift to recognize the core of a problem as well as its solution.

Diane Higgins, my editor, sought me out and expressed a desire to work with me at a time in my writing life when no others were beating a path to my door. More than anything I've ever written, this book represents a true collaboration between a writer and an editor. Diane was not simply present to oversee every one of the many stages of this book's revision; she was a crucial and irreplaceable part of its conception. There is not one sentence in these pages that does not reflect her exquisitely subtle ear and eye. In the years since this book's original publication, Nichole Argyres has contributed her thoughtful and perceptive oversight, as a valued editor and friend.

Finally, I want to say something about my parents, Max Maynard and Fredelle Bruser Maynard. Some dark and troubling aspects emerge in my portraits of them. To convey on the page two such complex and conflicted characters without those elements would have required the kinds of compromises my parents taught me to question, even as they found themselves forced to make many such compromises in their own lives. As painful as parts of this story may be, particularly to people who knew and loved my parents, I believe my mother and father would understand and even celebrate my having found, at last, the freedom to write as I do now. I cannot tell the story of our family, and the extraordinary and sometimes damaging way my parents raised my sister and me, without recognizing that if they had raised me differently, I might not possess the tools to tell this story. My father taught me how to see. My mother put the pen in my hand. I love them fiercely and deeply forever, for this and many other reasons.

An 18-Year-Old Looks Back on Life

by Joyce Maynard

Originally published April 23, 1972
The New York Times Magazine

EVERY GENERATION THINKS it's special—my grandparents because they remember horses and buggies, my parents because of
the Depression. The over-30's are special because they knew the
Red Scare of Korea, Chuck Berry and beatniks. My older sister is
special because she belonged to the first generation of teen-agers
(before that, people in their teens were *adolescents*), when being
a teen-ager was still fun. And I—I am 18, caught in the middle.
Mine is the generation of unfulfilled expectations. "When you're
older," my mother promised, "you can wear lipstick." But when
the time came, of course, lipstick wasn't being worn. "When we're
big, we'll dance like that," my friends and I whispered, watching
Chubby Checker twist on "American Bandstand." But we inherited
no dance steps, ours was a limp, formless shrug to watered-down
music that rarely made the feet tap. "Just wait till we can vote,"
I said, bursting with 10-year-old fervor, ready to fast, freeze, march
and die for peace and freedom as Joan Baez, barefoot, sang "We
Shall Overcome." Well, now we can vote, and we're old enough
to attend rallies and knock on doors and wave placards, and suddenly it doesn't seem to matter anymore.

My generation is special because of what we missed rather
than what we got, because in a certain sense we are the first and
the last. The first to take technology for granted. (What was a
space shot to us, except an hour cut from Social Studies to gather
before a TV in the gym as Cape Canaveral counted down?) The
first to grow up with TV. My sister was 8 when we got our set,

so to her it seemed magic and always somewhat foreign. She had known books already and would never really replace them. But for me, the TV set was, like the kitchen sink and the telephone, a fact of life.

We inherited a previous generation's hand-me-downs and took in the seams, turned up the hems, to make our new fashions. We took drugs from the college kids and made them a high-school commonplace. We got the Beatles, but not those lovable look-alikes in matching suits with barber cuts and songs that made you want to cry. They came to us like a bad joke—aged, bearded, discordant. And we inherited the Vietnam War just after the crest of the wave—too late to burn draft cards and too early not to be drafted. The boys of 1953—my year—will be the last to go.

So where are we now? Generalizing is dangerous. Call us the apathetic generation and we will become that. Say times are changing, nobody cares about prom queens and getting into the college of his choice any more—say that (because it sounds good, it indicates a trend, gives as symmetry to history) and you make a movement and a unit out of a generation unified only in its common fragmentation. If there is a reason why we are where we are, it comes from where we have been.

Like overanxious patients in analysis, we treasure the traumas of our childhood. Ours was more traumatic than most. The Kennedy assassination has become our myth: Talk to us for an evening or two—about movies or summer jobs or Nixon's trip to China or the weather—and the subject will come up ("Where were you when you heard?"), as if having lived through Jackie and the red roses, John-John's salute and Oswald's on-camera murder justifies our disenchantment.

We haven't all emerged the same, of course, because our lives were lived in high-school corridors and drive-in hamburger joints as well as in the pages of *Time* and *Life*, and the images on the TV screen. National events and personal memory blur so that, for me, Nov. 22, 1963, was a birthday party that had to be called off and Armstrong's moonwalk was my first full can of beer. If you want to know who we are now; if you wonder how we'll vote, or whether we will, or whether, 10 years from now, we'll end up just like all those other generations that thought they were special—with 2.2 kids and a house in Connecticut—if that's what you're wondering, look to the past because, whether we should blame it or not, we do.

I didn't know till years later that they called it the Cuban Missile Crisis. But I remember Castro. (We called him Castor Oil and were awed by his beard—beards were rare in those days.) We might not have worried so much (what would the Communists want with our small New Hampshire town?) except that we lived 10 miles from an air base. Planes buzzed around us like mosquitoes that summer. People talked about fallout shelters in their basements and one family on our street packed their car to go to the mountains. I couldn't understand that. If everybody was going to die, I certainly didn't want to stick around, with my hair falling out and—later—a plague of thalidomide-type babies. I wanted to go quickly, with my family.

Dying didn't bother me so much—I'd never known anyone who died, and death was unreal, fascinating. (I wanted Dr. Kildare to have more terminal cancer patients and fewer love affairs.) What bothered me was the business of immortality. Sometimes, the growing-up sort of concepts germinate slowly, but the full impact of death hit me like a bomb, in the night. Not only would my body be gone—that I could take—but I would cease to think. That I would no longer be a participant I had realized before; now I saw that I wouldn't even be an observer. What especially alarmed me about The Bomb (always singular like, a few years later, The Pill) was the possibility of total obliteration. All traces of me would be destroyed. There would be no grave and, if there were, no one left to visit it.

Newly philosophical, I pondered the universe. If the earth was in the solar system and the solar system was in the galaxy and the galaxy was in the universe, what was the universe in? And if the sun was just a dot—the head of a pin—what was I? We visited a planetarium that year, in third grade, and saw a dramatization of the sun exploding. Somehow the image of that orange ball zooming toward us merged with my image of The Bomb. The effect was devastating and for the first time in my life—except for Easter Sundays, when I wished I went to church so I could have a fancy new dress like my Catholic and Protestant friends—I longed for religion.

I was 8 when Joan Baez entered our lives, with long, black, beatnik hair and a dress made out of a burlap bag. When we got her first record (we called her Joan Baze then—soon she was simply Joan) we listened all day, to "All My Trials" and "Silver Dagger" and "Wildwood Flower." My sister grew her hair and started wearing sandals, made pilgrimages to Harvard Square. I took up the guitar. We loved her voice and her songs but, even more, we loved the idea of Joan, like the 15th-century Girl of Orleans, burning at society's stake, marching along or singing solitary, in a prison cell to protest segregation. She was the champion of nonconformity and so—like thousands of others—we joined the masses of her fans.

I knew she must but somehow I could never imagine Jackie Kennedy going to the bathroom. She was too cool and poised and perfect. We had a book about her, filled with color pictures of Jackie painting, in a spotless yellow linen dress, Jackie on the beach with Caroline and John-John, Jackie riding elephants in India and Jackie, in a long white gown, greeting Khrushchev like Snow White welcoming one of the seven dwarfs. (No, I wasn't betraying Joan in my adoration. Joan was beautiful but human, like us; Jackie was magic.) When, years later, she married Rumpelstiltskin, I felt like a child discovering, in his father's drawer, the Santa Claus suit. And, later still, reading some *Ladies' Home Journal* exposé ("Jacqueline Onassis's secretary tells all . . .") I felt almost sick. After the first few pages I put the magazine down. I wasn't interested in the fragments, only in the fact that the glass had broken.

They told us constantly that Oyster River Elementary School was one of the best in the state, but the state was New Hampshire, and that was like calling a mound of earth a peak because it rose up from the Sahara Desert. One fact of New Hampshire politics I learned early: We had no broad-based tax, no sales or income tax, because the anti-Federalist farmers and the shoe-factory workers who feared the Reds and creeping Socialism acquired their political philosophy from William Loeb's Manchester Union Leader. We in Durham, where the state university stands, were a specially hated target, a pocket of liberals filling the minds of New Hampshire's young with high-falutin, intellectual garbage. And that was why the archaic New Hampshire Legislature always cut the university budget in half and why my family had only one car, second-hand (my father taught English at the university). And The Union Leader was the reason, finally, why any man who wanted to be elected Governor had better pledge himself against the sales tax, so schools were supported by local property taxes and the sweepstakes, which meant that they weren't supported very well. So Oyster River was not a very good school.

But in all the bleakness—the annual memorizing of Kilmer's "Trees," the punishment administered by banging guilty heads on hard oak desks—we had one fine, fancy new gimmick that followed us from fourth grade through eighth. It was a white cardboard box of folders, condensed two-page stories about dinosaurs and earthquakes and Seeing-Eye dogs, with questions at the end. The folders were called Power Builders and they were leveled according to color—red, blue, yellow, orange, brown—all the way up to the dreamed-for, cheated-for purple. Power Builders came with their own answer keys, the idea being that you moved at your own rate and—we heard it a hundred times—that when you cheated, you only cheated yourself. The whole program was called SRA and there were a dozen other abbreviations, TTUM, FSU, PQB—all having to do with formulas that had reduced reading to a science.

We had Listening Skill Builders, too—more reader-digested minimodules of information, read aloud to us while we sat, poised stiffly in our chairs, trying frantically to remember the five steps (SRQPT? VWCNB? XUSLIN?) to Better Listening Comprehension. A Listening Skill Test would come later, to catch the mental wanderers, the doodlers, the deaf.

I—and most of the others in the Purple group—solved the problem by tucking an answer key into my Power Builder and writing down the answers (making an occasional error for credibility) without reading the story or the questions. By sixth grade, a whole group of us had been promoted to a special reading group and sent to an independent study-conference unit (nothing was a *room* any more) where we copied answer keys, five at a time, and then told dirty jokes.

SRA took over reading the way New Math took over arithmetic. By seventh grade, there was a special Developmental Reading class. (Mental reading, we called it.) The classroom was filled with audio-visual aids, phonetics charts, reading laboratories. Once a week, the teacher plugged in the speed-reading machine that projected a story on the board, one phrase at a time, faster and faster. Get a piece of dust in your eye—blink—and you were lost.

There were no books in the Developmental Reading room— the lab. Even in English class we escaped books easily. The project of the year was to portray a famous author (one of the 100 greatest of all time). I was Louisa May Alcott, and my best friend was Robert McCloskey, the man who wrote "Make Way for Ducklings." For this we put on skits, cut out pictures from magazines and, at the end of the year, dressed up. (I wore a long nightgown with my hair in a bun and got an A-plus; my friend came as a duck.) I have never read a book by Louisa May Alcott. I don't think I read a book all that year. All through high school, in fact, I read little except for magazines. Though I've started reading seriously now, in college, I still find myself drawn in bookstores to the bright covers and shiny, Power Builder look. My eyes have been trained to skip nonessentials (adjectives, adverbs) and dart straight to the meaty phrases. (TVPQM.) But—perhaps in defiance of that whirring black rate-builder projector—it takes me three hours to read 100 pages.

If I had spent at the piano the hours I gave to television, on all those afternoons when I came home from school, I would be an accomplished pianist now. Or if I'd danced, or read, or painted . . . But I turned on the set instead, every day, almost, every year, and sank into an old green easy chair, smothered in quilts, with a bag of Fritos beside me and a glass of milk to wash them down, facing life and death with Dr. Kildare, laughing at Danny Thomas, whispering the answers—out loud sometimes—with "Password" and "To Tell the Truth." Looking back over all those afternoons,

I try to convince myself they weren't wasted. I must have learned something; I must, at least, have changed.

What I learned was certainly not what TV tried to teach me. From the reams of trivia collected over years of quiz shows, I remember only the questions, never the answers. I loved "Leave It to Beaver" for the messes Beaver got into, not for the inevitable lecture from Dad at the end of each show. I saw every episode two or three times, witnessed Beaver's aging, his legs getting longer and his voice lower, only to start all over again with young Beaver every fall. (Someone told me recently that the boy who played Beaver Cleaver died in Vietnam. The news was a shock—I kept coming back to it for days until another distressed Beaver fan wrote to tell me that it wasn't true after all.)

I got so I could predict punch lines and endings, not really knowing whether I'd seen the episode before or only watched one like it. There was the bowling-ball routine, for instance: Lucy, Dobie Gillis, Pete and Gladys—they all used it. Somebody would get his finger stuck in a bowling ball (Lucy later updated the gimmick using Liz Taylor's ring) and then they'd have to go to a wedding or give a speech at the P.T.A. or have the boss to dinner, concealing one hand all the while. We weren't supposed to ask questions like "Why don't they just tell the truth?" These shows were built on deviousness, on the longest distance between two points, and on a kind of symmetry which decrees that no loose ends shall be left untied, no lingering doubts allowed. (The Surgeon General is off the track worrying about TV violence, I think. I grew up in the days before lawmen became peacemakers. What carries over is not the gunfights but the memory that everything always turned out all right.) Optimism shone through all those half hours I spent in the dark shadows of the TV room—out of evil shall come good.

Most of all, the situation comedies steeped me in American culture. I emerged from years of TV viewing indifferent to the museums of France, the architecture of Italy, the literature of England. A perversely homebound American, I pick up paperbacks in bookstores, checking before I buy to see if the characters have foreign names, whether the action takes place in London or New York. Vulgarity and banality fascinate me. More intellectual friends (who watch no TV) can't understand what I see in "My Three Sons." "Nothing happens," they say. "The characters are dull, plastic, faceless. Every show is the same." I guess that's why I watch them—boring repetition is, itself, a rhythm—a steady pulse of flashing Coca-Cola signs, McDonald's Golden Arches and Howard Johnson roofs.

I don't watch TV as an anthropologist, rising loftily above my subject to analyze. Neither do I watch, as some kids now tune in to reruns of "The Lone Ranger" and "Superman" (in the same spirit they enjoy comic books and pop art) for their camp. I watch in earnest. How can I do anything else? Five thousand hours of my life have gone into this box.

There were almost no blacks in our school. They were Negroes then; the word *black* was hard to say at first. *Negro* got hard to say for a while too, so I said nothing at all and was embarrassed. If you had asked me, at 9, to describe Cassius Clay, I would have taken great, liberal pains to be color-blind, mentioning height, build, eye color and shoe size, disregarding skin. I knew black people only from newspapers and the TV screen—picket lines, National Guardsmen at the doors of schools. (There were few black actors on TV then, except for Jack Benny's Rochester.) It was easy, in 1963, to embrace the Negro cause. Later, faced with cold stares from an all-black table in the cafeteria or heckled by a Panther selling newspapers, I first became aware of the fact that maybe the little old lady didn't want to be helped across the street. My visions of black-and-white-together look to me now like shots from "To Sir With Love." If a black is friendly to me, I wonder, as other blacks might, if he's a sellout.

I had no desire to scream or cry or throw jelly beans when I first saw the Beatles on the Ed Sullivan Show. An eighth-grader would have been old enough to revert to childhood, but I was too young to act anything but old. So mostly we laughed at them. We were in fifth grade, the year of rationality, the calm before the storm. We still screamed when the boys came near us (which they rarely did) and said they had cooties. Barbie dolls tempted us. That was the year when I got my first Barbie. Perhaps they were produced earlier, but they didn't reach New Hampshire till late that fall, and the stores were always sold out. So at the close of our doll-playing careers there was a sudden dramatic switch from lumpy, round-bellied Betsy Wetsys and stiff-legged little-girl dolls to slim, curvy Barbie, just 11 inches tall, with a huge, expensive wardrobe that included a filmy black negligee and a mouth that made her look as if she'd just swallowed a lemon.

Barbie wasn't just a toy, but a way of living that moved us suddenly from tea parties to dates with Ken at the Soda Shoppe. Our short careers with Barbie, before junior high sent her to the attic, built up our expectations for teen-age life before we had developed the sophistication to go along with them. Children today are accustomed to having a tantalizing youth culture all around them. (They play with Barbie in the nursery school.) For us, it broke like a cloudburst, without preparation. Caught in the deluge, we were torn—wanting to run for shelter but tempted, also, to sing in the rain.

To me, a 10-year-old sixth-grader in 1964, the Goldwater-Johnson election year was a drama, a six-month basketball playoff game, more action-packed than movies or TV. For all the wrong reasons I loved politics and plunged into the campaign fight. Shivering in the October winds outside a supermarket ("Hello, would you like some L.B.J. matches?"), Youth for Johnson tried hard to believe in the man with the 10-gallon hat. We were eager for a hero (we'd lost ours just 11 months before) and willing to trust. Government deceit was not yet taken for granted—maybe because we were more naive but also because the country was. Later, the war that never ended and the C.I.A. and the Pentagon Papers and I.T.T. would shake us, but in those days, when a man said, "My fellow Americans . . . ," we listened.

At school, I was a flaming liberal, holding lunchroom debates and setting up a 10-year-old's dichotomies: If you were for Johnson, you were "for" the Negroes, if you were for Goldwater, you were against them. Equally earnest Republicans would expound the domino theory and I would waver in spite of myself (what they said sounded logical), knowing there was a fallacy somewhere but saying only, "If my father was here, he'd explain it. . . ."

A friend and I set up a campaign headquarters at school, under a huge "All the Way with L.B.J." sign. (The tough kids snickered at that—"all the way" was reserved for the behavior of fast girls in the janitor's closet at dances.) The pleasure we got from our L.B.J. headquarters and its neat stacks of buttons and pamphlets was much the same as the pleasure I got, five years later, manning the "Support Your Junior Prom" bake-sale table in the lobby at school. I liked playing store, no matter what the goods.

And I believed, then, in the power of dissent and the possibility for change. I wrote protest songs filled with bloody babies and starving Negroes, to the tune of "American the Beautiful." I marched through the streets of town, a tall candle flickering in my hand, surrounded by college kids with love beads and placards (what they said seems mild and polite now). I remember it was all so beautiful I cried, but when I try to recapture the feeling, nothing comes. Like a sharp pain or the taste of peach ice cream on a hot July day, the sensation lasts only as long as the stimulus.

Ask us whose face is on the $5 bill and we may not know the answer. But nearly everyone my age remembers a cover of *Life* magazine that came out in the spring of 1965, part of a series of photographs that enter my dreams and my nightmares still. They were the first shots ever taken of an unborn fetus, curled up tightly in a sack of veins and membranes, with blue fingernails and almost transparent skin that made the pictures look like double exposures. More than the moon photographs a few years later, that grotesque figure fascinated me as the map of a new territory. It was often that way with photographs in *Life*—the issue that reported on the "In Cold Blood" murders; a single picture of a boy falling from an airplane and another of a woman who had lost 200 pounds. (I remember the faces of victims and killers from seven or eight years ago, while the endless issues on Rome and nature studies are entirely lost.)

Photographs are the illustrations for a decade of experiences. Just as, when we think of "Alice in Wonderland," we all see Tenniel's drawings, and when we think of the Cowardly Lion, we all see Bert Lahr, so, when we think of Lyndon Johnson's airborne swearing-in as President in 1963, we have a common image furnished by magazines, and when we think of fetuses, now, those cabbages we were supposed to have come from and smiling, golden-haired cherubs have been replaced forever by the cover of *Life*. Having had so many pictures to grow up with, we share a common visual idiom and have far less room for personal vision. The movie versions of books decide for us what our heroes and villains will look like, and we are powerless to change the camera's decree. So, while I was stunned and fascinated by that eerie fetus (where is he now, I wonder, and are those pictures in his family album?) I'm saddened too, knowing what it did to me. If I were asked to pinpoint major moments in my growing up, experiences that changed me, the sight of that photograph would be one.

Eighth grade was groovy. When I think of 1966, I see pink and orange stripes and wild purple paisleys and black and white vibrating to make the head ache. We were too young for drugs (they hadn't reached the junior high yet) but we didn't need them. Our world was psychedelic, our clothes and our make-up and our jewelry and our hair styles were trips in themselves. It was the year of the gimmick, and what mattered was being noticed, which meant being wild and mod and having the shortest skirt and the whitest Yardley Slicker lips and the dangliest earrings. (We all pierced our ears that year. You can tell the girls of 1966—they're the ones with not-quite-healed-over holes in their ears.)

I've kept my *Seventeen* magazines from junior high: vinyl skirts, paper dresses, Op and Pop, Sassoon haircuts, Patty Duke curls and body painting. My own clothes that year would have glowed in the dark. I remember one, a poor-boy top and mod Carnaby Street hat, a silver microskirt and purple stockings. (Pantyhose hadn't been invented yet; among our other distinctions, call us the last generation to wear garter belts. I recall an agonizing seventh-period math class in which, 10 minutes before the bell rang, my front and back garters came simultaneously undone.)

It was as if we'd just discovered color, and all the shiny, sterile things machines made possible for us. Now we cultivate the natural, homemade look, with earthy colors and frayed, lumpy macrame sashes that no one would mistake for store-bought. But back then we tried to look like spacemen, distorting natural forms. Nature wasn't a vanishing treasure to us yet—it was a barrier to be overcome. The highest compliment, the ultimate adjective was *unreal*.

I can understand the Jesus freaks turning, dope-muddled, to a life of self-denial and asceticism. The excesses of eighth-grade psychedelia left me feeling the same way and I turned, in 1967, to God. To the church, at least, anxious to wash away the bad aftertaste of too many Cokes and too much eye shadow. The church I chose, the only one conceivable for a confirmed atheist, wasn't really a church at all, but a dark gray building that housed the Unitarian Fellowship. They were an earnest, liberal-minded, socially-conscious congregation numbering 35 or 40. If I had been looking for spirituality, I knocked at the wrong door; the Unitarians were rationalists—scientists, mostly, whose programs would be slide shows of plant life in North Africa or discussions of migratory labor problems. We believed in our fellow man.

We tried Bible-reading in my Liberal Religious Youth group, sitting on orange crates in a circle of four, but in that mildewed attic room, the Old Testament held no power. We gave up on Genesis and rapped, instead, with a casual college student who started class saying, "Man, do I have a hangover." We tried singing: one soprano, two tenors and a tone-deaf alto, draped in shabby black robes designed for taller worshipers. After a couple of weeks of singing we switched, wisely, to what Unitarians do best, to the subjects suited to orange crates. We found a cause.

We discovered the Welfare Mothers of America—one Welfare Mother in particular. She was an angry, militant mother of eight (no husband in the picture) who wanted to go to the national conference in Tennessee and needed someone to foot the bill. I don't know who told us about Mrs. Mahoney, or her about us. In one excited Sunday meeting, anyway, the four of us voted to pay her way and, never having earned $4 without spending it, never having met Peg Mahoney, we called the state office of the Unitarian Church and arranged for a $200 loan. Then we made lists, allocated jobs, formed committees (as well as committees can be formed, with an active membership of four and a half dozen others who preferred to sleep in on Sundays). We would hold a spaghetti supper, all proceeds to go to the Mahoney fund.

We never heard what happened at the welfare conference—in fact, we never heard from our welfare mother again. She disappeared, with the red-plaid suitcase I lent her for the journey and the new hat we saw her off in. Our $200 debt lingered on through not one but three spaghetti suppers, during which I discovered that there's more to Italian-style fund-raising dinners than red-and-white-checked tablecloths and Segovia records. Every supper began with five or six helpers; as more and more customers arrived, though, fewer and fewer L.R.Y.-ers stayed on to help. By 10 o'clock, when the last walnut-sized meatball had been cooked and the last pot of spaghetti drained, there would be two of us left in our tomato-spotted red aprons, while all around, religious youth high on red wine sprawled and hiccupped on the kitchen floor, staggering nervously to the door, every few minutes, to make sure their parents weren't around. I never again felt the same about group activity—united we stand, and that wonderful feeling I used to get at Pete Seeger concerts, singing "This Land Is Your Land"—that if we worked together, nothing was impossible.

After the debt was paid I left L.R.Y., which had just discovered sensitivity training. Now the group held weekly, nonverbal communication sessions, with lots of hugging and feeling that boosted attendance to triple what it had been in our old save-the-world days. It seemed that everybody's favorite topic was himself.

Marijuana and the class of '71 moved through high school together. When we came in, as freshmen, drugs were still strange and new; marijuana was smoked only by a few marginal figures while those in the mainstream guzzled beer. It was called pot then—the words grass and dope came later; hash and acid and pills were almost unheard of. By my sophomore year, lots of the seniors and even a few younger kids were trying it. By the time I was a junior—in 1969—grass was no longer reserved for the hippies; basketball players and cheerleaders and boys with crewcuts and boys in black-leather jackets all smoked. And with senior year—maybe because of the nostalgia craze—there was an odd liquor revival. In my last month of school, a major bust led to the suspension of half a dozen boys. They were high on beer.

Now people are saying that the drug era is winding down. (It's those statisticians with their graphs again, charting social phenomena like the rise and fall of hemlines.) I doubt if it's real, this abandonment of marijuana. But the frenzy is gone, certainly, the excitement and the fear of getting caught and the worry of where to get good stuff. What's happened to dope is what happens to a new record: you play it constantly, full volume at first. Then, as you get to know the songs, you play them less often, not because you're tired of them exactly, but just because you know them. They're with you always, but quietly, in your head. My position was a difficult one, all through those four years when grass took root in Oyster River High. I was on the side of all those things that went along with smoking dope—the clothes, the music, the books, the candidates. More and more of my friends smoked, and many people weren't completely my friends, I think, because I didn't. Drugs took on a disproportionate importance. Why was it I could spend half a dozen evenings with someone without his ever asking me what I thought of Beethoven or Picasso but always, in the first half hour, he'd ask whether I smoked?

It became—like hair length and record collection—a symbol for who you were, and you couldn't be all the other things—progressive and creative and free-thinking—without taking that crumpled roll of dry, brown vegetation and holding it to your lips. You are what you eat—or what you smoke, or what you don't smoke. And when you say "like—you know," you're speaking the code, and suddenly the music of the Grateful Dead and the poetry of Bob Dylan and the general brilliance of Ken Kesey all belong to you as if, in those three fuzzy, mumbled words, you'd created art yourself and uttered the wisdom of the universe.

In my junior year I had English and algebra and French and art and history, but what I really had was fun. It was a year when I didn't give a thought to welfare mothers or war or peace or brotherhood; the big questions in my life were whether to cut my hair and what the theme of the Junior Prom should be. (I left my hair long. We decided on a castle.) Looking back on a year of sitting around just talking and drinking beer and driving around and drinking beer and dancing and drinking beer and just drinking beer, I can say, "Ah yes, the post-Woodstock disenchantment; the post-Chicago, postelection apathy; the rootlessness of a generation whose leaders had all been killed . . ."

But if that's what it was, we certainly didn't know it. Our lives were dominated by parties and pranks and dances and soccer games. (We won the state championship that year. Riding home in a streamer-trailing yellow bus, cheering "We're Number One," it never occurred to us that so were 49 other schools in 49 other states.) It was a time straight out of the goldfish-swallowing thirties, with a difference. We knew just enough to feel guilty, like trick-or-treaters nervously passing a ghost with a UNICEF box in his hand. We didn't feel bad enough not to build a 20-foot cardboard-and-crepe-paper castle, but we knew enough to realize, as we ripped it down the next morning, Grecian curls unwinding limply down our backs, that silver-painted cardboard and tissue-paper carnations weren't biodegradable.

I had never taken Women's Liberation very seriously. Partly it was the looks of the movement that bothered me. I believed in all the right things, but just as my social conscience evaporated at the prospect of roughing it in some tiny village with the Peace Corps, so my feminist notions disappeared at the thought of giving up eyeliner (just when I'd discovered it). Media-vulnerable, I wanted to be on the side of the beautiful, graceful people, and Women's Libbers seemed—except for Gloria Steinem, who was just emerging—plain and graceless. Women's Lib was still new and foreign, suggesting—to kids at an age of still-undefined sexuality—things like lesbianism and bisexuality. (We hadn't mastered *one*—how could we cope with the possibility of two?)

Besides, male chauvinism had no reality for me. In my family—two girls and two girl-loving parents—females occupied a privileged position. My mother and sister and I had no trouble getting equal status in our household. At school, too, girls seemed never to be discriminated against. (I wonder if I'd see things differently, going back there now.) Our class was run mostly by girls. The boys played soccer and sometimes held office on the student council—amiable figureheads—but it was the girls whose names filled the honor roll and the girls who ran class meetings. While I would never be Homecoming Sweetheart—I knew that—I had power in the school.

Then suddenly everything changed. A nearby boys' prep school announced that it would admit girls as day students. So at 17, in my senior year, I left Oyster River High for Phillips Exeter Academy.

The new world wasn't quite as I'd imagined. Exeter was a boys' school *("Huc venite pueri, ut viri sitis")* in which girls were an afterthought. We were so few that, to many, we appeared unapproachable. Like the Exeter blacks, the Exeter girls moved in gangs across the campus, ate together at all-girl tables and fled, after classes, to the isolated study areas allotted to them. The flight of the girls angered me; I felt newly militant, determined not to be intimidated by all those suits and ties and all the ivy-covered education. I wasn't just me anymore, but a symbol of my sex who had to prove, to 800 boys used to weekend girls at mixers, that I could hold my own. I found myself the only girl in every class—turned to, occasionally, by a faculty member accustomed to man-talk, and asked to give "the female point of view."

It makes one suspicious, paranoid. Why was I never asked to give the Scorpio's viewpoint, the myopic's, the half-Jewish, right-handed, New Hampshire resident's? Was being female my most significant feature? The subject of coeducation gets boring after a while. I wanted to talk about a book I'd read (having just discovered that reading could be fun) or a play I was in—and then somebody would ask the inevitable "What's it like to be a girl at Exeter?"

I became a compulsive overachiever, joining clubs and falling asleep at the typewriter in the hope of battering down doors I was used to having open, at my old school, where they knew me. Here someone else was the newspaper editor, the yearbook boss, the actor, the writer. I was the girl. All of first semester I approached school like a warrior on the offensive, a self-proclaimed outsider. Then, in the cease-fire over Christmas, I went to a hometown New Year's Eve party with the people I'd been romanticizing all that fall when I was surrounded by lawyers' sons. The conversation back home was of soccer games I hadn't been to and a graduation I wouldn't be marching in. The school had gone on without me; I was a preppie.

Something strange got into the boys at Exeter that year as if, along with the legendary saltpeter, something like lust for the country was being sprinkled into the nightly mashed potatoes. It wasn't just the overalls (with a tie on top to meet the dress code) or the country music that came humming out of every dorm. Exonians—Jonathan, Jrs. and Carter III's, Latin scholars and mathematicians with 800's on their college boards—were suddenly announcing to the college-placement counselor that no, they didn't want a Harvard interview, not now or ever. Hampshire, maybe (that's the place where you can go and study Eastern religion or dulcimer-making). But many weren't applying any place—they were going to study weaving in Norway, to be shepherds in the Alps, deckhands on a fishing boat or—most often—farmers. After the first ecological fury died down, after Ehrlich's "Population Bomb" exploded, that's what we were left with. Prep school boys felt it more than most, perhaps, because they, more than most, had worked their minds at the expense of their hands. And now, their heads full of theorems and declensions, they wanted to get back to the basics—to the simple, honest, uncluttered life where manure was cow s—, not bovine waste.

Exeter's return to the soil took the form of the farm project, a group of boys who got together, sold a few stocks, bought a red pick-up truck and proposed, for a spring project, that they work a plot of school-owned land a few miles out of town. The country kids I went to Oyster River with, grown up now and working in the shoe factory or married—they would have been amused at the farming fairy tale. In March, before the ice thawed, the harvest was already being planned. The faculty objected and the project died, and most—not all—went on to college in the fall. (They talk now, from a safe distance, about the irrelevance of Spenser and the smell of country soil and fresh-cut hay.) A friend who really did go on to farming came to visit me at school this fall. He looked out of place in the dorm; he put his boots up on my desk and then remembered he had cow dung on the soles. He laughed when I reminded him about the farm project. It's best they never really tried, I think. That way, in 10 years, when they're brokers, they'll still have the dream: tomatoes big as pumpkins, pumpkins big as suns and corn that's never known the touch of blight.

Gene McCarthy must have encountered blizzards in 1968, and mill towns like Berlin, N. H.—where I went to campaign for George McGovern last February—must have smelled just as bad as they do now. But back in '68 those things made the fight even more rewarding, because in suffering for your candidate and your dreams, you were demonstrating love. But now, in 1972, there's nothing fun about air so smelly you buy perfume to hold under your nose, or snow falling so thick you can't make out the words on the Yorty billboard right in front of you. No one feels moved to build snowmen.

Campaigning in New Hampshire was work. Magazines and newspapers blame the absence of youth excitement on McGovern and say he lacks charisma—he isn't a poet and his bumper stickers aren't daisy-shaped. But I think the difference in 1972 lies in the canvassers; this year's crusaders seem joyless, humorless. A high-school junior stuffing envelopes at campaign headquarters told me that when she was young—what is she now?—she was a Socialist. Another group of students left, after an hour of knocking on doors, to go snowmobiling. Somebody else, getting on the bus for home, said, "This makes the fifth weekend I've worked for the campaign," and I was suddenly struck by the fact that we'd all been compiling similar figures—how many miles we'd walked, how many houses we'd visited. In 1968 we believed, and so we shivered; in 1972, we shivered so that we might believe.

Our candidate this year is no less believable, but our idealism has soured and our motives have gotten less noble. We went to Berlin—many of us—so we could say "I canvassed in New Hampshire," the way high-school kids join clubs so they can write "I'm a member of the Latin Club" on their college applications. The students for McGovern whom I worked with were engaged in a business deal, trading frost-bitten fingers for guilt-free consciences; 1968's dreams and abstractions just don't hold up on a bill of sale.

* * *

The freshman women's dorm at Yale has no house mother. We have no check-in hours or drinking rules or punishments for having boys in our rooms past midnight. A guard sits by the door to offer, as they assured us at the beginning of the year, physical—not moral—protection. All of which makes it easy for many girls who feel, after high-school curfews and dating regulations, suddenly liberated. (The first week of school last fall, many girls stayed out all night, every night, displaying next morning the circles under their eyes the way some girls show off engagement rings.)

We all received the "Sex at Yale" book, a thick, black pamphlet filled with charts and diagrams and a lengthy discussion of contraceptive methods. And at the first women's assembly, the discussion moved quickly from course-signing-up procedures to gynecology, where it stayed for much of the evening. Somebody raised her hand to ask where she could fill her pill prescription, someone else wanted to know about abortions. There was no standing in the middle any more—you had to either take out a pen and paper and write down the phone numbers they gave out or stare stonily ahead, implying that those were numbers *you* certainly wouldn't be needing. From then on it seemed the line had been drawn.

But of course the problem is that no lines, no barriers, exist. Where five years ago a girl's decisions were made for her (she had to be in at 12 and, if she was found—in—with her boyfriend . . .), today the decision rests with her alone. She is surrounded by knowledgeable, sexually experienced girls and if *she* isn't willing to sleep with her boyfriend, somebody else will. It's peer-group pressure, 1972 style—the embarrassment of virginity.

Everyone is raised on nursery rhymes and nonsense stories. But it used to be that when you grew up, the nonsense disappeared. Not for us—it is at the core of our music and literature and art and, in fact, of our lives. Like characters in an Ionesco play, we take absurdity unblinking. In a world where military officials tell us "We had to destroy the village in order to save it," Dylan lyrics make an odd kind of sense. They aren't meant to be understood; they don't jar our sensibilities because we're used to non sequiturs. We don't take anything too seriously these days. (Was it a thousand earthquake victims or a million? Does it matter?) The casual butcher's-operation in the film "M*A*S*H" and the comedy in Vonnegut and the album cover showing John and Yoko, bareback, are all part of the new absurdity. The days of the Little Moron joke and the elephant joke and the knock-knock joke are gone. It sounds melodramatic, but the joke these days is life.

You're not supposed to care too much any more. Reactions have been scaled down from screaming and jelly-bean-throwing to nodding your head and maybe—if the music really gets to you (and music's the only thing that does any more)—tapping a finger. We need a passion transfusion, a shot of energy in the veins. It's what I'm most impatient with, in my generation—this languid, I-don't-give-a-s——-ism that stems in part, at least, from a culture of put-ons in which any serious expression of emotion is branded sentimental and old-fashioned. The fact that we set such a premium on being cool reveals a lot about my generation; the idea is not to care. You can hear it in the speech of college students today; cultivated monotones, low volume, punctuated with four-letter words that come off sounding only bland. I feel it most of all on Saturday morning, when the sun is shining and the crocuses are about to bloom and, walking through the corridors of my dorm, I see there isn't anyone awake.

I'm basically an optimist. Somehow, no matter what the latest population figures say, I feel everything will work out—just like on TV. I may doubt man's fundamental goodness, but I believe in his power to survive. I say, sometimes, that I wonder if we'll be around in 30 years, but then I forget myself and speak of "when I'm 50...." Death has touched me now—from Vietnam and Biafra and a car accident that makes me buckle my seat belt—but like negative numbers and the sound of a dog whistle (too high-pitched for human ears), it's not a concept I can comprehend. I feel immortal while all the signs around me proclaim that I'm not.

We feel cheated, many of us—the crop of 1953—which is why we complain about inheriting problems we didn't cause.

(Childhood notions of justice, reinforced by Perry Mason, linger on. Why should I clean up someone else's mess? Who can I blame?) We're excited also, of course: I can't wait to see how things turn out. But I wish I weren't quite so involved, I wish it weren't my life that's being turned into a suspense thriller.

When my friends and I were little, we had big plans. I would be a famous actress and singer, dancing on the side. I would paint my own sets and compose my own music, writing the script and the lyrics and reviewing the performance for *The New York Times*. I would marry and have three children (they don't allow us dreams like that any more) and we would live, rich and famous (donating lots to charity, of course, and periodically adopting orphans), in a house we designed ourselves. When I was older I had visions of good works. I saw myself in South American rain forests and African deserts, feeding the hungry and healing the sick, with an obsessive selflessness, I see now, as selfish, in the end, as my original plans for stardom.

Now my goal is simpler. I want to be happy. And I want comfort—nice clothes, a nice house, good music and good food, and the feeling that I'm doing some little thing that matters. I'll vote and I'll give to charity, but I won't give myself. I feel a sudden desire to buy land—not a lot, not as a business investment, but just a small plot of earth so that whatever they do to the country I'll have a place where I can go—a kind of fallout shelter, I guess. As some people prepare for their old age, so I prepare for my 20's. A little house, a comfortable chair, peace and quiet—retirement sounds tempting.

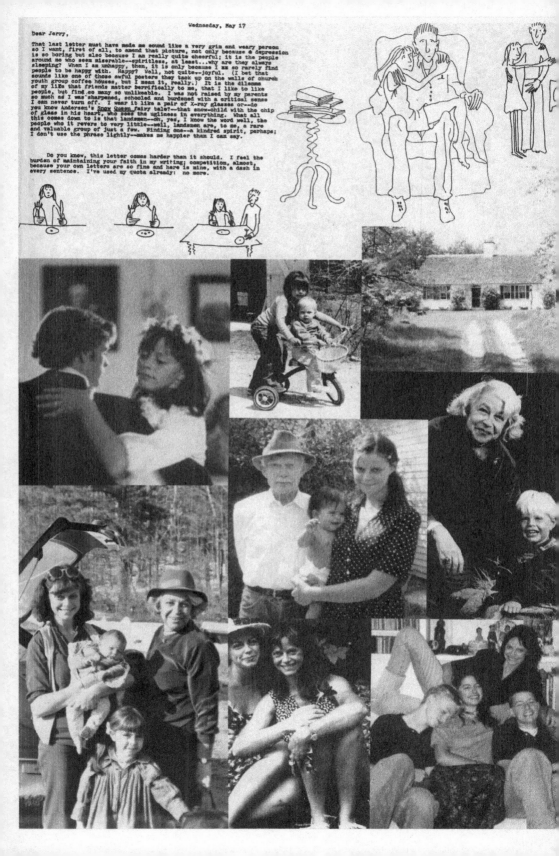

Wednesday, May 17

Dear Jerry,

That last letter must have made me sound like a very grim and weary person so I want, first of all, to amend that picture, not only because a depression is so boring but also because I am really quite cheerful; it is the people around me who seem miserable--spiritless, at least...why are they always sleeping? When I am unhappy, then, it is only because I am so rarely find people to be happy with. Happy? Well, not quite--joyful. (I bet that sounds like one of those awful posters they tack up on the walls of church youth group coffee houses, but I mean it, really.) It is the silliness of my life that friends matter terrifically to me, that I like to like people, but find so many so unlikeable. I was not raised by my parents so much as I was sharpened, schooled and burdened with a critical sense I can never turn off. I wear it like a pair of X-ray glasses or--do you know Andersen's Snow Queen fairy tale?--that snow-child with the chip of glass in his heart, who sees the ugliness in everything. What all this comes down to is that landsmen--oh, yes, I know the word well, the people who it revers to very little--well, landsmen are, to me, a rare and valuable group of just a few. Finding one--a kindred spirit, perhaps; I don't use the phrase lightly--makes me happier than I can say.

Do you know, this letter comes harder than it should. I feel the burden of maintaining your faith in my writing; competition, almost, because your own letters are so fine and here is mine, with a dash in every sentence. I've used my quota already: no more.